PARTY AND SOCIETY

PARTY AND SOCIETY
The Anglo-American Democracies

Robert R. Alford

Department of Sociology
University of Wisconsin

A Publication from the Research Program
of the Survey Research Center, University of California, Berkeley, California

Rand M\?Nally & Company • Chicago

RAND M꜀NALLY SOCIOLOGY SERIES

Edgar F. Borgatta, Advisory Editor

Alford, *Party and Society*

Nye and Hoffman, *The Employed Mother in America*

Warren, *The Community in America*

Copyright © 1963 by Rand M꜀Nally & Company
All Rights Reserved
Printed in U.S.A. by Rand M꜀Nally & Company
Library of Congress Catalog Card No. 63–12333
Second Printing, 1964

TO MY PARENTS

Foreword

THE last few years have witnessed a remarkable growth of survey research throughout the world. Academic, private, and public research organizations have sprung up in both Western and non-Western countries and have been regularly polling their respective populations on a wide variety of topics of social, economic, and political importance.

It is a characteristic of these surveys that they collect far more information than the investigators are concerned with or are able to use. Often, in fact, only the data having commercial or news value are culled, while great amounts of more fundamental, more interesting, and more complex information remain untouched and unheralded. It is not uncommon, for example, for national, regional, and community surveys to contain questions on the demographic characteristics of populations (age, education, and occupation, rural-urban residence, religion, income), their political characteristics (voting patterns, party preferences, response to leaders, political beliefs and attitudes), and their attitudes toward foreign affairs and foreign nations (perceptions of the U.S., the U.S.S.R., the U.N., the cold war, trade policy, foreign aid); the surveys frequently investigate patterns of social stratification and mobility, practices of child rearing, family life, education, religious worship, moral values, level of scientific belief, and dozens of similar topics. Often, the same or similar questions have been asked repeatedly in surveys taken at different times or in different countries, making parallel data available not only over time but across cultures.

These materials comprise a unique and rich body of knowledge on contemporary societies throughout the world. At relatively small cost, they can be subjected to secondary analysis for a wide variety of scholarly purposes in international, area, and comparative research. So far, however, they have been largely untapped. In part, this is because many scholars have not known of their existence. Furthermore, the difficulties of gaining access to these materials, as well as the time and energy required to become informed as to what is available, have been limitations to their use. There is now more than a promise that these obstacles will gradually be removed. A central library of survey materials has been established recently at the Elmo Roper Public Opinion Library at Williams College in Massachusetts. This library has already acquired a major portion of existing American and Canadian materials and is now beginning to store the results of the surveys conducted by various foreign research organizations as well. The Social Science Division of UNESCO is considering the possibility of establishing a European library center of survey data.

By way of adding to the resources for the scholarly use of these materials, the Survey Research Center of the University of California is setting up a Data Facility for Comparative Social Research as part of its ongoing operations. This facility is intended to provide faculty and students with information on available survey data, to aid them in obtaining international survey materials on deposit at the Elmo Roper Library and elsewhere, to give instruction in secondary analysis, and, when called upon, to arrange for the collection of new survey data in this country and abroad. In addition, the facility is seeking to demonstrate the potentialities of the secondary analysis of international survey materials by sponsoring research based on their exploitation.

A first fruit of this activity is Professor Alford's comparative study of political cleavages in Australia, Canada, Great Britain, and the United States. This study, carried out at the Survey Research Center, is based almost wholly on the secondary analysis of voting studies conducted in these four countries over the last two decades. It is concrete and eloquent testimony of the research possibilities which the storehouse of accumulated survey material affords.

Charles Y. Glock
Director, Survey Research Center
University of California (Berkeley)

Preface

WHETHER workers are becoming like middle-class people in their party loyalties is one of the fundamental factual questions raised by the conservative political temper and the apparently decreasing clarity of class lines in the relatively wealthy Western democracies since World War II. Whether *all* group-formations, not merely social class, are losing political relevance, and thus leaving no important mediating identifications between voter and nation is another frequently argued question. This view of the "mass society" can be tested by an assessment of the importance of regional and religiously-based political allegiances in comparison with those based upon social class. Secularization and the dwindling of various parochial identifications may actually be leaving social class as the strongest remaining source of political identity.

If class issues are blurring, if political parties are converging in their appeals and constituencies, and if local, ethnic, regional and religious bases for party loyalty are dwindling in highly industrialized societies, such tendencies should be most evident in the Anglo-American countries, the most "modernized" of any in the world heretofore. The subjects of this book are the relative importance of social class, regionalism, and religion for party divisions in Great Britain, Australia, the United States, and Canada, the causes of national differences in these patterns of political cleavage, and the pervasive pressures for change.

The principal focus of the study is upon those social factors related to party preferences which have been singled out as perhaps the most "durable" of all. The reasons for this can perhaps best be given by quoting a classic study:

the conditions underlying persistent voting cleavages seem to be 1) initial social differentiation such that the consequences of political policy are materially or symbolically different for different groups; 2) conditions of transmittibility from generation to generation; and 3) conditions of physical and social proximity providing for continued in-group contact in suceeding generations. In contemporary America these conditions are best met in *class*, in *ethnic*, and in *ecological* divisions of the population. They continue to provide, then, the most durable social bases for political cleavage.[1]

The empirical foundation of the study is over fifty public opinion surveys from the four countries, in which questions concerning occupation, religious membership, and political party preference were asked. A simple index of "class voting"—the degree of association of occupational position with party preference—was devised which was comparable in the four countries. The book also analyzes class voting among Protestants and Catholics and in various regions, states, or provinces. The basic concern is with relatively enduring constellations of political cleavages, not with the vicissitudes of particular elections. A secondary concern with *change* in the importance of these factors leads to consideration of surveys over as wide a time span as possible.

As will be shown, the polarization of the parties around different class, regional, and religious bases differs considerably in these countries. The order of class voting (in the early 1960's) is: Great Britain (highest), Australia, the United States, and Canada. In Britain, the regional cultures of Scotland and Wales and religious differentiation modify but do not erase the fundamental class basis of the Conservative and Labour parties. In Australia, less sharply class-divided politically, the Roman Catholics deviate sharply from others in similar class positions, and form the chief support for a new splinter Labor party, but there is little regionalism. The United States exhibits great diversity of support for the two major parties, with the southerners and the Catholics (most prominently in 1960) the most notable deviants from a national pattern.[2] In

---

[1] Bernard Berelson *et al.*, *Voting* (Chicago: University of Chicago Press, 1954), p. 75. (Italics in original.)

[2] Relatively less attention will be paid to the United States than to the three Commonwealth countries. A great many studies of the social bases of American politics have appeared, notably the series conducted by the Survey Research Center at the University of Michigan. See for example, Angus Campbell *et al.*, *The American Voter* (New York: Wiley, 1960). I have therefore treated the relevant themes more briefly.

Canada, regional and religious cleavages supersede class almost entirely as factors differentiating the support for national parties.

The methodological impulse behind this study is an attempt to show that public opinion surveys may be regarded as a source of information about political systems as well as about individual attitudes and opinions. Voting behavior is analyzed in this study not as a process of individual decision-making, but as an aspect of the social and political structure of nations. Survey data are considered to be "snapshots" of fundamentally historical processes of change and stability in the allegiance of social groups to political parties.

No one is more acutely conscious than the author of the discrepancy between the problems tackled in this volume and the data available which bear on these problems. Historians or political scientists with a knowledge of the Anglo-American countries and sociologists or survey researchers with a knowledge of the criteria for good survey data will find much in these pages that will not pass severe scrutiny. I can only justify this effort by pointing to the few existing attempts at systematic comparative analysis and expressing the hope that better ones will follow.

Robert R. Alford
May, 1963

Acknowledgments

TO Seymour Martin Lipset, Professor of Sociology at the University of California at Berkeley, I owe a great deal of intellectual inspiration. His never-ending wealth of exciting ideas has been a constant source of stimulation. Charles Y. Glock, Director of the Survey Research Center at Berkeley, gave the manuscript incisive, logical criticism. A special word of gratitude must go to Jack London of the Department of Education at Berkeley for his friendship and manifold aid.

This study, a revised version of a doctoral dissertation submitted to the University of California at Berkeley, forms part of a continuing program of research in comparative politics initiated by the Survey Research Center there. I made extensive use of its IBM card library and its data-processing resources. The staff at the Center was unfailingly helpful, and I want especially to thank Roderic Fredrickson, Director of Data-Processing, for help beyond the call of duty. Professor Philip K. Hastings, Director of the Roper Public Opinion Research Center at Williamstown, Massachusetts, from which much of the data came, gave vital assistance.

Since I cannot claim detailed familiarity with the political and social systems of the Anglo-American countries, I have prevailed upon persons in each country to comment upon various chapters. Whatever clarity my argument possesses owes a great deal to them. Among these I would like to mention: S. D. Clark of the University of Toronto, Philip Converse of the University of Michigan, Duncan MacRae, Jr., of the University of Chicago, Henry Mayer of the University of Sydney, Roy Morgan of Australian Public Opinion Polls, Peter Odegard of the University of California, Maurice Pinard of

Groupe de Recherches Sociales in Montreal, W. G. Runciman of Trinity College, Cambridge, Miss Byrne Hope Sanders of the Canadian Institute of Public Opinion, and T. C. Truman of the University of Queensland. Friends and colleagues at the Universities of California and Wisconsin (as well as at other scattered places since the days of Berkeley seminars) who have commented on various aspects of the study are too numerous to mention, but their suggestions were gratefully received. I cannot, unfortunately, ascribe to my many helpful critics any defects of knowledge, reasoning, or evidence.

I also wish to acknowledge aid from grants for research in comparative political behavior from the Behavioral Sciences Division of the Ford Foundation, from the Committee on Research, University of California, and from the Graduate Research Committee, University of Wisconsin. I am indebted to Marvin Dicker for numerous substantive suggestions and critical comments and to Darrow S. Bishop for accomplishing the laborious task of checking figures and footnotes. The editors of the *Western Political Quarterly* and the *Public Opinion Quarterly* have kindly consented to the inclusion of parts of articles originally appearing in those journals.

Finally, I want to express my gratitude to three former teachers —Reinhard Bendix, Kenneth Bock, and Robert Nisbet—who have continually urged that the social sciences analyze the historical as well as the structural aspects of events in human societies.

Contents

List of Tables*

* Unless otherwise indicated, all tables apply to four Anglo-American countries—Great Britain, Australia, the United States, and Canada.

List of Illustrations

Chapter 1

Party and Class in the
Anglo-American Democracies

THE Anglo-American countries—Great Britain, Australia, New
Zealand, the United States, and Canada—are alike in the important
respect that they may be termed "pluralist" political systems. In
such systems, political parties are free to organize and compete for
power, and pressure groups and interest groups of many kinds may
also compete for influence upon political decision-makers.[1] Voters
are not tightly integrated into enclaves of traditionalism which reinforce ancestral political loyalties. Parties must therefore compete
for support; they are not guaranteed a reliable national majority,
although they can count on many constituencies for consistent support.[2] In these countries, every person in the society is potentially
a full member of the political system—a citizen, regardless of social
and legal practices in some sections which bar the exercise of the
rights of that citizenship. The relatively early establishment of
manhood voting has given citizens of these countries, in contrast
with many others, a stake in the continuance of the existing political system.

[1] See William Kornhauser, *The Politics of Mass Society* (Glencoe, Ill.: Free
Press, 1959), for a recent discussion of political pluralism, and Alexis de
Tocqueville, *Democracy in America* (New York: Vintage, 1954), for the
classic statement of the preconditions of pluralism.

[2] The islands of traditionalism and enforcement of one-party voting, such as
the South in the United States, will be discussed in the chapters on the various countries. It should not be assumed that all enclaves disappear in modern
societies. Ethnically or religiously homogeneous suburbs are striking features of
many cities, and their political consequences are not yet known.

In this chapter, features of the political culture and institutions of the Anglo-American countries will be first described; then characteristics of their social class systems will be discussed.

POLITICAL CULTURE

The Anglo-American countries have the common heritage of British political culture and traditions. Where a common political culture—widespread values unifying a political system—exists, specific political institutions may differ, but the "spirit" or "climate" of politics may be remarkably similar. In spite of the parliamentary system and cabinet government in the Commonwealth and the presidential system in the United States, the countries share a common set of underlying political values: liberalism, individualism, and a pragmatic, non-ideological sense of compromise. There is a high level of consensus in these countries upon these values. The political scientist Gabriel Almond has described the political culture of these Anglo-American countries as "secular and homogeneous."[3] Alexander Brady, in his comparative study of several Commonwealth countries, makes the same point. Although he refers specifically to the overseas Dominions, his point applies to the United States as well:

> The overseas Dominions . . . share two common socio-political elements: first, extensive and sparsely peopled territories, situated chiefly within the temperate latitudes, where politics and social life have been penetrated in various degrees with the spirit of a frontier; and secondly, political institutions, mainly derivative, rooted ultimately in the law, culture, and liberal philosophy of the British people.[4]

A Canadian historian adds that although the United States, unlike the Dominion of the British Commonwealth, "shut [the] doorway to the past" by its revolution, it

> locked the stable door after the steed—that is, the traditional English institutions—had been securely tied inside. No one needs to be reminded that today, after nearly two centuries of separation, the

---

[3] Gabriel Almond, "Comparative Political Systems" in Heinz Eulau, Samuel Eldersveld, and Morris Janowitz, eds., *Political Behavior; A Reader in Theory and Research* (Glencoe, Ill.: Free Press, 1956), p. 36.
[4] Alexander Brady, *Democracy in the Dominions* (Toronto: University of Toronto Press, 1947), p. 1.

institutions of the entire English-speaking world have tremendous areas in common.[5]

Consensus

The Anglo-American political systems enjoy a high level of consensus on political procedures and on the political framework itself. More specifically, no social group feels itself so severely deprived by the operations of the system that it moves outside of the framework of existing political institutions to struggle for its demands. Also, no social groups are completely isolated from similar reactions to events affecting the nation.

Consensus may be distinguished from legitimacy, which refers to the belief by a population that the existence of their nation (or any institution or social practice) is right and proper. In sociological usage, the term is taken from the German scholar Max Weber's analysis of the ways in which different types of power and authority are "legitimated." The distinction between consensus and legitimacy is important here because, as will be shown in the case of Canada, the Anglo-American nations vary in the degree to which their citizens believe in the essential "rightness" of their political institutions. Political struggles may nevertheless be constrained by consensus on the "rules of the game."[6]

Voters in these countries seem to be even less concerned about which party wins than voters in other stable European democracies, which may indicate either a lack of burning issues or the failure of the parties to take a stand on such issues. The failure of more radical parties to gain a foothold also suggests that the relative unconcern of voters for the victory of their party reflects a high level of consensus.[7]

---

[5] A. R. M. Lower, "Theories of Canadian Federalism—Yesterday and Today" in A. R. M. Lower and F. R. Scott *et al., Evolving Canadian Federalism* (Durham, N.C.: Duke University Press, 1958), pp. 5–6.

[6] See Max Weber, *The Theory of Social and Economic Organization* (Glencoe, Ill.: Free Press, 1947), pp. 124–32, and Reinhard Bendix, *Max Weber: An Intellectual Portrait* (New York: Doubleday, 1960), pp. 294–300.

[7] An international Gallup poll in 1948 reported that the proportion of the population saying that it made a great deal of difference which political party won was between 40 and 47 per cent in Canada, Australia, and the United States; 52 per cent in Denmark; and between 59 and 69 per cent in three Scandinavian countries. (See Australian Gallup poll release, February-March, 1949.) A similar question asked in Britain in 1958 ("Do you think that there is any real important difference between the political parties in this country?") found that 40 per cent said yes. (British Institute of Public Opinion Survey No. 58, January, 1958.)

In spite of these similarities, there are probably important differences in the mechanisms which generate compromise in these countries. In Great Britain, consensus is probably built into individuals—with values of deference and accommodation being strongly held. In the United States, the levels of individual tolerance of differences are lower, but the absence of strong majority parties and the system of checks on majority rule force moderation upon the political system; institutional devices reinforcing concensus are required because consensual values are probably not deeply internalized.[8]

Although these societies are as unified by consensus on certain values as any societies in existence today, such consensus—whether based on unifying religious or secular values or on institutions—is always problematic. Assuming that it is an eternal characteristic obscures analysis of the actual mechanisms through which these political systems have attained some measure of stability. Any system exhibits a considerable degree of instability because of continuous struggles of competing values and interests. Various strains and tensions change political boundaries and agreements.[9]

The common political culture of the Anglo-American countries means that a comparative study of political cleavages is not complicated by widely varying political values and traditions. Also, the character of this political culture means that the pluralist political institutions of these countries are reinforced by appropriate values and traditions.

British political culture has become differentiated, however, to suit the particular circumstances of national development. The various English-speaking colonies adopted the particular facets of English political ideologies which suited their conditions. One observer distinguished the colonies as follows:

> . . . discussions in the United States seemed to be in the language of Locke or Adam Smith; in Canada there was a flavor of James

---

[8] See Harry Eckstein, *A Theory of Stable Democracy*, Research Monograph No. 10 (Princeton: Center of International Studies, 1961) for a discussion of the way in which certain patterns of congruence of authority patterns at different levels of social organization favor stable democracy.

[9] An important question worth investigating, in any political system, is: Under what conditions can a group which does not accept a particular set of unifying values or beliefs come to exert political influence so as to disrupt the political system?

Mill with a dash of John Stuart Mill; but in Australia the shadows of all the agitators and reformers from the Chartists to Henry George and the Fabians were over the land.[10]

These different ideological forebears are consistent with the idea that, although all of these nations accept representative government, it is with somewhat different nuances: Canada believes in a traditional elite restricting and guiding representative democracy, much more in the British vein, and therefore has less distrust of central government. The United States believes that the bourgeois can govern society far better than any government; whereas Australia believes that government must control society in the interest of the people. Thus, the style of politics exhibits a different flair, even though the cut of the costume is the same. The actual degree of centralization of government or the political role of the bourgeois may be quite different from that implied by a prevalent ideology, of course.

Complex historical processes obviously determined the outcomes of the political and social struggles which have shaped the present forms of the political cultures of these countries, and the details cannot be discussed here. In Canada and the United States, for example, parallel social movements took place in response to similar forces and situations, but with quite different outcomes. According to S. D. Clark, although "it is true that the American political society was born of revolution whereas the Canadian political society developed largely out of forces opposed to revolution," Canada did have its revolutions; they were unsuccessful.

> Forms of political organization in Canada . . . have actually represented an effort to hold in check the kind of political developments which [the frontier] experience engendered . . . the more radical principle of checks and balances [and] the politically irresponsible radicalism of the frontier.[11]

---

[10] Herbert Heaton, "Other Wests Than Ours," *The Tasks of Economic History,* Supplement VI of the *Journal of Economic History* (1946), p. 60.

[11] S. D. Clark, *Movements of Political Protest in Canada, 1640–1840* (Toronto: University of Toronto Press, 1959), pp. 3, 4, 10. Clark notes that as a consequence of the failure of revolution, the Canadian rebel, because of the weakness of the society as a legitimate order, "could not avoid the charge of disloyalty since what he sought threatened the very political existence of the society of which he was a member" (p. 10). In the United States, on the other hand, "the patriotism of the rebel in American society was seldom open to serious question . . . since he was indirectly fighting the battles of his governing authorities" (p. 9).

Such subtle variations in political culture may have definite effects upon the styles of behavior of officials. "Canadian foreign ministers of recent years have described their endeavors as . . . cautious, patient, compromising, flexible" in accordance with their non-revolutionary tradition. On the other hand, "from the American revolutionary tradition derives that characteristically American belief that some swift and spectacular stroke may permanently solve problems which in their nature admit only of amelioration."[12]

STRUCTURAL AND HISTORICAL FACTORS

The parliaments of the Anglo-American countries differ considerably in size: Great Britain has the most members in its lower House (630); the United States is next (435); then Canada (265); and finally Australia (121). It might be argued that larger parliaments would find it more difficult to maintain discipline, since so many factions could easily find numerical support. Also, the small constituencies upon which they would necessarily be based might mean that local or regional interests would have more impact upon their behavior than national ones. Since the largest parliament of these four also has centralized, disciplined parties, size can be ruled out as a decisive factor. It might be suggested that there is a "threshold" past which increasing size has no great effect upon the functioning of a social or political organization, and that probably all of these parliaments are beyond the threshold size. Past, say, fifty members, a political body is necessarily organized into numerous subcommittees which provide structural opportunity for whatever factionalism and localism is potentially present in the social features of the system.

Other differences in the character of the political institutions do exist, and their consequences for the pattern of political cleavage will be taken into account in appropriate chapters. The differences in the operations of the parliaments and the party systems will be discussed briefly in this chapter. Great Britain has a unitary state; the other three have federal systems. Federalism introduces an element of potential regionalism which is of varying importance. The United States government cannot be brought down by a vote of "no confidence" before its allotted term is up; the other govern-

---

[12] See James Eayrs, *The Art of the Possible: Government and Foreign Policy in Canada* (Toronto: University of Toronto Press, 1961), pp. 153–54.

ments are subject to constant challenge by the opposition party. This feature, part of the system of cabinet government, has unknown consequences for the social base of the parties. Does a party behave differently on this account? Even a tentative answer to this question is beyond the scope of this study. The system of the single-member constituency and simple majority is in effect for each of these nations except Australia, where a form of the preferential ballot is used. The Australian system apparently significantly affects the number and role of the political parties; this will be touched upon in Chapter 7.

Whether the sheer size of either nation or parliament affects the number and operations of political parties or the character of their strategies and appeals for support is problematic. The United States had a population in 1960 of about 180 million people; the United Kingdom, 52 million; Canada, about 18 million; and Australia, about 10 million. Great size may decrease the possibility that class groupings will organize effectively on a national basis and may increase the likelihood that regionalism—whether based upon ethnic or religious groups or simply on the domination of a region by a single economic interest—can maintain its hold. As will be shown, neither the two smaller nor the two larger countries are similar in their patterns of political cleavage, so it is reasonable to assume that size in and of itself is not a decisive factor.

In considering similarities and differences between nations, it can be too easily concluded that each feature being compared is "inevitable" in each country, that the British unitary state, for example, arises from fundamental features of British history or values or that American federalism springs from equally deep-rooted forces. It is difficult to keep in mind the possibility that historical "accidents"— personalities, specific events, political contingencies—may have accumulative consequences for political systems far out of proportion to the original triggering cause. However, the path which was actually taken was not "accidental" in the sense that what happened did happen because of forces and pressures working in that particular direction. When evaluating the origins of some feature of a society or state, both possibilities must be kept in mind simultaneously; the attribute may have been produced by overwhelming social and political forces or by relatively minor events and situations. The political boundaries of the present nation-state illustrate this point.

It is historically possible that the Anglo-Saxon countries might "look" much more similar than they do now. Suppose that Ireland had not seceded from the United Kingdom but had been satisfied with home rule and its own provincial parliament (like the present one in Northern Ireland) and that Scotland and Wales had been given their own provincial parliaments. Structurally and politically, the pattern of class and regional politics in Britain would be much closer to the other three countries than it now is. There is reason to believe that this is not a far-fetched possibility. A majority of delegates to the "Speaker's Conference" established in 1919 proposed to the Prime Minister in 1920 that bodies subordinate to the United Kingdom Parliament be established in England, Scotland, and Wales. The majority would have been even greater had not the Ulstermen (Northern Ireland) opposed the proposal. (Separatist pressures upon them from the Irish Nationalists forced them to take the position that no such changes could be allowed.) According to Sir Reginald Coupland, Lloyd George (or another leader) *could* have pushed for provincial parliaments and won.[13] Clearly, forces were at work which prevented this outcome, and yet the splitting up of the British unitary state was not an impossibility.

Similar "ifs" in the other direction can be advanced for Canada and the United States. If Quebec had successfully seceded from Canada, many of the pressures toward regionalism in Canada would have been removed, and consolidation of a legitimate, English-speaking nation would have been immensely facilitated. As a consequence, a far more homogeneous nation, undoubtedly exhibiting patterns of class politics much more like Britain's would exist. If the South had successfully seceded from the United States, it seems rather evident that the parties at the present time would not be weighted with Left and Right elements in the way that they are at present. The solid bloc of conservative southerners obscures the class basis of American politics and creates a pull toward regionalism. Suppose, also, that Australia had not adopted a "White Australia" policy or had given its aboriginals citizenship and a separate state. Regional blocs of Orientals and former primitive tribes might now exist within the Australian nation.

A principal task for any scholar analyzing social and political organization is to explain historical patterns as they exist, and, in ad-

---

[13] Sir Reginald Coupland, *Welsh and Scottish Nationalism: A Study* (London: Collins, 1954), p. 321. Scotland and Northern Ireland actually do have separate legal and judicial systems.

dition, to explain how much contingencies, situational reactions of individuals, and the accidents of personality, have altered crucial political decisions and left legacies of structure relatively unconnected to social values or political forces. As far as the problem of this book is concerned, it must be kept in mind that national boundaries are not iron "external conditions" which delimit inquiry but part of the problematic center of investigation. Some social or political conditions, whether strongly established values, successful strategies, or a series of fortuitous circumstances, hold a given political system together or split it apart, and determine its form. Similarly, the paths of action taken by political parties or social classes need not be assumed to have been historically inevitable or necessary— alternative possible actions by leaders or groups might have permanently altered not merely events, but the systems themselves.[14]

TWO-PARTY SYSTEMS

Each of the Anglo-American countries tends toward a two-party system, although three of the four here considered have more than two parties actually running candidates for national office.[15] Whether these countries are "really" two-party systems or not depends on the problem of interest, but both the legitimate way in which they constitute two-party systems and the reasons for the existence of more than two parties are important for the understanding of the pattern of political cleavages in these countries.

Political scientists, when distinguishing the Anglo-American countries from others, commonly consider them to be "two-party" systems, a theoretical rather than an empirical term referring to certain structural pressures and institutional imperatives common to all of these countries. According to the political scientist D. W. Brogan, countries which have had "British political training . . . fall naturally back to the two-party system, even a two-party system with little intellectual consistency."[16] Maurice Duverger re-

---

[14] For an excellent discussion of this point, see Barrington Moore, Jr., *Political Power and Social Theory* (Cambridge: Harvard University Press, 1958), pp. 148–59.

[15] All of these countries have many minor parties springing up over temporary issues or representing some particular aggrieved public, but only those parties which are recognized as having some national importance are referred to here.

[16] In Lord Campion *et al.*, *Parliament, a Survey* (London: George Allen & Unwin, 1952), p. 75.

fers to the "Anglo-Saxon two-party systems," contrasting them with the single- and multi-party systems of continental Europe.[17]

Such a description is most meaningful when these countries are contrasted with others more clearly of a multi-party or single-party type. The three countries within the British Commonwealth share a system of parliamentary government. Power is not divided between the executive and legislative branches in the American manner, but must necessarily be exercised across the board by one or the other of the two major parties. Power in Great Britain is transferred back and forth from the Labour to the Conservative party, the Liberal party playing a minor role. Power in Australia shifts from Labor to a coalition of the Liberal and Country parties. Power in Canada shifts from the Liberal to the Conservative party; the Cooperative Commonwealth Federation (CCF), its successor —the "New Democratic party"—and the Social Credit party have had no realistic hopes of gaining governmental power. The parties which form the government or the Opposition in these parliamentary systems may change, and the third or fourth parties may play crucial roles in influencing policies, but power is exercised by one of two major parties or coalitions. In the United States, without a parliamentary system, a two-party system has become stable partly because of the party primary, which allows flexible coalitions within the framework of both parties. The presidential and gubernatorial systems in the United States also encourage a two-party division, since these offices cannot be divided and coalitions tend to form around two candidates.[18]

The justification for saying that the Commonwealth nations have "two-party" systems rests primarily upon the institution of cabinet government, in which the single party which secures a majority of seats in the lower house forms a government. As a number of political scientists have pointed out, this creates a pressure for unity of opposition to the governing party. This pressure offsets the fragmenting effects of opposition: the tendency for groups and parties out of power to quarrel over the appropriate ideologies and organizational tactics which will return them to power.[19]

---

[17] Maurice Duverger, *Political Parties* (London: Methuen, 1954), p. 203.

[18] See Seymour M. Lipset, "Party Systems and the Representation of Social Groups," *European Journal of Sociology*, I (1960), 50–85.

[19] See E. E. Schattschneider, *Party Government* (New York: Farrar & Rinehart, 1942) for a discussion of the pressures upon the "out-groups" to coalesce. Such a theory suffers somewhat from the continuing existence of "third" parties in all of these countries except the United States.

Thus, although more than two parties run candidates for national office in these countries, the realistic alternative governments presented to the electorate—the main concern here—are only two. This is another factor which these countries have in common and which makes comparative generalizations more valid. The electorate is not fragmented into supporters of one or another small party hoping to gain a few seats and a voice in a coalition government.[20]

POLITICAL PARTIES: LEFT AND RIGHT

Political parties in the Anglo-American countries, more than those in most others, fall along the classic Left-Right continuum; they lack the complications introduced by strong totalitarian or religious parties that cut across the Left-Right dimension. The dominant political issues in these countries mainly relate to distribution of the national wealth. The degree of centralization of government necessary or desirable to accomplish a variety of social goals, the level of regulation of private business, and the level of public ownership essary or desirable to accomplish a variety of social goals, the level are Left-Right issues arising from the basic divisions of class interests in these societies. The parties in the Anglo-American countries differ in their stands on these issues and in their "distance" apart, but the systems themselves are not torn by conflict over the very existence of pluralist political institutions. The existence of parties primarily battling over Left-Right economic issues is in part a consequence of the moderate and compromising values of British political culture and in part a result of the relative wealth and high average standard of living of these countries. The character of the parties also shapes and reinforces a particular political culture, of course.

Unlike the parties of continental Europe, political parties in these countries are not usually polarized along *explicit* religious lines. Instead, a secular norm is dominant. Secular politics is, almost by definition, "interest" politics. The parties represent loose coalitions of diverse interest groups rather than clearly defined sets of ultimate values.

---

[20] Variations in the electoral system account for differences in the numbers of parties to some extent. The "preferential ballot" in use in Australia may account for the rise of small parties, which can thereby gain influence without weakening the major party to which they are linked. The "third" parties in each country will be considered in the appropriate chapters and their general functions for social groups in Chapter 10.

Table 1–1 (p. 13) attempts to place the parties in four Anglo-American countries on a Left-Right continuum in terms of domestic policies, on the assumptions that: (1) in all four, politics is a process of collective bargaining between different interest groups; (2) the Left-Right split is a major dimension dividing the parties; and (3) these four constitute a *single* major type of political system, so the parties may be compared along similar dimensions. These distinctions really fall at uneven intervals along a continuum. The constellations of policies and ideologies of specific parties cannot be neatly cataloged, particularly in consensual systems where the parties are open to many, and often contradictory, influences.

The radical Left does not exist in these countries except in minute and sectarian forms, nor does the reactionary Right exist in the form of parties. Movements such as Sir Oswald Mosley's in Britain or those of McCarthyites in the United States (including the John Birch Society) cannot command support as independent parties, so they operate as pressure groups upon the other parties. (In fact, the absence of extremist parties can be considered a defining characteristic of these systems; it is further evidence of a high level of consensus.) The typical ideology of parties of each type can be characterized as follows.

The social-democratic-Left parties follow the model of the European social-democratic parties, advocating expanded government social welfare activities and sometimes nationalization of industry but accepting moderate parliamentary procedures—and therefore serious compromises with their programs. The center-Left parties on many issues are indistinguishable from the center-Right parties. The former are usually for social reforms, but will split from the social-democratic-Left on the issues of nationalization, unconditional support of trade unions, and expanded government bureaucracies. The center-Left accepts an ideology of individualism and freedom—in practice, toleration of monopoly corporations as long as government exercises certain controls. It regards both capital and labor as undesirably tending toward monopoly control, and sees government as a necessary mediator between the two.

The center-Right parties are much less distrustful than the center-Left of the activities of the big businessmen and see their enlightened elements as the sources of economic progress. They view trade unions as an unavoidable necessity under modern circumstances which can be turned to responsible ends under the proper leader-

TABLE 1-1

Left and Right Parties

| | LEFT | | CENTER | | RIGHT | |
	Radical-Left	Social-Democratic-Left	Left	Right	Conservative-Right	Reactionary-Right
Great Britain	......	Labour	Liberal	Conservative	......	(Mosley)
Australia	......	Labor	Democratic Labor	Liberal	Country	......
United States	......	......	Democratic	......	Republican	(McCarthyite movements)
Canada	......	New Democratic	Liberal	......	Progressive Conservative	Social Credit

ship. Government activity is encouraged insofar as it serves as a bulwark to business enterprise, and even nationalization of weaker industries will be suffered, in practice if not in principle, in order to maintain the remainder of the private economic system as a going concern.[21] The conservative-Right parties cannot clearly be distinguished by specific beliefs, but often vacillate between center- and reactionary-Right policies.

The reactionary-Right movements reject the legitimacy of trade unionism and see many political movements and forces as part of a conspiracy to destroy institutions originating in the eighteenth and nineteenth centuries which have changed under twentieth century conditions. Such movements will advocate various nostrums —new taxation devices, new monetary plans, anti-political party measures—which will supposedly restore the society to its former purity. (The Social Credit party of Canada, originating in Alberta as an agrarian reform party, became a Right-wing party partly because of its monetary ideology, which originally was conceived of as an anti-monopoly, anti-capitalistic device. (See Chapter 9.)

Detailed evidence for these assertions cannot be presented here, since the concern of this book is not with party ideology or practices as such, but with the character of party support.[22]

---

[21] It may be noted that centralization of government is not necessarily the hallmark of leftist ideology. The forerunners of the present Progressive-Conservative party in Canada (Liberal-Conservatives under John A. Macdonald) and the present Republican party in the United States (the Federalists under Alexander Hamilton) believed in centralization as a means of advancing the development of nationally organized propertied, commercial, and industrial interests, which they saw as the agents of national integration and development. A belief in decentralization, conversely, has frequently been associated with radical agrarian movements. The function of any ideology must be seen in relation to the specific conditions which make it serviceable to a particular group.

[22] There is no good typology of ideological orientations of parties. For a very brief general discussion, see Maurice Duverger, *op. cit.* pp. 418–21. Also, for more specific distinctions see D. W. Rawson, *Australia Votes: The 1958 Federal Election* (Melbourne: Melbourne University Press, 1961), pp. 10–59, for a discussion of the ideologies and programs of Australian parties; The Times of London, *Guide to the House of Commons, 1959* (London, 1960), pp. 240–58, for a summary of the election manifestoes of the three British parties which reveal clear ideological differences; Clinton Rossiter, *Parties and Politics in America* (Ithaca, N.Y.: Cornell University Press, 1960), pp. 66–82; and Robert M. Dawson, *The Government of Canada* (2nd ed.; Toronto: University of Toronto Press, 1954), pp. 491–501. Ideological characterizations are more difficult for the American parties (both United States and Canadian) for reasons already indicated.

The scheme in Table 1–1 portrays the approximate way in which the parties in these countries correspond to these types. The Labor parties of Britain and Australia, and the New Democratic party (formerly the Cooperative Commonwealth Federation) are social-democratic-Left parties. The United States lacks such a moderate socialist party. All four countries have a center-Left party, but only in Canada (the Liberal party) and the United States (the Democratic party) is this type of party the major party of the Left. Center-Right parties are missing in the United States and Canada, but they are dominant on the Right in Australia and Great Britain. Conservative-Right parties are the major parties of the Right in the United States and Canada, but Australia also has such a party in the Country party.

It may be noted that what might be called the "center of gravity" of the political system is further to the Left in Great Britain and Australia. Although the party system is still polarized, the major parties in these countries are both further to the Left than are the major parties of the United States and Canada. That is, both the Liberal party in Australia and the Conservative party in Great Britain have accepted a far more "Left" program than has been necessary for the Progressive-Conservative party in Canada and the Republican party in the United States. Given a moderate, consensual political culture, it is only to be expected that the necessities of remaining a potential holder of power would pull the more conservative parties in Australia and Britain to the Left—or conversely, the more Left parties in the United States and Canada to the Right.

Tendencies bringing these party systems together will be discussed in the appropriate chapters; these involve mainly the attempted revival of the Liberal party in Britain and the growth of the Democratic Labor party in Australia, both here labeled center-Left parties. If these could become the dominant parties on the Left, presumably this would release the major Right parties in these countries from the pull to the Left, and the four systems would look even more alike than they do now.

It assumes that domestic politics is still the axis of polarization for the political parties in these countries. If, or when, foreign policy issues become of supreme importance, traditional ideological cleavages may lose much of their importance, although there may be some connection between a party's domestic and foreign policies. Parties of the Right tend to assume that they act in the national interest, partly because they represent political positions already established and legitimate which are therefore more easily covered with the aura of the "national interest." But either party, in consensual systems at least, can become leader of the nation in periods when foreign policy issues are crucial. The extent to which such issues have replaced domestic issues as the main basis for party cleavage is an important problem, but there seems to be no reason to assume that the classic Left-Right continuum has lost its relevance.

Another problem concerns the location of the line between Left and Right. Should the center-Right parties of Britain and Australia be classified as Left parties with respect to the parties of Canada and the United States? As characterized here, they certainly can be described as such, but this seems to be only an abstract consideration. In practice, there is no sharp dividing line between the parties of the Left and the Right, especially at the center; this is indeed a fundamental characteristic of these systems and need not be defined away.

Moreover, it must not be inferred from this classification that the functions of parties of the same type are the same in each system. Clearly, a party will operate differently where it is a minority and where it is a majority. Specific historical and institutional features of the different societies will affect the recruitment of leadership, the character of party support, and so one, and these in turn will press the party in various directions. An important problem for comparative research would be to analyze the ways in which internal organization, strategies, and even the platforms of the social-democratic, center-Left or Right, or conservative-Right parties are affected by their majority or minority status, their position Right or Left vis-à-vis other parties, and the contingencies of their historical situation.

Static distinctions such as those made do not portray pressures for change upon parties from changing historical conditions. Positions appropriately Right in one historical period may become the property of the Left in another period. For example, while a country remains "frontier" in character, and economic or territorial expansion is still an important possibility, centralized government may be the goal of conservative politicians and businessmen because only such a government can effectively establish the conditions for expansion. Such a government may be opposed by the farmers and workers of the time. Provincial or states' rights were the bulwark of the small farmer in both the United States and Canada, and in an earlier historical period were the backbone of the Left parties' programs. When a nation has become more urbanized and industrialized, and when economic or territorial expansion has become more an ideology than a reality, the relative emphasis on government centralization shifts; the Left party seeks to expand welfare programs, and the Right party attempts to hold the goals of government down to facilitating economic activity.

This implicit description of the parties as national bodies ignores the interplay of national and regional interests. Centralization must also be seen as a matter of tactics, shifting according to time and place. In a real sense, for example, the weighting of both major parties toward the Right in Canada and the United States (see Chapters 8, 9) has allowed conservative economic interests to use both the centralizing and the decentralizing possibilities inherent in the ambiguity of their constitutions to their own advantage.[23]

Another aspect of the positions of the parties which static distinctions do not reveal is their response, especially in consensual systems, to current social demands of politically important publics. A party which is "normally" a conservative-Right party may thus be drawn to the Left in order to win over what it perceives as a segment of the population it must lure away from another party. The Progressive-Conservative party of Canada moved far to the Left in 1957 in exactly such an attempt (see Chapter 9, pp. 279–80), and the Labour party in Britain may be under similar pressures to move to the Right (see Chapter 6, pp. 126–27). Whatever the complex causes of how parties react to the constant contradic-

---

[23] The courts, and not merely the parties, have been affected by conservative pressures, whether consciously or not. Canadian Left legislation was ruled to violate the British North America Act—both for failing to fall within the jurisdiction of the provincial government and for failing to fall within the jurisdiction of the Dominion government. For example, a tax bill passed by the Social Credit government in Alberta was ruled unconstitutional because it "coerced" the banks—not on the ground that the decision favored the existing financial structure, but on the ground that the province has no right to interfere with Dominion corporations. The Dominion power was asserted to protect the unity of the Canadian financial system. On the other hand, Left legislation paralleling American New Deal legislation was ruled unconstitutional because it was held that only the provinces could pass social insurance measures. See James R. Mallory, *Social Credit and the Federal Power in Canada* (Toronto: University of Toronto Press, 1954), pp. 51 ff. Undoubtedly parallel actions of the parties could be found.

tory pressures upon them, it is clear that parties do change their character. Few comparative studies of the conditions stabilizing or undermining an established party's character have been done, and here the relevance of such studies to the understanding of political cleavages can only be indicated.

Little attention will be paid to the social bases of party politics in New Zealand for the reason that no national surveys have been conducted in that country. A comparison of New Zealand with other countries would add further depth to the understanding of how essentially British institutions have been modified under new conditions. New Zealand is relatively non-industrialized, small in both area and population, with essentially the same political institutions as Britain. It has: fusion of legislative and executive bodies, unitary government, a two-party system (plus a small Social Credit party), and other similar features. It is too small to permit political regionalism—in the sense that a population in an area large enough to have an ideology of separatism cannot exist. It has a strong Labour party which differs from the British Labour party in that a core of intellectuals was not present from the beginning.[24]

SOCIAL CLASS AND CITIZENSHIP

Full citizenship and competitive parties have not eliminated class stratification in the Anglo-American countries. However, through a series of historical developments in England, a basic equality of rights has been established, and the previously much more rigid class system was eliminated. As T. H. Marshall has pointed out, this movement toward equality of rights has passed through roughly three stages: (1) the achievement of civil rights (of habeas corpus, freedom of the press, freedom to work at one's choice of occupation) in the eighteenth century; (2) political rights (to vote and to organize) in the nineteenth century; and (3) social rights (to a minimum wage and a certain level of economic security) in the twentieth century.[25] Clearly, none of these yet exists in fully developed form, and though the other Anglo-American coun-

---

[24] For a comparison of the British and New Zealand Labour parties, see Louise Overacker, "The British and New Zealand Labour Parties: A Comparison," *Political Science* (New Zealand), I (March, 1957), 23–36, and II (September, 1957), 15–33.

[25] T. H. Marshall, *Citizenship and Social Class* (London: Cambridge University Press, 1950).

tries did not go through the same historical process as England, they are in substantially the same position in the 1960's.

In Great Britain, political equality has not been completely achieved for all citizens, but the extent to which remaining inequalities are being challenged is an indication of the degree to which Britain is becoming like the other Anglo-American democracies, where there are no *institutionalized* differences in the political rights of individuals. One change is the gradual abolition of the special votes for the universities and for property-holders. Another challenge, still unsuccessful at this writing, concerns the hereditary right to a seat in the House of Lords.[26]

The emergence of these new political rights helped to stabilize the new form of class system. The "single uniform status of citizenship . . . provided the foundation of equality on which the structure of inequality could be built."[27] In a real sense, the achievement of citizenship legitimated sharp differences of wealth and property because the system seemed to be absolved of responsibility for the fate of individuals.

Citizenship in this sense was not (could not) be seen by Marx or by Marxists as having the profound political consequences which it in fact has had. If considered at all by Marxists, the idea of citizenship in a democratic order was included under the heading of "false consciousness," as a delusion engendered by the powerful agencies available to the capitalist class for convincing the workers that their needs could be met without a profound transformation

---

[26] In 1962, two persons inherited seats in the House of Lords but refused to accept them. Both were former members of the House of Commons, and one won an election to Commons after being elevated to the peerage. He was not allowed to take his seat. A committee in the same year was studying this decision, and the long-standing practice that a person cannot disavow his hereditary political privileges may be altered. (See the *New York Times,* June 27, 1962.)

[27] Marshall, *op. cit.,* p. 34. The view that the achievement of citizenship—full political and social integration into the larger society—by the working classes is a perennial problem of industrializing societies, a problem occasioned by the process of formation of the working class from a peasantry torn from village life and the land, is closely akin to the Marxist view of societal development. It accepts the idea of class struggle and sees large structural problems posed by certain tendencies of a society at a given level of economic development. However, this view (at least in its expression by such writers as T. H. Marshall and Reinhard Bendix) rejects the inevitability of socialism as the working-class political response to the social conditions of capitalist society. Citizenship and the equalitarianism it implies become a substitute for socialist forms of equality.

of existing property relationships. The legitimacy of British political culture and its institutions seemed to Marxists to be a temporary phenomenon which would be erased as the inadequacy of the system to contain class conflicts or to solve the problems of production and distribution in the national economy was increasingly perceived by the working class.

On the other hand, although the equalitarian political culture of these countries has probably reduced the political consequences of class stratification, there is no reason to suppose that the class structure is unrelated to the parties. In the following section, the similarities of class structure of these four countries are discussed, particularly with regard to the range of positions available, the prestige attached to different positions (using occupations as the measure of positions), the extent of social mobility and what has been called "class crystallization." These "structural" features of class systems need not be the most politically important, however, and the subsequent section will take up the subjective aspect of class stratification: class consciousness.

Structural Features of Social Class

The range of stratification positions available is roughly the same in each of these societies. Professionals, skilled craftsmen, small businessmen, executives, civil servants, salesmen, and laborers all exist in each of these societies. No important feudal segments remain.

Since these are all advanced industrial societies, the composition of their labor forces is similar. This is shown by a number of measures: the proportion of the population in non-agricultural pursuits, the distribution of employed persons in different occupations and industries, and the proportion of manual workers who are salaried or wage-earning as distinct from self-employed. Tables 1–2 to 1–5 show these various characteristics of the labor force of the four countries.

Although the proportion of the male labor force in non-agricultural occupations differs slightly from country to country, it is higher in the lowest of these countries (Canada) than in the average of the other European stable democracies (Table 1–2).

Tables 1–3, 1–4, and 1–5 are given in detail especially to show that Great Britain does not have a much larger proportion of manual workers or persons in manufacturing industries than the other

TABLE 1–2

Males in Non-Agricultural Occupations, circa 1950

COUNTRY	MALES IN NON-AGRICULTURAL OCCUPATIONS *(Per Cent)*
Great Britain	94
Australia	84
United States	85
Canada	77
Other European and English-speaking stable democracies	74

Source: United Nations, *Demographic Yearbook* (New York, 1956), Table 12, pp. 344–87. The other European or English-speaking stable democracies are Belgium, Denmark, Ireland, New Zealand, the Netherlands, Norway, Sweden, and Switzerland. For a number of other indices of economic development for these countries and other European and Latin-American countries, see Seymour M. Lipset, *Political Man* (New York: Doubleday, 1960), pp. 51–54.

countries. A number of scholars have implicitly assumed that Britain's politics was different from that of the other English-speaking countries because it has an extremely high proportion of manual workers in its population.[28]

The occupational composition of the labor force shown in Table 1–3 is quite similar in the four countries. Australia and Great Britain have a slightly higher proportion of persons in the three classifications which might broadly be called manual occupations, and a slightly lower proportion in the white-collar and professional occupations, but the differences are small compared to less industrialized countries. Even if service and farming, fishing, etc. are included as manual occupations, the countries are very much alike.

Table 1–4 distinguishes, within the occupations called "manual," between employers, self-employed persons, salaried workers and wage-earners, and unpaid family workers. The size of the purely salaried and wage-earning segments in manual occupations is also very similar in the four countries.

---

[28] See for example, Mark Abrams, "Social Class in British Politics," *Public Opinion Quarterly*, XXV (Fall, 1961), 342. Abrams' estimate is based on large sample surveys. John Bonham's calculations, reproduced in Table 6–2, p. 128, are based upon different categories from those employed here; they need not be incorrect, but they simply do not apply to an international comparison.

TABLE 1–3
The Economically Active Population, by Occupation, circa 1950

OCCUPATION	ECONOMICALLY ACTIVE POPULATION (Per Cent)			
	UNITED KINGDOM* 1951	AUSTRALIA† 1947	UNITED STATES 1950	CANADA 1951
Professional, technical and related	6	5	8	7
Managerial, administrative, clerical and related	12	18	21	20
Sales	10	8	7	6
Farming, fishing, hunting, lumbering, and related	5	15	12	19
Mining, quarrying and related	3 ⎫	⎫	1 ⎫	2 ⎫
Operating transport	8 ⎬ 42	⎬ 42	4 ⎬ 38	5 ⎬ 38
Crafts, production process, and others not elsewhere classified	31 ⎭	⎭	33 ⎭	31 ⎭
Service‡	14	7	10	8
Armed forces	2	1	2	1
Not classifiable	9	4	2	1
TOTAL	100	100	100	100
TOTAL NUMBER (000's)	(22,578)	(3,196)	(60,037)	(5,300)

Source: United Nations, *Demographic Yearbook* (New York, 1956), Table 15, pp. 458–99.
* Northern Ireland is excluded.
† Certain Australian occupational groups were not tabulated separately.
‡ Service occupations may or may not be "manual" in character.

TABLE 1–4

Total Economically Active Population in Manual Occupations Who Are Salaried and Wage-Earners, circa 1950

COUNTRY	ECONOMICALLY ACTIVE POPULATION		
	TOTAL NUMBER (000's)	IN MANUAL OCCUPATIONS (Per Cent)	IN MANUAL OCCUPATIONS WHO ARE SALARIED AND WAGE-EARNERS (Per Cent)
Great Britain (1951)	22,578	42	39
Australia (1947)	3,196	42	37
United States (1950)	60,037	38	34
Canada (1951)	5,300	38	35

Source: United Nations, *Demographic Yearbook* (New York, 1956), Table 15, pp. 458–99. The figures are for the census nearest to 1950. The distinction in the table refers to "occupation" and "status within that occupation." The manual occupations are mining, quarrying, operating transport, crafts, production process, and labor, as also shown in Table 1–3. The small differences between the percentages given above are due to the small numbers of persons in those occupations who are employers, self-employed persons, or unpaid family workers. Northern Ireland is excluded from the above table, but its comparable percentages are 47 and 42. Since its labor force is less than 3 per cent of the total British labor force, its inclusion would not change the above figures.

The industrial distribution of the labor force—as distinguished from its occupational composition—is shown in Table 1–5. Managers and executives of steel mills, as well as janitors, are included in the "manufacturing" category. England and Wales have a slightly higher proportion of persons in manufacturing and a slightly lower proportion in the so-called tertiary industries—those which do not either produce raw materials or process them, but service and distribute people and commodities. Again, however, the over-all distribution is quite similar.

In addition to similar occupational and industrial structures, these countries have similar levels of occupational mobility. A major conclusion of a recent study of social mobility in a number of industrial societies was that the level of intergenerational mobility from a manual occupation to a non-manual one (or back) is substantially the same in all industrial societies. Undoubtedly the level of mobility is even more similar for the Anglo-American countries

TABLE 1–5

Industrial Distribution of the Non-Agricultural Labor Force, circa 1950

INDUSTRY	NON-AGRICULTURAL LABOR FORCE (Per Cent)			
	ENGLAND AND WALES 1951	AUSTRALIA 1954	UNITED STATES 1950	CANADA 1951
Mining and quarrying	6	3	2	3
Manufacturing	40	33	33	34
Construction and utilities	12	16	12	13
Commerce	13 ⎫	19 ⎫	20 ⎫	18 ⎫
Transportation and communication "Tertiary Industry"	10 ⎬ 42	13 ⎬ 47	10 ⎬ 50	12 ⎬ 48
Services	19 ⎭	15 ⎭	20 ⎭	18 ⎭
Other	0	1	3	2
TOTAL	100	100	100	100
TOTAL NUMBER (000's)	(12,918)	(2,395)	(36,835)	(3,153)

Source: International Urban Research, Berkeley, California. Agricultural, forestry, hunting, and fishing industries are excluded.

than for countries just emerging from feudalism or rapidly industrializing.[29] Since the occupational composition of these countries is similar, similarity of levels of mobility also means roughly equal opportunities.[30]

Similarity of *rates* of mobility need not mean, of course, that the *mechanisms* of mobility are the same. Ralph H. Turner has suggested that the dominant norm in the United States favors "contest" mobility, in which individuals compete in an open contest; Britain's norm, on the other hand, favors "sponsored" mobility, in which potential elite members are chosen by institutions providing channels for upward mobility—the institutional embodiment of Britain's more sharply status-divided society.[31] (See Chapter 6, pp. 125–28.)

Not only are actual levels of mobility similar in these countries, the prestige of different occupations is also alike. A study comparing occupational prestige in a number of countries found that three English-speaking nations (and Germany) were more like each other than like the U.S.S.R. and Japan in the prestige rankings given to different occupations by samples of respondents.[32]

Corresponding to the similarity of prestige rankings is a similarity of wage-differentials in a number of industries. Lebergott found that in the United States, Canada, and the United Kingdom, the ranking of a number of industries in terms of the average wage paid

---

[29] Seymour M. Lipset and Reinhard Bendix, *Social Mobility in Industrial Society* (Berkeley: University of California Press, 1959), pp. 13–25. In a footnote on p. 29, the authors specifically dispute data from a Melbourne study which found that Australia has less mobility of this kind than other Western countries.

[30] *Ibid.*, p. 27. The authors note that if a country is 90 per cent peasant, "even with completely equal opportunity most children of peasants must remain peasants."

[31] Ralph H. Turner, "Sponsored and Contest Mobility and the School System," *American Sociological Review*, XXV (December, 1960), 855–67.

[32] Alex Inkeles and Peter Rossi, "National Comparisons of Occupational Prestige," *American Journal of Sociology*, LXI (January, 1956), 329–39. The countries considered in this study were Great Britain, the United States, New Zealand, Japan, and Germany. A parallel study done in Canada found equally high correlations. See Bernard R. Blishen, "The Construction and Use of an Occupational Class Scale," *Canadian Journal of Economics and Political Science*, XXIV (November, 1958), 521–31. The same British data are analyzed in more detail in C. A. Moser and J. R. Hall, "The Social Grading of Occupations" in David Glass, ed., *Social Mobility in Britain* (London: Routledge & Kegan Paul, 1954), pp. 29–50. Similar results are reported for Australia in Ronald Taft, "The Social Grading of Occupations in Australia," *British Journal of Sociology*, IV (June, 1953), 181–88.

was the same.[33] Thus, the sheerly economic factors differentiating one section of the working class from another may be relatively the same in these countries. (See Chapter 5, p. 119.) No comparative evidence for the economic position of the persons occupying non-manual positions is available.

In addition, no comparative data are available on the degree of "class crystallization," or the extent to which persons in these countries have consistent social statuses: the absence of such combinations as high income and low status occupation, little education but high status occupation. This is obviously related to the extent and level of social mobility. Presumably if the level of social mobility is high, many persons will possess contradictory status attributes. Yet two countries can probably have roughly similar rates of intergenerational mobility from manual to non-manual occupations (as already shown) and still the proportions of persons in inconsistent status positions may differ considerably. Studies of Detroit and Minneapolis in the United States have shown that a large proportion of the population has inconsistent status attributes (or, in terms of the city itself, a low level of "class crystalization" exists). Less class crystallization was found in large cities than in smaller cities when Detroit and Minneapolis were compared to Lloyd Warner's "Jonesville."[34]

The degree of "class endogamy"—the extent to which men tend to marry brides coming from occupational strata similar to their own—has been found in one preliminary comparison to be "probably about the same in the U.S.A. as it is in England and Wales," which lends further support to the assumption that the objective stratification system of at least these two countries is not substantially different.[35]

---

[33] Cited in Clark Kerr, "Wage Relationships—the Comparative Impact of Market and Power Forces" in John T. Dunlop, ed., *The Theory of Wage Determination* (New York: St. Martin, 1957), pp. 179–80.

[34] Gerhard E. Lenski, "Status Crystallization: A Non-Vertical Dimension of Social Status," *American Sociological Review*, XIX (August, 1954), 405–13. This study of Detroit was repeated for Minneapolis, and the latter is reported in G. Hochbaum, J. G. Darley, E. D. Monachesi, and C. Bird, "Socioeconomic Variables in a Large City," *American Journal of Sociology*, LXI (July, 1955), 31–38. Since Lenski also considered the dimension of ethnicity, he called the measure one of "status-crystallization." Where only education, occupation, and income are combined into a composite measure, the present author prefers the term "class crystallization."

[35] J. R. Hall, "A Comparison of the Degree of Social Endogamy in England and Wales and the U.S.A." in David V. Glass, ed., *Social Mobility in Britain*.

One might expect, therefore, that status inconsistency will increase with urbanization. Because of greater social and geographic mobility in large cities or urbanized countries, a lower correlation between income, education, and occupation than in towns or less urbanized countries will exist. These studies have not been replicated in other countries; they would fill in an important gap in the knowledge of variables affecting social mobility, class consciousness, and, presumably, the association of class and voting. Aside from any question of class consciousness, the "visibility" of the class structure is probably far higher in a country with a high level of class crystallization, since few workers are in contact with anyone with higher incomes or education than themselves.

The nature of the stratification systems in these countries is important for an understanding of the phenomenon of class voting. It has been shown that they are similar in a number of important respects: the shape and content of the occupational structure, the amount of occupational mobility, and the prestige attaching to different occupations. Differences in class voting, therefore, cannot be ascribed to gross differences in the structural features of their stratification systems.

One point to be emphasized is that all four countries are highly stratified in the fundamental sense that there are great differences in incomes, standards of living, and in the life-chances of children of poor families to live relatively free from worry about the next meal. Even in the most "affluent" of these societies—the United States—"poor families comprise one-fifth of the nation's families."[36]

(London: Routledge & Kegan Paul, 1954), p. 346. Hall compared three different occupation groups (non-manual, skilled manual, routine non-manual, and semiskilled and unskilled manual) and found that in all three, the United States actually had higher rates of class endogamy. While this may not be a statistically significant difference owing to variations of sampling and population, the consistency found in three strata suggests that possibly class endogamy may actually be higher in the United States, a finding which would controvert what even close observers of the social class systems of both societies have concluded.

[36] James N. Morgan, Martin H. David, Wilbur J. Cohen, and Harvey E. Brazer, *Income and Welfare in the United States* (New York: McGraw-Hill, 1962), p. 191. This book documents in great detail Michael Harrington's assertion that between 40 and 50 million persons in the United States live at or below the poverty level. Harrington's estimate is based upon the United States Bureau of Labor Statistics figure of $4,000 family income as the dividing line between mere "deprivation" and poverty. See Michael Harrington, *The Other America* (New York: Macmillan, 1962).

Since the majority of these impoverished people have not played a significant role in the political system, their needs do not become translated into effective political demands. A general economic slump might recreate the conditions for the emergence of class politics, or, on the other hand (as is shown in Chapter 8), a general demand by all strata for social change may arise. In any case, it should not be assumed that because these societies are the wealthiest in the world, potentially sharp class issues do not exist.

Subjective Features of Social Class

Apart from "objective" aspects of stratification such as have been discussed, "subjective" aspects—such as the social distance between persons and the extent to which style of life, accent, dress, or manners mark a person indelibly as a member of a high or low status-group—may be important factors solidifying loyalties to political parties. We would expect that where consciousness of gulfs between social statuses is sharply marked, group and party loyalties would be much stronger, partly because in such a society, it would be more difficult for men to lose their marks of origin (even if they actually managed to leave their original class position), and partly because the consequences of losing those marks would be more serious: the severance of family ties is only one such consequence.

Great Britain has the most clearly marked system of status differentiation of any of these four countries.[37] Some consider the system to be breaking down under the impact of prosperity and the slow equalization of educational opportunities for workers. (See Chapter 6.) If so, the Anglo-American societies will be alike in yet another respect.

The character of the British class system is reflected in T. H. Marshall's views. He stresses recognition by others as a certain *kind* of person as the hallmark of class. Admission to certain social relationships determines the class to which one belongs. The implication of this is that social class is a membership which is ascribed prior to gaining an education or entering an occupation. For Americans and probably Australians and Canadians, achieved status is most important; occupation and education determine class status.

---

[37] See Seymour M. Lipset, "Democracy and Social Structure" (MSS, University of California, Berkeley, 1962) for a summary of the evidence for this assertion.

For Britishers, class determines occupation and education. In the more equalitarian colonies, class membership is tenuous prior to adulthood; it is a social role which is learned. In Britain, social class is not a separate, differentiated role, but a characteristic permeating the entire being. Class in Britain is like nationality in the sense that it is not "detachable" from the basic identities of persons.[38]

Canada may be closest to Great Britain in its level of such status differentiation (although no systematic evidence is available). Australia, on the other hand, has probably gone to the other extreme—even further in the equalitarian direction than the United States. R. N. Rosecrance has plausibly explained some of these international differences:

> On the whole America was settled originally by members of the middle class who had not developed an articulate middle-class mentality. . . . The attitudes of the American bourgeoisie, then, did not partake of the doctrinaire hatred of the old aristocracy conjured with the fear of the rising lower classes. Such attitudes could be prevalent only after the industrial revolution had made unmistakably clear the separate and different interests of the several classes. . . .
>
> Having been populated after the industrial revolution, Australian society would inevitably be different. Australians were class conscious, and they were substantially lower class. They not only had to combat the pretensions of squattocracy in Australia; they previously had to fight the old society in England before arriving in Sydney. Americans did not have to fight a battle in Europe or America. The result was a curious blending of the American and European situations: Australians were class conscious and had scotched the class pretensions of native feudalism in the name of equality; Americans were not class conscious, and they were fundamentally of the same class.[39]

The same point was made by James Bryce, who noted that in Britain, the Reform Acts extending the suffrage and enacting other political rights were carried through by part of the upper class aided by the middle class—not as a result of any demand by the

[38] See Marshall, *op. cit.*, pp. 96–100. As will be indicated in Chapter 6, social changes in Britain are producing more equalitarianism. Canada has been exposed to both British and American influences, and probably both patterns exist there.

[39] R. N. Rosecrance, "The Radical Tradition in Australia: An Interpretation," *The Review of Politics*, XXII (January, 1960), 125. The consequences of this tradition will be analyzed briefly in Chapter 7.

masses.[40] Political reforms took place much more speedily in Australia, New Zealand, and the United States because of the lack of an aristocracy; they progressed more slowly in Canada because there the bourgeois revolution was not carried through. Equalitarian values related to the intensity and character of class consciousness have undoubtedly left varying marks on the political institutions of these countries.

Although no thorough and systematic comparison has been made, some evidence indicates that—in spite of these differences—the four countries are similar with respect to what might be called the structure (as distinct from the intensity) of class identification. Surveyors in Britain, Australia, and the United States asked persons what social class they belonged to and constructed a measure of the "distance" between occupational groups and working-class identifications. The rank order found for different occupations was approximately the same for the three countries: professionals, salaried employees, big-businessmen, small shop owners, clerical workers, and manual workers. The only exception occurred in Australia, where big-businessmen were less likely to see themselves as "working class" than were professionals. It may be noted also that this order is almost exactly the same as those for occupational prestige and for the actual socio-economic position of differing occupations.[41] (See Table 4–1, p. 78.)

In any of these class systems, however, status makes a profound difference in the way people are treated. George Orwell contrasted an injured miner to his own bourgeois position, and, although he was speaking of British society, the situation of American workers applying for unemployment compensation is not very different:

---

[40] See James Bryce, *Modern Democracies* (New York: Macmillan, 1929), pp. 31–34.

[41] William Buchanan and Hadley Cantril, *How Nations See Each Other* (Urbana: University of Illinois Press, 1953), p. 14. In this 1948 survey, the measure of class identification for a given occupational group was constructed by subtracting the percentage of persons (in the occupation) identifying themselves as "working-class" from the percentage identifying themselves as "middle-class" and adding to the result twice the percentage identifying themselves as "upper-class." The relations of the "subjective" aspects of social stratification such as class identification with the "objective" aspects previously discussed have not been traced comparatively. An initial study of Detroit found that two forms of class consciousness were indeed related to the crystallization of individual statuses. See Werner Landecker, "Class Crystallization and Class Consciousness," *American Sociological Review*, XXVIII (April, 1963), 219–29.

Watching this man go to the colliery to draw his compensation, I was struck by the profound differences that are still made by *status*. Here was a man who had been half blinded in one of the most useful of all jobs and was drawing a pension to which he had a perfect right, if anybody had a right to anything. Yet he could not, so to speak, *demand* this pension—he could not, for instance, draw it when and how he wanted it. He had to go to the colliery once a week at a time named by the company, and when he got there he was kept waiting about for hours in the cold wind. For all I know he was also expected to touch his cap and show gratitude to whomever paid him; at any rate he had to waste an afternoon and spend sixpence in bus fares. It is very different for a member of the bourgeoisie, even such a down-at-heel member as I am. Even when I am on the verge of starvation I have certain rights attaching to my bourgeois status. I do not earn much more than a miner earns, but I do at least get it paid into my bank in a gentlemanly manner and can draw it out when I choose. And even when my account is exhausted, the bank people are still passably polite.

This business of petty inconvenience and indignity, of being kept waiting about, of having to do everything at other people's convenience, is inherent in working class life. A thousand influences constantly press a working man down into a *passive* rôle.[42]

CONCLUSION

Thus, it might be said that America was born of revolution, Australia was born of revolutionaries without a revolution, Canada was born out of forces opposed to revolution, and modern Britain was not born at all, but has evolved under the guidance of the aristocracy to its present state. The marks of their historic origins unquestionably affect the character of the responses of social groups to political and economic events differently from country to country.

Considerable differences in sensitivity to class and status do exist, but these must not be overstated. As already indicated, equality is a strongly held value in all of these societies, and even Britain is under heavy pressure to create more equalitarian institutions. Such an achievement will not, however, wipe out the objective features of class stratification which have been documented. Even if all workers come to think of themselves as middle-class and perceive no important discrimination on grounds of status, it seems highly

---

[42] George Orwell, *The Road to Wigan Pier* (London: Victor Gollancz, 1937), p. 49. (Italics in original.)

unlikely that the wide gaps in income, power, and differential life-chances separating the main social strata will be eliminated.[43]

The class and political structures of these countries have been treated as if they were separable entities. Although it is possible to analyze the institutional structures of social classes and political parties separately, their mutual connections are vital for a study of political cleavages. Both the class structure and the nature of the party system are independent factors. For the Anglo-American countries, we may regard them as constants—at least for purposes of preliminary investigation. Although people more or less advantaged by the economic system exist and press their respective demands upon the parties and the government, the essence of politics in these countries is devising a strategy of gaining majority support without either endangering the stable social base of a party, losing the opportunity to win over part of another stratum, or moving too far away from the issues which are legitimately in the political arena at a given time.

In conclusion, it must be emphasized that the Anglo-American countries form a small cluster of highly developed (both politically and economically) nations and that the differences which are emphasized in this study are, from a world-wide point of view, minor indeed. The five Anglo-American countries would place high on any conceivable scale of national integration and political or economic development.[44] The similarity of these countries in contrast

---

[43] It has been argued that an "open society"—one which allows considerable mobility upward and downward—in an era of prosperity will be characterized by a breakdown of class identifications. The existence of many reference groups, often conflicting and therefore producing "cross-pressures," will affect political identifications. Changes in the salience of various reference groups and the consequences for orientations to the class structure are important research problems in this area.

[44] One of the first attempts to devise an empirical measure of "national political development" scored 77 independent nations in terms of the strength of political parties in the parliament and the method of selection of a chief executive over a twenty-year period. The five Anglo-American countries (together with Sweden and Switzerland) scored the highest of all on this measure and also on a "communications development" measure comprised of newspaper and newsprint consumption, the number of telephones, and the number of pieces of domestic mail per capita. The author notes that "the score a nation receives on communications development is itself highly dependent on the national level of educational development, urbanization, labor force movement out of agricultural employment, and economic development." See Phillips Cutright, "National Political Development: Measurement and Analysis," *American Sociological Review*, XXVIII (April, 1963), 253–65.

to most others in such measures of modernization adds greater significance, as will be discussed in Chapter 5, to the differences found
in the extent of class polarization in four of the Anglo-American
countries.

Chapter 2

The Bases of Political Cleavage

FEW researchers have investigated the variations in the importance of different political cleavages in a number of countries. Voting studies have almost without exception focused upon one community, one constituency, or one nation. Furthermore, few attempts have been made to compare patterns of voting between different communities or areas within a single nation.[1] Yet comparative analysis can clarify the way in which different national and regional contexts affect the relevance of various group memberships for political behavior.

The complex association between class interests and other group loyalties that become politically relevant has also been little investigated. To what extent, for example, is the connection between class position and voting behavior reinforced or negated by loyalties to party based on religion or region? Political behavior within regions,

[1] One United States study compares the presidential voting patterns in a predominantly Republican community, Elmira, New York, in 1940 with those in a predominantly Democratic community, Sandusky, Ohio, in 1948. The authors' chief comparative finding was that the political climate of the Republican community affected Democratic lower-class voters mainly when the latter were not surrounded by friends and relatives who agreed with them politically (and vice versa for the Republicans in the Democratic community). They called this the "breakage effect," implying that until the primary-group environment of the voter "broke," he was insulated from the political atmosphere of the community. The particular finding was one of the first results from the use of comparative voting data to investigate the effect of a different social context upon voting behavior. See Bernard Berelson *et al., Voting* (Chicago: University of Chicago Press, 1954), pp. 98–101.

as distinct from communities or constituencies, has received relatively little study although Democratic loyalties in, say, Birmingham, Alabama, are undoubtedly a result of regional factors rather than of those peculiar to the city.

Regions as used here mean those territorial entities less than the nation which are potentially capable of becoming the focus of political struggle and loyalties—in a sense, potentially capable of becoming nations themselves. Where regions within a nation command strong loyalties, class interests may not be the main source of political cleavage. The lack of class voting within a region in such an instance need not mean a lack of class cleavages, but only an overriding loyalty to a regional identity perceived as an alternative national identity. A lack of class voting in such a region is analogous to the pulling over of all strata in a nation to one party when a foreign policy crisis occurs. If the region did succeed in becoming a nation, presumably the class cleavages that exist within it would assert themselves, since the new political unit is no longer defending its autonomy or its dominant group interests against an external enemy. Examples of such regions are the South in the United States, Quebec in Canada, and Ireland in the United Kingdom.

Although it is known that religious affiliations and loyalties affect political behavior, little is known about how the association of class and vote varies in different religious groups. Where particular religions are associated with minority status or with a special politically relevant set of religious beliefs, we may expect that class interest may not be the main source of political cleavage *within* the religious group. As with regional identities, the lack of class voting within the religious group may mean not a lack of class cleavages, but an overriding loyalty to a religious identity which has come to be associated with a political identity.[2]

Few studies have investigated whether the association of class and vote persists within different religious or regional groupings. Most voting studies have focused mainly upon the manifold factors affecting *individual* decisions to vote and how to vote—factors such as religion, class position, rural-urban residence, and so forth—and

---

[2] By "identity" here is meant an attachment by most members of a given social group—identified as a group by means of either territorial residence or non-territorially defined social affiliations (residence in the American South or affiliation with the Catholic Church, for example)—to that residence or affiliation (or symbols of them) as a valuable social membership.

therefore have dealt only tangentially with this question. But these studies have not taken up directly the problem of the relative contribution of such factors to the total pattern of political support. Moreover, no studies have examined the variations from country to country in the relative importance of the various group interests affecting political behavior.

CLASS AND VOTING BEHAVIOR

Studies of voting behavior have routinely found a correlation between the social class position of voters and the party they typically vote for. Persons in business and sales occupations, persons in upper-income levels, or persons with more than a high school education, are more likely to vote for a party which stands for protection of business interests and little welfare legislation than persons in low-prestige occupations, with low incomes, or with little education. A growing body of voting studies has amply documented this generalization, both for the United States and Great Britain.[3] That class position and voting behavior are correlated is by now a commonplace.

Clearly not all occupations can be neatly placed in a "class interest" category, however. Some professions are an exception to this generalization for the probable reason that they have no direct link with economic interest groups. College teachers, social workers, and most civil servants are examples. On the other hand, nonsalaried lawyers, doctors, and others in "entrepreneurial" professions behave politically more like businessmen.

It is possible that the association of class and vote is declining. Continuing prosperity and the opportunities for education, higher incomes, and middle-class styles of life available to workers may be

[3] For the United States, Gallup polls of national samples have consistently found that middle-class people are more Republican than workers. Studies with similar results of single communities include: Paul Lazarsfeld, Bernard Berelson and Hazel Gaudet, *The People's Choice* (New York: Columbia University Press, 1948); and Bernard Berelson *et al., op. cit.* For Great Britain, Social Surveys, Inc. (formerly the British Institute of Public Opinion) has consistently found that middle-class people vote Conservative more than do workers. A study of single constituencies with similar results is: Mark Benney, A. P. Gray, and R. H. Pear, *How People Vote* (London: Routledge & Kegan Paul, 1956). A summary of the voting studies bearing on this point is presented in Seymour M. Lipset, *Political Man* (New York: Doubleday, 1960), chap. vii.

eroding the connection between class position and voting. The American political scientist, V. O. Key, for example, suggests that:

> Perhaps in the election of 1936 [in the United States] the party division most nearly coincided with differences of income and occupation. That coincidence declined, as class-relevant questions faded from the forefront, and in 1952 and 1956, Republicans won substantial support in the lower-income groups.[4]

A study of American voters has actually found that the correlation of the occupational status of voters with their party preferences dropped in the three successive presidential elections from 1948 to 1956. Although no studies of changes in the association of class and vote have been done in England, a study of the 1959 general election in Great Britain suggested that the prosperity and social mobility in Britain during the 1950's might be reducing the bases for class politics.[5]

Regardless of what changes may be taking place, an association between class position and voting behavior is natural and expected in the Western democracies because of a number of factors: the existence of class interests, the representation of these interests by political parties, the regular association of certain parties with certain interests, and the tendency of voters to choose the party historically associated with social groups to which they belong—groups with both a class and non-class character. Given the character of the stratification order and the way political parties compete for support from various groups, it would be remarkable if such an association were not found.

Class interests compete for advantage in many ways in the Western democracies. James Madison's classic essay on factions in American society summarizes a state of affairs which exists in all of these societies even now:

> Those who hold and those who are without property have ever formed distinct interests in society. Those who are creditors, and

---

[4] V. O. Key, Jr., *Politics, Parties and Pressure Groups* (4th ed.; New York: Thomas Y. Crowell, 1958), p. 274.

[5] For the United States, see Angus Campbell *et al.*, *The American Voter* (New York: Wiley, 1960), p. 347; and P. E. Converse, "The Shifting Role of Class in Political Attitudes and Behavior" in E. Maccoby, T. Newcomb, and E. Hartley, eds., *Readings in Social Psychology* (3rd ed.; New York: Henry Holt, 1958), pp. 388–99. For Great Britain, see D. E. Butler and Richard Rose, *The British General Election of 1959* (London: Macmillan, 1960), pp. 14–16.

those who are debtors, fall under a like discrimination. A landed interest, a manufacturing interest, a mercantile interest, a moneyed interest, with many lesser interests, grow up of necessity in civilized nations, and divide them into different classes, actuated by different sentiments and views.[6]

Although class interests are universal in these societies, they are not completely homogeneous. Precisely because of this, class interests form a crucially important but not the sole basis for political action. Income, occupation, property, and education—the chief components of life-chances—do not divide the population into two huge camps of the privileged and the oppressed. Persons in the same economic position may more or less permanently unite for a common political or economic purpose, but such class-based solidarities do not constitute a permanent majority of the population. Although some minority economic interests are usually dominant in a given society, the degree to which economic elites tend to coalesce is an important but not relevant problem.

Class interests are politically relevant in different degrees in the Western democracies. Group interests based upon incentives as strong and stable as economic ones are constantly struggling for *political* advantage. In the modern democratic state, the political parties have developed largely as instruments of various class interests. But, partly because of the lack of monolithic unity among groups sharing common economic interests and partly because of the character of the party system itself as a device for straddling many kinds of social conflicts,

the party-system is the democratic translation of the class-struggle. It postulates national unity beneath the divisions of class. It postulates the rationalization of class interests so that these can make appeal on the grounds of their service to or compatibility with the national interest.[7]

---

[6] Saul K. Padover, ed., *The Complete Madison* (New York: Harper, 1953), p. 52.

[7] Robert M. MacIver, *The Web of Government* (New York: Macmillan, 1947), p. 217. The phrase "democratic class struggle," referring to the party system, is an enticing one, uniting as it does Jeffersonian democracy and Marxism. It was used in the title of a work in political sociology by H. D. Anderson and P. E. Davidson, *Ballots and the Democratic Class Struggle* (Stanford, Calif.: Stanford University Press, 1943) and as a chapter heading in Lipset, *op. cit.* See also Max Lerner, *America as a Civilization* (New York: Simon & Schuster, 1957), pp. 536–41.

Thus, political parties usually have a dual and conflicting role: to represent group interests and to unite group interests. The intensity, scope, and direction of class interests at a given time, and the extent to which they are cross-cut or reinforced by other social cleavages, will determine the degree to which those interests become or remain politically relevant.

Political parties historically have come to represent specific coalitions of class interests. Parties adopt programs, encourage legislation, and appeal to voters in ways which tend to make them the representatives of specific sets of class interests. And it is probably justified to infer that this representation is consistent with the class composition of the support for a given party. The sociologist Seymour M. Lipset asserts that "even though many parties renounce the principle of class conflict or loyalty, an analysis of their appeals and their support suggests that they do represent the interests of different classes."[8] And Robert M. MacIver concludes that: "wherever parties divide on serious issues, and above all on economic issues, the more advantaged or well-to-do are certain to show preference for one party or group of parties and the less advantaged for the other."[9] It cannot be assumed, however, that in a given historical period a party will consistently act on behalf of the class interests corresponding to the position of most of its supporters. Parties may change their policies but still retain the social base which gave them their initial strength. Citizens vote as they do partly because of attachments to groups in which membership carries with it a certain political predisposition—groups such as trade unions, families, and religious associations. Such voting in accordance with group loyalties is different from that assumed by classical democratic theory, which postulates a free and rational mind deciding on the basis of issues and facts. Group loyalties, whether to trade unions or to religious or ethnic cultures, imply stable political predispositions which most individuals do not willfully or arbitrarily deny or reject.

Because of these several factors—the existence of class interests, the representation of those interests by political parties, the association of certain parties with certain interests, and the likelihood that persons will vote in accordance with group loyalties (includ-

[8] Lipset, *op. cit.*, p. 220.
[9] MacIver, *op. cit.*, p. 123.

ing those related to their class position)—a consistent association of social class position and voting behavior may be expected.

The association of social class and the support for a party is likely to be affected by the political structure of a given system. The character of the parliamentary system, the balance between national and local organs of government, the number and structure of parties, will either encourage or deflect the polarization of parties around certain class bases.

The way in which a historically high level of class voting affects the formal institutions of the political system may be equally important. The class base of the parties, once in existence, may become an independent political force of its own. A high level of class voting may constrain the shifts of a party to the Left or Right. If the Labour party, for example, draws most British manual workers and very few middle-class people, this may discourage those in the party who want to convert it into a center-Left party. The simple lack of a broad social base may be a powerful political deterrent against potentially sacrificing the supporters a party does have for a possible new base. In a real sense, a party supported by a narrow class base (or a narrow regional or religious base), may be relatively inflexible in the kinds of policy changes it can contemplate. Party leaders may find it hard to say to one section of their supporters: "We cannot fulfill this demand of yours because that would alienate another section of our supporters, and we must remain united to win." There is thus a constant interaction between the historically-based association of a party with a fairly stable class base and the needs of political strategy at any given moment.

It should be emphasized again that class stratification must vary in the extent of its political relevance. Workers might have a lively sense of class consciousness, be militant union members, but vote for a Right party on non-class grounds (such as its anti-communist stand, it stand on religion or foreign policy, or a host of other reasons). Many self-conscious members of the middle class might, conversely, vote for the Left party because of its stand on non-class issues. Regardless of whether persons in working-class occupations actually have some economic interests or aspirations in common with middle-class persons (owning stock, property, or aspiring to own a small business), non-class issues in and of themselves reduce the association between social class and voting. Since issues vary in their salience from election to election and in their impact on various subgroups within the broad economic interest groups, considerable variation in the association of class and vote over time is to be expected as well.

METHODS FOR STUDYING CLASS VOTING

Where direct evidence on the class position of voters has not been available, studies of the association of class and vote have been based on inferences from other kinds of evidence. The "ecological" type of study draws inferences as to the character of party support from a correlation between the party strength in an area and such demographic characteristics of the area as religious or occupational composition. The classic study of this type was done by the French political scientist Andrè Siegfried in his study of voting patterns in France from 1871 to 1912.[10] A study of southern politics in the United States relies heavily on this method to infer characteristics of voters.[11] A more recent study of the South uses the ecological method to infer the extent of urban Republicanism among different income groups.[12]

Another method of studying the association of class and vote has been to make inferences from the occupational positions of a party's representatives in parliament. The Canadian political scientist Alexander Brady draws his plausible conclusion that the Labour party in England was based largely on the working class from the election of fifty-three working-class Members of Parliament in 1906 and from other changes in the composition of the British governing elite in the nineteenth century.[13] The nature of party programs and the content of party appeals for support have also been used to infer the characteristics of party supporters.

None of these methods guarantees the discovery of the real class composition of the support for a party. It is easy to assume that voters are likely to vote for candidates in occupations similar to their own or for parties supporting legislation congruent with their

---

[10] André Siegfried, *Tableau Politique de la France de l'ouest sous la Troisième République* (Paris: Librairie Armand Colin, 1913).

[11] V. O. Key, Jr., *Southern Politics in State and Nation* (New York: Knopf, 1949).

[12] Donald S. Strong, *Urban Republicanism in the South* (Birmingham: University of Alabama, Bureau of Public Administration, 1960).

[13] Alexander Brady, "The British Governing Class and Democracy," *Canadian Journal of Economics and Political Science*, XX (November, 1954), 405–20.

class interests. But, because class interests are cut across by many other group interests, such assumptions may be contrary to fact. A party may have historically derived bonds to certain ideologies, pressure groups, and programs which do not at all reflect the needs and desires of its actual constituency. Particularly in the present period, when the class bases of politics may be dwindling, it is dangerous to infer anything concerning the social bases of the parties from such indirect evidence as ecological correlations (especially since geographic mobility is high), the occupational composition of parliamentary delegations, or the content of platforms and speeches.

Where public opinion has been surveyed, the association of class and vote can be studied by means of direct information on the class position of voters. The newer techniques of survey research have been utilized by many of the studies cited, although most of them have been more concerned with the social-psychological factors linked to party identification and voting than with the social bases of the parties as such.

POLITICAL REGIONALISM

A nation exhibits political regionalism, in the sense used here, when political parties exist which are peculiar to a given region, when a national party consistently draws disproportionate support from a given region, or when regions shift from election to election in opposing directions, thus indicating that the impact of national political currents affect regions in contradictory ways. Those factors which produce a temporary shift of a region toward a particular party in a given election or which throw up a temporary alliance calling itself a party are not of concern here. Rather, the problem concerns those relatively enduring concentrations of interests and values held by social groups in given regions which result in relatively stable deviations from national patterns of political cleavage.

All of the Anglo-American countries exhibit some variety of political regionalism. Britain and Australia have nationally-oriented parties which draw only regional support. The Liberal party in Britain gets strong support only in Wales. The Democratic Labor party in Australia is strongest in Victoria. The United States and Canada have regionally-oriented parties which also draw support only from their own regions.[14] The southern Dixiecrats in 1952 and 1956 and the Quebec *Union Nationale* are cases in point. Canada is more complex because its two formerly regional parties—the Cooperative Commonwealth Federation of Saskatchewan and the Social Credit party of Alberta—began in the 1950's to bid for a national position. As will be seen in Chapter 9, however, Canada's parties may still be described as predominantly regional. No party in Canada can truly be described as a "national" party in the sense that it draws consistent and relatively equal support from all regions.

These countries differ considerably in the degree of relative support from election to election among various regions for a given party, with British and Australian regions exhibiting more consistent patterns than the other countries.

These three aspects of political regionalism—regional parties, disparity of support, and shifts from election to election—are portrayed to some extent by Table 2–1 (p. 45), which shows the support for major parties on the Left for at least three elections in the 1950's in each region of each country. In Canada, the extent of regional diversity is more visible when the support for two parties is given. The regions are ranked in the order of their level of Left voting insofar as is possible.

The relative stability of British regions, and, at the other extreme, the tremendous variation and volatility of party support in the Canadian regions are shown by Table 2–1. In Britain, there is hardly an exception to the ordering of regions in terms of Labour strength in the three elections from 1951 to 1959. Also, in almost every case, each region followed the national drift away from Labour in this decade—even Wales, where Labour is strongest. Northern Ireland, where the Conservative party wins overwhelmingly (see pp. 144–45), is the only area where Labour voting has dropped below 40 per cent. The Liberal party draws about the same vote in each region other than Wales. (See pp. 153–59.)

The Australian states exhibit a few more exceptions to a consistent rank order over time than Britain, but they are almost as consistent in their shifts upward and downward. The Australian Labor party's vote is almost always highest in South Australia and lowest in Queensland. Possible reasons for this are discussed on

---

[14] I am indebted to Professor Juan Linz of Columbia University for some of the formulations in this section.

TABLE 2–1

Preference for the Left Parties in Various Regions, 1950–1962 (National Elections)

	GREAT BRITAIN (LABOUR VOTE)				
	ELECTION			1959 TOTAL VOTE (000's)	RANK-INDEX SCORE*
REGION	1951	1955 (Per Cent)	1959		
Welsh boroughs	63	60	58	437	3
Welsh counties	59	56	56	1,054	6
London boroughs	55	53	49	1,592	10
Scottish burghs	51	50	50	1,257	11
English boroughs	50	48	46	11,216	15
English counties	45	44	40	10,319	19
Scottish counties	44	43	43	1,410	20
Northern Ireland	13	5	8	576	24
TOTAL	49	46	44		

	AUSTRALIA (LABOR VOTE)						
	ELECTION					1961 TOTAL VOTE (000's)	RANK-INDEX SCORE
STATE	1951	1954	1955 (Per Cent)	1958	1961		
South Australia	48	52	47	48	50	501	8
New South Wales	48	50	48	47	51	2,043	8
Tasmania	46	49	45	47	52	178	14
Victoria	47	49	37	40	41	1,515	21
Western Australia	43	46	45	35	40	365	25
Queensland	41	43	43	37	47	783	28
TOTAL				43	47		

Sources: The British figures are taken from The Times of London, *Guide to the House of Commons* (London, 1951, 1959). The 1951–1958 Australian figures are estimated from graphs in S. R. Davis, ed., *The Government of the Australian States* (Melbourne: Longmans, Green, 1960), pp. 641–46, and the 1961 figures appear in the *Australian Journal of Politics and History*, VIII (May, 1962), 104.

* The rank-index score is a crude way of ordering the regions in terms of their "usual" level of Left voting. For each election, a rank order was constructed, and the sum of the ranks was computed. In this table, the regions are listed in the order of this rank-index score.

TABLE 2–1—Continued

UNITED STATES (DEMOCRATIC VOTE)

REGION	1952	ELECTION 1956 (Per Cent)	1960	1960 TOTAL VOTE (000's)	RANK-INDEX SCORE
East South Central	53	50	47	3,042	6
South Atlantic	51	47	52	6,890	8
West South Central	50	45	47	2,201	12
Pacific	43	44	49	8,521	13
Middle Atlantic	44	39	52	15,069	14
New England	43	38	56	4,979	15
East North Central	43	40	48	16,163	15
West North Central	41	43	46	6,873	21
Mountain	40	40	46	2,643	24
TOTAL	44	42	50		

CANADA (LIBERAL AND NEW DEMOCRATIC VOTE)

PROVINCE	1953 Lib	1953 NDP	1957 Lib	1957 NDP	1958 Lib	1958 NDP	1962 Lib	1962 NDP	1962 TOTAL VOTE (000's)	RANK-INDEX SCORE
Newfoundland	67	1	61	..	54	..	59	5	154	6
Saskatchewan	38	44	30	10	19	28	23	22	423	12
Nova Scotia	53	7	45	4	38	4	42	10	421	19
Quebec	61	2	57	2	45	2	40	4	2,090	19
Manitoba	40	24	26	23	21	19	31	19	387	20
Ontario	47	11	37	12	32	10	42	17	2,685	22
New Brunswick	53	3	47	1	43	2	44	5	249	25
British Columbia	31	27	20	23	16	24	27	31	683	27
Prince Edward Isl.	51	1	46	1	37	..	44	5	73	32
Alberta	35	7	28	6	14	4	20	8	502	40
TOTAL	49	9	40	11	33	9	37	14		

Sources: The United States figures are compiled from state figures given in U.S. Bureau of the Census, *Congressional District Data Book* (districts of the Eighty-seventh Congress), a *Statistical Abstract* supplement (Washington, D.C.: United States Government Printing Office, 1961). The United States is divided into regions, as given in Appendix D. The Canadian figures appear in Howard A. Scarrow, *Canada Votes* (New Orleans: Hauser Press, 1962). Totals and percentages may be slightly inaccurate because of rounding. U.S. figures refer to Presidential voting.

page 188. The emergence of the Democratic Labor party in 1955 has altered the regional balance of the parties somewhat, since it has drawn about 15 per cent of the vote in Victoria but only 5 to 7 per cent in the other states (see Chapter 7). Australia has no state that deviates from the national level of Labor vote as much as does Northern Ireland.

The United States regions—groups of states—are internally quite heterogeneous; therefore the true regional diversity of the country is not adequately shown by the summary figures in Table 2–1. The United States regions show a fairly consistent rise and fall with the national trend, but there is considerable deviation in the rank order of Democratic vote within the regions. The 1960 election shows sharp deviations: the Democratic vote rose sharply in the eastern seaboard and either dropped or rose very slightly in the southern states. (For the possible connection of this change with special regional or religious reactions, see Chapter 11.) Generally, the Democratic vote is highest in the southern regions and lowest in the mountain region.

The political diversity of the Canadian provinces is vividly shown in Table 2–1, where the support for the Liberal and New Democratic (or CCF) parties from 1953 to 1962 is given. The Liberal vote is generally highest in Newfoundland and lowest in Alberta. The New Democratic vote is highest in Saskatchewan and British Columbia, but almost nothing in several provinces. Differences in the support for a Left party are great from province to province, whether the two parties are considered separately or together as the "potential" Left vote. In the 1962 Canadian election, for example, the New Democratic vote ranged from 4 per cent in Quebec to 31 per cent in British Columbia. On the other hand, the trends of change in the Liberal vote from election to election are almost always consistently in the same direction, despite the radical divergence of the absolute level of Liberal voting. This is testimony to the penetration of national political currents into each province, regardless of its degree of devotion to a given party. The vote for the other parties (Progressive-Conservative and Social Credit) also vacillates tremendously. Social Credit, for example, received almost no votes in Quebec in 1957 and 1958, but jumped to the 26 per cent mark in 1962. One of the questions to be discussed in Chapter 9 is whether this lack of stable party loyalties in Canada is a mark of tradition or of political maturity.

Three chief factors probably making for political regionalism may be distinguished: the economic structure of a region, the concentration of an ethnic or religious group in an area, and constitutional provisions allowing important degrees of sovereignty to political units smaller than the nation as a whole. These are considered in more detail in Chapter 11.

Where a substantial area contains only one economic stratum or where one stratum has managed to gain undisputed political sway (by winning over the rest of the population or by rendering it politically ineffective), regional parties or a one-party region may emerge which defends the regional economic interests against threat from national economic groups. Examples of economically homogeneous areas (at least until the 1950's) are Saskatchewan and Alberta in Canada (one-crop wheat areas) and the rural South in the United States (until its spurt of industrialization). In Britain, Wales has been predominantly a mining area, and the Midlands, an industrial area. The conditions which determine whether the existing parties are flexible enough to contain such regional interests as pressure groups within national parties or whether those interests are driven to form a separate party are outside the scope of this study.

Where a certain ethnic or religious group is concentrated in an area, it may provide a "cultural" basis for political regionalism. If such a group has minority status in the society, the political consequence of concentration may be a sense of nationalist or semi-nationalist oppression which finds expression in representation by a political party. If the group has a distinctive culture, even if it is not a minority in the strict sense of numbers, it may perceive itself to be threatened by the majority culture in other regions. The fact of concentration may, on the other hand, have no political relevance if there is no distinctive culture to be defended.

Where constitutional provisions allow important degrees of sovereignty to regional political units, a third base for political regionalism may be created. However, such regionalism is not a necessary consequence of constitutional guarantees of partial sovereignty (most frequently in the form of federalism). Aside from the probability that economic and cultural bases for regionalism usually exist within a political unit, under certain conditions the political unit itself may become valued, especially if it is under attack as inefficient or obsolete. Under those conditions, parties may come to be defenders of the integrity of the political unit, regardless of the degree to which the unit actually serves the economic interests or the distinctive values of groups residing within its jurisdiction. "Nationalist" ideologies, whether on the national or state (provincial) levels, play a political role which cannot be reduced to economic interests or cultural values.

The most pronounced form of political regionalism—a regional party overwhelmingly supported by the residents of the area—may be expected where all of these factors are combined—where the residents share economic interests and a common ethnic and religious identity setting them apart from other regions and where they also constitute the overwhelming majority of a region which is the bulk of a political unit. If such a region is large enough, it constitutes a potential nation in its own right, and clearly secession may be either a real possibility or its threat may constitute an instrument of political struggle with the rest of the nation.[15] The degree to which political regionalism in each of the four countries is associated with these factors will be discussed briefly in the chapters on each country and more generally in Chapter 11.

The foregoing discussion has assumed that characteristics of groups within a region or the relations of those groups to groups in other regions are the main *causes* of political regionalism. But the defense of economic interests or cultural integrity may not be the only, nor even the most important, reasons for the *maintenance* of political regionalism (although they may be the principal causes of its initial emergence). From the point of view of political power and the relations of national and regional elites, political regionalism may serve as a means by which certain local elites maintain their political and social power. Ideologies calling for the defense of the regional economy, cultural integrity, or political sovereignty may often mask manipulations of the regional population by those elites in an attempt to maintain their special privileges. Their goal, therefore, may not be primarily the defense of the autonomy of the region or of the dominant group interests of the region against an external enemy, but rather the maintenance of their position of

---

[15] See Richard Hartshorne, "The Functional Approach in Political Geography," *Annals of the Association of American Geographers*, XL (June, 1950), 95–130, for a discussion of the forces affecting the boundaries of regions, states and nations. His article presents a host of hypotheses concerning the relation between social and political factors and the geographical boundaries of nation-states.

power and privilege against other groups *within* the region. Locally dominant groups, oligarchically organized, can use the ideology of the external enemy and the need for regional solidarity to defend their own positions.

Since it is not the goal of this study to investigate the political role of regional loyalties, this subject is raised merely to emphasize the complexity of relations between regional and national loyalties and interests. Many examples of these various types of regionalism could be given. In the United States, where a great diversity of economic interests is organized into a strongly entrenched federal system, the political rights of regions (or states, in this case) are either fought for or attacked by various interest groups, depending upon their perception of the immediate advantages.

As Vile puts it:

> The cry of "States' Rights" has always been used to defend plural interests as well as geographical ones. The greatest defenders of States' Rights have been prepared to use the national power to further class interest, and the proponents of strong central government have jumped behind the barricade of State powers when their economic interests were threatened by the exercise of the national power they had championed.[16]

This comment undoubtedly applies to regional versus national conflicts in all four countries.

RELIGION AND POLITICS

The connection between religion and politics arises as a problem only in nations which are not religiously homogeneous. Classical political thinkers such as Aristotle took it for granted that religious homogeneity was a condition of political stability, and they were right. Where opposing beliefs about ultimate values enter the political arena, they exacerbate struggles by preventing compromise.[17]

---

[16] M. J. C. Vile, *The Structure of American Federalism* (London: Oxford University Press, 1961), p. 38.

[17] For a modern form of the argument that religious homogeneity is necessary for political stability, see Leicester Webb, "Churches and the Australian Community" in E. D. French, ed., *Melbourne Studies in Education, 1958–1959* (Melbourne: Melbourne University Press, 1960), pp. 89–131, and his lecture "Politics and Polity" (Canberra, Australian National University, 1960). Western societies, as he sees it, are unified by certain political values closely associated with Christianity: the idea of justice and the concept that the polity is something toward which men who are conscious of moral freedom and responsibility will naturally be drawn.

In modern non-homogeneous societies, three changes (occurring in different degrees in different societies) may have moderated conflicts over ultimate values: secularization, the weakening of religious belief in general; compartmentalization, the separation of religion from other areas of life; and homogenization, the convergence of many religions upon a vaguely-defined consensus on teaching and practice.[18] Actually all of these processes, or contradictory forms of them, may be going on simultaneously.

The largely Protestant societies such as the Anglo-American countries have possibly moved farther along these three paths of change than other countries. Protestantism, with its emphasis upon the separation of Church and State, undoubtedly has encouraged a secular norm in the behavior of parties and voters. Even where religious issues and motives exist, they have had to remain covert, because they are illegitimate in the political realm.

In this respect, the Anglo-American countries differ greatly from the continental European countries. Religious parties do not exist in the Anglo-American countries, in sharp contrast to such continental nations as Italy, France, Belgium, Norway, and the Netherlands. No parties based almost exclusively upon an appeal to religious values and identifications have gained any appreciable strength in the Anglo-American countries. Although some parties have gained most of their support from particular religious groups (the nationalist parties *Bloc Populaire* and *Union Nationale* in Quebec, and the splinter Labor party in Australia gain the great bulk of their support from Catholics), the parties have never based their appeals or programs upon this characteristic of their supporters. This difference between the Anglo-American countries and some of the continental European ones is, as suggested in Chapter 1, almost a defining characteristic of the former: they are "secular, homogeneous" political systems.

One reason for this difference may be suggested. In the continental countries where religious parties are strong, religious freedom was won at the same time and was linked with the achievement of political freedom. The consequence was that to this

---

[18] See Gerhard Lenski, *The Religious Factor* (New York: Doubleday, 1960), p. 9, for this usage of the term "compartmentalization." However, Lenski later uses the word for the opposite phenomenon: the tendency for the whole of life to be organized around religious membership. He cites the Netherlands and Lebanon as the best examples of the latter (p. 326 ff.).

day, religion, class, and politics have been closely linked. In Britain, on the other hand, these issues emerged separately and were solved separately; as a result, not only were Church and State legally separated, but also the development of legitimate issues and parties connecting the two was prevented.

Certain features of the Reformation in England in the 1500's, unlike those of the Reformations on the continent, may have contributed to the relatively high degree of separation of church and state and the legitimacy of religious pluralism in British political culture. Since varying political stratagems rather than a constant religious ideal initiated the English Reformation, a number of religious options came to exist. The political authority in England undertook to break Catholic power without any single religious ethic or ideology guiding its efforts; it followed a continually oscillating course of strategy vis-à-vis the Church in the period 1530–1560. The crown of England itself passed through many hands during this period, and every change of government brought a sharp change of position regarding the Church. After three decades of policy fluctuation, the political authority could no longer re-establish a single dominant religion. A minority of the population remained firmly Roman Catholic, but other minorities just as firmly adhered to one or another of the many church reforms and systems of dogma which had been pressed upon the English people in the preceding decades. The English state had by the 1560's missed its historic opportunity, as no other European state had, to take religious decisions out of the hands of the people. Religious pluralism and the separation of the state from a single coercive church were thereby established in England—and subsequently in its colonies—as in no other country.[19]

Thus, a firmer historical basis for the secularization of politics has existed in the Anglo-American countries than in certain continental nations. In the colonies, the institutional domination of Protestantism was even less of an issue, and the Catholic church has never been more than a minority religion except in certain regions such as Quebec.[20] It must be emphasized again, however, that po-

---

[19] Taken from a summary of results in Herbert Schoeffler, *Wirkungen der Reformation*. [Effects of the Reformation] (Frankfort am Main: Vittorio Klostermann, 1960), pp. 322–24. I am indebted to Reinhard Bendix for this source.

[20] See Seymour M. Lipset, *Political Man* (New York: Doubleday, 1960), pp. 83–85, for a discussion of the ways in which historical resolution of issues colors subsequent political struggles.

litical secularization need not imply the secularization of the whole society. These are two parallel processes which need not be associated.[21]

Another reason for the rise of religious parties in continental Europe and their lack, so far, in the English-speaking countries has been the simple fact that the latter are predominantly Protestant, the former, predominantly Catholic. Where Catholics have made up a majority of the population, and therefore have had an opportunity to carry out Catholic social policies by political means, Catholic parties have arisen and Protestant parties have formed in reaction.[22] In the Anglo-American countries, the autonomous authority of the Catholic church to educate its own members has not been seriously challenged, and that church, as a consequence, has not made militant attempts to influence political life. A modus vivendi has been worked out which has not only strengthened the legitimacy of the national political system, but has made it unnecessary for religious parties to emerge. No religious group of any size in these systems has challenged one fundamental premise of a legitimate democratic state: either a secular political culture must exist in a society with more than one important religious group, or homogeneity of religious composition must exist within a state with an explicitly religious basis. It is a measure of the viability of Protestantism, combined with British political institutions and traditions, that each of the Anglo-American countries has to a great degree been able to assimilate the Catholics into a secular political culture.

This achievement stands out even more when the particular situation of Quebec in Canada is considered. Here most of the conditions favoring the development of a religious party are present: a minor-

---

[21] In the Netherlands, for example, the percentage describing themselves as "free thinkers," with "no fixed religion," or as "churchless" has increased steadily in each subsequent Census since 1879 to a high of 17 per cent in 1947. Although undoubtedly this figure does not indicate the "real" degree of secularization—since in a country where so few are areligious there must be some pressure to admit being religious—even this trend does not accord with the contrary trend toward religious parties. See M. Fogarty, *Christian Democracy in Western Europe, 1820–1953* (London: Routledge & Kegan Paul, 1957), p. 357.

[22] See Seymour M. Lipset and Juan Linz, "The Social Bases of Political Diversity in Western Democracies" (MSS, Center for Advanced Studies in the Behavioral Sciences, Stanford, Calif., 1956) for some of the general formulations of this section.

ity religious group is the majority within one of the two largest political units within a federal state; ethnic differences are present; a different language is spoken; and a sense of opposition is felt toward a political party with a historical association with another religion and ethnic group (the Conservatives, based upon English Protestants). Yet no religious party has developed; rather, nationalistic parties flourish. In Latin Europe, in contrast, the connection between a distinctive ethnic culture and Catholicism has produced strong Catholic parties.[23]

In Canada alone of the four Anglo-American countries might we expect such a consequence. Catholics in the United States and Australia are more diverse ethnically and geographically than in Canada, and in Britain the secession of Ireland deprived that issue of its saliency (although even the Irish issue had more of a nationalistic than a religious flavor). This example indicates again that something distinctive about the political culture of the Anglo-American countries affects even the regions and religious groups presumably most isolated from its influence. Quebec has taken the path of an extreme emphasis upon "Canadianism," stressing cultural autonomy within the framework of the Canadian federal union rather than struggling for a separate religiously homogeneous state or forming a religious party.[24]

French-Canadian nationalist parties have not even stressed their religious differences with English-Canada, although they could have easily done so. This failure to emphasize a possible source of regional political solidarity is another mark of the difference between the political culture of the Anglo-American and continental systems. The 1942 nationalist party in Quebec—the *Bloc Populaire*—grew in spite of the refusal of Catholic Action and Cardinal Villeneuve in Quebec to support the party. It clearly had a possible religious appeal and base, however, for the lower clergy welcomed it, seeing the new party as a possible avenue for reversing the "effects of the wartime industrialization upon French-Canadian family life and

---

[23] R. V. Burks, "Catholic Parties in Latin Europe," *Journal of Modern History*, XXIV (September, 1952), 269–86.

[24] Clearly Quebec's policies are determined by many factors, including the fear of joining the "melting pot" United States, but the point here is simply that its nationalistic tendencies have not been reinforced by a serious attempt to raise religious issues. Religion has been only one of the aspects of French-Catholic culture which have been seen by Quebec nationalists as necessary to maintain.

morals."[25] A religious appeal could conceivably have offset the new party's internal divisions over economic policy. Some of the leaders were crusaders for nationalization of industry, some were big businessmen, and an overriding appeal for religious unity could have temporarily dissolved those differences; yet none was made.[26]

Thus, the primary fact about the political relevance of religion in the Anglo-American countries is that it is *not* the primary fact of political life. The problem then becomes the extent to which religious groups exhibit distinctive patterns of political behavior, and to link this to differences and similarities in social and political processes. As will be shown in later chapters, while the designation "secular and homogeneous" applies when comparing these societies with others, religion is relevant to political behavior in these countries, although in varying degrees. For reasons to be discussed in Chapter 4, the main focus will be upon Protestant-Catholic differences.

The distinctive political behavior of Catholics will be of chief concern here. Catholics in each of these countries are more likely to vote for the major Left party than are Protestants. In the United States, they are disproportionately Democratic; in Great Britain and Australia, Labor; in Canada, Liberal.[27]

---

[25] Mason Wade, *The French-Canadians, 1760–1945* (London: Macmillan, 1955), p. 956.

[26] The assimilation of Quebec to a secular political culture must not be overstressed. The Catholic Church in Quebec has a number of rights not possessed by other churches. In addition, there are Catholic trade unions and other religious penetrations into institutions normally secularized in the Anglo-American countries. This in itself makes the extent of political secularism more notable.

[27] Documentation is given in the appropriate chapters, but major sources may be mentioned here. For the United States, see Bernard Berelson *et al., Voting* (Chicago: University of Chicago Press, 1954), pp. 71, 333; and Angus Campbell *et al., The American Voter* (New York: Wiley, 1960), pp. 301–6. For Great Britain, see P. Campbell *et al.,* "Voting Behavior in Droylsden in October, 1951," *Journal of the Manchester School of Economic and Social Studies,* XX (1952), 63; and Hans J. Eysenck, *The Psychology of Politics* (London: Routledge & Kegan Paul, 1954), p. 21. For Australia, see Louise Overacker, *The Australian Party System* (New Haven: Yale University Press, 1952), pp. 305–6; and R. N. Spann, "The Catholic Vote in Australia" in Henry Mayer, ed., *Catholics and the Free Society: An Australian Symposium* (Melbourne: F. W. Cheshire, 1961), pp. 115–41. For Canada, see Robert M. Dawson, *The Government of Canada* (Toronto: University of Toronto Press, 1954), p. 510; and W. Filley, "Social Structure and Canadian Political Parties: The Quebec Case," *Western Political Quarterly,* IX (December, 1956), 900–14.

Possible causes of the distinctive political behavior of Catholics in these four countries lie partly in their special religious beliefs which find expression in political issues, but also partly in their position historically as an immigrant and low-status minority in each country. Even in Britain, the Catholics have largely been of Irish descent and have been treated and have regarded themselves as an ethnic minority. Catholics entered the other countries as immigrant minorities and went into low-status occupations. These several characteristics have combined to produce a tendency to vote for the Left party. The Right parties have tended to represent the upper classes, which have also been Protestant and from majority ethnic groups; the Left parties have tended to represent the lower classes, which have been more likely to be Catholic and have minority ethnic status.

Some of these reasons for political differentiation along religious lines are likely to disappear, but some are relatively permanent— again depending on general processes of secularization and homogenization in the society at large. Distinctive Catholic values and institutions are not likely to disappear: thus the issues of religious education and political representation are always present in these countries. These issues take different forms in each nation, and to the extent that they exacerbate Catholic consciousness of minority status, either culturally or religiously, their voting patterns may deviate from those of Protestants. The historical association of a party with a low-status immigrant group may disappear more readily as Catholics move up in social status and ethnic differences disappear. To put it another way, the purely religious dimension of distinctive political behavior may emerge more clearly after the class and ethnic associations disappear.[28]

The lack of legitimacy of either religious parties or explicitly religious political appeals or even explicitly religiously-motivated voting in the Anglo-American countries does not necessarily mean that distinctive patterns of religious voting are likely to disappear even if the Catholics become completely assimilated ethnically and socio-economically. A compelling argument for the continuation of a Catholic deviation is the continuing failure of the Anglo-American societies to live up to Catholic social policies. The very notion of the separation of Church and State is against traditional Catholic

---

[28] The problem of what happens when a minority religious group becomes socially mobile is discussed with special reference to Australia in Chapter 7.

stands.[29] Until the State becomes Catholic or Catholics abandon certain fundamental tenets—such as religious education, opposition to birth control, and other positions—such issues will always be a potential source of religiously-based political cleavage. This distinctiveness does not necessarily have to be exhibited by loyalty to their traditional party, of course.

Catholic voting behavior in these countries is under a complex set of contradictory cross-pressures. Assuming that there is an association between class and party, and one between religion and party, almost every possible combination of class position and party identification involves cross-pressures for Catholics. The matter is further complicated by the contradictory tendencies within Catholicism itself, for it is at one and the same time profoundly conservative religiously and, sometimes, powerfully progressive socially. The very success of the Church in holding its members close may intensify these cross-pressures, since religion cannot as easily become compartmentalized for Catholics as for Protestants.

Middle-class Catholics are under cross-pressures because their class position and the conservative component of Catholicism predisposes them to vote Right. But the historical association of their minority status and ethnic position with the Left party leads them to vote Left.[30] Working-class Catholics are also under cross-pressures because the class and ethnic components of their status and the progressive component of Catholicism predispose them toward a Left vote, but the conservative element of Catholicism draws them toward a Right vote. The political consequences of these complex cross-pressures have not been satisfactorily analyzed comparatively and are beyond the scope of this volume. However, cross-pressures have been held to lead to withdrawal from political activities.[31]

Two recent studies have found, in contrast to the earlier one, that

---

[29] The attempts by American Catholic intellectuals such as John Courtney Murray to reconcile pluralism with Catholic social theology are testimony both to the secular norm of the Anglo-American societies and the necessity for Catholic theology to remain essentially unquestioned.

[30] Apparently, as shown in Chapter 8, not only middle-class status but also subjective middle-class identifications are necessary to reduce Catholic distinctive political behavior, at least in the United States.

[31] The finding of the 1940 Erie County study in the United States was that persons in cross-pressured situations voted less often and delayed their voting decision more than persons not under cross-pressures. See Paul F. Lazarsfeld, *et al., The People's Choice* (New York: Columbia University Press, 1948).

Catholics do not withdraw from voting in situations of predicted cross-pressures. A study of voting among Catholics in Kingston, Ontario, in 1953 and 1955 found that Catholics in a conservative political climate voted as heavily as anyone else. And a study of middle-class Catholics in Detroit in 1957 and 1958 found that they did not withdraw from political activity.[32]

The conclusions to be drawn from these specific findings may be: (1) that the cross-pressures upon Catholics have lost their importance; or (2) that Catholics are not under cross-pressures because one of the presumed bases of pressure is not one in reality or because through some other process the person or group is "shielded" from such pressures; or (3) that the cross-pressure theory is invalid —membership in groups with differing political predispositions does not tend to reduce the level of political activity or does so only under certain special circumstances.

The conservative influences of Catholic religious beliefs and values are shown by a number of studies. Contrary to what one might expect, Catholics (in the United States and Canada, at least) who usually attend services and are involved in church-related activities are *not* more likely to vote for the traditional Left party of their group; they are, indeed, less likely to do so than those more removed from their church. Conversely, Catholics more involved in the social and associational life of the Catholic community (apart from its religious dimension), as one might expect, are more likely to vote for the traditional party than those less involved in such community life.[33]

These studies indicate the dual and sometimes contradictory political effect of Catholicism as an aspect of an ethnic subculture and Catholicism as a distinctive set of values embodied in religious institutions. Unfortunately, within the range of data available for

---

[32] John Meisel, "Religious Affiliation and Electoral Behavior: A Case Study," *Canadian Journal of Economics and Political Science*, XXII (November, 1956), 481–96. See also Lenski, *op. cit.*, p. 132.

[33] See Lenski, *op. cit.*, p. 165; and Meisel, *op. cit.*, pp. 492–94, for parallel findings for the United States and Canada on this point. Meisel found that sisters and lay nurses in Canada were more likely to be Conservative voters than were rank-and-file Catholics. Lenski found that Detroit Catholics who attended church frequently were more likely to be Republican than non-attending Catholics, but that Catholics who associated frequently with Catholics were more Democratic than Catholics who associated frequently with Protestants. See Chapter 6 for a discussion of the "natural" conservatism of British Catholics, although the data do not permit a direct test of this point.

this study, no specification of these consequences in the Anglo-American countries can be undertaken.

It need not be assumed that distinctive voting patterns are the only expression of religious values in politics or that a religious party is incapable of adjusting to changing situations. In the Netherlands, although the support given to various parties has changed little in the last fifty years, governmental coalitions have changed in their composition, and varying social philosophies have been implemented. Although almost all Catholics vote for the Catholic party, for example, conflicts of interest between Catholic workers and Catholic employers take place *within* the Catholic party. Shifts of power and influence are reflected in changes of leadership and, thereby, shifts of the alliances within the parliamentary coalitions (from alliances with the Protestants to cooperation with the socialists, or vice versa). Such methods may allow political differences to be resolved as effectively as do the methods more common in the Anglo-American countries.[34]

In conclusion, this study will examine, insofar as the data will allow, the simultaneous effect of regional, religious, and class factors in voting behavior in order to discover the relative importance of these three major components of political cleavage in the Anglo-American countries. In addition, some attention will be paid to changes in the importance of these factors. It can be argued that major pressures against religious and regional politics have been created by social changes due to urbanization and industrialization in countries with secular and universalistic political cultures. If fundamental religious and regional differences decline, even if the symbols of identity remain, these social bases of political cleavage may become irrelevant. As the problems faced by government become more national in scope, politics may increasingly be based upon the competitions of large organizations with national social bases, competitions with an "interest" or "class" content.

---

[34] I am indebted to Carlos Kruytbosch for pointing this out to me. See Fogarty, *op. cit.*, for a detailed analysis of the religious parties in continental Europe.

Chapter 3

Problems of Comparative Survey Analysis

THE use of survey data for comparative studies of political cleavages is a relatively new undertaking. This chapter discusses some general and specific problems and presents the specific sources for the data of this study, as well as the measure of voting used.

PROBLEMS IN THE COMPARATIVE USE OF SURVEY DATA

Three separate problems connected with the use of survey data for a study of comparative political behavior will be considered: (1) the use of survey data in general, (2) their use for the study of political behavior, and (3) their use for comparative purposes.

First, the general difficulties in the use of survey data. An article by sociologist T. R. Williams illustrates a number of the common criticisms of the use made of responses to interviews. According to Professor Williams, the assumption that the behavior of the respondent corresponds to his responses in the interview situation is unwarranted, and the corollary assumption that such responses are equivalent and therefore susceptible to legitimate statistical manipulation is highly doubtful. With sociologist Herbert Blumer, Williams asserts that causal relationships in human behavior are more likely to be found in the context of social groups. Causes of human behavior cannot be discovered with the atomized, psychologically naïve view of human behavior which survey research implies.[1]

Some of these criticisms are irrelevant to the present study— though their merit when applied to survey studies of individual behavior is a serious question. Survey responses may be interpreted so as to (1) avoid inferring deeply held values or attitudes from an answer and (2) avoid equating similar answers to the same question by individuals who have widely differing values and social experiences. The main assumption of survey research called into question by these critics is the view that survey responses represent the attitudes and probable behavior of a single human being. If the unit of analysis is not the individual but social groups, however, these particular criticisms lose their relevance.

Survey data may be regarded as indicating the expected patterns of response of persons belonging to a certain social group or category. This is precisely what an answer to an interview question constitutes. By regarding responses in this way, we assume nothing about the predictability of behavior or the depth of belief. First, responses are no longer regarded as measures of individual opinion or behavior, but are used to produce a statistical aggregate representing the modal pattern of a social group. Second, the public character of the response is no longer ambiguously confused with private behavior or belief. Inferences are made from a public response (public in the sense that it is made to a stranger, the interviewer) to a public pattern of beliefs, attitudes, and behavior characteristic of a social group. This interpretation of survey responses is consistent with a common-sense view of what people say to interviewers: people say what they think people like themselves are supposed to say. When the concern is with the behavior (political or otherwise) *expected* of persons with certain group affiliations, the distinction between what individuals *really* think and what they think they are *supposed* to think is perhaps not too important. The deviations of individuals from the norms of their groups are important, but not for the purposes of this study.

---

[1] Thomas R. Williams, "A Critique of some Assumptions of Social Survey Research," *Public Opinion Quarterly*, XXIII (Spring, 1959), 55–62. Professor Blumer's position is stated in his article, "Public Opinion and Public Opinion Polling," *American Sociological Review*, XIII (October, 1948), 542–54. For a discussion of various ways of interpreting statements that a group (workers, farmers, Catholics) votes for party X, see H. Daudt, *Floating Voters and the Floating Vote* (Leiden: H. E. Stenfert Kroese NV, 1961), pp. 25 ff.

Thus, where the research is concerned with the public norms of political behavior associated with membership in certain social categories—religious, regional, or class—whether or not survey data tell us much about private belief or the social context of behavior is irrelevant.

Whether answers to questions are really predictive of other kinds of behavior is a problem which must eternally plague survey researchers. Again, probably this is less relevant where the typical pattern of response of a social group is of concern than where the behavior of individuals is the focus. In this study, one central problem is to ascertain the *association* of class and vote, i.e., a relationship between *two* or more social categories, *compared* in four countries. Probably this kind of research problem is less affected by the inevitable problem of predictability than studies of individual variations.

A second problem related to the use of survey data for the study of political behavior is that existing research has not studied significant *political* problems. The social-psychological studies of voting choice are mainly studies of the importance of a variety of social pressures for those decisions; those studies do not consider many problems really important for the political process, a few of which will be mentioned. Whether survey data can be used for these problems is an important question; this study of the Anglo-American countries is intended as a step in that direction.

Articles by several leading social scientists have been concerned with the kind of contribution which surveys have made and could make to the problems of understanding political systems and processes. Political scientist Avery Leiserson has pointed out that survey studies of political behavior have not been integrated with political theory, but have relied on non-political models of decision-making. He asserts that in political systems resting on consent (or consensus), such as the Anglo-American democracies, the political party is the distinctive political institution connecting the individual and his group-affiliations with the law-making and administrative structure of government. Leiserson suggests that the area of comparative politics is the most promising one for the reintegration of the "macro" institutional approach of political theory with the "micro" approach of political behavior.[2]

---

[2] Avery Leiserson, "The Place of Parties in the Study of Politics," *American Political Science Review*, LI (December, 1957), 943–54.

Sociologist Herbert H. Hyman has contrasted the sophisticated indexes developed to handle "the individual and his opinions" (in the voting studies cited in Chapter 2) with the need for:

> new modes of index construction which characterize and capture relevant features of the social distribution of opinion. . . . We need indices of *public* opinion that parallel the current indices of individual opinion. When is the social geography of opinion too polarized? When is consensus breaking down?[3]

Hyman considers this "fundamental aspect of a theory of public opinion; the aspect that relates public opinion to the political process, to political forms of society" to have been neglected. He implies that political behavior has not yet been approached using available theoretical concepts concerning social and political systems.

Political scientist V. O. Key, Jr., has made a similar point. He argues that most survey research into political behavior has not been *politically* relevant; that is, it has not sought answers to questions of crucial importance to the political process: "the operation of the state apparatus," historical shifts of political allegiances, the changing conditions under which different social variables affect voting behavior. In part, this neglect has been because any given survey is only a "snapshot" of historical processes, but also partly because survey researchers have been more interested in the motivational and attitudinal differences between individuals which affect their political behavior than in structural and historical factors affecting the modal behavior of groups. Key considers the survey method appropriate for the study of politics but advocates the comparative study of many surveys over time, and under many different social and political conditions, in order to attack further the "truly refractory problems of politics."[4]

Survey data have not yet been used enough for systematic comparative research.[5] This is partly due to difficulties which are be-

---

[3] Herbert H. Hyman, "Toward a Theory of Public Opinion," *Public Opinion Quarterly*, XXI (Spring, 1957), 59. (Italics in original.)

[4] V. O. Key, Jr., "The Politically Relevant in Surveys," *Public Opinion Quarterly*, XXIV (Spring, 1960), 54–61.

[5] One example of such research is Stein Rokkan and Angus Campbell, "Norway and the United States of America," *International Social Science Journal*, XII (1960), 69–99. A study by Seymour M. Lipset and Juan Linz, "The Social Bases of Political Diversity in the Western Democracies" (MSS, Center for Advanced Studies in the Behavioral Sciences, Palo Alto, Calif., 1956) attempts to systematize existing research into a comparative framework. See also Philip E. Converse and Georges Dupeux, "Politicization of the Electorate in France and the United States," *Public Opinion Quarterly*, XXVI (Spring, 1962), 1–24.

lieved to be inherent in the data. An implicit assumption of much research in comparative government and politics is that its subject matter comprises a number of unique configurations of social and political phenomena which must be studied as wholes or not at all. Attempts at isolating variables which can be compared across national lines are viewed as tearing out aspects of the phenomena from their legitimate context, thereby divorcing them from their meaningful relations with the particular society and political system within which they exist. This particular philosophical view is mentioned only to make explicit the view that this assumption is no more warranted than the alternative one that political systems and factors affecting political behavior are unique in some respects and not in others, in exactly the same way as are all phenomena in nature. Comparisons of factors affecting political behavior within different systems can be made without necessarily violating the meaning or nature of the phenomena.[6]

In one respect, however, this argument concerning the historical uniqueness of political configurations makes an important relevant point. When survey data are used within a comparative framework, their essential historical character is much more obvious than when the social system within which individual responses occur is taken for granted. Survey data, like all data in any science, are essentially historical in their nature; they refer ultimately to events and actions located in a particular place at a particular time. All generalizations rest upon a process of abstraction; analogies and contrasts are drawn from the historical specificity of the data to allow statement of generalizations which are applicable to more than the specific conditions under which the events occurred. Since ultimately all generalizations rest upon observation of historical realities, they cannot apply to social (or physical) conditions which depart "too much" from those from which the original data were drawn.[7]

---

[6] For discussion of the problems of comparative research in the social sciences, see Gideon Sjoberg, "The Comparative Method in the Social Sciences," *Philosophy of Science,* XXII (April, 1955), 106–17; and Oscar Lewis, "Comparisons in Cultural Anthropology," *The Yearbook of Anthropology* (New York: Wenner-Gren Foundation for Anthropological Research, 1955), pp. 259–92. Sjoberg stresses the problems of establishing invariant reference points, sampling, and standardizing observations. Lewis emphasizes the wide range of kinds of comparisons made by anthropologists.

[7] For a discussion of the implications of the comparative-historical framework for social science, see Kenneth E. Bock, *The Acceptance of Histories,* University of California Publications in Sociology and Social Institutions (Berkeley and Los Angeles: University of California Press, 1956), III, No. 1, esp. 122–29.

This, however, is precisely the ambiguous ground upon which the generalizations of all science rest: are the situations from which data are drawn really comparable in their crucial aspects—so that the particular relationships we perceive are not accidental? The problem is formulated differently in different sciences. In experimental sciences, as many variables are held constant as possible to minimize any extraneous effect upon the experimental relationship. Yet the constant underlying ambiguity (and it must be always present to some degree) is always whether some crucial factor affecting the relationship has been missed. In non-experimental science, the problem of sampling is crucial. Have we established comparable populations from which the samples are drawn? Have we drawn a sample which is representative of the crucial variables affecting the relationship of concern to us? These are questions which cannot be answered a priori but, paradoxically, only after the investigation is completed. Only if a replication discloses the operations of other factors or if logical analysis of the results uncovers a confounding variable, can the results be upset. This implies that the scientist himself can have no guarantee, at the time of investigation, of the accuracy of his assumptions concerning the comparability or generality of his units of analysis.

This study involves four kinds of samples:

(1) A sample of *countries*—those with two-party parliamentary systems. A number of cases are not included because of a lack of data: New Zealand, Uruguay, and possibly Turkey.[8] In practice, the countries are restricted also to those with dominant British political culture, which omits only New Zealand. A number of questions which will be raised by the data can be answered only by means of comparisons with entirely different types of cultures or political systems.

(2) A sample of *persons* within countries. The problems of this kind of sample will be discussed later in this chapter.

(3) A sample of *variables*. For reasons discussed earlier, the main empirical focus is limited to class, regional, and religious factors as they affect voting. Conceivably other social cleavages (tribalism, ethnicity, race, bureaucracy, for example) might be more important in a specific system. Ideological factors might be more important than any group factors in some systems.

---

[8] Maurice Duverger, *Political Parties* (London: Methuen, 1954), pp. 208–11.

(4) A sample of *time periods*. Availability of data and limitations of time and resources have restricted the data to roughly the period 1936 to 1962, which need not adequately represent the universe of historical time in which two-party parliamentary systems of this type have existed.

Clearly no research, in the present state of development of the social sciences, can fulfill rigorous sampling requirements, except possibly studies relating to samples of individuals. Even here, where the implicit population of concern is a universal one, there is usually a non-random sampling of countries, cultures, and time periods. Ordinarily we hope that factors outside of our control do not severely damage the relationships we observe. Too often, however, the logic of sampling is neglected.

The implications of these considerations for the comparative use of survey data are several:

(1) Comparable units of analysis must be established to avoid the possibility that the relationships studied are due to factors beyond the range of the study. In Chapter 1, the similarity of the political and class structures of the Anglo-American countries was documented.

(2) Maximum replication must be sought to avoid the possibility that the historical time-place character of a particular sample of the population produces the results. As will be shown, the major findings of this study are replicated by utilizing more than one national survey for each country and election, if possible.

(3) The possibility of change over time must be examined to avoid the likelihood that a particular historical period may reflect temporary forces and not a stable relationship. Here, surveys are cited from a period of almost twenty years for each country in an attempt to separate apparently stable social bases of politics from changing ones. The effect of using only one survey at one point in time is to assume that sampling variability is minimal and thus that a whole variety of social and political conditions left unspecified do not alter the general relationships found. In a comparative study, these assumptions cannot be made, although they are reasonable for a cross-sectional analysis of voting patterns for a given community or nation.

The problem of the comparability of survey questions across national boundaries is a difficult one, but the comparisons made here are probably as legitimate as is possible, particularly since they are made within a common political culture. In the case of the present study, there is reason to believe that a comparison between nations is just as meaningful as a comparison within nations. We have no grounds for assuming a priori that the South of Britain is more like the North of Britain than it is like New England or Ontario, or that Catholics in Quebec are more like Catholics in Ontario than they are like Catholics in Victoria. In fact, we might want to predict just the opposite. The units of analysis are so complex and so heterogeneous that comparisons either between nations or between groups and regions within nations are equally legitimate (or illegitimate).

The problem of the meaning of questions to individual respondents is parallel: we need not worry lest questions concerning voting or occupation or religion are any more ambiguous for Canadians than for Britishers. If the validity of national studies is accepted, then international studies have equal validity, at least within the boundaries of a single political culture and language. (The case of French-speaking Quebec shows that comparisons of Quebec with Ontario may be more dangerous than that, say, of Ontario with New South Wales.)

The novelty of attempts to use empirical data for comparative purposes has been well described by Robert K. Merton:

> Because statistical indices of such attributes of social systems [as heterogeneity, integration, or cohesion] have seldom been utilized in conjunction with indices of individual behavior, comparative sociology has been largely limited to loose and indecisive findings. . . . When statistical indices of group attributes have been adopted —for example, variations in racial proportions among groups— these have typically not been *combined* with systematic comparisons of the behavior of like-statused people within these distinctive groups. And, correlatively, when relatively precise measures of individual attitudes have been obtained, these have seldom been combined with similarly definite measures of social structure.[9]

In this study, an index of social structure (the index of class voting, described in the next chapter) is developed from data deriving from aggregates of individuals. Such an index is comparable to the one mentioned by Merton (the racial proportion of a group) in the sense that it is also derived from individual data and is not an organizational or structural property. Other characteristics of

---

[9] Robert K. Merton, *Social Theory and Social Structure* (Glencoe, Ill.: Free Press, 1957), p. 261. (Italics in original.)

"like-statused" persons are then compared within systems differing in the attribute of class voting.

SURVEY DATA FROM THE ANGLO-AMERICAN COUNTRIES

The basic data for this study comprise fifty-three separate surveys of the electorate in Great Britain, Australia, the United States, and Canada, conducted by both academic and commercial organizations. All surveys were conducted between 1936 and 1962, though the period varies for each country. Data from fourteen are reported in various studies in a form which was usable for the generalizations of concern here. IBM cards for a total of thirty-nine other surveys were tabulated for the specific purposes of this study: eight from Australia (between 1943 and 1961), nine from Great Britain (between 1943 and 1962), and eleven each for the United States and Canada (between 1936 and 1960 and between 1945 and 1961, respectively). In each of these surveys, information on the occupation and party preference of the respondent was available, and this information forms the basis for the index of class voting to be discussed in the next chapter. For some of these surveys, the religion and region of residence of the respondent were also available.

The particular surveys used here were not selected randomly from the entire range of surveys available. Most of the Commonwealth surveys used are deposited at the Survey Research Center at the University of California, Berkeley. Other surveys used are deposited at the Roper Public Opinion Research Center, Williamstown, Massachusetts. Where possible, surveys were selected which were taken within three months prior to a major election and which asked questions concerning occupation, voting intention, religion, region of residence, age, and sex. Table 3–1 summarizes the sources of data. It includes only surveys from which an index of class voting was computed.

As noted, more than one survey, where possible, was tabulated for each time period, usually before a national election. The variations in the results for various surveys will be discussed at pertinent points in the analysis of the data. The questions used referred mainly to the voting intention of the respondent in a national election (for the parliaments of the Commonwealth countries, for President in the United States). Where both information on the past vote and the voting intention and/or the party identification of the

TABLE 3–1

Sources of Data on Class Voting*

COUNTRY	SEPARATE NATIONAL SURVEYS CITED	SURVEYS SPECIFICALLY TABULATED FOR THIS STUDY	TIME COVERED
Great Britain	12	9	1943–1962
Australia	12	8	1943–1961
United States	15	11	1936–1960
Canada	14	11	1940–1961
TOTAL	53	39	1936–1962

* See Appendix A for a list of all of the tabulated surveys, their dates, and sources. See Appendix B for the exact questions asked in each survey, the occupational divisions used for each survey, the numbers of cases in each sample, and the date of each survey. Shown here are the numbers of surveys used for the basic evidence on class voting in each country. To minimize sampling error, more than one survey for each election period was used if possible. The first column above gives the total number of national samples of each population from which the index of class voting was computed. In some cases the index was estimated from other studies. These estimates account for the discrepancy between the first and second columns.

respondent were available, they were used to check on the reliability of the question on voting intention and the stability of the index of class voting when different questions were asked.

The first systematic survey of the voting intentions of a national cross-section of the population occurred in the 1936 presidential election in the United States, when the American Institute of Public Opinion (the "Gallup Poll") began its continuing series of political studies. Since then, organizations springing from the American parent have been established in a number of countries. The Gallup organizations in Canada (the Canadian Institute of Public Opinion), Australia (Australian Public Opinion Polls), and Great Britain (formerly the British Institute of Public Opinion, now Social Surveys, Incorporated) have conducted election surveys since their beginning, and their data constitute the basic evidence for the character of political cleavages in those countries.

In the United States, the sources of data are more diverse and of varying quality. Both Gallup and Roper organization surveys have been used, as well as data from the University of Michigan national studies of voting behavior, if available. Other studies not primarily intended as studies of political behavior, but containing questions on the voting intention or past vote of the respondent, have also been used.[10]

The University of Michigan Survey Research Center uses a probability sample; therefore its results have been accepted as most nearly correct. Their data have been plotted in the graphs appearing in subsequent chapters—instead of those of the commercial survey organizations, which use quota samples. A sampling error cannot be computed for a quota sample, and the biases of interviewers enter to a far larger degree than in a probability sample. In some cases, the results of the Gallup and Roper surveys are remarkably close to the Michigan results; in others, discrepancies are great.

The sizes of the samples for the studies used range from 600 to over 5,000, most being between 1,000 and 2,000. In the earlier years of surveys, samples tended to be larger. Gallup polls in the 1930's usually sampled at least 3,000 respondents. With advances in the methods of sample selection, a higher level of accuracy of prediction became possible with a smaller sample. In this study, the sources of error due to sampling bias are of minimal importance for several reasons. First, the concern here is with a *relationship* of class and vote, not with a prediction of actual percentages of voting. A relationship of two or more variables is probably less vulnerable to errors of sampling than a single percentage based on answers to a single question. Second, the study relies upon a number of surveys, both over time and for the same election, so that the errors of a given survey are less important. Where a systematic sampling bias exists that affects all the surveys, such an expedient would not solve the problem. The principal systematic bias is likely to be in the direction of underrepresenting lower-income groups, but where such groups are themselves a basic unit of analysis, this bias is also reduced in importance. As long as the *kinds* of people actually in-

---

[10] Early Gallup results from a number of countries are reported in Hadley Cantril and Mildred Strunk, eds., *Public Opinion, 1935–1946* (Princeton: Princeton University Press, 1951). The Michigan studies are reported in a series of volumes, beginning with Angus Campbell, Gerald Gurin, and Warren E. Miller, *The Voter Decides* (Evanston, Ill.: Row, Peterson, 1954), a study mainly of the 1952 electorate, but including also a 1948 study. A Michigan study of the 1954 congressional election was reported in Angus Campbell and H. C. Cooper, *Group Differences in Attitudes and Votes* (Ann Arbor, Mich.: Survey Research Center, 1956). The 1956 presidential election is analyzed in Angus Campbell and others, *The American Voter* (New York: Wiley, 1960). Another study from which data were used was reported in Samuel Stouffer, *Communism, Conformity and Civil Liberties* (New York: Doubleday, 1955).

TABLE 3–2

Typical Occupational Codes for Surveys*

AUSTRALIA	CANADA	UNITED STATES	GREAT BRITAIN
Manual Occupations			
Skilled, including boot-repairer, etc., who must have shop	Skilled labor or tradesman	Skilled worker	Manual workers in:
	Semi-skilled and unskilled	Unskilled worker and operative	Factory
Semi-skilled			Transport industry
		Service worker, domestic and protective	Building industry
Unskilled			Farm
Farm labor		Farm laborer	All other manual occupations
Non-Manual Occupations			
Professional	Professional and semi-professional	Professional	Professional
Owner and executive of large business	Major and junior executive; owner of large business	Business, executive	Director, proprietor, manager
Owner of small business		Clerical	Shop; personal service
Clerk, shop assistant	Proprietor of small business	Sales worker	Office and other non-manual
	Clerical		Student
	Outside salesman		
	Service and inside salesman		
Not Included in Any Tables			
Pensioner	Retired or unemployed	Retired and unemployed	None
Serviceman	Student; armed forces	Farmer and farm manager	
Farm owner			
	Farmer		

* The above codes are standard for British and Australian Gallup polls, except for one British survey done in 1943 for which the codes are given in Appendix B. The Canadian code given is for Survey No. 258 (May, 1957), and the United States code is for Survey No. 573 (October, 1956), both done by the Gallup organizations. Other occupational codes for the latter countries vary somewhat, but complete details are given in the footnotes accompanying the tables in Appendix B. Housewives are included under their husbands' occupations wherever possible. Exceptions are noted.

terviewed are representative, their underrepresentation is less important when they constitute a unit for analysis.

The underrepresentation of manual workers in the early years of polling is probably not a serious source of bias interfering with generalizations about changes in the level of class voting. Although no estimate is possible of changes in the degree of underrepresentation, the relationships here are relatively less affected because manual workers are a basic unit of analysis. It is assumed only that, regardless of any occupational bias in the samples, the manual workers who were included were the "same kind of people" as those who were excluded. Again, if prediction of the actual percentage of answers to a given question were of concern, this would be an important problem. Since the samples are divided along manual–non-manual lines, and since only the association of class and vote, not the actual vote itself, is of concern, this bias is not as important as it might be. Table 3–2 shows the way in which specific occupational groups were classified into manual and non-manual strata from typical surveys in each country.

THE MEASURE OF VOTING

Party preference in national elections is used as the measure of political behavior. No actual measure of the voting behavior of persons in different occupations is possible because of the secret ballot, and the questions asked in surveys are the closest available substitute. The most common form for the question, when asked prior to an election, was: "If the national election were today, for which party would you vote?" Variations in the questions are given in Appendix B.

Voting for the political unit which is the chief focus of national politics was used for each country: Voting for President in each election since 1936 in the United States and for the House of Representatives (or Commons) in each of the Commonwealth countries for each election since 1940 (if available). In some cases, only the past vote was available, but this is explicitly mentioned where it is used.

Persons who did not know whom they were going to vote for are omitted from every table. This introduces an unknown amount of bias into the results. In some of the surveys as much as 25 per cent of the persons in the sample were undecided as to their party preference. Here, as in other connections, the particular research problem of concern makes this bias of less importance than if the actual voting behavior of different social groups were to be predicted. In general, including the "don't knows" in a few computations from selected surveys did not affect the level of class voting appreciably, and none of the other relationships analyzed was altered.

No attempt was made to assess whether respondents were more or less likely to vote. In the Michigan studies already cited, elaborate controls were inserted to allow some prediction of whether a given individual was really going to vote or not. Since these controls are not possible in a secondary analysis, the responses of all persons expressing a party preference were accepted as of equal weight. The population of concern is thus in effect the entire eligible electorate save for the farmers.[11]

---

[11] In Chapter 1 it was noted that the politics of farmers and the social base of purely agrarian parties would not be considered. Therefore farm owners have been excluded from all tables included here except for the surveys from Great Britain. It was not possible to distinguish farmers in the British surveys, and, in any case, farmers form less than 5 per cent of the population in Great Britain. Farm laborers in Australia and the United States are included in the manual category. The Canadian surveys do not distinguish between farm laborers and farm owners; therefore they have been excluded completely.

Chapter 4

Measures of Social and Political Cleavage

THIS chapter presents simple measures of the association of social class position, religion, and region with voting behavior. A discussion of the suitability of the measure for comparative research on two-party parliamentary systems follows some consideration of the problems of empirically defining social class.

INDEXES OF SOCIAL CLASS AND VOTING

An appropriate measure of social class from surveys in modernized societies depends entirely on the theoretical purposes and assumptions of a particular research problem. No single social characteristic of individuals can adequately measure their economic life-chances, their community prestige, or their power over other individuals. In addition to this general difficulty, social changes now most marked in Western societies have created severe problems for the analysis of the influence of social class upon political behavior. The decreasing size of a visible "working class" and its apparently decreasing organizational solidarity deprive single indexes of social class of much significance. Neither subjective class identification nor a composite measure of objective class position (measures which, for example, combine education, income, and occupation) are of great help because both hide the very complications which should be analyzed: i.e., the discrepancies between these measures and the different kinds of attitudes and behavior which the discrepancies produce. By trying to establish the "best" measure of social class, researchers may reify the concept even if they are conscious of its complexities. When they find that such a composite measure does not predict behavior very well, they may conclude too readily that social class is no longer of much importance.[1]

But, where the stratification order is itself not the principal object of study (the dependent variable), occupation can probably be used as a convenient way of measuring objective social class position. For a comparative study of voting behavior, occupation is probably the best single indicator.[2] But, the effect of other status characteristics should be examined as well—not to show the deficiencies of occupation as an index of class position, but to clarify the complex ways in which people in roughly similar social positions may differ politically. If the changing importance of status or class position for political behavior is of concern, then comparing groups defined in a roughly similar way at a number of points in time should reveal any tendency to come together politically as well. If the political meaning of being in a "middle-class" or a "working-class" occupation has shifted or differs from country to country, it can be discovered by such research.[3]

---

[1] A recent study of class and party in a Norwegian village found that occupational differences remained the chief basis of stratification and political cleavage even though no substantial differences of income and prestige were present. See George K. Park and Lee Soltow, "Politics and Social Structure in a Norwegian Village," *American Journal of Sociology*, LXVII (September, 1961), 152–64. This suggests that, under some conditions, using occupation as an index of stratification may lead to somewhat different relationships than using income or prestige, and possibly may give a more static picture (not necessarily a more distorted one). By comparison, a study of political behavior in some future United States election might find that if income were used as the index of stratification, no relation would be found between it and political behavior. Such a result would show that this particular criterion of stratification was no longer relevant for attitudes and behavior, not that stratification itself did not exist or have consequences. In a period of social change, the validity of indexes of major structural phenomena such as stratification may need to be reconsidered over a period of time.

[2] The authors of *The American Voter* note that, among the objective indicators of class, "occupation tends to predict political attitudes and voting most efficiently." Angus Campbell and others, *The American Voter* (New York: Wiley, 1960), p. 344. See also A. H. Birch, *Small Town Politics* (London: Oxford University Press, 1959), pp. 104–8, for a brief discussion of the problems of classifying occupations into "classes."

[3] For discussions of changes in the class structure of the United States, see Kurt Mayer, "Recent Changes in the Class Structure of the United States" in *Transactions of the Third World Congress of Sociology* (1956), pp. 66–80, and Ely Chinoy, "Social Mobility Trends in the United States," *American Sociological Review*, XX (April, 1955), 180–86. Similar patterns of change have been foreseen for most of the two-party, parliamentary nations, which are the wealthiest nations in the world.

The best empirical measure of class probably will differ depending on whether the problem is to locate individuals within a given stratification system or to locate strata characterized by a number of predominant attributes. Much discussion of the methodological problems of defining classes assumes that the main problem is that of locating individuals.[4] If the location and attributes of strata are the main concern, then the intercorrelation of various attributes of status becomes a principal methodological line of attack upon the problem of identifying classes.[5]

The implication of this argument for the construction of an index of social class and voting is that a number of single empirical indexes can probably be used which more or less efficiently indicate the existence of social strata with certain attributes (income, education, occupation, prestige, style of life, historical continuity, etc.). Whether survey data on income, education, subjective class identification, or occupation are adequate, and which item is the best such indicator, are empirical questions; but several studies seem to show that the best predictor of other such attributes (both of individuals and of strata) is occupational position. A comparison of nineteen different indexes of status has been made using the method of factor analysis, and the variable most closely related to the first factor extracted was occupation. Although this conclusion was based only on United States data, it may hold for a number of Western societies.[6]

Such a single index has obvious shortcomings because of the probable low level of consistency of various attributes of status (in the United States at least), but it is particularly suitable for comparative research. The differences between countries, cities, or re-

---

[4] Leonard Reissman's excellent analysis of *Class in American Society* (Glencoe, Ill.: Free Press, 1959) is a case in point. He suggests that "four kinds of criteria have been used to identify social classes . . . 1) How the person lives; 2) What others think of him; 3) What he thinks of himself; and 4) What he does" (p. 116). All of these criteria assume that the location of individuals is the key problem, not the location of strata.

[5] See Werner Landecker, "Class Boundaries," *American Sociological Review*, XXV (December, 1960), 868–77, for one of the first such empirical attempts to delineate strata, utilizing survey data.

[6] Joseph A. Kahl and James A. Davis, "A Comparison of Indices of Socio-Economic Status," *American Sociological Review*, XX (June, 1955), 317–25. A detailed discussion of the problems of classifying occupations, primarily for use in comparative research on social mobility, appears in S. M. Miller, "Comparative Social Mobility," *Current Sociology*, IX (1960), 10–14. Miller utilizes the manual-non-manual classification for somewhat the same reasons as are pertinent here.

gions in the level of what has been called "status (or class) crystallization" constitute an important problem, but such differences do not preclude the use of a single measure of class position.[7] First, as already mentioned, occupation is probably the best single predictor of other class characteristics (and this may well be true in other countries as well as in the United States). Second, the very imperfection of occupation as an index is an integral part of stratification in this type of society and political system. The prosperity, high level of social mobility, and relative wealth of the countries with two-party parliamentary systems implies that a relatively high proportion of their populations is moving upward or downward, is in contact with other social classes or persons from other social origins, and has "contradictory" class attributes and experiences.

Arthur Kornhauser has concluded, from the undeniable fact that many attributes can be used as *indicators* of social class, that "one can hardly escape serious misgivings about the scientific feasibility of analyzing public opinion in relation to so complex an assortment of factors."[8] But any complex characteristic of either a society or an individual is difficult to measure, and the practical problem here is to find a relatively unambiguous measure which is obtainable at moderate cost in time and money, which correlates relatively highly with logically related measures of the same abstract characteristics, and which is meaningful across national or regional boundaries. Occupation seems to fulfill these conditions most clearly.

For the purposes of constructing an index of the association of social class and voting, an additional manual–non-manual distinction has some theoretical justification. The move across the manual–non-manual "line" seems to have a similar meaning in most Western societies. The shift from a blue-collar to a white-collar job has more

---

[7] No comparative research has been done using the concept of status or class crystallization, although it would certainly be possible. Existing studies have focused upon single cities or national samples without regard for regional or other areal variations, and the failure to find more differences in behavior between persons with consistent and discrepant statuses may be due to the lack of a comparative focus, not to the lack of importance of this as an independent variable. See Gerhard E. Lenski, "Status-Crystallization: A Non-Vertical Dimension of Social Status," *American Sociological Review*, XIX (August, 1954), 405–13, and Irwin W. Goffman, "Status Consistency and Preference for Change in Power Distribution," *American Sociological Review*, XXII (June, 1957), 275–81.

[8] Arthur Kornhauser, "Public Opinion and Social Class," *American Journal of Sociology*, LV (January, 1950), 338.

significance—personally and socially—than a shift within each category, although the relative prestige and life-chances of various occupations differ considerably within either broad category.[9] But more important, the remaining contrasts between the middle class and the working class in styles of life, education, and values probably justify calling the manual–non-manual division a "class" distinction which would be blurred if the constant empirical focus were upon political differences between professionals and white-collar workers, or skilled and unskilled laborers. Such differences are important, however, and the focus on class neglects many important differences within the middle-class and the working-class electorates.[10]

Support for the manual–non-manual distinction (for the United States, at least) is given by the finding that "on the scale of the socio-economic index, there is a fairly sharp separation between the lowest of the white-collar groups (sales and clerical) and the highest manual group (craftsmen, etc.)." Table 4–1 shows the index for selected occupational groups. Unfortunately, no similar data on the other Anglo-American countries are available.[11]

This usage of the term "class" is similar in one respect to Max Weber's usage, which distinguishes a class from a community or self-conscious status group. "Classes" merely represent possible and frequent *bases* for communal action to Weber, who specifies that a class exists when a "number of people have in common a specific causal component of their life-chances in so far as this component

---

[9] This generalization is probably most questionable for shifts from skilled worker to an owner of a very small business. Also, the problem of how to classify farming occupations, or farm–non-farm occupational shifts in terms of social mobility has not been satisfactorily solved. Since agrarian politics is usually distinctive in most countries, for purposes of an empirical index, those social strata most characteristic of industrial societies—manual and non-manual occupations—can probably be examined without regard for the farming population.

[10] The further decision to dichotomize the various occupational groups into manual and non-manual can also be justified on practical grounds, particularly if comparative secondary analysis of existing surveys is contemplated. Specific occupational categories are classified differently in various surveys, and the manual–non-manual distinction is the most unambiguous one for comparative purposes. Also, the data are much more easily handled when only two social strata are compared, instead of the eight or ten occupations usually available in a survey.

[11] Albert J. Reiss, Jr. and others, *Occupations and Social Status* (New York: Free Press of Glencoe, 1961), p. 155.

TABLE 4–1

A Socio-Economic Index for Selected Occupation Groups, United States, 1950

OCCUPATION GROUP	SOCIO-ECONOMIC INDEX*
Non-Manual	
Professional and technical	75
Managers, officials and proprietors (except farm)	57
Sales workers	49
Clerical workers	47
Manual	
Craftsmen and foremen	31
Operatives	18
Service workers (except private household)	17
Private household workers	8
Laborers (except farm and mine)	7

Source: Albert J. Reiss, Jr. and others, *Occupations and Social Status* (New York: Free Press of Glencoe, 1961), p. 155.

* The socio-economic index was computed from aggregate income and education data for males and adjusted for the age composition of the occupations. Farming occupations are omitted here as are other parts of the original table.

is represented exclusively by economic interests in the possession of goods and opportunities for income, and is represented under the conditions of the commodity or labor markets."[12]

In the sense that the "specific causal component" of life-chances is probably more disadvantageous for skilled workers than for clerks and small businessmen, the manual–non-manual distinction suggested as the measure of class is a reasonable one. But by the same token, the limitations of using the manual–non-manual division are clear. The distinction is too general, because sales clerks are not in

---

[12] Hans Gerth and C. Wright Mills, eds., *From Max Weber: Essays in Sociology* (New York: Oxford University Press, 1946), p. 181.

the same "class situation," in Weber's sense, as either professionals or executives of large businesses.

The use of the term "class" here does not imply any implication of consciousness of membership in a social class. Whether manual or non-manual workers are conscious or not of a collective identity and whether they associate this collective identity with a political party representing a collective interest, are of course important empirical questions, but ones which should be kept separate from that of the degree of political divergence of objectively defined strata.

Since voting as such can be analyzed at any political level, the index of class voting to be suggested can be applied to communities, regions, or nations (or to any social group within these areal entities). Since the parties in the class and political systems of reference usually represents the Left and Right on a number of issues (welfare, taxation, regulation of business and trade unions, and other similar issues), for purposes of empirical comparison parties can usually be divided in this way.

Where two major parties are the main contenders for power, it is assumed that dividing the vote into Left and Right fairly represents the fundamental political division in the electorate. Since minor parties exist in most "two-party" systems, some decision must be made concerning the character of their appeals, parliamentary alignments with a major party, and legislative policies, in order to classify them as part of a Right or Left political alliance. For purposes of an empirical index, such a decision might vary from country to country and from election to election. Chapter 1 has discussed the Left-Right character of the parties in the Anglo-American countries.

AN INDEX OF CLASS VOTING

The extent to which manual and non-manual strata divide in their support for political parties can be summarized in a simple numerical "index of class voting." As with an index of class itself, any such measure has inherent limitations as well as advantages, depending on the problem of concern.

The suggested index of class voting is computed very simply as follows: *Subtract the percentage of persons in non-manual occupations voting for Left parties from the percentage of persons in man-*

ual occupations voting for Left parties.[13] The hypothetical figures
given in the accompanying example indicate that the statistic computed as shown did not change in value during the three elections

Per Cent Voting Left (Hypothetical Figures)

		Votes for Left	
	1948	*1952*	*1956*
		(Per Cent)	
Manual Occupations	70	60	50
Non-Manual Occupations	50	40	30
Per Cent Difference	+20	+20	+20

from 1948 to 1956. Therefore, according to this index, class voting
did not change in that period, despite a move away from the Left
party in both social strata.

This index thus assumes that it is the gap between the voting
patterns of manual and non-manual occupations that is vital for
assessing class voting, not the over-all level of Right or Left voting.
The problem of how to interpret a shift to the Right or the Left is
not basically that of determining the choice of an index of class
voting since the problem of interpretation would remain regardless
of which index is chosen. This particular index embodies the assumption that the deviation of either the manual or the non-manual
stratum from any given level of vote for one of the major parties is
the important fact relevant to an assessment of class voting. Adding
up the deviation (with regard to the sign) produces this index. Although the method of computation just given does not make this
clear, a reinterpretation of the above example will. For the 1952
figure, for example, the manual stratum split 60–40 for the Left and

[13] The logic behind the use of such an index is that used by Donald J.
Bogue in his computation of a "coefficient of dissimilarity" measuring the
"total amount of dissimilarity between any two percentage distributions in
which the two sets of percentages are distributed by the same classes and refer
to the same units." See Donald J. Bogue, *The Structure of the Metropolitan
Community* (Ann Arbor: Horace H. Rackham School of Graduate Studies,
University of Michigan, 1950), p. 72. Here, an index of class voting is suggested only for dichotomies, but nothing in the nature of the index prevents it
from being used for more numerous categories. Another use of the same index
is presented in O. D. Duncan and Beverly Duncan, "Residential Distribution
and Occupational Stratification," *American Journal of Sociology*, LX (March,
1955), 493–503.

Right parties respectively, i.e., 10 per cent more in their expected (Left) direction than a 50–50 split. The non-manual stratum split 40–60 in the opposite direction, i.e., 10 per cent more in their expected (Right) direction than a 50–50 split. Adding these two 10 per cent deviations from a 50–50 split in each stratum, we get an index figure of 20, which is exactly the same as the simpler computation given. (The same index would result if deviations from any other base-line percentage were computed.)

But what if the voting figures upon which the index was based were as follows?

Per Cent Voting Left

Manual Occupations	20
Non-Manual Occupations	0
Per Cent Difference	+20

Clearly this is a radically different situation from the one producing the figures just given. The political significance of class has changed, as has the whole political system, and that is just the point. Here we have the virtual destruction of support for one major party, and complete unanimity in one stratum. The index is meaningless for such a situation even though it shows an unchanged figure of +20. Clearly, the conditions affecting the social bases of the parties have changed to such an extent that any simple statistic such as this lacks any relevance to an understanding of what has happened. But assuming for the moment that no such catastrophic change has occurred, it is still difficult to interpret the change. The lack of any Left voting among non-manuals may mean that they are extremely class-conscious and are voting Right for pure class reasons. On the other hand, the 20 per cent of all manual workers voting Left may mean that most workers have taken on middle-class aspirations and are expressing them politically by voting Right. A total decline in the significance of social class as a determinant of voting need not be implied even by such outlandish figures as those. One stratum may be extremely class-conscious and voting for a party representing its felt interests; another stratum may be voting for the same party for completely non-class reasons.

Any empirical index, regardless of its particular construction, applies only to a given set of social and political conditions. But given such conditions, why compute the index in this particular way? To answer this question, we must bring in further assumptions concerning the character of this type of political system.

The index reflects the assumption that both major parties respond to issues salient to the voters and attempt to gain as much support as possible; neither party tries to isolate its social base from political influence. Parties change with the changing importance of issues and are susceptible to influence from social currents and conflicts within the electorate. Clearly this is true only of certain societies and in certain historical periods. Computing the index as a simple percentage difference between the Left support of the two social strata assumes that it is easy to change parties in these political systems and that it is no harder for the average Left vote of either stratum to go from 40 per cent to 50 per cent than from 50 per cent to 60 per cent. This point deserves some elaboration, since it reflects an important assumption relative to the problem of change in the level of class voting. (See Appendix E for further discussion.)

The index suggested assumes that major social strata tend to be affected similarly by political and social currents to the Right and to the Left—that, in other words, a high level of consensus exists. No social group is impervious to national social trends. Evidence to this effect has been found in at least two United States studies. An early study of voter-registrants in Santa Clara County, California, found that a trend toward Democratic registration occurred among *all* occupational groups, not just those presumably benefitting most from the New Deal.[14] A recent study of voting change has shown the reverse shift to have occurred in the 1948 to 1956 period, when all occupational groups moved in a Republican direction.[15]

If this is the way that political shifts have occurred in this type of political system, then only a movement in both strata toward the same percentage for each party would be a true decline of the importance of social class as a systematic factor differentiating the support of the parties. This would be a move away from the normal predispositions in both strata. Actually, as already pointed out, changes in other directions could occur. The Left vote could decline steadily in both strata. This might mean that both strata were becoming middle-class in their values but that the Left party was stubbornly maintaining its identity as the party of workers. Or con-

---

[14] See H. Dewey Anderson and P. E. Davidson, *Ballots and the Democratic Class Struggle* (Stanford, Calif.: Stanford University Press, 1943), p. 370.

[15] Campbell and others, *op. cit.*, pp. 346–47.

versely, both strata might be radicalized and move away from both traditional parties toward revolutionary parties if the old parties maintained conservative appeals.

The index of class voting is independent of what the authors of *The American Voter* have called "class-solidarity," the degree to which the manual or non-manual stratum deviates from unanimous support of the Left or Right party, respectively.[16] If we assume an equal number of persons in each stratum, then what might be called "relative class solidarity" (the percentage-point difference between the degree to which manual workers deviate from a 100 per cent vote for the Left party and the degree to which non-manual persons deviate from a 100 per cent vote for the Right party) stays the same regardless of the level of class voting (assuming that class voting is either 0 or positive). The level of relative class solidarity is determined by the absolute level of Left voting, not by the level of class voting.

The suggested index of class voting must not be overinterpreted to imply the importance of class issues in the programs of the parties or the meaning of class issues to the voters. Whether a high level of class voting (as measured by this index) is related to class appeals and a high level of class consciousness is an important question, but no inferences from the index itself can be made. It measures simply the extent to which social strata, as defined by manual and non-manual occupations, diverge in their support of a major political party.

The question might be raised: Why not deal only with one class or stratum? It would be easy to refer only to, say, the proportion of workers voting for the Left party and consider that a measure of class voting. But such a measure pertains neither to the entire class system nor to the entire political system. Also, such a measure may not adequately distinguish between nations because the workers in Great Britain may vote no more heavily Labour than the workers in the United States vote Democratic. As indicated before, the feature of the association of stratification and politics of concern here is not how heavily one stratum votes for a party, but how distant this level of support is from that given by another stratum to the same party.

This particular index does leave aside two important aspects of

---

[16] *Ibid.*, p. 348.

the relation of social classes to parties: the degree of political distinctiveness of the working class (the absolute level of Left voting by workers) and the degree of class distinctiveness of the Left party (the proportion of support for the Left party drawn from workers).[17]

Four limiting cases are illustrated below. Type I illustrates the case where the Left party draws almost exclusively from the working class *and* the working class supports no other party. Party and class lines are sharply drawn. Such a state of affairs might well constitute a revolutionary situation. We need not expect that the Anglo-American countries will exhibit this pattern in the historical period dealt with here. Type II illustrates the case where the working class divides its support between the two parties but the Left party subsists almost entirely on its working class votes, and Type III the opposite case, where the workers vote almost exclusively for the Left party, but the middle class divides its support between the two parties. The index of class voting does not differentiate these two types. Type IV illustrates the case where neither party nor class can be sharply distinguished by their support or composition.

In a comparative study which took into account a wider range of political cultures and social structures, these dimensions of the class-party relationship—the political distinctiveness of the working class and the class distinctiveness of the Left parties—would need to be taken into account. For present purposes this inadequacy of the index of class voting can be neglected.

In these four countries, the working-class vote for the Left party varies between 50 and 70 per cent, and the working-class segment of the Left party's support is usually no higher. The main exception is in Britain, where the working class supplies roughly three-quarters of the Labour party's support. But the situation in Britain may still be quite different from that in Norway, for example, where workers give heavy support to the Socialists (over 80 per cent) but the middle-class support for that party is also relatively high.

How to interpret shifts as Right or Left in a three- or four-party system is a problem tacitly ignored by the index. The subsequent chapters on each country attempt to remedy this inadequacy by considering the role of the "third" party in the various countries. The index of class voting must not be seen as a simple "empirical" index

---

[17] I am indebted to Stein Rokkan for noting this point.

TYPE I
High Political Distinctiveness of the Working Class
High Class Distinctiveness of the Left Party

| | Vote for Party | | |
	Left	*Right*	*Total*
		(Per Cent)	
Manual Occupations	90	10	100
Non-Manual Occupations	10	90	100
Index of Class Voting	80		

TYPE II
Low Political Distinctiveness of the Working Class
High Class Distinctiveness of the Left Party

| | Vote for Party | | |
	Left	*Right*	*Total*
		(Per Cent)	
Manual Occupations	60	40	100
Non-Manual Occupations	10	90	100
Index of Class Voting	50		

TYPE III
High Political Distinctiveness of the Working Class
Low Class Distinctiveness of the Left Party

| | Vote for Party | | |
	Left	*Right*	*Total*
		(Per Cent)	
Manual Occupations	90	10	100
Non-Manual Occupations	40	60	100
Index of Class Voting	50		

TYPE IV
Low Political Distinctiveness of the Working Class
Low Class Distinctiveness of the Left Party

| | Vote for Party | | |
	Left	*Right*	*Total*
		(Per Cent)	
Manual Occupations	60	40	100
Non-Manual Occupations	40	60	100
Index of Class Voting	20		

based upon exactly comparable questions and categories, but as a "theoretical" index based upon assumptions concerning the similarity of the class structures of these countries, the Left-Right character of the two-party systems (despite the continuing "third" parties) and the pluralist, moderate character of the political process in these countries. Any comparative statements to be made rest upon the validity of these assumptions.

STATUS POLARIZATION AND THE AMERICAN VOTER

A recent work utilizing survey data for an analysis of American voting behavior computes an identical index of the association of social class and vote, but calls it "status-polarization."[18] It was, however, put to different uses. The concept of "status-polarization" used in *The American Voter* is a social-psychological one in line with the theoretical focus of the Michigan voting studies upon the factors affecting individual voting decisions.[19] Status polarization, in the authors' definition, refers to the extent of "identification" of individuals with a class or status-group. Occupation, religion, and education are treated as "external" characteristics of individuals which may or may not indicate an identification with a social group. This theoretical orientation produces a concern with what the study calls "short-term fluctuations" of the importance of status or class factors in voting behavior. The authors conclude from their data that class factors were much more important in polarizing the electorate in 1948 than in 1952 or 1956. They explicitly recognize that long-term changes in the importance of status and class and religious factors may be occurring, but, by and large, such problems are outside their selected scope.

"Status-polarization" is considered a measure of the "intensity and extent of class identification" in a society. "When polarization is

---

[18] See Campbell and others, *op. cit.*, p. 347. The index of status polarization is based upon a manual–non-manual division. I am indebted to Professor Philip Converse of the University of Michigan for clarifying the definition.

[19] Other publications by various members of the staff of the Survey Research Center, University of Michigan include: Angus Campbell, G. Gurin, and W. E. Miller, *The Voter Decides* (Evanston: Row, Peterson, 1954); Angus Campbell and H. C. Cooper, *Group Differences in Attitudes and Votes* (Ann Arbor: The Survey Research Center, 1956); and P. E. Converse, "The Shifting Role of Class in Political Attitudes and Behavior" in E. Maccoby, T. Newcomb, and E. Hartley, eds., *Readings in Social Psychology* (3rd ed.; New York: Holt, 1958).

high, most of the citizenry must have perceived a conflict of interests between strata and have taken on class identifications with fair intensity. When polarization is low, either few people are identifying, or extant identifications are weak, or both."[20] Such polarization may be expressed in different areas, economic or political, but the concept as such refers only to the feeling of solidarity of individuals with persons in similar social positions, as contrasted with persons in other positions. There are degrees of polarization in the sense that a general polarization may exist on many issues and grounds or only on a few issues. The sense of polarization (or "antagonism") may be high in only a few people or in many. These dimensions of identification are called the "area," the "scope" and the "intensity" dimensions of polarization.

The key idea in their concept of status polarization is thus the movement of two (or more) status groups toward greater self-identification as entities. This implies that the strata "perceive" a conflict of interest between them. But, as I shall try to show, the legitimate concern of the authors with short-range change and with such social-psychological factors leads them to neglect certain interpretations of their empirical index of status polarization which contribute to an understanding of the role of class factors in political behavior.

Although the shifting importance of class identifications for individuals is the main concern of the authors of *The American Voter*, the distinction between self-identification and objective status is not kept clear.[21] Sometimes "status voting" is used to refer to the association of occupation with vote, sometimes to the association of subjective class identification with vote.[22] But the association of objective status with voting may not be a good measure of the extent of class identifications. Since voting is largely in accordance

---

[20] Campbell and others, *The American Voter, op. cit.*, p. 339.

[21] In making this point, I do not want to imply that they fail to deal with actual measures of group identification and its effect upon political behavior. The most important contribution of their chapter on class is to show how degrees of political involvement, actual subjective class identification, and self-awareness as a member of a group interact with objective status to alter individual political behavior.

[22] "Status voting" in Figures 13–3 and 13–4 of Campbell and others, *The American Voter, op. cit.*, pp. 352, 354, refers to the correlation of subjective status and vote, but in Figure 13–2 (p. 347) "status-polarization" refers to the correlation of objective status and vote. The two terms seem to be used interchangeably.

with traditional group memberships, voting in accordance with the political predispositions of one's occupational associates or other status affiliations may remain at a high level even though class identifications have become weak.

A figure on page 345 of *The American Voter* illustrates different levels of status polarization. Three pictures of the voting behavior of two social strata are given, illustrating "depolarization" (where 50 per cent of each stratum votes conservatively), "complete polarization" (where all upper-class members and no lower-class members vote conservatively), and an "intermediate stage" (where there is equal crossing over of both groups).

The "intermediate stage" is an extremely ambiguous one mainly because it covers a range of alternatives encompassing most of the possibilities for variation in a consensual parliamentary political system. The only numerical figures given corresponding to the "intermediate" coefficient of status polarization shown (0.50) are 75 per cent of the upper class voting Right and 25 per cent of the lower class voting Right.

The difficulty with this way of interpreting status polarization is that it does not give the actual range of possibilities for a given numerical coefficient. If the one actual example is to be taken at face value, the coefficient is computed by subtracting the percentage of lower-class people voting conservatively (25 per cent) from the percentage of upper-class people voting conservatively (75 per cent), producing a coefficient of 0.50. But all of the upper class could vote conservatively and half of the lower class could vote conservatively (or vice versa), with the same numerical coefficient of status polarization resulting (100 per cent minus 50 per cent equals 0.50 either way). Would this mean that one class was extremely conscious of its interests and that the other was imbued with "false consciousness"?

The important point here is that for nations with stable party and parliamentary systems there may be relatively great shifts from Right to Left (from conservative to liberal governments) but little change in the level of polarization—as measured by such an index. A more important question is: Does a move to the Right or Left mean a substantial change in the *gap* between the political behavior of social strata?

The picture of the range of status polarization presented in *The American Voter* does not exhaust the possibilities of variation in still another sense. One group may become more homogeneous than another. The upper class may become more solidly Right at the same time that the lower class is becoming more solidly Left *or* remaining the same. This kind of variation is not included in the concept of status polarization presented in *The American Voter*. The authors may have an image of polarization as an *individual* matter, to be arrived at for the whole political system by adding up the class antagonisms and identifications assumed to be felt by voters as individuals. At this point, one can say only that this concept of status polarization does not convey the realistic range of possibilities of variation found in the Western democracies. The authors' "intermediate stage" covers a multitude of possibilities of variation in the importance of status and class factors for the political behavior of individuals, and ignores the kinds of change possible for entire social strata.

Although in a given election (or series of them), certain candidates and issues may pull normally Left voters to the Right party, these voters may remain identified *even on a class basis* with the other party. Oscar Glantz has shown that American voters for Eisenhower differed greatly in their political attitudes. Workers voting for Eisenhower remained Democratic, by and large, in their party identifications and remained Left in their opinions on a number of issues.[23] Non-party factors accounted for the appeal of Eisenhower to about three-quarters of the working-class ex-Democrats and about two-thirds of the middle-class Democratic defectors. Glantz concludes that the "interest-group basis of political behavior" was not destroyed by the Eisenhower pull.

"Temporary" non-class issues and candidates therefore do not necessarily completely nullify class allegiances and their political channels. There is a danger of overinterpreting one election or trend. The move to the Right in 1952 by normally Democratic workers was not, from this evidence, a permanent shift of allegiances away from an identification of their class interests with the Democratic party.

The authors use the term "behavior" to cover two types of political change: by the social group and the individual. It is used to refer both to the typical voting preferences of Catholics, workers, or Negroes (a "statistical" statement) and to the particular preferences of

---

[23] Oscar Glantz, "Unitary Political Behavior and Differential Motivation," *Western Political Quarterly*, X (1957), 833–47.

one person (a "clinical" statement). But the conditions which cause a particular Catholic worker to vote Left are not the same as those which cause 70 per cent of Catholic workers to vote Left. The former are personal phenomena, having their roots in the life history and social experiences of the person; the latter are social and historical phenomena, having their roots in the historical experiences of ethnic and religious groups.

Ignoring this difference allows the authors to term as "surprising" the origins of a present party commitment by an individual in the far distant past of his ethnic ancestors. As they put it:

> if we trace a party commitment [and ambiguity begins here, because whether this term refers to an individual or to the modal behavior of a social group is not made clear] deep enough into the past, we must sooner or later encounter recognizable "beginnings," and . . . these beginnings are likely to involve pressures arising outside the political order as narrowly defined. True as this may be, such a tracing leads with surprising frequency to events lying years or even generations behind us, in such remote circumstances as a ravaged Georgia plantation or a job for a bewildered Boston immigrant. It is such roots of current choice that provide a strange commentary on the view of the democratic process as a periodic re-evaluation of contemporary events.[24]

But it is not really at all surprising that social mechanisms exist which transmit political values and loyalties from one generation to another. Such historical experiences explain the typical political loyalties of a social group, not the political choices of an individual. One has not yet explained why a given individual votes a certain way when one finds out why a group to which he belongs has a predominant political loyalty.[25]

The inferences drawn by the authors of *The American Voter* from their data contribute importantly to our knowledge of the pressures upon individual voters and the processes by which voting preferences change or stabilize. But the extent of class identification and antagonism which exists in a political system need not be inferred from the degree of political divergence of objectively defined social strata.

---

[24] Campbell and others, *The American Voter, op. cit.*, p. 292.

[25] Wherever a comparison of *rates* of behavior for one group as compared to another has been made, it seems more reasonable to refer to social rather than to individual factors to account for the observed differences.

INDEXES OF RELIGIOUS AND REGIONAL VOTING

Whether voting behavior is oriented toward religious or regional rather than class loyalties is difficult to assess, especially since in some cases they may reinforce each other. Where Catholics, for example, hold predominantly lower-status occupations *and* are in a minority in a Protestant country where they are treated as such, they have a double incentive for voting for a certain party. Where a certain social class is in an overwhelming majority in a certain region, it is difficult to separate the class and the regional origins of a propensity to support a certain political party.

Survey data allow an approximate separation of these factors, although it cannot be claimed that by merely locating persons within certain regions or who acknowledge a religious affiliation one can learn anything about the exact character or strength of the political identities which result.

Generally, it will be assumed here that if a region or a religious group has a special political identity—the southerners or the Catholics with the Democrats in the United States, for example—the effects should appear within *both* manual and non-manual strata. More specifically, the percentage-point difference in Left voting between religious groups (mainly Protestant and Catholic) within a given class will be termed "religious voting." If this is close to zero, it will be interpreted as indicating that religious loyalties are not politically relevant. The same procedure will not be used for regional differences because more regions are being compared, and a simple dichotomy is not possible. Therefore, only regional differences in class voting will be compared.

This procedure holds constant the proportion of persons within a region or a religious group who happen to be in a certain social class and therefore removes one possible source of confusion of religious or regional political identities with class-based political identities.

If Catholics have the same index of class voting as Protestants—even though Catholics, both manual and non-manual, have a higher level of Left vote than Protestants in similar strata—then religion does not offset the effect of class but is added to it. As will be shown, this is indeed the case in a number of elections in the various countries; religion affects party loyalties but does not reduce the level of class voting. In other cases, religion seems to act in the opposite direction. Frequently, a complicated interaction occurs between class, religion, and region as they affect voting, with a sharp polarization occurring along class lines in some regions and religions but not in others. Neither the data nor the scope of this study allow for intensive explorations of the meaning of such a complex interaction of the factors. Ideally, in order to see the independent effect of region (or religion) upon class voting, both occupation and religion (or region) should be held constant. In practice, this has not often been possible because of a lack of cases.

Precisely because there is interaction between class, regional, and religious bases of political cleavage, these factors cannot be considered to vary independently. If religious voting were at its maximum (assuming equal numbers of Protestants and Catholics divided equally into manual and non-manual strata), class voting would have to be zero (or vice versa). The limits of religious voting are therefore set by the range of class voting actually found, as is also the case with regional voting. Since the distribution of classes within religious groups, and of both within regions, is not uniform, the practical limits of any particular type of cleavage set by another form of cleavage are not easy to set.

In practice, however, the limits of religious and regional voting are fairly broad for any given level of class voting. The over-all association of class and vote in these nations is determined largely by Protestants and by the highly industrialized-urbanized regions— since Protestants are in a heavy majority and urban-industrial regions are the most populous. Therefore, the deviation of Catholics and of the smaller, more rural regions (those more likely to exhibit regionalism) from national patterns of class voting can be fairly great.

Assessment of the importance of various social bases of party support would be complicated enormously if it was determined that the parties had drastically shifted their appeals and policies during this period. If, for example, the Catholic middle class voted heavily Democratic in 1944 because of the educational policies of Roosevelt at that time but shifted over to the Republicans in 1952 because the Republicans took over those policies, this would not necessarily mean any decline in the distinctive ideologies or values of the Catholics. Catholics might shift parties (even in a direction presumably in line with their class) precisely because of their particular religious values in order to maintain a connection with a party which furthered the values. (A partial check on such a shift, of course, would be whether Catholic manual workers as well as middle-class people shifted, and this is what the measure of religious voting is designed to show.)

Since no serious effort can be made here to assess the degree to which the parties themselves have made attempts to change their social base by appealing specifically to groups not traditionally in their camp (the United States Republicans to the southerners and to Catholics, the Canadian Conservatives to Quebec residents, for example), it will be assumed that no important changes have taken place within this period. Some of the empirical findings can undoubtedly be explained by such a shift by the parties, however, and further research might show some such connections.

Chapter 5

Class Voting in the Anglo-American Countries

THE class structure and the party systems in the Anglo-American countries indicate that class and voting are associated, but nothing said thus far implies identical relationships. This chapter is devoted to: first, a discussion of the differences in the level of class voting indicated by historical and institutional features of these societies; second, a presentation of the evidence on class voting from a great number of public opinion surveys taken between 1936 and 1962; and third, a discussion of some correlates of class voting which may help to explain why differences exist despite the similarities of political culture and class structure.

WHY CLASS VOTING SHOULD BE HIGHER IN GREAT BRITAIN AND AUSTRALIA

Considerable historical and institutional evidence indicates that the association of class and vote should be higher in Great Britain and Australia than in the United States and Canada. In particular, the explicit links of the trade unions with the Labor parties of Great Britain and Australia might seem to be prima facie evidence that manual workers are far more likely to support the Labor party than non-manual workers. But this is not a necessary connection. The links of a class organization with a party bearing the name of "labor" do not guarantee that the actual character of the support of the party is sharply differentiated from that of the other party. Particularly in this historical period, when, according to authors already cited, class lines are blurring and the working class in advanced industrial societies is losing its distinctive identity and consciousness as it takes on middle-class values and aspirations, there is no reason to assume that working-class and middle-class persons are still sharply divided in their political loyalties.

Before presenting the actual evidence, the views of political scientists on a few of the historical differences between these four political systems which probably affect the level of class voting should be noted. Since this is a large topic in itself, only a few representative and current works will be cited. The point is obvious: class organizations and class ideologies have been much more explicitly linked to the political parties in Great Britain and Australia than in the United States and Canada.

The Labour party of Great Britain was from the first an instrument of class organizations—the trade unions.

> The Labour party was founded by the trade unions to secure Labour representation in Parliament and to support by political action the objectives sought by the trade unions in the interests of their members. . . . What produced that party was the discovery by the urban workers that they could secure better conditions of service by combinations among themselves, and the threat by the employers to seize the initiative by employers' federations which could also act as pressure groups in Parliament.[1]

Even today, the trade unions raise most of the money for the Labour party, and are officially represented in the "National Council of Labour," composed of representatives of the Labour party, the Trades Union Congress, and the Cooperative party.[2] Although in practice the Labour party has a high degree of independence, the "constitutional law" of the party holds that it is bound by the decisions of the annual Parliamentary Labour Conference, in which the unions are officially represented.

However, though actual relationships exist between the trade unions and the Labour party in Great Britain, they are complicated and often strained, and in no sense do the trade unions dictate to the Labour party. The party is not the creature of working-class organizations; the very moderation of British political culture pre-

---

[1] Sir Ivor Jennings, *Party Politics, II: The Growth of Parties* (Cambridge: Cambridge University Press, 1961), pp. 235, 237.

[2] *Ibid.*, pp. 256–57; Robert T. McKenzie, *British Political Parties* (London: Heinemann, 1955), p. 529.

vents any coincidence of class and party views. But clearly the trade unions—unquestioned instruments of working-class interests —and the Labour party are historically and publicly linked. On this ground alone, we might expect that political loyalties in Great Britain might be explicitly class-linked.[3]

The Labor party in Australia is equally solidly linked to working-class organizations.

> The Labour Party was created by the trade unions and their Trades and Labour Councils. The solid core and the majority of its membership, as of its electoral support, came and have ever since come from trade unionists and their families. Most of its Parliamentarians, Federal and State, have risen through the trade union ranks. For many years it was little more than the trade-unions-in-politics—in earlier times, in some States at least, it was known as the "Labour-in-politics" movement, implying just that.[4]

The class-structure of Australia is similar to that of the other countries. From these two factors, we might expect that the level of class voting in Australia is close to that of Britain.

But one feature of Australian history might lead to a level of class voting different from that in Great Britain. The Australian Labor party has always had higher prestige and authority than the British Labour party. From the very beginning of Australian nationhood in 1901, the Labor party has existed as a political force and has shaped the political traditions of its country far more than the Labour party of Great Britain did. The British Labour party arose partly as a means of breaking the dominance in Parliament of the industrial and owning classes and of gaining recognition of the legitimacy of class organizations. The Australian Labor party arose partly as an instrument for the unification of Australia as an independent nation and partly as a representative of strongly organized and militant unions mainly composed of workers in "rural" occupations such as

---

[3] A common Conservative accusation against Labour is that it is dominated by "special interests" and therefore cannot represent the nation as well as the Conservative party. McKenzie devotes much of his book on British political parties to a demonstration that the Labour party is no more (and no less) bound to outside pressure groups than the Conservative party. See McKenzie, *op. cit.*, chap. 1.

[4] L. F. Crisp, *The Australian Federal Labour Party: 1901–1951* (London: Longmans, Green, 1955), p. 182. See also Donald W. Rawson, *Australia Votes: The 1958 Federal Election* (Melbourne: Melbourne University Press, 1961), p. 2.

sheep-shearing. Its dominance is noted by American political scientist Louise Overacker:

> The position of the Labor Party, both as to program and actual strength in Parliament, is a determining factor from which the politicians calculate their course, right or left. . . . The matrix of Australian politics is the Labor Party, and Australian politics reflects working-class rather than middle-class thinking.[5]

The dominant role of the Labor party in Australia might produce either higher or lower levels of class voting in Australia than Great Britain. Where the Right party has the halo of tradition and defender of the nation and is supported by widespread values of deference toward the aristocracy as in Great Britain, we might expect that a large minority of the workers would vote Conservative for non-class reasons. Even if middle-class persons voted consistently Conservative in accordance with *their* class interests, Conservative "deferential voting" among workers would reduce the level of class voting. On the other hand, the middle class in Australia might be more likely to vote Labor because of the legitimacy and nationalism associated with the Labor party in that country, reducing the level of class voting there.

Both of these arguments are plausible, and both may be wrong. Actually, the greater legitimacy of the Right in Great Britain and of the Left in Australia may negligibly affect the voting of either social class. This point has been raised simply to underline the difficulty of predicting the level of class voting from information on only the historic links of class organizations to political parties.

But regardless of the differences between Australia and Great Britain, historical and institutional evidence does indicate that class voting is likely to be higher in both of these countries than in the United States and Canada.

Occupational differences in the composition of the lower houses of the parliaments of the countries are consistent with this prediction, as Table 5–1 shows, for various years. In Britain and Australia, 19 per cent of Members of Parliament were either manual workers

---

[5] Louise Overacker, *The Australian Party System* (New Haven: Yale University Press, 1952), p. 81. Part of the quote was taken from C. Hartley Grattan, *Introducing Australia* (New York: John Day, 1942), p. 153. Here, as is the case with the British Labour party, such origins and political role do not mean that the party has a consistent ideological position or that it is not willing to compromise.

or trade union officials, while in the United States and Canada, only 3 per cent and 1 per cent, respectively, came from such occupations. The class composition of the lower house in the latter two countries is like the composition of the Right parties in Britain and Australia.[6]

TABLE 5–1

Members of the Lower House from Working-Class Occupations, by Parties

COUNTRY	MEMBERS FROM WORKING CLASS (Per Cent)		
Great Britain, 1959	Conservative	Labour	Total
	0	47	19
Australia, 1951	Liberal	Labor	Total
	4	45	19
United States, 1949	Republican	Democratic	Total
	..	..	3
Canada, 1945	Conservative	Liberal	Total
	..	..	1

Sources: Information was not available for all persons, nor for the parties separately in the United States and Canada, although the differences could not possibly be great.

Great Britain: Computed from D. E. Butler and Richard Rose, *The British General Election of 1959* (London: Macmillan, 1960), p. 127. The percentages given include labor union officials, who hold 12 per cent of the Labour seats in the House of Commons. One Conservative was a manual worker.

Australia: Compiled from the *Australian Parliamentary Handbook, 1952* (Sydney: Angus and Robertson, 1952), pp. 265–300. The percentages given include labor union officials, who hold 15 per cent of the Labor seats in the House of Representatives.

United States: From Donald R. Matthews, *The Social Background of Political Decision-Makers* (New York: Random House, 1954). The percentage given refers to either wage-earners or low-salaried workers. It may be noted that of the state legislators in thirteen states (including most of the highly urbanized states, where trade unions are most likely to be politically active), 7 per cent in this period were wage-earners or low-salaried workers.

Canada: From Norman Ward, *The Canadian House of Commons: Representation* (Toronto: University of Toronto Press, 1950), p. 132. Each member was classified according to as many as three "occupations and economic interests." Ward notes also that "in no single province has there been a serious and continuing difference of occupational structure between the major groups composing each party in the legislature" (pp. 135–36).

The Left political parties in the United States and Canada do not have public and historic links with trade unions and other class organizations which might repel the middle class and attract the

---

[6] Middle-class professionals comprise almost equal proportions of the Left and Right parliamentarians in both Australia and Britain (between 35 and 40 per cent), despite the dominance of class groupings in the parties. Presumably such groups should be a moderating influence upon class conflicts, having less of a direct stake in the struggle. Lawyers are more highly represented in the British than in the Australian parliament.

working class, producing a high level of class voting. As R. M. MacIver has put it:

> party government can under certain conditions operate with considerable indifference to class stratification. Thus for long periods and over large areas in the United States and in Canada there was little relation between class and party, the struggle between parties being essentially a contest of the "ins" and the "outs" for the spoils of office. When this happens, however, parties are hardly distinguishable from one another with respect to principles or to objectives.

MacIver infers that when, as in the 1930's, "both in Canada and the United States, one or another party came to propose important economic changes," the tendency of the more well-to-do to support one party and the poorer to support another showed again.[7]

That the political parties in the United States and Canada historically have been competing political elites—the "ins" and the "outs"—and not the direct representatives of class organizations does not clearly distinguish them from the parties of Australia and Great Britain, however. In all four societies, each party has in practice consented to whatever legislation has been passed and has even adopted some policies likely to be favored by the class base of the other party in order to win over support. In Australia, "Labor's political opponents have accepted many of Labor's policies," and in Great Britain, most markedly in recent years, the policies of the parties have been well-nigh indistinguishable.[8] Thus it cannot be maintained that the actual policies of the parties in Australia and Great Britain are so different from those in the other two countries—aside from historic traditions and organizational links—that we may expect sharp differences in the level of class voting.

There is another ground on which class voting may not be expected to be sharply higher in Australia and Great Britain—at least higher than in the United States. The public images of the two parties in the United States sharply define them as representatives of distinctive class bases:

---

[7] Robert M. MacIver, *The Web of Government* (New York: Macmillan, 1947), p. 123. MacIver offers no evidence for his assertion that when the parties differ in their objectives class voting is likely to increase, although it is certainly a plausible inference.

[8] Overacker, *op. cit.*, p. 81; and Jennings, *op. cit.*, chap. 9 ("Sham Fight"), pp. 327–42.

a consistent majority—at times as high as two-thirds to three-quarters—of the adult population of the United States perceives a clear distinction in ideological and interest-group propensity between the two major parties. The polls tend to verify the commonly accepted caricature that the Democratic Party is the party of the poor and of labor and the Republican Party is the party of business and of the rich. . . . These stereotypes may be less important as accurate descriptions of party differences than as reflections of the public's belief that the parties actually provide meaningful alternatives in many areas of policy, even though there are important areas of consensus.[9]

Thus, even though there are no explicit links of class organizations to particular parties, and regardless of the degree to which the parties *actually* represent distinctive class interests, American political parties are viewed by voters as representing different social classes. A much higher level of class voting in Australia and Great Britain than in the United States may not therefore be expected.

In Canada, on the other hand, none of these factors favoring a high level of class voting exists. Except for the New Democratic party, one of the minor parties, no political party has any explicit links with class organizations, and such links are, in fact, sedulously avoided. The parties are not ideologically linked with any distinctive class interests historically, and are not identified with specific class bases at present. Therefore, class voting might be low. But, again, this need not be true. Class interests exist in Canada as they do in the United States, and certainly the political parties represent them to some degree. A complete absence of class voting is not, therefore, to be expected. It is also true that the class bases of Canadian politics need not be much different from those of other countries in the British tradition. Since much of its population originated in Great Britain, similar kinds of political expectations and loyalties might exist among Canadians, shaping the parties around specific class bases.

The Liberal party in Canada has not been linked historically to class organizations in the way that the Labor parties of Australia and Great Britain have. This is partly due to the frontier character of Canada (and the frontier has had similar effects upon American

---

[9] Stephen K. Bailey, *The Condition of Our National Political Parties* ("An Occasional Paper of the Center for the Study of Democratic Institutions" [New York, 1959]), p. 22. Evidence for this statement was provided by the Roper Public Opinion Research Center, Williamstown, Massachusetts, which tabulated every question in American public opinion polls since 1946 that dealt with public images of the two parties.

politics) since class struggles were vitiated by the availability to dissatisfied workers of land to the West. The continual expansion of Canada and the domination of certain regions by agriculture has emphasized sectional conflicts of East and West based on urban-financial versus rural-agricultural conflicts rather than on the classical struggle between industrialists and workers. Therefore, working-class organizations have been relatively weak and relatively irrele vant politically.

The Conservative party took the lead in the policy of national development and in the unification of Canada—while the Labor party led in those matters in Australia—and therefore has historically benefitted from this identification with the national interest. The Liberal party has been the defender of provincial autonomy, mainly due to its long association with the French-Catholic minority in Quebec, and this link has further deterred its identification as the party of the working class.[10]

The parties in Canada have therefore not been identified as class parties, but not for the reason that class interests do not exist or receive political expression in Canada. Class interests have been cross-cut by so many other politically relevant cleavages—sectional, religious, ethnic—that they have not emerged as the chief basis for political loyalties. We may expect that class voting is lower in Canada than in Great Britain and Australia but not necessarily lower than in the United States, where so many diverse cleavages have also determined the strategies and appeals of the political parties.

We may now turn to the evidence on the relation between social-class position and voting in these four countries derived from a large number of public opinion surveys and summarized by means of the index of class voting.

DIFFERENCES IN CLASS VOTING: SURVEY RESULTS

A number of public opinion surveys taken between 1952 and 1962 indicate that class voting is consistently higher in Australia and Great Britain than in Canada and the United States. The coun-

---

[10] For general descriptions of the links of the Canadian political parties to sectional, class, and urban-rural interests, see R. McGregor Dawson, *The Government of Canada* (2nd ed.; Toronto: University of Toronto Press, 1954), pp. 500–30; and H. M. Clokie, *Canadian Government and Politics* (Toronto: Longmans, Green, 1944), pp. 75–95. These points are discussed further in Chapter 9.

tries may be ranked in the following order: Great Britain, Australia, the United States, and Canada. Table 5–2 and Figure 5–1 summarize these results. (See Appendix B for details.)

TABLE 5–2

Class Voting, 1952–1962

| COUNTRY | INDEX OF CLASS VOTING* | | | Based on Number of Surveys |
	Mean	Lowest	Highest	
Great Britain	40	35	44	8
Australia	33	27	37	10
United States	16	13	23	5
Canada	8	—1	17	10

* The index of class voting was computed by subtracting the percentage of non-manual workers voting for "Left" parties from the percentage of manual workers voting for "Left" parties. For Great Britain, the Labour party was used; for Australia, the Australian Labor party; for the United States, the Democratic party; for Canada, the CCF (or NDP) and Liberal parties. Where two parties were classified as "Left," their votes among each strata were combined. For a discussion of the index, see Chapter 4. See Appendix B for the exact questions asked in each survey, the occupational divisions used, the dates of polls, and the numbers of cases in manual and non-manual occupations. The surveys were taken at various times between 1952 and 1962. All questions referred to voting intention or past vote in a national election.

Class voting is almost always above zero; only one Canadian survey falls below that mark. Great Britain is consistently higher than Australia in the 1952–1962 period; it has a mean index of 40 and a range of 35 to 44. Australia is consistently higher than the United States and has a mean index of 33 and a range of 27 to 37. The United States is consistently higher than Canada, except for one 1958 Canadian survey, and has a mean index of 16 and a range of 13 to 23. Canada always has the lowest level of class voting, with the single exception mentioned.[11]

Particular shifts in each country and the contribution of each social stratum to class voting will be discussed in the chapters on each country, but it must be stressed that no particular figure has any great significance. It is probable, however, that the over-all patterns of differences from country to country override any possibilities of sampling error.

The "true" level of class voting may actually have shifted, as Figure 5–1 indicates. Given the lack of tight integration of social

---

[11] Table 5–2 includes only the 1952–1962 period for summary purposes. Prior data are more unreliable for the various countries because of greater sampling variability and the unavailability of really comparable British data prior to 1955.

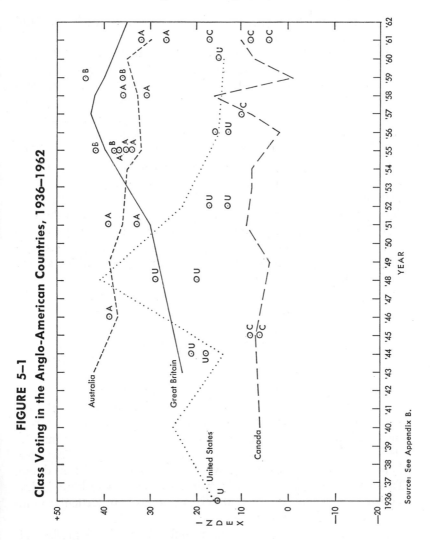

FIGURE 5-1

Class Voting in the Anglo-American Countries, 1936–1962

Source: See Appendix B.

groups, whether they be social classes or others, and the lack of close correspondence of class and party, a rather high level of shifting back and forth of the social bases of the parties is likely, as different issues both class and non-class become salient, and as the parties jockey for support from various groups. But what is striking here is not the variation within the countries, but that, regardless of that variation, the differences in class voting between the countries are so sharp and consistent.

But before these results are accepted, we must consider the possibility that they are due to particular social groups within each country. It is possible, for example, that the solid Democratic loyalties in the South account for the lower level of class voting in the United States than in Australia. It is possible that the solid Liberal loyalties of Quebec (until 1958) account for the lower level of class voting in Canada than in the United States. It is possible that class voting is manifested in Great Britain and Australia mainly among older persons, in whom class loyalties are more deeply felt and depressions and oppression more bitterly remembered, on one side, or callously forgotten, on the other. If the differences between the four Anglo-American nations disappear when certain subgroups of the population are examined, then the difference between political systems is a statistical artifact produced by strong antipathies among certain segments of the population and equally strong ties overriding those of class among other segments.

As Table 5–3 shows, the differences in the level of class voting between the four Anglo-American countries do not disappear when class voting is examined within different age groups, within two religious groups (Protestants and Catholics), within the regions highest and lowest in their level of class voting, and in large cities. By and large, the rank order of class voting is not affected. Within each age-group, among either Protestants or Catholics, Great Britain has the highest class voting of any of these countries; Australia is next followed by the United States and then Canada. It may be noted that the difference between Britain and Australia disappears when the regions highest and lowest in class voting are considered. (To some extent the figures are artifacts of extremely high or low component index figures, so that here, as before, no particular number has any great significance.)

Table 5–3 shows that regionalism and religion have marked effects upon class voting in each country—in that class voting is consistently higher among Protestants than among Catholics and that a considerable difference appears between the regions with the highest and the lowest average levels of class voting. The problems of interpreting these differences will be dealt with in the chapters on each country and in Chapters 10 and 11.

The differences between the countries remain when class voting

TABLE 5–3

Class Voting within Selected Demographic Groups, between 1952 and 1962

	MEAN INDEX OF CLASS VOTING*								
	AGE-GROUP†				RELIGION		REGION‡		CITIES
COUNTRY	20–30	30–40	40–50	50–60	Protes-tants	Catholics	Highest	Lowest	OVER 100,000
Great Britain	39	36	37	42	46	44	47	23	41
Australia	30	28	35	39	36	29	47	22	36
United States	13	13	22	13	21	16	31	4	20
Canada	5	9	13	9	10	2	26	—12	11

Sources: The surveys upon which the figures are based are:
Great Britain, CQ 82 (1955), CQ 1717 (1957), CQ 116–118 (1959), and CQ 275 (1962); *Australia,* Nos. 115 (1955), 135 (1958), 140 (1960), 149 (1961), and 154 (1961); *United States, Michigan* (1952); Nos. 573 (1956), 636K (1960), and 75 (1960); *Canada,* Nos. 238 (1954), 250 (1956), 266X (1958), 285 (1960), 286 (1961), and 292 (1961). Not all information was available on every survey. See Appendixes A and B for details on the surveys.

* Computation of the index of class voting is discussed in Chapter 4. Figures given here are means of a number of index figures for each country.

† The age-groups for Michigan 1952 and the British surveys are not precisely as indicated above.

‡ For Michigan 1952, the regions are slightly different from those used in the other United States surveys, and the "urban" category is a combination of urban and suburban metropolitan areas. All figures are + except as indicated.

in cities of over 100,000 population is considered. Urbanization does not (or has not yet) reduce the international differences in class voting. (It may be noted here that two surveys of urban constituencies in New Zealand found a level of class voting very close to Great Britain's.)[12]

As a final check on the validity of the differences between these political systems in their level of class voting (and as a check on the adequacy of the manual–non-manual distinction as a measure of class), it is possible to define social class more narrowly in terms

[12] Class voting in one metropolitan area of New Zealand (Dunedin Central) was +40 in a 1961 election. The figure was computed from Austin Mitchell, "Dunedin Central," *Political Science* (New Zealand), XIV (March, 1962), 27–80. A detailed breakdown of occupations allowed a recombination into a manual–non-manual dichotomy. A 1958 survey of voting in a New Zealand urban constituency (Wellington Central) showed parallel results, although precise comparisons are not possible since the data were not given in sufficient detail. See Robert S. Milne, "Voting in Wellington Central, 1957," *Political Science* (New Zealand), X (September, 1958), 34–37.

of two criteria of class position instead of one and to compute a more refined measure of class voting. It seems reasonable to predict that the validity of the principal finding of the differences in class voting will be reinforced if the rank order remains when social class is defined in terms of either education, income, subjective class identification, or trade-union membership in addition to occupation. Table 5–4 shows that the rank order of class voting in the four countries remains the same even when a more narrow (one should say more rigorous) definition of the social class position of the respondents is used. The level of class voting is indeed higher in each country when social

TABLE 5–4

Class Voting Defined by Two Class Characteristics, between 1952 and 1962

	MEAN CLASS INDEX*			
COUNTRY	Education and Occupation	Income and Occupation	Subjective Social Class and Occupation	Trade-Union Membership and Occupation
Great Britain	57	52	53	51
Australia	43	46	47	46
United States	26	31	35	22
Canada	10	11	12	16

* Figures given are means computed from the same surveys listed under Table 5–3 where the question was asked. In Australia, education and class identification were asked only in No. 154 (1961). In Canada, class identification was asked only in No. 292 (1961). In the United States, class identification was asked only in Michigan (1952). Otherwise the figures are derived from at least two surveys in each country. All figures are +. The figures are based upon a definition of "working class" and "middle class" defined by two class characteristics, as follows:

Great Britain: Manual workers were included who either (1) left school before the age of fifteen, (2) were judged to be in one of the lower two positions on a four-point socio-economic status scale by interviewers, (3) identified themselves as "working-class" when asked: "What social class would you say you are in?" or (4) had a member of a trade union in their family. Non-manual persons were included who either (1) remained in school past age fifteen, (2) were judged to belong in one of the higher two positions on a socio-economic status scale by interviewers, (3) identified themselves as "lower-middle-class" or higher, or (4) did not have a trade-union member in the family.

Australia: Manual workers were included who either (1) had primary, secondary, some technical or commercial education, who finished technical or commercial school, or who had an intermediate certificate; (2) were judged to be in one of the lower two positions on a four-point socio-economic status scale by interviewers; (3) identified themselves as "working-class," or (4) had a trade-union member in the family. Non-manual persons were included who either (1) had some university training or a university degree, or either a leaving or a matriculation certificate, (2) were judged to belong in one of the upper two positions on a four-point socio-economic scale by interviewers, (3) identified themselves as "middle-class" or higher, or (4) did not have a trade-union member in the family.

United States: Criteria in the United States surveys varied considerably. For education, the division was between high school or less for manual workers, and some college or more for persons in non-manual occupations. The income criteria for the Gallup and Roper surveys were parallel to the British and Australian surveys, but for Michigan (1952), manual workers were included who earned less than $3,000 per year and non-manuals who earned more than $7,500.

Canada: The educational criteria were the same as in the United States; the others, the same as Britain and Australia.

classes are defined more narrowly than by manual and non-manual occupations, but the differences between the four countries remain the same.

Survey data from four Anglo-American countries have shown that clear and consistent differences between the countries exist, regardless of whether class voting is examined for the total electorate divided into manual and non-manual occupations, for the same division within various demographic groups, or for a more rigorous definition of classes. Great Britain and Australia have higher levels of class voting than the United States and Canada. Some of the correlates of different levels of class voting which may be causal factors are discussed in the next section.

In none of these countries is the voting of one stratum for "its" party unanimous. Political consensus in these countries is shown by the constant shifting back and forth from Right to Left, but never does the vote by manual workers for the Right party, or non-manual workers for the Left party, drop below about 20 per cent. Never does the index of class voting rise above 60 percentage points (80 per cent of the manual workers voting Left, 20 per cent of the non-manual workers voting Left, for example) even when, as in Table 5–4, classes are defined more narrowly than by occupation only. This narrower definition leaves out so much of the potential electorate that it is meaningless as an over-all measure of class voting. The imperfect "status crystallization" of these four countries produces a high level of "cross-class" voting, no matter how class is defined. The fairly even impact of politically relevant events upon the classes is also shown clearly by the parallel moves to the Right or Left in most election periods. (See Figure 1 in each of the following four chapters.)

POSSIBLE CAUSES OF THE DIFFERENCES IN CLASS VOTING

A search for political and social differences between the Anglo-American countries which parallel the differences in class voting and which might account for them suggests four possibilities: (1) the parties in countries where class voting is higher might more consistently *represent* class interests; (2) the parties in countries where class voting is higher might more consistently *appeal* to class interests; (3) the parties where class voting is higher might simply possess the historical loyalties of certain classes, regardless of how they appeal to or represent class interests; (4) regardless of historical loyalties or the actions of parties, the social classes in these societies might be differently exposed to situations in which the political relevance of class interests becomes apparent; i.e., the social structure of these countries might be sufficiently different (despite similarities in the range and number of class positions, in the prestige of different occupations, and in the level of social mobility) that a high level of class voting is more likely in one country than another.

Whether the parties in Australia and Great Britain more consistently represent or appeal to class interests is a crucial problem for an adequate understanding of the emergence of class patterns of support for the parties. That all of the parties in each country strive to win support from all social classes does not contradict the existence of real differences between parties in their appeals and representativeness. Only a few speculative suggestions can be offered here.

The historical links of the trade unions in Great Britain and Australia to the Labor parties certainly suggest that the Labor parties there are more likely both to appeal to and to represent working-class interests than the Left parties of the United States and Canada. Upon that assumption, Table 5–5 suggests a connection between the differences in class voting actually found and possible differences of appeal and representation. Parties in Great Britain both appeal to and represent class interests; voters rationally respond by dividing their support more clearly along class lines. Parties in Australia appeal to, but less clearly represent, class interests (this is

TABLE 5–5

Class Voting and Representation of or Appeals to Specific Class Interests

COUNTRY	PARTIES REPRESENTING CLASS INTERESTS	PARTIES APPEALING TO SPECIFIC CLASS INTERESTS	LEVEL OF CLASS VOTING
Great Britain	+	+	High
Australia	+ —	+	Medium High
United States	+	—	Medium Low
Canada	—	—	Low

only speculation). Parties in the United States represent class interests as much as the Australian parties but do not specifically appeal for support in class terms. Last, the parties in Canada neither consistently represent distinctive class interests nor appeal to different class bases for support.

Two characteristics of working-class ideology in these countries might affect the level of class voting, other things being equal: the level of class consciousness and the degree of equalitarianism. Qualitative evidence suggests that the countries should be differentiated as shown in Table 5–6.

TABLE 5–6

Class Ideologies

COUNTRY	CLASS CONSCIOUSNESS	EQUALITARIANISM
Australia	+	+
Great Britain	+	—
United States	—	+
Canada	—	—

Table 5–6 suggests that Australian workers have a sharp working-class consciousness and strong feelings of equalitarianism. Their leaders are not seen as "any better" than they are. British workers, in contrast, are class-conscious but accept the leadership of the aristocrats and the well-educated. (Obviously these are relative statements.) American workers are not particularly class-conscious but are equalitarian; Canadian workers are neither class-conscious nor equalitarian in this sense. If such a schema accurately sums up differences between the countries (and assuming that the middle class is similarly differentiated), we would expect the level of class voting to be in line with them, given similar class structures, and therefore that class voting should be higher in Australia than in Britain. Since it is not, other social and economic differences to be discussed may be more crucial explanatory factors than ideological differences.

These differences between the parties and the prevalent ideologies of social classes in the four countries might completely account for the differences in class voting, but because the interest here is in class voting as a structural fact of their socio-political systems, we may look further for correspondences of the rank order of class voting with other characteristics of the four societies.[13] Do we find correspondences of the order of class voting with other social characteristics of these societies?

At first glance this might seem unlikely. These four societies were picked precisely because they were similar in political and social type. On any measure of economic and social development—urbanization, wealth, industrialization—all four countries will be included in the first ten nations.[14] Their similarity of political culture, party systems and parliamentary systems has also been documented. But precisely because of this great similarity, correlations between class voting and certain other social characteristics are more plausible as causal relationships, since the correlations cannot be ascribed to gross differences of social or political structure.

For comparative purposes, some of these socio-economic measures are given for the other European or English-speaking stable democracies as well (for Belgium, Denmark, Ireland, New Zealand, the Netherlands, Norway, Sweden, and Switzerland).[15] Although the comparisons with these other countries will not be discussed separately, it may be noted that in almost every instance, each of the four Anglo-American countries here analyzed is more urbanized, has a higher per capita income, and a higher percentage of employed males in the non-agricultural labor force, than the average of the other stable European democracies. Since the European and English-speaking democracies are far more "developed" than any other group of countries in turn, it is clear that these four countries are among the most economically developed and wealthy countries in the world.

In spite of the gross similarities of wealth and industrialization,

---

[13] The last possible cause of differences in class voting—historic loyalties—is, for our purposes, merely a residual category; if neither social-structural differences nor differences in party appeals and representation of class interests are correlated with class voting, we could ascribe differences between the countries to historical loyalties of certain strata to certain parties. Traditionalism of one kind or another—class-based traditionalism in Great Britain, non-class traditionalism in the United States or Canada—may be a historical factor of great importance.

[14] See, for example, Thomas O. Wilkinson, "Urban Structure and Industrialization," *American Sociological Review*, XXV (June, 1960), 358, in which data from forty-nine nations are compared.

[15] For other indexes of wealth, urbanization, industrialization, and education, including figures for Latin-American and European unstable democracies and dictatorships, see Seymour M. Lipset, *Political Man* (New York: Doubleday, 1960), pp. 51–54.

even differences in the level of economic growth and development seem to be consistent with differences in the level of class voting. The countries with higher levels of class voting are expanding more slowly—which may reduce opportunities, restrict mobility, and therefore maintain the solidarity of classes to a greater degree. On four related measures of economic growth, the rank order was Australia (lowest), Great Britain, the United States, and Canada.[16]

All other factors being equal, we might expect that more urbanized societies (and societies which had been urbanized for a longer period of time) would have higher levels of class voting than less urbanized societies. A considerable amount of sociological and political research has indicated that urbanism breaks down loyalties to community, region, and religion, and substitutes class loyalties as the basis for political behavior.[17] We might also expect that relatively poorer societies with a relatively larger working class would have higher levels of class voting, simply on the grounds that class interests would be more explicit, and working-class parties more easily organized.

Also, more "closed" societies—societies with lower levels of educational opportunities, less chance for upward social mobility, and less chance for individuals to "escape" via a frontier—might have a higher level of class voting. In these four societies, where education is a real symbol of class status, lack of educational opportunities for bright working-class children might strongly reinforce class voting (and this might be the case even though in actual fact as many working-class children move up into non-manual positions) for both manual and non-manual voters. Manual workers would be more likely to vote Left out of resentment; non-manuals would be more likely to vote Right as a symbol of their privilege. If, in addition,

---

[16] The measures showed the rise per year (in the post-World War II years) in gross domestic product, gross national product, net domestic product, and net national product. Measures of investment and savings rates were also fairly consistent for both the late nineteenth and early twentieth century periods, but ratios indicating net capital formation were not consistent with class voting. See Simon Kuznets, "Quantitative Aspects of the Economic Growth of Nations," V: "Capital Formation Proportions: International Comparisons for Recent Years" and VI: "Long-Term Trends in Capital Formation Proportions," *Economic Development and Cultural Change*, VII, Part II (July, 1960), 1–96, and IX, Part II (July, 1961), 1–124.

[17] The works of the political scientist A. N. Holcombe are the American classics taking this point of view. See his *The New Party Politics* (New York: Norton, 1933), and *The Middle Classes in American Politics* (Cambridge: Harvard University Press, 1940).

there were important differences in the character of social mobility (despite the similarities in over-all rates, as shown in Chapter 1), the objective gap between social classes might be greater in one society than another.

Another aspect of a "closed" society—the lack of a frontier—also should increase class voting. Where no escape is possible from the urban class struggle, manual workers stay and fight. Where open land is available, many who might form the leadership of working-class organizations leave.

Clearly these factors are not necessarily independent, and where they all exist, class voting should be reinforced accordingly. Relatively poor, highly urbanized societies where manual workers have little educational opportunity and few avenues for escape should have high levels of class voting. And in fact such is the case. It is impossible here to explore these relationships deeply and establish in fact their independent effect upon class voting, but the data available are highly suggestive. Statistics on each of the factors mentioned show that the rank order on each factor is almost the same as the rank order of class voting.

The extent of urbanization of a society is itself an index of many other social processes, which can be interpreted in various ways, but the statistics are quite consistent both for recent times and in the late nineteenth century. If urbanization is an index of the extent to which the population is freed from traditional ties to locality and church, and therefore is rendered susceptible to class appeals, then at least as far back as 1890 the British have been less traditionalist in these respects than any of these other three peoples. The striking fact about these statistics is that on every index of urbanization, the rank order is almost exactly the same as that of class voting. Several indexes of urbanization are given, and the consistency for several such measures shows that the result is not an artifact of the particular way of computing the urban proportion of the population. See Table 5–7.

Another measure of lack of traditionalism associated with urbanization is the birth rate. In countries which have lost the rural traditions of big families and the exclusively family-centered pattern of social life, birth rates have dropped fairly consistently. And persons less exposed to such traditional family controls—more willing to restrict their family size—are presumably less likely to respond to political appeals in traditional, non-class ways. If such a relation-

TABLE 5–7

Cumulative Percentage of the Population Living in Cities of Different Sizes, 1890 and circa 1950

CUMULATIVE PERCENTAGE OF POPULATION IN CITIES, BY SIZE

1890

COUNTRY	2,000+	10,000+	20,000+	20–100,000	100,000+
England and Wales	72.0	61.7	53.6	21.8	31.8
Scotland	65.4	49.9	42.4	12.6	29.8
Australia (7 colonies)	..	41.4	38.8	9.7	29.1
United States	37.7	27.6	23.8	8.3	15.5
Canada	27.3	17.1	14.2	6.0	8.2

1950

	2,000+	10,000+	20,000+	100,000+	IN METROPOLITAN AREAS
United Kingdom (1951)	79.7	74.0	66.9	36.1	77.0
Australia (1947)	71.5	55.4	43.9	51.4	55.4
United States (1950)	59.8	49.0	43.0	29.4	55.9
Canada (1951)	50.7	40.2	35.1	23.3	45.5
Other European Stable Democracies	..	..	38.0	23.3	33.7

Sources: The 1890 figures are from Adna F. Weber, *The Growth of Cities in the 19th Century* ("Columbia Studies in History, Economics and Public Law," Vol. XI [New York: Macmillan, 1899]), p. 144. The *circa* 1950 figures are taken from Jack P. Gibbs and Kingsley Davis, "Conventional versus Metropolitan Data in the International Study of Urbanization," *American Sociological Review,* XXIII (October, 1958), 506–7.

ship holds for the Anglo-American countries, it is even more likely
to be significant, because these countries are already among the
least traditional countries in which the birth rate is already lower
than in most countries of the world. But, in fact, the Anglo-
American countries with the lowest birth rates have the highest
levels of class voting. See Table 5–8. It may be noted that the sharpest difference in birth rates is between the "Old World" and the
"New" even though the rank order is the same.

TABLE 5–8
Range of Crude Birth Rate, 1947–1955*

COUNTRY	RANGE OF CRUDE BIRTH RATE
Great Britain	15.4–20.7
Australia	22.5–24.1
United States	23.5–25.8
Canada	27.1–28.9

Source: United Nations, *Demographic Yearbook* (New York, 1956), Table 20, pp. 610–21.
* The consistency over a period of eight years in the differences between the countries shows
that the differences are not due to some yearly variation. Since differences in the age structure of
these countries are not great, the crude birth rate may be used here. The same rank order is found
when measures which control for age and sex composition (either the intrinsic birth rate or the net
reproduction rate) are computed.

The differences in per capita income between these countries
show that the poorer countries—Australia and Great Britain—have
higher levels of class voting. See Table 5–9. Further research might
show that the pattern of *distribution* of wealth is also more uneven
in those countries than in the United States and Canada.

TABLE 5–9
Per Capita Income, circa 1950

COUNTRY	PER CAPITA INCOME (United States Dollars)
Great Britain	773
Australia	679
United States	1,453
Canada	870
Other European Stable Democracies	658

Source: United Nations, Statistical Office, *National and Per Capita Income in 70 Countries* 1949
(Statistical Papers, Series E, No. 1 [New York, 1950]), pp. 14–16.

The relative size of the middle class in the Anglo-American countries may also be related to class voting. It would seem natural that a country with a larger middle class would have less class voting. Regardless of the level of Left voting of manual workers, the middle class is more likely to vote Left in such a country (and therefore reduce the gap between the Left vote of manual and non-manual strata) for two reasons. First, in a country with a small middle class, the members are more likely to think of themselves as occupying a favored position vis-à-vis workers and therefore are more likely to vote Right. Second, in a country with a large middle class, many members are "fresh" from the working class and might be expected to retain their traditional Left allegiances for a certain period of time. These two factors would tend to raise the Left vote among persons in non-manual occupations. Therefore, we should expect that the Anglo-American countries with higher levels of class voting—Australia and Great Britain—should have a smaller middle class proportionately.

Some evidence of this does exist, again although these four countries are very highly industrialized and urbanized and therefore very much alike, as has been shown in Table 1–5, where the industrial distribution of their populations was given. This table does show slight differences between the countries, however, which are in almost the same order as the level of class voting. Combining the "tertiary" industries from Table 1–5, the obtained results are as shown in Table 5–10. The United States has the highest propor-

TABLE 5–10

Males in the Non-Agricultural Labor Force in Tertiary Industry, 1950

COUNTRY	MALES IN TERTIARY INDUSTRY* (Per Cent)
Great Britain	42
Australia	47
United States	50
Canada	48

Source: International Urban Research, Berkeley, California.
* "Tertiary industry" includes workers in commerce and finance, transport and communication services, and other service industries. See Table 1–5, p. 24 for the complete industrial distribution of the labor force. The term "tertiary" is taken from Colin Clark, *The Conditions of Economic Progress* (London: Macmillan, 1940).

tion of workers in tertiary industries; otherwise the rank order is the same as the order of class voting. (It may be noted also from Table 1–2 that the percentage of males in the non-agricultural labor force is also almost in the rank order of class voting.)

Another indicator of the proportion of middle-class or white-collar workers is the proportion of salaried employees to wage-earners in manufacturing establishments. Table 5–11 shows that the countries with higher levels of class voting have a lower proportion of salaried workers to wage-earners. Admittedly, the rank order here is not the same as that of class voting, but in none of these correlations do the two countries highest in class voting change positions with either of the countries lowest in class voting.

TABLE 5–11

Ratio of Salaried Workers to Wage-Earners in Manufacturing Establishments, 1954–1957

COUNTRY	MANUFACTURING ESTABLISHMENTS (000's)	WAGE-EARNERS (000's)	SALARIED	RATIO
Great Britain	57.2	6,216	1,406	.22
Australia	52.8	870	135	.16
United States	300.0	13,135	4,044	.30
Canada	37.4	1,052	301	.28

Source: United Nations, *Statistical Yearbook* (New York, 1958), pp. 157–63. Data from previous years are given in the same table. The British data are for 1954; data for the other countries are for 1956–57.

Educational opportunities are quite different in the four countries, and again, in the same direction as the level of class voting. The countries with higher class voting have fewer students per 1,000 in the population in either higher education or primary education, as Table 5–12 shows, and Great Britain and Australia are below the other European democracies in this respect.

The greater opportunities for education in the United States and Canada than Britain and Australia suggest that the character of social mobility must be quite different in the former countries, in spite of the gross similarity of movement found in the studies mentioned in Chapter 1. Possibly, ". . . the distance moved occupationally

TABLE 5–12

Students in Higher Education and in Primary Education, Per 1,000 Population, circa 1950

| | STUDENTS PER 1,000 POPULATION IN: | |
COUNTRY	*Higher Education*	*Primary Education*
Great Britain	1.6	90
Australia	2.9	131
United States	17.8	124
Canada	5.4	138
Other European Stable Democracies	3.2	113

Source: Figures on higher education are from UNESCO, *World Survey of Education* (Paris, 1955), pp. 24–25. Figures on primary education are from United Nations, *A Preliminary Report on the World Social Situation* (New York, 1952), pp. 86–98.

is commensurately greater [in the United States and Canada]; or, because of increased educational achievement in the United States, manual to non-manual occupational mobility involves traversing a greater social distance than a comparable move in Western Europe."[18] In spite of the similarity of over-all rates of social mobility, it is possible that such differences as exist may help account for differences in the level of class voting—if mobility is relatively low where class voting is high. Unfortunately few truly comparable data exist.[19] However, more elaborate distinctions between types of mobility and directions of movement show some international varia-

---

[18] A. H. Feldman, "Economic Development and Social Mobility," *Economic Development and Cultural Change*, VIII (April, 1960), 316. This hypothesis is only one of several suggested by Feldman to account for the seeming contradiction between the findings that mobility rates are equal in highly industrialized countries, that education is a key path for upward mobility, and yet that educational opportunities are so different.

[19] One study comparing a British with an American study found that mobility was actually slightly higher in Britain for each of three occupational status categories (the proportion of sons remaining in their father's status). However, the authors note that the American sample was urban, the British sample national, and that "the biases almost certainly produce an artificially high index of association" of sons' and fathers' occupations for the United States. See J. R. Hall and W. Ziegel, "A Comparison of Social Mobility Data for England and Wales, Italy, France and the U.S.A." in David Glass, ed., *Social Mobility in Britain* (London: Routledge & Kegan Paul, 1953), p. 265.

tions which may be of significance in interpreting the data on class voting.

While upward mobility (the movement of sons of fathers in manual—including farming and working-class urban—occupations into non-manual occupations)is fairly similar in Great Britain and the United States, downward mobility of the sons of non-manual fathers is far higher in Britain. Of the "manual" British fathers, 25 per cent have "non-manual" sons. The comparable figure is 29 per cent in the United States. However, 42 per cent of the sons of non-manual fathers are in manual positions in Britain, as compared to only 25 per cent of the sons of non-manual fathers in the United States.[20]

The greater downward rate of mobility in Great Britain—the replenishing of the manual working class from the non-manual strata —may be a significant cause of the higher level of class voting in that country. Miller raises the question: "Is it true that the easier the drop, the more the concern with status and social distance?" If such a constant interchange between strata occurs, then downwardly mobile Britishers must become Labour voters very quickly (and vice versa). The implications of this will be discussed in Chapter 6.[21]

If, regardless of how *many* of the manual workers achieve non-manual status in a given generation, there is a relatively large dropback of non-manual persons into the manual strata, the impetus for class voting would seem to be reinforced. Recent recruits to the non-manual strata might feel that they had an insecure hold upon their new status and try to adopt the political attitudes they felt to be appropriate to their position; whereas the manual workers, both those in stable positions and those recently downwardly mobile, might react negatively to their experiences by higher rates of Left voting.

---

[20] See S. M. Miller, "Comparative Social Mobility," *Current Sociology*, IX, No. 1 (1960), p. 36.

[21] *Ibid.*, p. 33. Australia also had the pattern of high upward mobility and high downward mobility, but data were available only for Melbourne, not for national samples as in Britain and the United States. Two United States studies found the pattern of high upward mobility and low downward mobility. No study was available to Miller for Canada, and therefore it is impossible to determine whether the patterns of mobility are completely consistent with the level of class voting.

The only Canadian study of intergenerational mobility was done in the province of Quebec. The authors did find, however, that urban French-Canadians had about the same rate of mobility as was found in national studies in France, England, and the United States. This conclusion may or may not be generalizable to Canada as a whole.[22]

Comparison of Britain with the United States in the level of "elite mobility" indicates that in this respect also mobility is higher in the United States. Miller analyzed the rate of movement into "elite" occupations (the higher business and independent professional occupations) and found that the rate of movement of *both* manual and non-manual strata into the highest occupational positions was higher in the United States than in Britain.[23] Thus, both a crude measure of intergenerational mobility from "manual" to "non-manual" occupations, and a more refined measure of movement into the highest positions indicate differences between Britain and the United States that seem consistent with the variation between countries in class voting patterns.[24]

Political appeals on class lines may evoke a more homogeneous response in Britain and Australia than in the other countries—if there is greater objective stratification *within* working-class occupations where class voting is lower. Some evidence for this is found in the smaller gap between the wages of skilled workers and those of unskilled workers in the United Kingdom and Australia than in

---

[22] Yves de Jocas and Guy Rocher, "Inter-Generation Occupational Mobility in the Province of Quebec," *Canadian Journal of Economics and Political Science*, XXIII (February, 1957), 66. English-Canadians had a much higher rate of mobility than French-Canadians in this study. Unfortunately, the Quebec data were only for an urban sample. If urban mobility rates are higher than rural rates in such societies, as seems likely, then the over-all national rates might be quite similar. An important area for further research is a comparison of rural vs. urban mobility rates. International gross similarities may conceal sharp internal differences in rural-urban rates, differences related to the speed and direction of industrialization and the rates of internal migration to small areas (urbanization).

[23] Miller, *op. cit.*, p. 38.

[24] Miller (*ibid.*, p. 36) computed an index of "inequality of opportunity," which showed that opportunities were most unequal in Britain, less in Australia, and least in the United States. On the other hand, an index of "equality of opportunity" was almost the same, reflecting the fact that the life-chances of middle-class sons in Great Britain were lower than in any of the eighteen countries for which data were available.

Canada and the United States.[25] A difference in the wage-rates of skilled and unskilled workers might be expected to have political consequences—skilled workers being less likely to vote Left in countries where the skilled are much more highly paid than the unskilled, and vice versa where the income differential is small. Lack of differentiation of the working class might also demarcate the line between worker and middle class more sharply, since it seems unlikely that the similarity of wages of skilled and unskilled would bring them both closer to the non-manual level rather than farther from it.[26]

The almost complete absence of class voting in Canada cannot be explained by relatively greater economic security of the working classes if a gross measure of unemployment can be considered a rough criterion. A careful compilation of available statistics on unemployment rates in the three Commonwealth countries between 1916 and 1950 shows that while unemployment rates were lower in Canada than in either Australia or the United Kingdom for thirteen of the sixteen years between 1916 and 1931, unemployment was actually higher in Canada than in either of the other countries in sixteen of the nineteen years between 1932 and 1950.[27] Unless it be argued that the non-class character of the Canadian parties was determined prior to the Great Depression, and that therefore the

---

[25] A comparison of the average wage of unskilled urban laborers with the average wage of five types of skilled workers (furniture-makers, engineers, garage mechanics, construction workers, and truck drivers) found that the gap was almost uniformly narrower in 1953 in both Britain and Australia than in either the United States or Canada. Fifteen of eighteen possible comparisons were in this direction. See Colin Clark, *The Conditions of Economic Progress* (3rd ed.; London: Macmillan, 1957), pp. 526–31. Similar figures are given for over forty other countries. It may be noted that the pattern was the same in New Zealand, where class voting is also apparently high, as in Britain and Australia.

[26] In 1940, at least, the average wage of unskilled laborers was lower in Britain and Australia than in the United States and Canada. See Karl Deutsch, *Nationalism and Social Communication* (New York: Wiley, 1953), p. 36. The real question, however, may be whether wages of manual workers are *relatively* lower than others. Political reactions may be due largely to relative, not absolute, deprivation.

[27] Walter Galenson and Arnold Zellner, "International Comparison of Unemployment Rates" in National Bureau of Economic Research, *The Measurement and Behavior of Unemployment* (Princeton: Princeton University Press, 1957), pp. 455–56. The monograph deals with six other countries as well, and over a slightly longer period of time for some of the nine, and contains extensive methodological discussion. Data were not available for the United States.

present lack of class differentiation is a "cultural lag," the low level of Canadian class voting cannot be explained by any great insulation of Canadian workers from the vicissitudes of the business cycle. As will be shown in Chapter 9, cultural factors largely account for the Canadian pattern.

The extent to which these countries have "frontiers" which offer an escape from intense class struggles and a safety valve reducing the strains of political conflict (and therefore class voting) is difficult to judge. According to most historians, the United States and Canada are the classic frontier countries, having great expanses of land to the west. Their lower levels of class voting are therefore understandable for yet another reason. Great Britain, enclosed within its island, clearly is not a frontier country, and therefore its high level of class voting is reinforced on this score also. Australia is perhaps the more puzzling case because of its wide areas of uninhabited land.

Yet Australia is not a "frontier" country in any acceptable sense of the word. Its unpopulated areas have practically no rainfall and are not really available for "frontier" purposes. Australia is actually an urban country, par excellence. It has the highest proportion of its population of any of the four countries in six cities of over 100,-000 population—the capitals of the six states. It is second only to Great Britain in the proportion of the population in cities over 20,000, and only a shade under the United States (but considerably under Great Britain) in the proportion of its population in "Standard Metropolitan Areas." Canada, by contrast, is lowest on all of the urbanization indexes. This high level of urbanization, combined with the lack of real opportunities in the unpopulated areas, imply that Australia is not a true frontier country. Its relatively high level of class voting is therefore not inconsistent with this factor.

In the search for possible causes of the differences in class voting between the Anglo-American countries, a number of fairly consistent correlations have fit our expectations as to factors which should affect class voting. In general, the poorer and more urbanized societies also have a slightly smaller proportion of the labor force in "middle-class" occupations, have lower educational and other opportunities, and offer less opportunity to escape via the frontier. They also have higher levels of class voting, which seems rather understandable.

SUMMARY

Consistent and striking differences between the Anglo-American countries in the level of class voting—as defined by the index developed in Chapter 4—have been found. These differences exist despite similarities of class and political structure and the maintenance of consensus on the parties and the form of government. Correlations between the level of class voting and various social factors such as: (1) the degree of urbanization, (2) the proportion of middle-class persons in the labor force, (3) the per capita income, (4) educational opportunities, (5) mobility, (6) income stratification among workers, and others are consistent with expectations concerning possible causes of class voting.

These are, however, only gross characterizations of the level and causes of class voting. Several questions remain: How do regional and religious factors affect class voting in the four countries? What are the changes in the level of class voting in the last twenty years in each country, and what are the implications of these changes for the future? What is the role of the minor parties in each country? The succeeding four chapters will take up these questions.

Chapter 6

Great Britain:
"Pure" But Declining Class Politics?

SOCIAL class is usually presumed to be the fundamental social membership affecting voting behavior in Great Britain. A number of studies of voting behavior in particular constituencies have offered this conclusion. According to a study of Greenwich (London) during the 1950 General Election:

> one common finding has stood out in all the tables so far presented —that of the factors we have studied the one most strongly associated with differences in vote is social class. The other differences which have been traced, between men and women, old and young, those with only elementary education and those with higher education, and between trade union members and nonmembers, provide only minor variations on this dominant theme.[1]

The authors of a study of Bristol North-East in 1951 found:

> on examining various social characteristics of electors, that a distinct association exists between some of these characteristics and the party for which the electors vote. The most important and strongest of these associations is that between social class, both subjective and objective, and voting.[2]

---

[1] Mark Benney, A. P. Gray, and R. H. Pear, *How People Vote* (London: Routledge & Kegan Paul, 1956), p. 113.

[2] Robert S. Milne and H. C. Mackenzie, *Straight Fight* (London: Chiswick Press, 1954), p. 50.

The inference from these studies, and the common interpretation of British politics, is expressed by one of the co-authors of the Greenwich study:

> of all the democracies, England is the one in which there is the most consciousness of class and most awareness of class distinctions and the pattern of social intercourse which flows therefrom . . . most of our informants voted for what they considered their class-interests.[3]

Furthermore, non-class factors such as regional and religious loyalties are considered to have very little bearing upon voting behavior. According to John Bonham, the author of a study of middle-class voting patterns:

> the simplicity of the British social structure, the high degree of national unity, and the two-party system, have helped to concentrate attention on the distribution of wealth between classes. British politics are almost wholly innocent of those issues which cross the social lines in other lands—for example race, nationality, religion, town and country interests, regional interest, or the conflict between authoritarian and parliamentary methods.[4]

This sense of class membership presumably is both reinforced by and reinforces loyalties to a political party. A factory worker in such a system "naturally," by the logic of the social and political structure, thinks of himself as both a worker and "Labour." An Eton-educated professional thinks of himself, equally naturally, as upper-class and "Conservative." Class lines sharply divide both the sense of personal solidarity and the sense of political solidarity.

However, as the American political scientist Samuel Beer puts it, this fundamental cleavage is mitigated by a consensus across class lines on "basic social and political values which endures through sharp conflicts of class and party and which may provide the means for their resolution."[5]

SOCIAL CHANGES AFFECTING CLASS VOTING

But British society is not standing still. A number of social and political trends seem to suggest a lessening of solid class and party

---

[3] From the Introduction to Benney *et al.*, *op. cit.*, p. 6.

[4] John Bonham, *The Middle-Class Vote* (London: Faber & Faber, 1954), pp. 194–95.

[5] Samuel H. Beer, "Pressure Groups and Parties in Britain," *American Political Science Review*, L (March, 1956), 2.

identifications. Consecutive Labour losses in General Elections since 1950, an expanding middle class, the greater educational opportunities for working-class children provided by the 1944 Education Act, all point toward a decline of the class bases of British politics. As Leslie Lipson suggests, there is now agreement across party lines on many of the main issues that "energized party combat for virtually a century and a half: the democratizing of a constitution which aristocracy had operated, the extension of public social services to provide security for the underprivileged, the choice of policy in foreign, imperial and Commonwealth affairs, and the determination of the functions that the state should perform in the economic process." Lipson suggests that the issues which may emerge or re-emerge are particular problems of prosperity: mass consumption, leisure, and the two educational systems. Echoing a thesis of T. H. Marshall, Lipson asserts that Britain has achieved political and economic equality, but that social equality is lagging behind.[6] Whether social inequality—the persistence of sharp status distinctions based on heredity, where one is educated, accent, etc.—alone will maintain the polarization of classes along party lines is a moot question.

By political and economic equality, both Lipson and Marshall mean equality of opportunity, not absolute equality. Not all agree that the former has been achieved in Britain. One Labour spokesman, Member of Parliament C. A. R. Crosland, suggests that there has been less "convergence" of the support for the parties in Great Britain than in any of the other Anglo-American democracies. He asserts that class issues are still most relevant in Britain—the highly discriminatory educational system, the highly unequal distribution of income—and, therefore, ample reasons still exist for British politics to remain polarized around social classes.[7]

In spite of this, a number of trends seemingly presage a decline of class voting. Labour lost three consecutive General Elections between 1951 and 1959, each by increasing numbers of seats. But, as

---

[6] Leslie Lipson, "Common Ground and Emerging Conflict between the British Parties," *Political Quarterly*, XXVII (1956), 184. See also Thomas H. Marshall, *Citizenship and Social Class* (London: Cambridge University Press, 1950) and the discussion in Chapter 1, above.

[7] See C. A. R. Crosland, "New Moods, Old Problems," *Encounter*, XVI (February, 1961), 3–4. Crosland objects to the doctrinaire Left position on this question, however, and is in the "Right" wing of the Labour controversy over policies and programs.

Table 6–1 shows, the change of the total vote has not been as striking as the loss of seats. The margin between Labour and Conservative voting totals has not been more than 5 per cent, except in 1945,
when Labour drew 8 per cent more than the Conservatives. The
tendency of a two-party system to reward the majority party with

TABLE 6–1
Votes and Seats, British House of Commons, 1945–1959

YEAR	TOTAL VOTING (000's)	PER CENT OF VOTES Labour	Conservative	Liberal
1945	24,979	48.0	39.9	9.0
1950	28,769	46.4	41.7	9.1
1951	28,602	48.8	48.0	2.5
1955	26,761	46.3	49.8	2.7
1959	27,863	43.8	49.4	5.9

YEAR	Conservative	SEATS Labour	Conservative minus Labour
1945	212	394	—182
1950	298	315	— 17
1951	321	295	+ 26
1955	345	277	+ 68
1959	365	258	+107

Source: The Times of London, *Guide to the House of Commons* (London, published after each
election). The figures for the 1945 seats are as of the time of dissolution just prior to the 1950
election. The Conservative figures include the minor party candidates associated with the Conservatives. The total vote percentages do not add to 100 because other minor party candidates are not
included.

more than its share of seats provides a visible semblance of political crisis for the losing party, although the Labour vote was only 5
per cent less in 1959 than it was in 1945. But parties must win elections, and if permanent alterations of the social structure account
for the drop of the Labour vote, the crisis may be firmly founded,
despite the possibility of an equally great shift of the electorate
back to the Left.[8]

An opposing interpretation of Labour's successive defeats has
been offered by Ralph Miliband, who argues that British society
remains essentially a class society, and that Labour must rest its

[8] Since 216 Liberals ran in 1959 and only 110 in 1955, and the Liberal
party vote increased from 2.7 to 5.9 per cent, the loss by Labour could conceivably be due to a switch to the Liberals by 1955 Labour supporters, but
even so, this switch is not in itself of a magnitude to serve as a portent of
political doom.

policies upon a socialist appeal, rather than upon spurious "national" policies. He indicates that there is:

> nothing to suggest that a multitude of men and women, who are not of the working classes, have in the past found the class character of the Labour party a bar to their support for it, or that support for it would wane if its leaders were to adapt their policies to that fact.[9]

Such alternative explanations and the lack of any ready resolution point not only to deep political gulfs separating various Labour and Left segments, but also to a lack of factual data on the characteristics of voters in Britain and on the relevance of different issues to stability or change of voting patterns.[10]

Of more import for the crisis of British Labour are the social changes of which the political trends are seemingly only a consequence. The decline of Labour voting since 1945 seems to be only the beginning of a greater decline. Labour losses are blamed upon the reluctance of the Labour party to abandon its trade-union links, its appeal to class consciousness, its program of nationalization of industries—in short, its identity as a "working-class" party. This theory of Labour losses considers the expanding middle class, the growing homogeneity of styles of life of workers and middle classes, and the continuing prosperity of Britain, to be evidence of the obsolescence of class appeals and class issues. Britain is becoming a middle-class society, the argument runs, and Labour must change with the times.[11]

---

[9] Ralph Miliband, *Parliamentary Socialism: A Study in the Politics of Labour* (London: Allen & Unwin, 1961), p. 348.

[10] Advocacy of research which could answer such questions does not imply belief that any political party should govern its strategy by the findings of a survey. Mr. Miliband himself would certainly hold that the Labour party should undertake a "task of political conversion," as he puts it (*ibid.*, p. 349), rather than focus upon victory above all.

[11] For examples of these arguments or discussions of them, see Mark Abrams, Richard Rose and Rita Hinden, *Must Labour Lose?* (London: Penguin, 1960); D. E. Butler and Richard Rose, *The British General Election of 1959* (London: Macmillan, 1960), pp. 14–16; and a series of articles by Seymour M. Lipset in the American journal, *The New Leader* (November 7 and 21, 1960; February 6, 1961). The pages of British political journals have been filled with debates on the proper way the Labour party can meet the needs of the new kind of society which is emerging. The change has not apparently been only a postwar one. Even in 1941, George Orwell could write that "one of the most important developments in England during the past twenty years has been the upward and downward extension of the middle class." See *A Collection of Essays* (New York: Doubleday Anchor Books, 1954), p. 280.

The middle class in Great Britain has indeed grown markedly in the last thirty years, but the political consequences of this growth are difficult to assess. Although the proportion of small businessmen has declined, the proportion of persons in the lower professions and in white-collar occupations (teachers, clerks, office workers, technical assistants of various kinds, minor officials) has increased considerably. The proportion of workers in manual labor has decreased slightly. Table 6–2 shows the change from 1931 to 1951.

TABLE 6–2

Persons in Various Occupational Groups, Great Britain, 1931 and 1951

OCCUPATIONS	PER CENT OF POPULATION	
	1931	*1951*
Proprietor, Managerial	14.1 (4,100)	12.6 (4,300)
Higher Professional	1.6 (450)	2.6 (900)
Lower Professional	3.8 (1,100)	4.4 (1,500)
White-Collar	7.6 (2,200)	10.8 (3,700)
Intermediate	4.8 (1,400)	5.0 (1,700)
Manual Wage-Earning	68.1 (19,800)	64.6 (22,100)
TOTAL	100.0	100.0

Source: John Bonham, *The Middle-Class* Vote (London: Faber & Faber, 1954), p. 113. Men and women are included, with an estimate of the number of "unoccupied adults associated with each group" (i.e. housewives). See p. 22 for a description of the occupational composition of the four countries using comparable categories which produce figures somewhat different from those Bonham gives.

Whether many of the "new middle class" think of themselves as middle-class, or even if they do, whether they are deserting the Labour propensities of their class of origin, are questions for any study of current British politics to answer. G. D. H. Cole holds that the character of these new occupations does not produce a "middle-class mentality," but, on the contrary, that many low-salaried persons will join trade unions and feel themselves part of the working class.[12]

Although Professor Cole is referring mainly to the possibility that the new middle class will accept collective trade-union action as appropriate to its new status, his remark applies equally well to the probability of its continuing as Labour supporters. If he is right,

[12] G. D. H. Cole, "The Conception of the Middle Classes," *British Journal of Sociology* (December, 1950), pp. 275–90.

the association of class and voting should be declining, not because of the desertion of Labour by manual supporters, but because of the recruitment of these new non-manual workers to Labour. (This leaves aside the question of their subjective class identity.)

The beginnings of change in the educational system may also imply a decline of the close connection of class and party. The expansion of secondary schools and universities begun by the Education Act of 1944 seems to be another wedge which can break down class consciousness and solidarity—another step away from the social inequality which may still be reinforcing class loyalties to Labour. A study of working-class and middle-class adolescents in grammar and secondary schools in London in 1951 (seven years after the Act) found that there was less underrepresentation of the upper working class in the grammar schools, although the lower working class continued to be underrepresented. More to the point, though lower achievers than middle-class boys of the same intelligence, "the working-class boys seemed aware of the significance of a grammar-school education for upward movement in social status, and in their vocational expectations and aspirations they showed themselves the most upwardly mobile group."[13] The possible connection between these social changes, particularly manifest in the London area, and a decline of the association of class and party will be discussed in a later section.

If a substantial portion of the new middle class continues to vote Labour, then class voting should be declining from this one consideration alone. An expansion of the middle class may be taking place without a decline of the political divergence of social classes, however. Even if a relatively small proportion of the new middle class turns Conservative and relatively few workers abandon Labour in a period of prosperity and consolidation of gains, the net effect will be a decline of the Labour vote and a seeming convergence of the class bases of the parties.[14]

---

[13] H. T. Himmelweit, "Social Status and Secondary Education Since the 1944 Act" in D. V. Glass, ed., *Social Mobility in Britain* (London: Routledge & Kegan Paul, 1954), p. 159.

[14] See David Lockwood, "The 'New Working Class,'" *European Journal of Sociology,* I (1960), 248–59, for a discussion which calls into question the easy prediction of a trend toward Conservative voting among a more prosperous working class. Lockwood notes that such an argument neglects "almost completely the structure of social relationships by which class attitudes are generated, sustained, or modified (p.249).

It is possible that mobility in England breaks traditional loyalties to party very quickly. Newly middle-class persons may not stay Labour but quickly shift to Conservative. The British political and class system, with a high and visible association of classes with parties *and* sharp status distinctions, would seem to put real pressure upon upwardly mobile persons quickly to shed their Labour loyalties.[15] Whether downward mobility has the opposite effect is an important question.

CLASS AND VOTE IN BRITAIN

Survey data may offer some tentative answers to the questions implied by the previous discussion. Figure 6–1 shows the Labour vote in manual and non-manual strata from 1943 to 1962 (see also Appendix B). Class voting is indicated by the width of the gap between the Labour vote of the two occupational strata. Assuming that the earlier figures are comparable (and some question might reasonably be raised about the comparison), the figure shows that the increase of class voting between 1943 and 1962 is almost entirely due to the drop of Labour voting within the middle class. The manual workers have stayed relatively constant in their Labour vote.[16]

Manual workers are more likely to vote Conservative than non-manual persons are to vote Labour. Seldom does the Labour vote of the middle class rise above 20 per cent; seldom does the non-Labour vote of the workers drop below 40 per cent. The interdependence of party and class is clear; Labour's electoral fate depends largely on gaining more of the middle-class vote (since even in the "Labour" election of 1945 it could not muster more than 60 per cent of its "natural" support) and a Conservative victory rests inevitably upon heavy working-class support.

---

[15] For a discussion of the class structure of British society and the possible consequences of the Education Act of 1944 for social mobility and a blurring of the status lines, see Anthony Richmond, "The United Kingdom" in Arnold Rose, ed., *The Institutions of Advanced Societies* (Minneapolis: University of Minnesota Press, 1958), pp. 54–65. See also C. A. R. Crosland, *The Future of Socialism* (New York: Macmillan, 1957), pp. 185–89.

[16] Despite the relatively sharp divergence of the classes, consensus is still demonstrated, in that in almost every case the patterns of movement are in the same direction. The divergence of class voting between 1951 and 1957 was not produced by opposite movements but by movements in similar direction in both classes—though in smaller degree in one class than another.

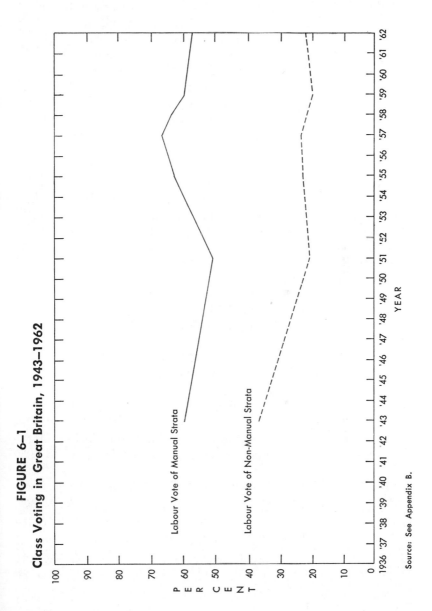

FIGURE 6-1
Class Voting in Great Britain, 1943-1962

Labour Vote of Manual Strata

Labour Vote of Non-Manual Strata

PERCENT

100 90 80 70 60 50 40 30 20 10 0

1936 '37 '38 '39 '40 '41 '42 '43 '44 '45 '46 '47 '48 '49 '50 '51 '52 '53 '54 '55 '56 '57 '58 '59 '60 '61 '62

YEAR

Source: See Appendix B.

Although the data will not be presented, a check upon the results using other indexes of class position (education and income) indicates that the percentage-point difference in Labour voting between groups dichotomized into "upper" and "lower" economic status, and groups divided into those who left school at fifteen and those who had schooling after the age of fifteen, is almost identical with the measure of class voting based on occupation used in the tables.[17]

The new middle class, drawn from the working class and therefore presumably from a Labour background, has apparently not retained its original Labour predispositions. Most of the socially mobile workers classified as "non-manual" in the 1957–1959 studies must have shifted to the Conservative party (unless every other non-manual worker went to Labour, an unlikely possibility). There is no evidence that the mobile workers went to the Liberal party. The electoral fears of Labour may be justified in one respect: socially mobile workers may quickly shed whatever Labour loyalties they may have had (unless the mobile workers are already Conservative, a real possibility).

Unfortunately, it appears that no data on the relation of mobility to political behavior are available in any existing British study. Thus the implications for the Labour vote of the finding that Britain has a high level of *downward* mobility compared to the United States can only be speculative. (See Chapter 5, p. 118.)

Manual workers are probably little less likely to vote Labour now than they were in the 1945 election. Only in a survey taken in June, 1959, did the percentage of manual workers voting Labour drop below the 60 per cent figure marked up in the 1943 survey.[18] This drop may of course be the forerunner of a larger decline of the Labour vote among manual workers, but the evidence up to 1959

---

[17] The British pollster Mark Abrams reports almost precisely the same figures for class voting from his own surveys of the British electorate. In a recent article, he notes that "when on an occupational basis the electorate is divided into two groups—middle-class and working class—we find that three-quarters of the former vote Conservative and nearly two-thirds of the latter vote Labour." This is a level of class voting of 40 or more percentage points. Mark Abrams, "Social Class and British Politics," *Public Opinion Quarterly*, XXV (Fall, 1961), 344. This level, he says (without giving any specific data), was about the same for the elections of 1945, 1950, and 1951.

[18] Note that these figures are for the three-party total of voting intentions. The figures estimated from John Bonham (*loc. cit.*) are ignored here because they were calculated on bases impossible to reconcile with the figures calculated directly from the original data of the British Institute of Public Opinion.

does not substantiate any sizable loss of Labour loyalties among manual workers. Since we lack data on the political solidarity of individual voters, this cannot be determined definitively.

A detailed consideration of the shifts of more specific occupations is not within the scope of this study; we shall not investigate whether the lower non-manual and skilled manual segments follow the same pattern as the more inclusive strata, but the conclusion seems warranted that no substantial shift of the class bases of British politics has taken place. The British electorate remains sharply divided along class lines. No decline of the differences between classes as such or of the political predispositions connected with occupational status has occurred. The shift of the occupational structure has undermined the objective basis of Labour support by reducing the actual size of the working class, and this change probably accounts for part of the loss of Labour votes. Labour's traditional electorate may be as solid as ever.

Rural location does not affect class voting. Two community studies have shown that class voting is not significantly lower in small, isolated towns in Britain. A 1950 survey in Banbury, a town of 19,000 in the middle of England with a strong element of traditionalism, found a level of class voting as high as the national level.[19] In another traditionalistic community, Glossop, where Labour is not strong, class voting was +30 in 1951.[20]

Class voting is apparently higher, however, in heavily Labour urban constituencies. In the London constituency of Greenwich in 1950 (a predominantly lower-middle-class and working-class area), class voting was +55, according to a recomputation of figures from an election survey in that year.[21] This high level of class voting justifies the authors' assertion, already quoted, about the primacy of social class.

But how "pure" is class politics in Great Britain? Religious and regional deviations from the class pattern of voting can be exam-

---

[19] See Margaret Stacey, *Tradition and Change: A Study of Banbury* (London: Oxford University Press, 1960), p. 43. A crude index of class voting was computed from Table 11 by combining occupational status levels 1 to 4 and 5 to 7. The results are not strictly comparable since routine non-manual occupations were classified with skilled manual occupations. Nevertheless, class voting was +38 for all voters (including "floaters" and those with no preference) and +42 for the three-party total.

[20] Anthony H. Birch, *Small Town Politics* (London: Oxford University Press, 1959). The figure was computed from a table on p. 106.

[21] Benney *et al., op. cit.,* p. 118.

ined by turning to the patterns of class voting within different religious and regional groupings.

RELIGION AND CLASS VOTING

Whether there is any consistent tendency for religious membership to override class position is the concern of this section. The connections between religion and politics exist in Britain as in every country, but this broad topic cannot be dealt with here in detail. Since the Established Church—the Church of England—was associated with the gentry and the aristocracy, it was natural for the budding working-class movements of the nineteenth century to become Nonconformist or atheist, and it might be expected that some of this historical association of politics and religion would be manifested in a greater tendency of working-class Nonconformists to be Labour, or working-class Church of England members to be Conservative. Since the concern is here not with the effect of religion alone upon voting, but rather with the interaction of religion and class voting, the general character of religious loyalties in themselves is not relevant.

About 50 to 60 per cent of the British population is associated with the Church of England, although not all of these attend church regularly. About 10 per cent are Methodists, and 3 per cent belong to various small "non-conformist" sects, such as the Baptists and the Congregationalists. Catholics comprise about 8 per cent of the population.[22] This section will focus upon the Catholics insofar as they differ politically from other "protestant" religions, and not upon variations within the Protestant denominations, although this subject will be touched upon. In each Anglo-American country, Catholics constitute the major religious group with distinctive values and practices. Whether or not they deviate politically from Protestant persons in similar class positions in Great Britain is the problem to be discussed here.

Voting studies offer little information on the effect of religion upon voting. A 1950 study of Greenwich found that Catholics and irreligious persons were slightly more likely to vote Labour than members of other churches. No link between Nonconformity and

---

[22] See Richmond, *op. cit.*, pp. 107–9, for statistics on the religious composition of the British population.

Labour politics was found.[23] Too few cases were obtained to control for social class. Another study, of Droylsden in 1951, also found that "Roman Catholics are more likely to vote Labour than Anglicans and members of the free churches."[24] However, these conclusions were based upon samples taken in single constituencies. No national surveys holding social class constant have been analyzed to discover the voting patterns of different religious groups. If only class factors affect voting in Great Britain, there should be no significant differences in class voting within different religious groups; or if differences exist, they should not regularly affect both strata in the same direction. On the other hand, if we find that in Great Britain both manual and non-manual Catholics exhibit consistently higher Labour preferences than other religions, it may be that a sense of minority status has produced a religious deviation toward the Left party.

Three surveys taken by the British Institute of Public Opinion had questions on religious membership. Tables 6–3 and Figure 6–2 present the level of Labour voting and class voting in different religious groupings. For reasons of comparability with the other countries, the non-Catholic denominations have been considered together as "Protestants," although the differences between them are at least as important as those between the Catholics and any other religious group.

Table 6–3 gives a mixed picture of the level of religious voting in Britain and the variations in class voting within different religious groups. Religious voting is relatively low in Britain as compared to the other Anglo-American countries. (There was an exception among manual workers in a 1962 survey.) A possible explanation for the voting pattern of the Catholic manual workers, who were the least likely of any religious group to prefer Labour in a 1957 survey (but the most likely in a 1962 survey) will be discussed later. As can be seen from Table 6–3, Catholics, in either manual or non-manual occupations, do not deviate more than 8 percentage points (with the exception noted) from the average

---

[23] Benney *et. al., op. cit.,* p. 111.

[24] P. Campbell, D. Donnison, and A. Potter, "Voting Behaviour in Droylsden in October, 1951," *Journal of the Manchester School of Economics and Social Studies,* XX (January, 1952), 63. Essentially the same finding was reported by Birch, *op. cit.,* p. 112. Birch suggests that "religion and politics have been more closely linked [in the Northwest] than elsewhere," and that Glossop in particular exhibits the effects of traditional religious-political links (p. 111).

TABLE 6-3
Labour Preference, by Religion and Occupation Type, Great Britain, 1943–1962

OCCUPATION TYPE	Total	PER CENT PREFERRING LABOUR						Total Protestant*	Religious Voting†
		Church of England	Nonconformist	Catholic	Scottish	Other	None		
1943									
Manual	60 (1,064)‡	55 (489)	69 (185)	65 (112)	53 (92)	69 (144)	59 (42)	58 (766)	+ 7
Non-Manual	37 (378)	30 (177)	35 (74)	37 (32)	44 (25)	59 (61)	22 (9)	33 (276)	+ 4
TOTAL	54 (1,442)	48 (666)	59 (259)	59 (144)	51 (117)	66 (205)	53 (51)	51 (1,042)	+ 8
Index of Class Voting	+23	+25	+34	+28	+9	+10	+37	+25	
1957									
Manual	67 (742)	66 (403)	64 (98)	58 (78)	74 (47)	72 (29)	76 (87)	66 (548)	− 8
Non-Manual	24 (558)	22 (316)	26 (91)	29 (45)	14 (59)	33 (27)	55 (20)	22 (466)	+ 7
TOTAL	49 (1,300)	47 (719)	46 (189)	37 (123)	41 (106)	54 (56)	72 (107)	46 (1,014)	− 9
Index of Class Voting	+43	+44	+38	+29	+60	+39	+21	+44	
1962									
Manual	57 (537)	56 (350)	53 (51)	78 (50)	47 (32)	48 (27)	71 (24)	55 (433)	+23
Non-Manual	22 (434)	20 (275)	18 (45)	19 (26)	20 (35)	32 (31)	50 (20)	19 (335)	0
TOTAL	41 (971)	40 (625)	36 (96)	58 (76)	33 (67)	40 (58)	61 (44)	40 (768)	+18
Index of Class Voting	+35	+36	+35	+59	+27	+16	+21	+36	

Source: British Institute of Public Opinion (BIPO) Surveys Nos. 104, 1717, and 275. The totals include only those persons indicating a preference for one of the three parties. The question was: "What religious denomination do you belong to?"
* Includes Church of England, Nonconformist, and Scottish voters.
† Percentage by which the Catholic Labour vote exceeded the "Protestant" Labour vote.
‡ Total number of respondents in parentheses.

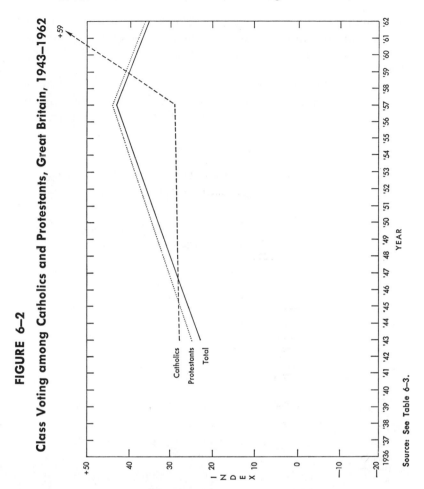

FIGURE 6-2

Class Voting among Catholics and Protestants, Great Britain, 1943-1962

vote of "Protestant" denominations in three surveys widely separated in time.

Class voting was slightly higher among Catholics than the average for the nation in 1943. It dropped in 1957 (because of the low
level of Labour voting among manual workers), and rose to an extremely high point in 1962 (again because of the manual workers).
Members of the Scottish Church also exhibit great variability in class
voting (as does Scotland as a whole, to be discussed later). Figure
6-2 portrays the level of class voting among Catholics as compared

to "Protestants" in the three surveys. There is no tendency for Catholics to vote according to their religion consistently, nor is there any consistent difference between Protestant and Catholic levels of class voting.

The interesting group to examine in more detail is the Catholic manual worker group. See Table 6–4. In 1957, the Catholic manual workers voted Labour less than Protestants in similar class posi-

TABLE 6–4

Labour Preference of Manual Workers, by Selected Demographic Variables and Religion, Great Britain, 1957 and 1962

DEMO-GRAPHIC VARIABLES	PER CENT PREFERRING LABOUR					
	1957			1962		
	Catholics	Protestants	Religious Voting Index	Catholics	Protestants	Religious Voting Index
Socio-Economic Level						
"Average Minus and Below"	61 (72)*	69 (502)	—8	76 (41)	56 (387)	+20
Subjective Social Class "Working"	76 (57)	77 (329)	—1	82 (28)	67 (257)	+15
Sex						
Male	56 (52)	71 (297)	—15	64 (25)	65 (209)	—1
Female (Housewives)	62 (21)	63 (227)	— 1	89 (18)	45 (191)	+44
Age						
16–34	70 (27)	69 (207)	+1	80 (15)	60 (124)	+20
35–44	50 (22)	74 (114)	—24	78 (14)	58 (92)	+20
45 Plus	52 (29)	60 (227)	—8	67 (15)	51 (191)	+16
Region						
Greater London and South	65 (23)	59 (186)	+6	69 (13)	53 (205)	+16
TOTAL	58 (78)	66 (548)	—8	75 (44)	56 (408)	+19

Source: BIPO Nos. 1717 and 275.
* Total number of respondents in parentheses.

tions, but just the reverse was found in a 1962 survey. Non-manual Catholics were slightly more Labour than the average in 1957, but no different in 1962. Thus the effect of Catholicism is not uniform upon both strata. The table shows the level of Labour voting within selected social categories among manual workers divided into Protestants and Catholics.

The general findings of the two surveys on religious voting remain for certain subgroups but not for others. In the Greater London and Southern region, the national pattern remains as it does in more refined social class groupings. Age does not alter the general direction of religious voting. (However, the younger voters, both Protestant and Catholic, are more likely to prefer Labour in both surveys. See pages 162–63.) Sex differences are striking, although not in the expected direction. Female Catholics are more likely to vote Labour than male Catholics in both surveys, a result not consistent with the usual belief that being a woman and being a Catholic both predispose in a conservative political direction. As far as religious voting by sex is concerned, Table 6–4 shows that in 1957 Catholic men were considerably less likely to vote Labour than Protestant men, while there was no difference between Catholic and Protestant housewives. In 1962, there was no difference between the men, but the Catholic housewives were heavily Labour.

Women, and particularly Catholic women, have been found to be more conservative than men in a number of studies. Here they contribute to a higher, not a lower, Labour vote among Catholics.

It is possible that the variable patterns exhibited by these data are entirely due to sampling error. The number of cases of Catholics is small in both surveys, and no strict probability methods were employed. But assuming that the data, in general if not in detail, reflect some "real" pattern of inconsistency and change among Catholic manual workers in Britain, some tentative explanation for these variations may be essayed.

The "natural" conservatism associated with being a Catholic may operate unevenly in the British political system, which in this respect seems to be markedly unlike the other Anglo-American countries. If Catholics are less secularized than Protestants, this may help account for the lower level of Labour voting among Catholics, particularly in Britain where class politics dominates and where the Left party is also a secular party. The 1957 survey offers some data on these points. Catholics do go to church more often than members of other religions. (Conservative Catholics go more often than Labour Catholics, Liberal Catholics less than either.)[25] More Catholics than persons of any other religion believe in life after death; more Catholics believe that religion has more influence than politics on the way people live. (In these respects there is no difference between Labour Catholics and Conservative Catholics.) As contrasted with non-Catholics, more Catholics believe that the church should express views on social and political questions (and more Labour supporters than Conservative supporters believe this, among the Catholics). Catholics similarly are least likely to want to delete religious instruction in schools. (But Catholics are more willing than those in any other religion to open theaters on Sunday; they are not like the more puritanical Protestants in this regard.)

Thus, British manual Catholics are less secularized than Protestant manual workers, as shown by a 1957 survey. There is no reason on these grounds that they should support Labour; precisely the reverse. Catholics in Great Britain, as in the other Anglo-American countries, are more religious than Protestants, and therefore are presumably more affected by the anti-socialist political tendencies of the Church. This may be the main reason why they are less likely to vote for the secular Left party than are Catholics in the other Anglo-American countries. In Great Britain, the conservatism of Catholicism should assert itself in patterns of Conservative voting.

But this explanation is inconsistent with the 1962 data, where Catholic manual workers, especially women, were found to be heavily Labour. The only way to reconcile the two sets of data would be to find some intervening "conservative" factor which is actually characteristic of the Labour party and which allows Catho-

---

[25] These and the following inferences are based on the 1957 British Institute of Public Opinion (BIPO) Survey which asked about the religious beliefs and practices of Britons. The data supporting them are not given in detail. The statements apply specifically to Catholic and Protestant manual workers, although most of the generalizations would also apply to non-manual members of the different religions. A similar argument is made by Gerhard Lenski in *The Religious Factor* (New York: Doubleday, 1960) which is based on a 1957 Detroit survey. Lenski found that for Catholics church attendance was associated with Republican voting, while frequent association with Catholic friends and relatives was associated with Democratic voting. He explained this in terms of the parallel response of the Church and the Republican party to the moral aspects of politics, rather than to issues related to class and status (p. 165). See also pp. 50–58 above.

lic women to perceive the Labour party as a legitimately conservative party. If this factor were related to some religious basis for Labour voting, it could be said that religious traditionalism still operated in Britain. Unfortunately, the data were not collected for the purpose of tracing the complex associations of religion and politics and do not allow for further explorations of possible causes.

The evidence on religious voting is inconclusive in the sense that three separate national surveys, taken over nineteen years, do not give consistent results. Yet one thing can be said with some certainty: religious membership does not unite Britishers across class lines. Even in the 1962 survey in which Catholic manual workers were considerably more Labour than "Protestants," the level of religious voting was nowhere near the level of class voting. And perhaps more important, this "religious effect" was found only among manual workers. Middle-class Catholics were no more likely to be Labourites than middle-class persons in other religions. Therefore, class voting among Catholics was extraordinarily high. It seems clear that connections between religion and politics remain close in Britain, but the effects of religious membership are not unilinear and simple, cutting across all other cleavages, as they do in Canada most prominently.

REGIONALISM AND CLASS VOTING

As with religious factors, a discussion of regionalism and political behavior in Great Britain cannot be exhaustive. Attention will be given primarily to variations in class voting within different British regions. This is particularly significant because the only speculations about this have been based upon the ecological method, which has shown that mining regions are heavily Labour, that Wales is more Liberal, and so forth. The ecological approach cannot discover whether the non-manual workers within regions with a distinctive regional identity, or even a historic nationalism, are pulled over to solidary support of the regional party. Do "regional parties" exist in Great Britain, in the sense of the "Solid South" behind the Democrats in the United States or the traditional Liberalism of Quebec? Only survey data can give even a tentative answer, but no national studies of British voting behavior have attempted to treat this question.

Clear bases for regionalism seem to exist in Scottish and Welsh nationalism.[26] The issue of Northern Ireland is still alive, of course, but since no data are available on the social bases of the parties there, this problem will not be discussed. The overwhelming majority of the voters in Northern Ireland support the Ulster Unionist party (a version of the Conservative party), and in a sense this is a kind of reverse regionalism: a regional support for a party attempting to reinforce the unity of the United Kingdom, not disrupt it.[27]

The Liberal party has long based one of its appeals for support upon Scottish and Welsh nationalism, and its 1959 election manifesto indicates at least the remnants of the regional identity of these two peoples:

> The Scots and Welsh are separate peoples, each with a great and distinctive tradition. Each country has special problems, including severe unemployment and depopulation, problems which cannot possibly be solved by a Government based on London. Liberals would give Wales and Scotland Parliaments of their own . . .[28]

A federal parliament has been suggested intermittently as a means of recognizing the cultural integrity of the Welsh and Scottish peoples.[29]

"Pseudo-federal" elements in the British system allow for recognition of a degree of distinctiveness in Scottish, Welsh, and Northern Irish regional sentiments. Both Scotland and Wales have a "Grand Committee" within the United Kingdom House of Com-

---

[26] See Reginald Coupland, *Welsh and Scottish Nationalism* (London: Collins, 1954). If language can be considered a crucial index of the cultural basis for regional separatism, then clearly Wales ranks higher than Scotland; for in 1931, 37 per cent of the Welsh population spoke Welsh, while only 2 per cent of the Scottish population spoke Gaelic (p. 396).

[27] See J. R. V. Prescott, "The Function and Methods of Electoral Geography," *Annals of the Association of American Geographers*, XLIX (September, 1959), 296–304, for a summary of the election returns to Stormont (the Northern Ireland parliament) since 1920. Only one constituency has not gone either always Unionist or always Nationalist. The most fertile areas colonized by English and Scottish Protestants are now Unionist. The less fertile, mountainous areas have populations descended from indigenous Irish stock, and are still Catholic. According to Prescott, the communication between these areas and Eire was better than with the rest of Northern Ireland and Great Britain, and these areas are still Nationalist.

[28] Quoted in The Times of London, *Guide to the House of Commons* (London, 1959), p. 258.

[29] M. Lloyd George, "Regional Parliaments," *Parliamentary Affairs*, VIII (1955), 430–35.

mons composed of members from the region, which handles some of the bills concerning only their areas. The Scottish Committee, in existence since 1907, handled two-thirds of the bills that dealt especially with Scottish affairs between 1948 and 1957.[30] Northern Ireland has its own regional parliament, as well as members sitting in the United Kingdom House of Commons. Both Scotland and Northern Ireland have their own legal and judicial systems.

Besides historic ties of culture, there are economic reasons for a regional pattern of voting that might cut across class lines. As the Liberal Party Manifesto suggests, these two areas, partly because of the dominance of mining in Wales, partly because of the backward technological character of Scottish industry, are suffering economically and may blame their troubles on the centralized government in London.[31] In fact, a movement for Scottish separatism, propagated by the Scottish Covenant Association and the more extreme Nationalist party, became of such importance that a Royal Commission was established to investigate it in 1952.[32]

In Wales, the Plaid Cymru nationalist movement has consistently run candidates in General Elections, seldom if ever winning any seats. The Labour party has dominated Welsh politics since 1923, winning over 50 per cent of the votes cast at every general election since that date and over 70 per cent since 1945.[33] Welsh nationalism is apparently growing, not dying, and is manifested in numerous local associations, in a new emphasis on the Welsh language, and in the "increasing numbers of 1st generation middle-class people who associate themselves with nationalist policies." This movement is not thought likely to impress the workers, however.[34]

---

[30] See J. H. Burns, "The Scottish Committees of the House of Commons, 1948–1959," *Political Studies* (Oxford), VIII (1960), 272–96.

[31] See Alexander K. Cairncross, *The Scottish Economy* (London: Cambridge University Press, 1954).

[32] Sidney A. Burrell, "The Scottish Separatist Movements: A Present Assessment," *Political Science Quarterly*, LXX (September, 1955), 358–67.

[33] Tom Brennan, E. W. Cooney, and H. Pollins, *Social Change in Southwest Wales* (London: Watts, 1954), pp. 146–47.

[34] *Ibid.*, p. 172. The combination of a distinctive culture plus an emergent middle class seems to produce, not a growing conservatism, but a cultural nationalism which takes the form of a desire for rapid economic development and political autonomy. These goals are seen as the only means of preserving the culture of the area—as a way of defending the culture against its own people—in a sense. Wales is rapidly becoming anglicized as it becomes permeated with mass culture. The nationalist movement, led by a new bourgeoisie, tries to protect the people against their own vulnerability to the alien culture. This middle-class nationalism is paralleled by recent developments in Quebec.

These few points are sufficient to underline the likelihood of regional deviations from class politics in Great Britain, particularly in Scotland and Wales. Both have suffering economies which could lead to nationalistic interpretations of "colonial" discrimination on the part of the English, and both have distinctive cultures and ways of life that might well produce unified political loyalties.

Yet neither of the major parties expresses whatever aspirations for political autonomy may exist among these peoples. The Labour and Conservative parties are not essentially federal bodies. If the major parties do not represent any aspirations for regional autonomy, and are not federally organized, then we should expect that no party in Wales or Scotland is identified as a regional party, receiving support cutting broadly across class lines. One ecological study of Southwest Wales does suggest that as the proportion of persons in service industries increases, the proportion of Labour votes declines, indicating a class basis for the Labour vote.[35]

If class politics is truly dominant in Great Britain, then we might expect that, regardless of the depth of regional loyalties in Welsh and Scottish hearts, they would be irrelevant to voting patterns. They would exist above and between party and class identities but would not override them. If this is the case, then the regional patterns of class voting would be far different from those to be documented in the United States and Canada, where regional loyalties in the South and in Quebec pull both manual and non-manual strata over to one party.

The pattern of class voting in Wales and Scotland is indeed distinctive in Great Britain, but the distinctiveness is exactly the opposite of that to be shown in the one-party regions of the United States and Canada. In the regions with presumably the greatest degree of regional identity, class voting is not lower but is usually higher. Wales has the highest level of class voting of any region in three out of five 1957–1962 British surveys; it has the lowest level of class voting in one survey. Scottish class voting is above the average in three out of five of the same surveys (highest in one), but has the lowest level of class voting in one. This very inconsistency may indicate the contrary pulls to and away from a class party and a regional identity. But regardless of this, clearly the regional patterns are far different from those of the United States and Canada.

---

[35] *Ibid.*, p. 170.

Both strata are not pulled over to one party. Class cleavages dominate regional loyalties.

Figure 6–3 shows the level of class voting in British regions from 1957 to 1962. (See Table 6–5 for the original data.) Unfortunately too few surveys were available to distinguish reliably between sampling error and either trends or consistent patterns, so that generalizations cannot be offered with great confidence.

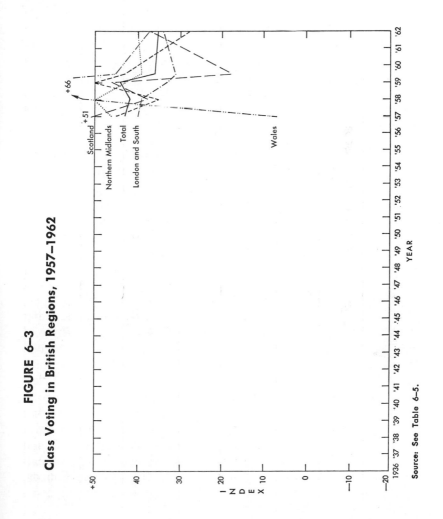

FIGURE 6–3

Class Voting in British Regions, 1957–1962

Source: See Table 6–5.

TABLE 6–5

Labour Preference, by Region and Occupation Type, Great Britain, 1957–1962

OCCUPATION TYPE	PER CENT PREFERRING LABOUR					
	Southern	Midlands	Wales	Northern	Scotland	Total
February, 1957						
Manual	61 (253)*	71 (154)	64 (33)	68 (225)	74 (78)	67 (743)
Non-Manual	21 (214)	26 (103)	57 (28)	22 (154)	23 (57)	24 (556)
Index of Class Voting	+40	+45	+7	+46	+51	+43
August, 1958						
Manual	61 (305)	59 (183)	75 (48)	70 (237)	60 (96)	64 (869)
Non-Manual	22 (268)	24 (157)	22 (27)	20 (178)	22 (64)	22 (694)
Index of Class Voting	+39	+35	+53	+50	+38	+42
February, 1959						
Manual	52 (109)	69 (102)	78 (23)	65 (119)	65 (40)	63 (393)
Non-Manual	19 (108)	19 (57)	12 (17)	22 (77)	19 (43)	19 (302)
Index of Class Voting	+33	+50	+66	+43	+46	+44

TABLE 6–5 (Continued)

PER CENT PREFERRING LABOUR

OCCUPATION TYPE	Southern	Midlands	Wales	Northern	Scotland	Total
			May–June, 1959			
Manual	53 (318)	63 (212)	64 (44)	59 (227)	45 (95)	57 (896)
Non-Manual	22 (232)	20 (130)	19 (36)	20 (157)	27 (64)	21 (619)
Index of Class Voting	+31	+43	+45	+39	+18	+36
			June, 1962			
Manual	53 (177)	54 (125)	62 (21)	61 (167)	59 (49)	57 (537)
Non-Manual	19 (148)	25 (94)	25 (20)	21 (136)	22 (36)	22 (434)
Index of Class Voting	+34	+29	+37	+40	+37	+35

Source: BIPO Surveys Nos. 1717, 82, 103, combined surveys Nos. 116 and 118, and 275. Definitions of the British regions will be found in Appendix D. Figure 6–3 presents the same data in the form of a graph.

* Number of respondents in parentheses.

Table 6–6 summarizes the rank order of regions in the level of class voting, from data in Table 6–5. Wales has the highest level of class voting in three of the five surveys, followed by the North, Scotland, the Midlands, and finally, the London and Southern region.

TABLE 6–6

Rank Order of Class Voting in the British Regions, 1957– 1962

| | NUMBER OF SURVEYS IN WHICH REGION RANKED: | | | | | |
	1st	2nd	3rd	4th	5th	RANK-INDEX SCORE
Wales	3	1	0	0	1	10
Northern	1	2	1	1	0	12
Scotland	1	1	1	1	1	15
Midlands	0	2	1	0	2	17
London and Southern	0	0	1	3	1	20

Source: Based on data from Table 6–5. Ties were counted twice in a single rank.

The period of time covered by these surveys is too short to give any valid picture of change or stability in the regions. The high level of vacillation in some regions, notably Wales and Scotland, is probably due not to real shifts of party loyalties in such a brief period, but to sampling biases. By the same token, the tendency toward decline of class voting in the London and Southern region may be equally fictitious.

Further evidence of the lack of regional identities in Britain is afforded by the relation of class voting to the history of unemployment in the various areas. It might be assumed that the high level of Labour voting in the regions of high unemployment in the 1930's (shown in Table 6–7) was a cross-class phenomenon reflecting the dissatisfaction of all persons in the area with economic conditions. One would expect this if there was a sense of regional identity and therefore a sense of outrage that one's fellow Welshmen were suffering. No such effect is found, since the classes are further apart where unemployment is high than where it is low. Class grievances served to polarize the electorate in Wales, Northern England, and Scotland.

TABLE 6–7

Unemployment and the Labour Vote in British Regions

REGION	PER CENT OF NATIONAL AVERAGE OF UNEMPLOYMENT IN THE 1930's	LABOUR VOTE 1950 (Per Cent)	CONSERVATIVE SWING SINCE 1945
Wales	More than 160	58.1	0.3
Northern England	More than 130	49.6	3.2
Scotland	More than 120	46.2	3.1
Midlands	About average	50.9	2.2
Southern England except for:	Less than 80	38.2	3.3
London and Suburbs	Less than 60	47.2	6.4
Whole Country	100	46.8	3.4

Source: H. G. Nicholas, *The British General Election of 1950* (London: Macmillan, 1951), p. 298. The original source for the unemployment data was M. P. Fogarty, *Prospects of the Industrial Areas of Great Britain* (London: Methuen, 1945), p. 5.

Does this contradict the assumption of consensus—that all strata tend to move together in each historical period, and that therefore there may be a common political response to events which have a very different effect upon different social strata? Not necessarily, because we have no historical evidence showing that a *change* occurred in the level of class voting when unemployment became high. Probably the same conditions produce both class voting and unemployment, and the processes of consensus operate in both types of regions. (It may be recalled from Chapter 5 that the relatively poorer countries with fewer educational opportunities have higher levels of class voting. The same may be true of regions within countries—at least in Great Britain, where cultural factors affecting class voting do not apparently operate to the same degree as in the other countries.)

Besides showing that the special regional loyalties of Wales and Scotland do not reduce class voting, Table 6–5 has some implications for the possible decline of class voting. If regional social change tends toward the expansion of urban populations, educational opportunities, and the middle class, and if these changes are associated with lower levels of class voting, the total level of class voting may be expected to drop.

Table 6–6 shows that the average level of class voting was lowest in the London and Southern region which includes the metropolitan areas of Great Britain. This region is the most urbanized of any in the country. It has the highest percentage of the population in commerce and financial occupations (in both 1931 and 1951), and the lowest percentage in agriculture. It had the highest number of physicians per 1,000 population in 1951, the highest proportion of clerks and typists, and the highest proportion of the population in full-time education. Also a study cited earlier demonstrated that the 1944 Education Act opened up educational opportunities for bright working-class children, particularly in the London area.[36] As Table 6–7 showed, the Southern region suffered least during the Great Depression.

The Greater London area is probably more like the United States in general level of social and economic development than are other British regions; therefore it may be most like the United States in its level of class voting. This fact may have real implications for the future of the class bases of British politics, if other regions go through the same process of social change.[37]

This evidence on regionalism seems to contradict the major thesis of this chapter—that the class structure in Britain is changing, but not the class bases of politics. The low level of class voting in the Southern region is due to a lower level of Labour voting by man-

---

[36] Himmelweit, *op. cit.*, pp. 141–59. The data on social characteristics of regions in England and Wales are taken from *Census, 1951, General Report* (London: Her Majesty's Stationery Office, 1958), p. 113, and the *Census 1951, Occupation Tables* (London: Her Majesty's Stationery Office, 1956), Table A, p. 620. The 1931 and 1951 regions are not exactly comparable, but are probably close enough for the rough comparison here. These data are only for the "London and Southeast" region, comprising (in 1951) the Counties of Essex (part), Hertfordshire (part), Kent, London, Middlesex, Surrey, and East and West Sussex. In the data reported from the BIPO surveys, the Southern and Southwest regions of England are also included, but they do not alter the findings.

[37] Intercorrelation of a number of economic characteristics of British regions showed that the London and Southeast region was quite different from all other regions in the country. The author of this study, concerned primarily with the methodology of regional accounts, does not discuss his substantive results. See Richard Stone, "A Comparison of the Economic Structure of Regions Based on the Concept of Distance," *Journal of Regional Science*, II (Fall, 1960), 1–20. The metropolitan areas in the Southern and Eastern regions of Britain are also growing faster than the other regions. See Leo Schnore, "Metropolitan Development in the United Kingdom," *Economic Geography*, XXXVIII (July, 1962), 223–24.

uals, not to a higher level of Labour voting by non-manuals. This may mean that the manual workers in these areas are in fact losing their Labour loyalties. Or it may mean that the "manual" category is too general, and in fact that these workers are predominantly skilled, have fairly good incomes, and do not vote differently from similar kinds of manual workers in other regions. If the latter is the case, then the shift in the class structure may be the cause of the declining Labour vote and not a change in the *kinds* of people supporting Labour. There may simply be fewer poorer workers in the London area.

The preceding two sections have attempted to show that the patterns of religious (particularly the Catholic) and regional (particularly the Welsh and Scottish) deviation from the national pattern of class voting do not contradict the dominance of class politics in Britain but rather manifest that dominance. A religion with a conservative ideology does not unite its members across class lines; a region with economic problems predisposes its working-class residents to vote especially strongly Labour, but whatever regional subculture may exist does not produce disproportionate Labour voting among the middle class.

THE LIBERAL PARTY AND CLASS VOTING

The assumption that Liberal party voting could be ignored must now be examined for its implications for the possible change in the character of class voting. It is possible that voting for the Liberal party has become a natural path of political transition for working-class and new-middle-class persons who are restive under the burden of a Labour party still strongly identified with the trade unions and still seen as "standing for the working class."

The Liberal party may fulfill, on the other hand, one of the several functions of a third party within a predominantly two-party system—in particular that of relieving temporary strains and tensions between parties and their supporters. (See Chapter 10.) If, for example, the Liberal party's support in terms of percentage of the electorate does not change, but its actual composition does change consistently, then it may be suggested that this is a structural consequence of a system dominated by class politics. The support of a party does not change proportionately, but it is constantly getting new recruits and losing old supporters. What might be called "structured alienation" takes place, in which a relatively constant proportion of the electorate is swinging away from or back to the two old parties at any given time. The proportion is constant (at least in this historical period) because of the homogeneity of British society and the resulting equivalence of the strains upon various sections of the electorate at any given time.

Changes in the social composition of the Liberal party supporters may give a clue to whether it is the beneficiary of any incipient tendencies toward a decline of class politics, or whether it still remains an adjunct of a political system dominated by class factors. The major hypothesis of this chapter suggests that the latter is the case. Since no decline of class voting has been shown and since the traditional bases of class politics remain strong, no large shift of certain categories of persons toward the Liberal party is to be expected. On the other hand, since the class structure is shifting, the Liberal party may benefit from the stratification strains which must exist.

The Liberals do not draw their support from a distinctive class base. Table 6–8 shows that since 1943, the Liberals have drawn roughly equal support from both manual and non-manual strata.[38] But if manual Liberals are better off than manual Labourites, or if non-manual Liberals are poorer, this might indicate that the Liberals draw disproportionate support from the upper levels of the manual workers and the lower levels of the non-manual workers (who might be the upwardly mobile manual workers voting Liberal instead of Conservative when they became non-manual). No evidence of this appears in these surveys. If anything, the poorer manual workers and the better-off non-manual workers are slightly more likely to vote Liberal. (No tabular presentation of these data is given.) But, in general, there seem to be no striking evidences of differences between Liberals on any class basis. The better-educated, better-off non-manual group is the only one considerably more likely to support the Liberals.

The only *social* bases for Liberal support which appear at all

[38] The one exception to the roughly equal support from both strata—the 21 per cent of non-manual persons in the August, 1958, survey reporting themselves as intending to vote Liberal—is another warning that more than one sample is necessary for any kind of judgment as to actual marginals. However, the relationships of one factor with another are not likely to change even if the sampling of voters is as far off as this survey apparently was.

TABLE 6–8

Liberal Party Preference, by Occupation Type, Great Britain, 1943–1959

SURVEY	PER CENT WITH LIBERAL PREFERENCE MANUAL	NON-MANUAL
December, 1943	12 (1,060)*	10 (378)
February, 1957	8 (743)	12 (558)
January, 1958	8 (415)	7 (344)
August, 1958	12 (874)	21 (692)
February, 1959	10 (397)	9 (309)
May–June, 1959	13 (871)	12 (606)

Sources: BIPO Surveys Nos. 104, 1717, 58, 82, 103, and combined surveys Nos. 116 and 118. These figures are for the three-party total. More people probably report themselves as intending to vote Liberal than actually do so. Just as Liberals fare better in by-elections in Great Britain, where it does not "count," so in surveys, people report that they intend to vote Liberal when they probably do not actually do so. In the 1955 General Election, 2.7 per cent of the voters voted Liberal; in the 1959 General Election, 5.9 per cent voted Liberal. These figures indicate, therefore, only the kinds of persons who say that they "might" vote Liberal.
* Total number of respondents in parentheses.

significant are Nonconformity, Welsh and Greater London residence, and middle-class self-identification. The first two are remnants of the regionalism of Wales and its association with the nonconformist religions. In the region with the lowest level of class voting—Greater London and South—the Liberal party does best among middle-class non-manuals. In this region a center, non-class party much like the Democratic party of the United States or the Liberal party of Canada appeals to an important emerging middle class. Table 6–9 shows the demographic groups within each region and class stratum giving the Liberal party more than 20 per cent support. The lack of cases available for such a complex cross-tabulation means that some Liberal groupings may not appear in the table simply for lack of cases; the table can therefore only be suggestive of a pattern of regularities in Liberal support across Britain.

If there is no or little class base for the Liberals, what is the nature of the Liberal support? As suggested previously, the Liberals may be an "ideological" third party, drawing support from people disgruntled with the bureaucratized and centralized major parties. Several findings from the national surveys show the ideological character of the Liberal voters (although, as also suggested earlier, Liberal support is not constant).

TABLE 6–9

Demographic Groups in Which the Liberal Vote Is over 20 Per Cent, by Region and Occupation Type, Great Britain, 1957

DEMOGRAPHIC GROUP	PER CENT VOTING LIBERAL				
	South	Midlands	Wales	North	Scotland
			Manual Occupations		
Age					
Sex			Males 22 (18)*		
Religion	Minor Religions 22 (9)		Nonconformist 27 (15)	Nonconformist 36 (11)	
Socio-Economic Status			Average Minus 27 (22)	Average 20 (15)	
Subjective Class			Lower Middle-Class 50 (8)		

TABLE 6–9 (Continued)

DEMOGRAPHIC GROUP	PER CENT VOTING LIBERAL				
	South	Midlands	Wales	North	Scotland
	Non-Manual Occupations				
Age	35–44 21 (65)				
Sex					
Religion	Nonconformist 29 (31)		Nonconformist 29 (7)	Minor Religions 62 (8)	
Socio-Economic Status					
Subjective Class	Middle-Class 20 (189)	Lower Middle-Class 25 (20)			Middle-Class 20 (15)

Source: BIPO Survey No. 1717, February, 1957.

* Total number of respondents in parentheses.

This table is a condensation of five: the separate cross-tabulation of region, social class, and vote by age, sex, religion, SES, and subjective class. Only the resulting Liberal percentages above 20 per cent appear in the table. In a sense, it represents the replication of the connection of each of the five independent variables with Liberal voting within each of two social strata and each of five regions. The lack of cases may prevent many possible relationships from appearing.

Liberals appear "in the middle" between Conservatives and La-bourites on three "class" issues on which questions were asked in a 1958 survey. (These results are given only as a sampling of such answers. In each available survey, Liberals are between Conserva-tives and Labourites on a number of political attitudes.) For exam-ple, when asked whether they agreed with: (1) "the right to strike," (2) "strikes should be illegal," or (3) "strike when arbitration fails," Liberals were more likely than supporters of other parties within either manual or non-manual strata to choose the "middle" position that strikes were permissible when negotiation and compromise had failed. On the question of whether respondents "approved of the measures the government has taken to deal with our economic difficulties," again the Liberals were almost exactly between the Labourites and the Conservatives. Among manual workers, the proportions of Conservatives, Liberals, and Labourites saying "yes" were 77, 49, and 20, in that order. Among non-manual workers, the proportions saying "yes" were 84, 50, and 25.

The opinions of party supporters within occupational strata on whether they "generally" approve of trade unions is probably a good indication of the "center" character of the Liberal ideology in Great Britain. As Table 6–10 shows, Liberals are slightly more likely than Conservatives to think that trade unions are a "good thing." The Liberals are much more likely to answer "don't know" to this question, which may be an even better indication that they are torn between wanting to recognize the legitimacy of trade unions and wanting to preserve the "freedom" of the individual worker.

Note that opinion on trade unions seems to be related to "party" far more than to "class." The differences between supporters of var-ious parties are much greater than those between workers in various occupations. This is shown more clearly by the total in each stra-tum believing that unions are a "good thing." The difference was only 13 per cent between manual and non-manual strata, with 69 per cent of the manual and 56 per cent of the non-manual workers holding that opinion. Within strata, however, there was a 26 per cent difference between Conservative and Labour manuals, and a 34 per cent difference between Conservative and Labour non-manuals. This shows how class issues are politicized in a situation where class politics is dominant. Clearly, also, this is an issue cre-ating real strain for the Liberals, who are seeking a middle ground between both classes and both parties.

TABLE 6–10

Answers to the Question, "Generally, Do You Think Trade Unions Are a Good Thing Or a Bad Thing?" by Party Preference and Occupation Type, Great Britain, 1958

OPINION	PARTY			
	Conserva-tive	Labour	Liberal	Total
Per Cent of Manual				
Good	52	78	57	69
Bad	27	5	15	11
Don't Know	22	17	28	20
Total Number	(217)	(569)	(102)	(888)
Per Cent of Non-Manual				
Good	48	82	50	56
Bad	33	5	15	23
Don't Know	19	13	35	21
Total Number	(398)	(153)	(149)	(700)

Source: BIPO Survey No. 82, 1958. Of the manual workers, 57 per cent of the persons without a party preference favored unions; of the non-manuals, 55 per cent of the persons without a party preference favored unions.

Liberal ideology is that of the "middle way." The Liberal program accentuates personal freedom, humanistic values ("People Count" was their 1959 election slogan), and a struggle against both private and public monopolies. It is natural, therefore, that the Liberal party should attract persons temporarily or permanently disaffected from big labor, the aristocracy, or the bureaucratic major parties.[39] A recent study of the attitudes of supporters of the three British parties derived from analysis of a large number of polls, found that the Liberals consistently occupied a position be-

[39] See R. B. McCallum, "The Liberal Outlook" in Morris Ginsberg, ed., *Law and Opinion in England in the 20th Century* (Berkeley: University of California Press, 1959), pp. 63–78, and A. Holt, "The Liberal Attitude to Contemporary Problems," *Political Quarterly*, XXIV (1953), 249–58, for statements of Liberal ideology. Other articles assessing the Liberal position in Great Britain include E. J. Cleary and H. Pollins, "Liberal Voting at the General Election of 1951," *Sociological Review*, I (December, 1953), 27–41, and P. Fothergill, "The Liberal Predicament," *Political Quarterly*, XXIV (1953), 243–49, and Abrams *et al.*, *op. cit.*, pp. 95 ff.

tween the supporters of the two larger parties on foreign policy questions—not only the domestic ones indicated by the data presented here.[40]

It has been shown that the Liberal party has no stable class base and that its supporters have centrist political opinions. But Liberal support is not consistent: the people who have these opinions do not regularly support the Liberals. Most of the Liberal support at any one time is shifting from or to another party.[41] Each of the surveys available (four all together) shows that less than one-third of the total Liberal vote was constant. Most of the Liberal voters were previous Conservative or Labour voters. And more of the Liberal vote came from Conservatives than from Labourites.

If workers with middle-class identifications are much more likely to be Liberals than those with working-class identifications, it would seem plausible to conclude that the Liberal party is likely to benefit from any strong shift of class identifications. Some slight evidence suggests that manual workers with middle-class identification are more Liberal. Of the manual workers calling themselves "middle-class," 12 per cent were Liberals; of the manual workers calling themselves "lower-middle class," 14 per cent were Liberals; whereas of the manual workers calling themselves "working-class," only 7 per cent were Liberals. This was also true for the nonmanual workers, as might be expected. Fewer of those with working-class identifications were Liberal.[42]

In conclusion, the evidence concerning the social bases of the Liberal vote suggests that the Liberal party functions as an "ideological outlet" for the strains of a highly class-divided political system. Although benefitting slightly from Nonconformist and Welsh

---

[40] Morris Davis and S. Verba, "Party Affiliation and International Opinions in Britain and France, 1947–1956," *Public Opinion Quarterly*, XXIV (Winter, 1960), 590–604. In a 1959 survey, however, Liberals were found to be closer to Conservatives than to Labourites in their views on the proper amount of power that business and labor organizations "should have." (British Social Surveys release, August, 1959).

[41] The data on this point are only suggestive, since they are based on reports of past voting intention of persons asked in 1957, 1958, or 1959. Since fewer Liberals ran in 1955, there is no way of telling how many persons switched out of choice or out of necessity. A survey obtained after the 1959 election, in which Liberals ran in about one-third of the constituencies, would show this much more clearly.

[42] These results were consistent in two surveys, BIPO Surveys Nos. 1717, February, 1957, and 103, February, 1959.

religious and regional deviations from a pure class politics, the Liberal party draws a small but consistent proportion of the electorate in every demographic group, with an emphasis upon persons identifying themselves as middle-class. Since most of its support is shifting back and forth at any given time, the alienation from the major parties which produces Liberal voting is a structural consequence of the domination of class in the British political system. This function of the Liberal party contrasts sharply with the "transition" function served by the Australian Democratic Labor party (discussed in Chapter 7) and with the "representative" functions served by some of the Canadian political parties. Where class politics is not dominant, but various parochial and local identities such as those to regional, ethnic, or religious subcultures prevail, third parties give social groups a sense of representation far more than they provide an ideological outlet for the strains of a highly stratified political order. (See Chapter 10 for a general discussion of third parties.)

AGE AND CLASS VOTING

One of the alleged trends pointed to by those who foresee a decline in the class bases of British politics is the tendency of young people to think of themselves as more middle-class, to identify the Conservative party with the middle class and with progressive ideas generally, to identify less (among working-class youth) with the trade unions and the Labour party, and therefore to be ready to move to the Right politically. The historic allegiance of young people to the Left in Great Britain is in danger of being broken, according to persons who see class politics as declining in Britain.

The most recent example of this view is a little Penguin book called *Must Labour Lose?* which starts from the undeniable fact that the Labour vote dropped steadily, albeit slowly, from 1950 to 1959.[43] The book attributes this drop to a number of causes; only the supposed Conservative trend of young voters is relevant at this point, however. According to the authors, "at least until the 1959 General Election new recruits to the voting registers could be ex-

---

[43] The book is based upon a national sample of 724 British voters taken in January and February, 1960. Originally published as a series in *Socialist Commentary*, the report on the survey is reprinted, together with a section on the British party system and a section drawing some implications for Labour policy, as Mark Abrams *et al.*, *Must Labour Lose?*, *op. cit.*

pected to vote Labour solidly; there was, however, no such uniformity about their behavior last October." And they conclude,
after analyzing the evidence from the survey, that ". . . there is
among young people today a complex of barely conscious Conservative sympathies which have still not yet fully expressed themselves in overt party affiliations."[44] However, no evidence on the
changes of Labour support among young people is presented to
support that assertion. In fact, no studies of differences between
age-groups at different time periods are available, and the one study
available to this writer is for 1943 and is obviously inadequate to
measure change, although some suggestive hypotheses are possible.

The studies of constituencies in the 1950 and 1951 elections
found that, within the different socio-economic strata, younger
voters were more likely to vote Labour than older voters. The 1950
Greenwich study found that in each social class the young voted
Labour more often than the old, but the difference was much more
marked among working-class people.[45] The authors of *Straight
Fight*, the study of Bristol North-East in 1951, concluded that the
age differences were really class differences, due to the comparative recency of the Labour party (and its consequent lack of a
"traditional" hold upon older voters) and to class differences in
death rates.[46] Neither of these studies advanced any hypotheses
concerning change. But they generally saw the age differences as
consequences in various ways of the class bases of British politics.
Similarly, the book *Must Labour Lose?* attributes the alleged dwindling Labour vote among youth to the changing character of class
loyalties and class identifications.

However, according to several surveys, young people are no less
likely to identify themselves as working-class than their elders, although those young people who do consider themselves to be "middle-class" are slightly less likely to vote Labour than older people
with the same class identifications. (These results are not presented
in any table.) But since this is a crucial point in any attempt to
predict the future of class voting in Great Britain, the differences
between age-groups must be examined in more detail, and the evidence presented in *Must Labour Lose?*, assessed.

The alienation of youth from Labour has become an easy cliché

[44] *Ibid.*, pp. 47, 58.
[45] Benney *et al.*, *op. cit.*, pp. 104–7.
[46] Milne and Mackenzie, *op. cit.*, pp. 58–59.

of the political journals. In the American journal *The Reporter*, George Steiner wrote that

> Socialism, it would appear, has become the political creed of the old and the disenchanted. Voters coming of political age in a prosperous economy where there is a labor shortage, except in a small number of pockets of technological depression, obviously find it difficult to identify themselves with a party whose deepest historical and emotional roots are the remembrance and fear of unemployment and economic crisis. Today the young vote Tory, and it is in old-age homes that the fires of socialism are kept burning most brightly.[47]

Plausible rhetoric, but is it true? Our central hypothesis that the change in the fortunes of the Labour party is due to a shift of the entire class structure and not a shift of the traditional bases of party support suggests that this is too easy a generalization. In order to cast doubt upon it, it is not necessary to show that younger people vote Labour *more* than older ones, but only that there is little difference between them. The concern here is not to establish a positive relationship but to show that the negative finding cannot be supported.

The evidence is fairly clear from a number of national samples that younger people are not less inclined to vote Labour than older ones (Table 6–11). Evidence from four surveys taken between January, 1958, and June, 1962, show that within either manual or non-manual strata, younger people are, with only four exceptions, no less likely to vote Labour than older people. Taking only the four more recent surveys, and considering "under thirty" to embrace most young people, twenty-four separate comparisons are possible (the age-groups between sixteen and twenty, twenty-one and twenty-four, twenty-five and twenty-nine within two strata for each of the four surveys). In twenty of the twenty-four comparisons, the persons in these age-groups were more likely to prefer the Labour party than the average for all ages in the same class. Young people are still more likely to vote for the Labour party than their elders.

The small numbers of cases do not allow any reliable statement

---

[47] "The Decline of the Labour Party," *The Reporter*, September 29, 1960, p. 33. Butler and Rose, *op. cit.*, p. 197, assert that it was in the twenty-one-to-twenty-nine age-group that Labour lost heavily in the 1959 election, but they do not give supporting evidence.

TABLE 6–11

Labour Preference by Age and Occupation Type, Great Britain, 1943–1962*

OCCUPATION TYPE	PER CENT PREFERRING LABOUR AGE GROUP								TOTAL

	21–29	30–49	Over 50	*December, 1943*					
Manual	70	60	57						60
	(137)†	(539)	(384)						(1,060)
Non-Manual	35	41	34						37
	(52)	(183)	(143)						(378)
Index of Class Voting	+35	+19	+23						+23

	16–20	21–24	25–29	30–34	35–44	45–49	50–64	65+	TOTAL
				January, 1958					
Manual	57	72	71	75	62	53	71	74	67
	(21)	(25)	(38)	(53)	(84)	(58)	(73)	(65)	(417)
Non-Manual	56	31	31	29	30	13	24	17	26
	(16)	(16)	(29)	(44)	(76)	(68)	(66)	(30)	(345)
Index of Class Voting	+1	+41	+40	+46	+32	+40	+47	+57	+41

				August, 1958					
Manual	89	67	69	63	71	61	54	58	64
	(35)	(72)	(99)	(106)	(172)	(135)	(153)	(120)	(891)
Non-Manual	44	25	29	18	23	18	16	20	22
	(34)	(52)	(70)	(76)	(149)	(119)	(138)	(65)	(703)
Index of Class Voting	+45	+42	+40	+45	+48	+43	+38	+38	+42

				May and June, 1959					
Manual	57	73	47	59	53	54	58	58	57
	(35)	(86)	(125)	(76)	(174)	(82)	(193)	(124)	(895)
Non-Manual	31	21	15	34	19	16	19	27	21
	(39)	(48)	(128)	(76)	(123)	(44)	(113)	(48)	(619)
Index of Class Voting	+26	+52	+32	+25	+34	+38	+39	+31	+36

				June, 1962					
Manual	59	59	69	56	59	45	57	51	57
	(22)	(29)	(52)	(64)	(127)	(55)	(112)	(74)	(537)
Non-Manual	46	18	39	24	27	16	9	8	22
	(28)	(34)	(36)	(55)	(102)	(56)	(85)	(38)	(434)
Index of Class Voting	+13	+41	+30	+32	+32	+29	+48	+43	+35

Sources: BIPO Surveys Nos. 104, 58, 82, 116 and 118 (combined), and 275.
* These are the three party totals and the complete age breakdowns given in each study.
† Total number of respondents in parentheses.

of trends within each age-group, but a comparison with the 1943 figures is suggestive. Within manual occupations, those in the age-group from twenty-one to twenty-nine were considerably more likely to prefer Labour than the older age-groups. But young middle-class persons were no different from their elders. This has changed. Middle-class youth are now even more likely to vote Labour than formerly and are considerably more likely than their elders to do so.

It may be noted here that despite the lack of low Labour voting among young people, class voting is not significantly or consistently lower among young people. The gap between the Labour vote of young manual and non-manual persons remains about the same as in the total population.[48]

These results are not an artifact of regional and religious differences in the relation of age and vote. Among both Protestants and Catholics, both manual and non-manual young people (under thirty) are considerably more likely to vote Labour than older persons in the same religion and class. As for regional effects, among the twenty-nine comparisons of the voting patterns of age-groups under thirty possible within five British regions (in the 1957 survey), in only seven of the twenty-nine was the Labour voting of the youth below the average for the region and the class. Although the numbers of cases do not make a secure interpretation possible, it may be significant that three of the seven exceptions to the general pattern occurred in the London and Southern region. This region has the lowest level of class voting generally, and it seems that young people in this region exhibit a greater tendency than in others to move away from Labour. This would be consistent, if true, with the general tendency of the area with the highest mobility oppor-

---

[48] The question may be raised as to whether these relationships remain when the proportion of young persons not knowing their party preference is considered. Such uncertainty may reflect an ambiguous class position possibly characteristic of a changing Britain. However, young people were only slightly less likely to have a party preference than older people. And even if every survey showed that young persons were uncertain politically, this is no certain evidence that their class identifications were weak. The political immaturity of young people, and their lack of involvement in occupational subcultures which reinforce political predispositions, can just as plausibly account for political uncertainty as weak class identifications. In any case, this point cannot account for the level of Labour vote among middle-class British youth. The whole question of age and generational differences has been insufficiently studied within a comparative framework.

tunities to exhibit a weakening of the traditional class bases of politics.

It seems plausible to conclude from these data that young British voters have not moved away from the Labour party. It remains to determine why the recent study reported in *Must Labour Lose?* could conclude that the drift of young voters away from Labour was a fatal omen. As will be seen, both the data and the interpretations made in that study are inadequate to support the generalization that young voters are now a potential Conservative voting bloc.

The chapter in *Must Labour Lose?* entitled "Young Voters" is based upon the assumption that until 1959 young people were "solid Labour voters," but now have "barely conscious Conservative sympathies," and that therefore a change must have taken place.[49] However, no evidence is presented either that young voters did not have the same sympathies previously, or that they are voting Labour less now than before, or even that "barely conscious" or even conscious Conservative sympathies are inconsistent with "solid Labour" voting. By the nature of a moderate politics of consensus, all kinds of "sympathies" cross party lines. Political behavior and attitudes are not consistent, and it cannot be assumed so easily that political sympathies are always reflected in parallel political behavior. All of these inferences are plausible, and may even be true, but surely more solid evidence than this of a *change* in the behavior and sympathies of young voters is necessary.

The conclusions of *Must Labour Lose?* are based solely upon one cross-section of the British population taken early in 1960. The basic evidence that is presented concerning the political tendencies of young Britishers is as follows:

> If we ignore the 10 percent whose political views were so unformed that they could not be described even as "leaning" towards any party, then it appears that 52 percent of young people today are Conservatives, 43 percent are Labour supporters and 5 percent Liberals. This Conservative lead has two sources: 35 percent of all working-class young people are ready to identify themselves with the Conservative Party, and only 10 percent of middle-class young people support the Labour Party. In the light of the voting behavior of young people over the past 25 years it is this latter finding which is perhaps the most striking; i.e., the almost complete

---

[49] Abrams *et al., op. cit.,* p. 58.

failure of the Labour Party to attract the interest and sympathy of young middle-class people. Indeed, it seems to be losing them: among middle-class people aged twenty-five and over in our sample less than 15 percent were prepared to describe themselves as Labour supporters. This, then, is the first significant finding about today's young people—they are further to the right than their elders were 10 and 15 years ago, and this move to the right is almost complete among the middle-class young.[50]

The other results from the survey, on attitudes and images of the parties, are designed to clarify or interpret what is considered a basic decline in Labour support from young people, particularly middle-class young people.

About this finding, first, the evidence given does not show *change* of voting patterns. The author makes the implicit inference that young people today are more to the Right than "their elders were 10 and 15 years ago," implying that the Labour vote of *older* people *now* can be interpreted as the same as the Labour vote of *younger* people *before*. Clearly this is not necessarily true. Possibly both young and old are now more Conservative than they were, or even conceivably young people are now less Conservative than young people were fifteen years ago. No evidence is presented which shows that the 10 per cent of middle-class young people found to be Labour in February, 1960, is not *higher* than the Labour proportion among young middle-class people in 1945. As several surveys have shown, middle-class young people are now more likely to be Labour than their elders, as compared with fifteen years ago.

Thus the conclusion that young voters are moving from Labour is based upon, first, a methodological error in the interpretation of the meaning of age, and, second, a conclusion from a single sample which is not consistent with at least four or five other national samples of the British electorate over a period of fifteen years.

But we may concede that if other evidence of lack of sympathy with the Labour party is found, especially among youth, an incipient Conservative trend may be under way.

A main source of evidence on the attitudes toward the political parties of young voters is one question on the most important attributes of a "good political party" and another on how these attributes "fit" the various parties. It turns out that the attributes of a

---

[50] *Ibid.,* pp. 47–48.

good party considered most important are: "would really work to prevent nuclear war," "would do most for world peace," and "would make the country more prosperous," each gaining the assent of over 40 per cent of people eighteen to twenty-four and people twenty-five and over. Whether a party "stands mainly for the working class" was considered a "most important" attribute of a good party by only 14 per cent of both age-groups. The table showing these results is juxtaposed to another giving younger and older persons' answers to the question concerning how these attributes "fit" each party. Certain conclusions were drawn that the young voters are more likely to see the Labour party in "unattractive" terms. In their words:

> When asked to go over the list and indicate which of the attributes applied more to one party rather than the other, young people were much more emphatic than their elders in seeing Labour as overwhelmingly the party which stands mainly for the working class, as out to help the underdog and to abolish class-differences. None of these traits seemed of much significance to young people when they indicated the most important features of a good political party. On the item they put at the top ("would really work to prevent nuclear war") over half saw no difference between the Labour Party and the Conservative Party, and on their second and third priorities ("would do most for world peace" and "would make the country more prosperous") they were as ready as their elders to recognize the Conservatives as being much more likely to be effective. In short, young voters see the Labour Party even more sharply than do their elders in the very terms which have apparently made that party generally unattractive to many voters in recent years.[51]

On the face of these statements that "over half saw no difference" and then were "as ready as their elders," it hardly seems justified to conclude that young voters see the Labour party in a certain way "even more sharply." But a more fundamental criticism can be made. When juxtaposing two *separate* results in this way, the authors run the danger of the "ecological fallacy": concluding from separate relationships that an inner relationship exists. In other words, they infer from findings that (1) more people stress prevention of nuclear war and fewer people stress "standing for the working class" as goals of "good parties," and that (2) more younger people than older people apply "standing mainly for the

---

[51] *Ibid.*, pp. 48–49.

working class" to the Labour party, the conclusion that (3) the Labour party is suffering from an "unattractive image" (standing for the working class) and that this image is particularly strong among young people, and that they therefore oppose the Labour party on those grounds. But it simply does not follow (although it may be plausible) from the way people see a party that therefore they either oppose or favor it. No evidence is presented that the *same* people who see the Labour party "standing for the working class" also *oppose* the Labour party. It is perfectly possible that all of those people support it.

The same point applies to the inference that because over half of the young voters saw no difference between the Labour party and the Conservative party (on the question of which party would "really work to prevent nuclear war") this was grounds for their rejection of the Labour party. Here again, the author does not say whether the people who say they favor a party working to prevent nuclear war are also the ones who attribute this more to the Conservative party *or* (and this is perhaps the most significant of all) whether they are the same ones supporting the Conservative party. No evidence is given of this link, although it is crucial to the argument. It must be shown that the people who both think that this goal is important and consider the Conservative party to further it better than Labour are also likely to *vote* Conservative. Not to give at least some evidence on this point implies the assumption that people vote in accordance with a rational assessment of parties and issues (or even in accordance with their "image" of the party), and most voting studies show that these are unwarranted assumptions.

Let us go back to the finding that a high proportion of persons choose "would really work to prevent nuclear war" as the most important attribute of a party. The only point selected to bolster the conclusion that "young people see the Labour Party even more sharply than do their elders . . . in . . . unattractive terms" is that over half of young people saw no difference between the Labour party and the Conservative party in this respect. But surely it is more important, first, whether young people thought the Conservative party to be more likely to prevent nuclear war than the Labour party, and second, whether more young people than older people thought the Conservative party to be more likely to prevent nuclear war than the Labour party. On both these scores, the data fail to support the conclusions drawn. Table 31 (p. 50) of *Must Labour*

Lose? shows not only that more young people see the Labour party as working to prevent nuclear war than see the Conservatives as seeking that goal (26 per cent see Labour in these terms, 18 per cent see the Conservatives as working to prevent nuclear war), but also that more young people than older people apply the statement to Labour and not to the Conservative party (26 and 23 per cent).

CONCLUSION

The high level of class voting in Britain does not necessarily reflect a polarization of political culture along class lines. As mentioned in Chapter 1, the traditional aristocracy in Britain has an enormous legitimacy and therefore undoubtedly the class ideology of Labour need not represent a polar opposite, but rather a cross-pressure upon Labour voters. As a recent study of the Tory worker puts it:

> Conservative voters in the working class appear to enjoy greater congruence between behavior and broad perceptions of the parties than do Labour voters, who seem to be linked to Labour almost entirely in terms of class interest. In a political culture which values so highly the Burkean themes of consensus and national identity, this suggests that working-class Conservatives may be under less ideological cross-pressures than Labour voters.[52]

The authors suggest, however, that the basis for Conservative voting may be increasingly "secular" rather than "deferential," in the sense of a belief that the traditional elite should govern. Younger and higher-income manual workers were less likely to give "deferential" reasons for being Conservative than older, lower-income workers. The former group of working-class Conservatives was also more concerned with mobility and was more "leftist" in its opinions. If the *basis* of working-class Conservatism is shifting toward a prag-

---

[52] Robert T. McKenzie and Allan Silver, "Conservatism, Industrialism and the Working-Class Tory in England" (Paper prepared for the Fifth World Congress of Sociology, Washington, D.C., September, 1962), pp. 8–9. The paper was based on a 1958 survey of 604 urban working-class voters, including 178 Conservatives. It may be suggested that the Right party in any consensual system may be seen by supporters of *both* parties as the most legitimate upholder of conservative values, most of which are shared by most voters. Left supporters merely weight other values or interests more heavily. The resulting cross-pressures may produce much of the party-shifting in such a system.

matic, secular evaluation of what a party can "do for me," then a justified inference (made by the authors) may be that the traditional working-class Conservative vote may be coming to be vacillating and untrustworthy at the same time that the working-class Labour vote may be losing its solidarity. That is to say, here is another piece of evidence that the British class and political system is becoming more like, say, the American one.[53]

It must not be inferred from the sharp class cleavages in party support, or from the polarization in the Parliament produced by party discipline, that the opinions of either the electorate or the members of the House of Commons are sharply split. On the contrary, on international issues at least, very little difference (in one study) was found either within or between party supporters. The authors note that "a high degree of unity within a party is not so much evidence that the party tends to unify the sentiments of its supporters as that it expresses the sentiment of a highly unified nation."[54] Whether there is such consensus on domestic issues is of course still problematic (it has been shown that "party" seems to organize opinions on domestic issues even more than "class"), but there is still a broad area of consensus.

Likewise, the opinions of Members of Parliament do not reveal suppressed antagonisms to the basic goals of the opposition. It might be argued that the degree of acceptance by the British Conservative leaders, for example, of the changes introduced by Labour in its period of power 1945–1951 does not reveal disaffection among Conservative rank-and-file Members of the House of Commons (so-called "backbenchers"). Party discipline and the realiza-

---

[53] McKenzie and Silver, *ibid.*, suggest that British political culture may be coming to be more homogeneous not only because working-class Conservatives are secularized, but also because working-class Labourites are becoming more deferential. It is also possible that American and Australian equalitarianism and populism are shifting toward a new version of a "deferential" system: the acceptance of political elites operating through large-scale organizations. If populism (legitimate mass pressure exerted outside of institutionalized political channels) is now politically more difficult, then we may see the equivalent of deference in an equalitarian system emerge. That is, if Americans are more likely now to see leadership and decision-making as being influenced almost solely through "channels," there has been a move toward an elitist system. (The relatively great difference remaining between the United States and Britain in the proportion of persons willing to use informal political channels— see Table 10–1, p. 297—indicates that such a move, if it exists, has not erased the difference between the political systems).

[54] Davis and Verba, *op. cit.*, p. 601.

tion of Conservative leaders that their political fortunes depended on maintaining their hold on a substantial minority of working-class voters may have forced acceptance of Labour reforms. However, a study of the opinions of the backbenchers in the 1955 to 1959 period, as expressed through their "Early Day Motions" (the "spontaneous unwhipped backbench manifestos" of members of any party), reveals "no evidence of violent disagreement on social questions." That is, given the opportunity to express spontaneous disapproval of the continuance of Labour-sponsored institutions, few Conservatives chose to do so. Whether some of them held strong beliefs that the welfare state should be abolished or not is irrelevant; the point is that such members apparently realized that even a gesture of opposition was politically completely unrealistic.[55]

To summarize, we have verified John Bonham's hypothesis quoted at the beginning of the chapter that very little except class matters for politics in Great Britain. In addition, we have discovered little evidence of a decline of the association of class and party. The entire class structure of Great Britain is shifting, however. The middle class is expanding, and apparently workers entering the middle class are fairly rapidly shifting to the Conservative side. The Labour party is probably no better off in this situation than it would be if the working class were becoming less class-conscious or less loyal to Labour. In fact, the situation is even more difficult than might have been predicted if the entire society were becoming "middle-classified." The Labour party is caught in a situation in which the remaining workers are still as heavily Labour as ever. Therefore, if the party tries to change its "image" as a working-class party by dropping its links to socialist goals and to the trade unions, it may merely alienate this still-strong section of the working class without necessarily winning over any of the climbing workers and newly-middle-class persons.

The features of the social bases of British politics which have

---

[55] See Samuel C. Finer, H. B. Berrington, and D. J. Bartholomew, *Backbench Opinion in the House of Commons, 1955–59* (London: Pergamon Press, 1961), pp. 7, 100. The authors analyzed patterns of sentiment among members of each major party as revealed in the Early Day Motions and related those patterns to occupational and educational background, age, political sponsorship, the year entering Parliament, and other social and political characteristics of the person and of his parliamentary seat. It is worthy of note that one of the sharpest splits within the Conservative party was between Oxford and Cambridge graduates.

been discovered—the dominance of class factors, and the inconsistent effect of regional and religious loyalties—are to be expected in a nation highly polarized around social classes but possessing a political culture with a sense of moderation and compromise. Where politics is so decisively based upon "interest" cleavages, additional "value" cleavages—entrenched religious and regional loyalties—would probably endanger the stability of the political system. Eire (Southern Ireland) was probably impossible to retain within a nation with a highly class-divided political system such as Britain's, since it piled a divisive "value" cleavage on top of already deep "interest" cleavages. Great Britain's high level of consensus and homogeneity has been gained at the price of secession.[56]

The present political and social homogeneity of British society is perhaps best shown by the unanimity of change from election to election. In the last five British elections,

> scarcely a seat has changed hands in a direction opposite to the national trend. At any election too the figures show that a change of mind by one voter in 100 in one direction or by two voters in 100 in the other would be decisive. So fine a balance can be maintained and endured because the basis for agreement is broad.[57]

It might be added that such a fine balance is maintained not only because the basis for agreement is broad, but because the basis for cleavage is equally broad and is diffused equally throughout the nation.

---

[56] In 1923 Eire—the Irish Free State—was formed out of the southern and western counties of Ireland, leaving six counties in Northern Ireland still part of the United Kingdom. For the story of the Irish War of Independence, see Edgar Holt, *Protest in Arms* (New York: Coward-McCann, 1961). Holt notes that Northern Ireland was more industrialized than Southern Ireland, as well as largely Protestant, and therefore had both an economic and a cultural stake in remaining with the United Kingdom (p. 32). Here is a case indicating that political integration is favored by industrialization and cultural homogeneity; regionalism, by the dominance of agriculture and cultural heterogeneity. See the discussion in Chapter 11.

[57] Kingsley B. Smellie, *The British Way of Life* (New York: Praeger, 1955), pp. 158–59. The various Nuffield studies document the uniformity of the swing, even in areas overwhelmingly for one party. See, for example, David E. Butler, *The British General Election of 1951* (London: Macmillan, 1952), pp. 249–64.

Chapter 7

Australia: The Politics of Class and Religion

CLASS voting is lower in Australia than it is in Great Britain, as already shown in Chapter 5. This chapter will (1) consider the historical and present importance of social class for the social bases of Australian politics, (2) show the relative absence of regionalism, despite the federal organization of the nation, and (3) examine the religious factor in Australian politics. The bulk of the chapter will be devoted to a case study of the Democratic Labor party (DLP), formed in 1955 as the Anti-Communist Labor party. The emergence of this Australian party is of special interest because it is an exception to the general absence of parties with an almost exclusively religious basis in the Anglo-American countries.

CLASS VOTING IN AUSTRALIA

Australia's politics have been dominated by class cleavages before and since its formation as a nation in 1901.[1] Class politics in

---

[1] The following discussion is based largely upon Alexander Brady, *Democracy in the Dominions* (Toronto: University of Toronto Press, 1947); A. Campbell Garnett, *Freedom and Planning in Australia* (Madison: University of Wisconsin Press, 1949); and Louise Overacker, *The Australian Party System* (New Haven: Yale University Press, 1952). For a discussion of Labor party ideology in Australia since its founding, and a brief discussion of the concept of "social class," see D. W. Rawson, "Labour, Socialism and the Working Class," *Australian Journal of Politics and History*, VII (May, 1961), 75–94. It may be noted that the spelling "Labor" will be used here, despite some inconsistencies on the part of Australians themselves, undoubtedly reflecting the twin influences of England and the United States.

Australia is not infused with the sharp status differentiation which is embedded in British society, and probably the level of class voting in Australia reflects the actual structural cleavages of the society in as bare a form as possible. As a young *émigré* to England put it, the class consciousness of the Australian worker stems from a keen awareness that "other people own the country . . . and this makes him a worker," but he "knows nothing of the emotional and psychological implications of belonging to a subject class, which has so constricted the outlook of the British proletarian."[2] It is possible, as suggested in Chapter 6, that the status differentiation of British society has maintained class-based political loyalties at a higher level than warranted by the class issues and actual differential economic interests in the society.

The reasons for the early domination of class politics in Australia can only be briefly suggested here, but may include (in contrast with the United States) the substitution of a radical rural proletarianism for an individualistic tradition fostered by small farmers, the substitution of an accentuated urbanism for a real frontier tradition, and greater ethnic homogeneity.

Australia's ecological conditions encouraged the formation of large pastoral estates rather than small farms. The laborers on these estates (located in the "outback," or expanses of land inland from the urban fringe around the southern rim of the continent) were extremely mobile, and did not form those local ties which prevent class consciousness. As one author put it,

> almost every observer of outback life has been forcibly struck by the extreme mobility of the pastoral population, and especially of the wage-earning part of it. . . . This mobility has naturally resulted in a diffusing of attitudes and values throughout the interior regardless of state boundaries.[3]

The rural "industries"—wheat, sheep, cattle—required little labor, and there was little contact between owner and worker but much contact between the workers. These essential prerequisites for the development of class consciousness resulted in early and unusual militancy for workers nominally in agrarian occupations. The outback philosophy of "mateship" which developed was not the kind

---

[2] Murray Sayle, "As Far as You Can Go," *Encounter*, XIV (May, 1960), p. 27.
[3] Russel B. Ward, *The Australian Legend* (Melbourne: Oxford University Press, 1958), p. 7.

of frontier equalitarianism found in the United States, but a more proletarian solidarity resulting in trade unionism and early political consciousness.[4]

The dominance of the pastoral industries by large owners (called "squatters") produced a "big man's frontier," as compared to the "small man's frontier" in the United States. "Nineteenth century Australia was composed of a few flockmakers, bankers and merchants, and a numerous peon class." While the small man's frontier stimulated American individualism, "Australia owes much of its collectivism to the fact that the frontier was hospitable to the large man instead."[5]

It is possible, on the other hand, that the dominance of a "proletarian" consciousness in Australian rural life, and the receptivity to a centralizing, collectivist ideology, did not stem from a paucity of small farmers or even ecological conditions preventing small farming. Rather, the difference between Australia and America may be due to differences in the ideologies of groups which migrated to these countries. Australians who went to the rural areas may have come from socialist European backgrounds and simply did not believe in decentralization, the "yeoman" virtues of the small farmer, and the individualistic virtues of small communities. Individualism in the United States, in contrast, may have been due to the migration of men believing in the freedom and independence conferred by the ownership of land.[6]

The differences in the ideology of rural life are not due, as a matter of fact, to a lower proportion of small farmers in Australia than in the United States and Canada. Australia has actually almost as high a proportion of persons in "primary industries" (farming, hunting, lumbering, and fishing) as Canada and, within primary industries, almost as many small farmers. Thus, "ecological" or climatic condi-

---

[4] For an interpretation of Australian national values along these lines, see Ronald Taft and Kenneth W. Walker, "Australia" in Arnold M. Rose, ed., *The Institutions of Advanced Societies* (Minneapolis: University of Minnesota Press, 1958), pp. 144–48.

[5] Brian Fitzpatrick, *The British Empire in Australia: An Economic History* (Melbourne: Melbourne University Press, 1941), pp. 188–91. Part of the quote was taken from Carter Goodrich, "The Australian and American Labor Movements," *Economic Record* (Melbourne), IV (November, 1928), 193–208. See also Fred Alexander, *Moving Frontiers, An American Theme and Its Application to Australian History* (Melbourne: Melbourne University Press, 1947).

[6] See Henry Nash Smith, *Virgin Land: The American West as Symbol and Myth* (New York: Vintage Books, 1957), esp. pp. 138–46.

tions may not have been the crucial factor in shaping Australian ideologies.[7]

Another factor possibly favoring the emergence of class politics has been the centering of Australian commercial and political life in the six capital cities, especially Melbourne and Sydney, the capitals of the most populous and industrialized states (Victoria and New South Wales). The lack of small towns in the interior, the need for central ports to funnel pastoral production into world markets, and the concentration of almost 60 per cent of the total population of 10 million in the six capital cities has favored an urban politics, and urban politics is usually class politics. What Alexander Brady has called the "highly accentuated metropolitanism" of Australian life has encouraged the powerful labor movement.[8]

Ethnic homogeneity has also encouraged class politics, mainly by preventing disruptive splits among the labor unions and the Australian Labor party (ALP). The so-called "White Australia" policy, agreed upon by most political elements, kept Australia 90 per cent British in national origin until after World War II.[9] The partly ethnic basis of the Catholic allegiance to the ALP will be discussed later.

Early organization of both trade unions and a labor party thus may have been the result of a collectivist ideology among the rural proletariat, the lack of an individualistic frontier, early and dominant urbanism, and the lack of ethnic diversity. By 1914 there were over 500,000 trade union members in Australia; while Canada, by contrast, with 2 million more citizens, had less than 200,000 at the same date.

The trade unions have been the organizational and financial

---

[7] The percentages of persons in primary industries in the four countries are: Great Britain, 5; Australia, 14; United States, 12; Canada, 19. The percentages, within primary industries, of persons "working on own account" (the closest approximation of small farmers) were (in 1956): Great Britain, 1; Australia, 8; United States, 7 (includes both employers and "workers on own account"); and Canada, 10. See the United Nations, *Demographic Yearbook* (New York, 1956), Table 15, pp. 458–99.

[8] Brady, *op. cit.*, p. 139.

[9] In the beginning of 1960, five hundred Asians were entering Australia each year, about half on long-term permits. As of then, there were still only fifty-two hundred Asians in Australia, and this was an increase of 30 per cent over the figure five years before. (*New York Times*, January 3, 1960). The possible political consequences of the wave of new immigration from eastern Europe will be considered later.

backbone of the ALP, which was formed even before the six states were federated into a nation in 1901. The ALP has maintained a socialist tradition but has refrained from putting much of its ostensible program into practice. (Actually, much of public ownership has been enacted by non-Labor governments.) Its socialist program is now under debate under much the same circumstances as that of the socialist program of the British Labour party, since the ALP has lost a series of national elections since 1949 (the ones in 1955 and possibly 1958 and 1961 because of the defection of the Democratic Labor party).

As a result of these historical factors, the Australian parties have distinctive class bases. The ALP is based upon the trade unions and industrial and agricultural workers. The Liberal party—the major party of the Right—is the party of "town capital": professionals, businessmen, and the middle class. The Country party is largely the party of "country capital": the defender of the interests of the "big men" who are successors of the squatters, although many small farmers (in Victoria, for example) might otherwise vote ALP.[10]

The importance of social class in the social bases of Australian politics is clearly shown by public opinion surveys, both national and in smaller areas. After analyzing results from a sample of Melbourne voters, O. A. Oeser and S. B. Hammond concluded that objective class position is an important determinant of voting behavior in Australia.[11] A survey in a suburban mixed-class area around Melbourne found a level of class voting (using the index suggested here) of 26 in 1960.[12] The author notes that there is an "absence of any sharp sense of social identity growing out of occupation or class" in this area. The level of class voting discovered in such an area is within the range to be suggested as that of structurally based class voting in these countries—a range toward which many

---

[10] The Country party, formed in 1919, participates in governing coalitions with the Liberal party in the federal Parliament. Australia has the preferential ballot, which allows minor parties to exist within a dominant two-party system without endangering the position of a major party. Further comment on this electoral system with special reference to the DLP will be made later.

[11] See their *Social Structure and Personality in a City* (London: Routledge & Kegan Paul, 1954), p. 312.

[12] Recomputed from a table in Creighton Burns, *Parties and People* (Melbourne: Melbourne University Press, 1961), p. 74. Class voting did not change if either the total choosing one of the major parties or the total of all persons in the sample was used as the basis of computation.

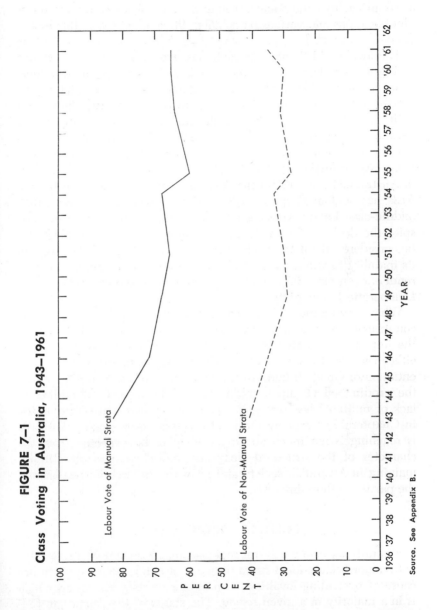

FIGURE 7-1

Class Voting in Australia, 1943–1961

Labour Vote of Manual Strata

Labour Vote of Non-Manual Strata

PERCENT

YEAR

Source. See Appendix B.

areas in each of the countries may be moving as traditional class identifications and various parochial political identities both weaken. (See Chapter 11.)

The level of ALP voting in each class from 1943 to 1961 is shown in Figure 7–1. The gap between the two lines represents the level of class voting, shown graphically together with the similar results for the other three countries in Figure 5–1, page 103. Both class voting and the Labor party vote declined fairly consistently in this period. Labor receives a higher proportion of the vote of both manual and non-manual strata in Australia than it does in Great Britain, possibly further evidence of the greater legitimacy of the Left in Australia. In the 1950's the Australian middle-class vote for the ALP has seldom dropped below 30 per cent; while the British middle-class Labour vote has been little more than 20 per cent. Despite the decline of its vote, the Australian Labor party must still be considered the normal "majority party" of the country in spite of its inability to win a national election from 1951 to 1963. This fact renders even more important an assessment of the character of the Democratic Labor party.

What may be more clearly evident in Australia than in the other countries is the secular erosion of the class bases of politics under the impact of a period of prosperity and social mobility. Lacking either the social diversity of the United States or the status differentiation of Great Britain, Australian politics has shown more easily the eroding effects upon traditional solidarities of an additional lack of militant class issues. Yet (and this thesis will be expanded in Chapter 11) probably the level of class voting which Australia is reaching is not much above the level to be expected from the character of the structural cleavages and class interests still remaining in Australian society and from the differential response of the parties to those interests.

POLITICAL REGIONALISM

Australia lacks any cultural regionalism. In none of the states are both major occupational strata drawn to a single political party because of overriding loyalties to an ethnic or religious group which is in a majority in a given region. The states of the Australian federal structure do not therefore represent distinctive subcultures, but are purely "political" units. Australia is a federal state, with only "constitutional" regionalism, in the sense defined in Chapter 2.

Australia's several colonies, which formed the present states, might well have provided the nucleus of a regionalism like Canada's if it had not been for the ethnic homogeneity of the immigrants. In the 1850's there was no true Australian national identity, and the first consequences of the campaigns for self-government were "parochialism and intercolonial rivalries." The digger demonstrations in 1853, for example, were against "Melbourne, not London," and a combination of class antagonisms with ethnic ones might well have produced a regional impetus. But, of the diggers, "the majority were British, recent arrivals and loyal by habit."[13] In other words, because the continent held only British colonies, nationalist impulses were not reinforced by separatist ones. British nationality was, in a sense, a surrogate for Australian nationality, producing a sense of cross-colony solidarity which prevented the development of an exaggerated political regionalism.

Economic regionalism exists, but largely within rather than between states. The regional elements which do exist are associated with two forms of cleavage: rural versus urban splits within states which are based on class interests; and large versus small states—the grievances of the four less developed and populous states (Tasmania, South Australia, Western Australia, and Queensland) against the two more populous states (Victoria and New South Wales) which dominate the nation. The federal machinery gives the special economic interests in the smaller states a voice but does not really embody any other political or cultural loyalties.

The dominance of class politics and the existence of parliamentary discipline and centralized parties have reduced the significance of a number of federal institutions nominally designed to maintain the voice of the separate states. The federal Senate, for example, has become subject to strong party discipline. The lack of any association of the states with distinctive social groupings—in sharp contrast to Canada (discussed in Chapter 9)—has meant that fed-

---

[13] Charles S. Blackton, "The Dawn of Australian National Feeling, 1850–1856," *Pacific Historical Review*, XXIV (May, 1955), 123, 132. Blackton notes that already "the pattern of Australia's future political life was forming—political cliques based on economic interests, political programs concerned mainly with economic results" (p. 137).

eralism has no obvious remaining justification except administrative, and its functions and desirability are therefore under fairly continuous debate.[14]

One Australian political scientist asserts that "the States no longer correspond with distinct interests or attitudes: there are no longer any solid economic or social foundations for the political divisions within the federal structure. . ." The states are now only political units, "not coherent social and economic groups."[15] Another author disagrees, pointing out that this may be true of the two more populous states, having both financial-industrial and rural centers, and therefore economically "balanced," but not of the other four states, which still possess distinctive local industries (Queensland sugar, Western Australia gold, Tasmania fruit, for example).[16] Whether or not the distinct economic interests of the states require the continuation of federalism does not contradict the assertion that such regionalism as exists is based upon special economic interests and not upon regional subcultures.

The class basis of the argument over federalism is shown by another Australian legal scholar who notes that the arguments for and against increased federal powers:

> increasingly . . . develop into arguments between socialists and anti-socialists. The former tend to favour federal power, because there is a reasonable chance of the ALP securing majorities in both federal houses, with the necessary financial resources and ability to nationalize on a national scale. The anti-socialists, for the same reason, tend to favour state rights.[17]

---

[14] See Brady, *op. cit.*, chaps. vii and viii, and Overacker, *op. cit.*, chap. i, for brief summaries of the Australian governmental system. See also Leslie F. Crisp, *The Parliamentary Government of the Commonwealth of Australia* (3rd ed.; London: Longmans Green, 1961) and Geoffrey Sawer, *Australian Government Today* (Melbourne: Melbourne University Press, 1961).

[15] P. H. Partridge, "The Politics of Federalism" in G. Sawer, ed., *Federalism: An Australian Jubilee Study* (Melbourne: Cheshire, 1952), p. 195. Although the Australian states have consistently been represented in the cabinet, this representation is not as linked with special cultural or economic groups as the parallel kind of "federalization" is in Canada. According to MacKirdy, "none of the Australian portfolios has become associated with a particular state in the manner that fisheries, agriculture and the interior have, at times, been identified with various Canadian regions." See K. A. MacKirdy, "The Federalization of the Australian Cabinet, 1901–1939," *Canadian Journal of Economics and Political Science*, XXIII (May, 1957), 223.

[16] John D. B. Miller, *Australian Government and Politics* (2nd ed.; London: Duckworth, 1959), p. 121.

[17] Sawer, *Australian Government Today, op. cit.*, p. 98.

Even the secession movements that developed have been based not upon nationalist sentiments but upon economic grievances or interests. In 1933, Western Australia voted two-to-one to secede from the federal union, but this vote was probably due to the economic depression at the time, which was wrongly attributed to the defects of the federal government.[18] That the anti-secessionist ALP won the state election soon afterward by a large margin is a sign that the majority for secession was largely a protest against supposedly detrimental Commonwealth economic actions, and not a reflection of strong secessionist sentiments.

In Queensland and New South Wales, there have been persistent sentiments for withdrawal of certain regions from the present states, but these also are based upon economic grievances, mainly of the farmers. The separatist movement in Queensland is supported mainly by sugar growers. In New South Wales, various farmers' associations—and through them the Country party—have supported a new state. This proposal was particularly strong in 1915 and 1916 because of insufficient state expenditures on railways and roads, especially when New South Wales rejected a proposal by Victoria to build new railways into the Riverina area.[19]

The ethnic and social homogeneity of Australia have thus meant that secession and separatist movements in Australia have been based upon economic interests, not upon regional subcultures with distinctive values and a concern for autonomy.

The consequences of this homogeneity for Australian political behavior are summarized by an Australian political scientist in a volume on state politics as follows:

> While for some purposes State boundaries define separate units of political action, yet in all the things which determine the content of political behavior—in their class relations, in their family structure, in the manner in which they gain their wealth, pursue pleasure, instruct their children, worship their gods, in their shibboleths and aspirations, in their dress, speech, diet and interests, there is,

---

[18] See Brady, *op. cit.*, p. 166, and Solomon R. Davis, *The Government of the Australian States* (London: Longmans, Green, 1960), p. 474. Western Canada's secessionist tendencies in the 1930's were also based on economic grievances. See Chapter 9.

[19] See D. R. Hall, "Non-Labour Parties" in Walter G. K. Duncan, ed., *Trends in Australian Politics* (Sydney: Angus & Robertson, 1935), p. 24, and Robert R. Bowie and Carl J. Friedrich, eds., *Studies in Federalism* (Boston: Little, Brown, 1954), p. 772.

despite the great differences in area, vegetation and climate, little
to distinguish the mode of life in Camooweal and Fitzroy Crossing,
in Cairns and Carnarvon, Collie and Collinsville, or Wagga Wagga
and Wagin; and little to mark the passage from the "Banana" State
to the West except for a casual cyclone gate, a modest wooden
bridge, or an elusive stone in the Nullarbor Desert.[20]

A review of the results of public opinion surveys conducted in
Australia from 1941 to 1955 found that very few attitudes varied
from state to state. This review concluded:

> The overwhelming impression which emerges from an analysis
> of some 127 surveys conducted between 1941–55 is the simi-
> larity of State opinion on the majority of questions polled by this
> agency [the Australian Gallup poll, from which the surveys for
> this study were also drawn]. This is particularly so on questions
> touching Australian national feelings, defence and foreign affairs,
> government ownership of industry and a large number of social
> issues such as women's status, criminal punishment and so on. The
> significant cleavages which express themselves on these issues are
> based either on party, occupation, age, sex, town and country resi-
> dence, but rarely the State in which the respondent lives.[21]

The absence of political regionalism is confirmed by the lack of
sharp differences between regions in patterns of class voting in the
Australian states; see Figure 7–2 and Table 7–1. (The data of Table
7–1 are summarized in Table 7–2.) In none of the states is class
voting as low as it is in the United States as a whole, and in South
Australia and Queensland in particular, class voting is as high as or
higher than the British average.

The high level of class voting in South Australia cannot be fully
explained here, but a few suggestions will be offered. The parties
are more polarized in this state than elsewhere in Australia. The
South Australian Labor party has "usually been regarded as a 'left-
wing' party compared with the party in Victoria and New South
Wales."[22] Also, Catholic influence is less marked (South Australia
has the lowest proportion of Catholics of any state), and the DLP
was weaker in South Australia than in any other state except New

---

[20] Solomon R. Davis, "Diversity in Unity," in Davis, *op. cit.*, pp. 560–61.

[21] *Ibid.*, pp. 562–63. The author goes on to qualify this broad conclusion by
citing specific issues and occasions when opinions differed between states.

[22] R. L. Reid *et al.*, "The Government of South Australia," in Davis, *op. cit.*,
p. 366.

FIGURE 7-2

Class Voting in Australian States, 1946–1962

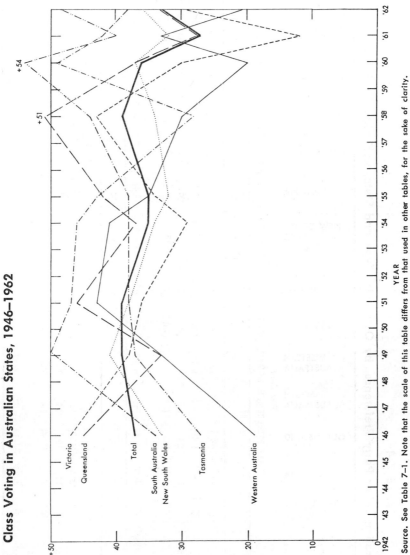

Source. See Table 7–1. Note that the scale of this table differs from that used in other tables, for the sake of clarity.

TABLE 7–1

Australian Labor Party Preference, by Occupation Type and State, Australia, 1946–1961

Per Cent ALP PREFERENCE, SAMPLE NO. 1†

OCCUPATION TYPE	NEW SOUTH WALES	VICTORIA	QUEENSLAND	SOUTH AUSTRALIA	WESTERN AUSTRALIA	TASMANIA	TOTAL*
1946							
Manual	70 (524)§	73 (396)	73 (119)	77 (80)	68 (71)	78 (36)	72 (1226)
Non-Manual	26 (306)	26 (191)	28 (85)	43 (72)	49 (47)	51 (33)	35 (834)
Index of Class Voting	+34	+47	+45	+34	+19	+27	+37
1949‡							
Manual	66 (389)	71 (315)	65 (133)	79 (85)	63 (67)	58 (43)	68 (1032)
Non-Manual	25 (305)	33 (213)	32 (114)	29 (62)	30 (43)	21 (29)	29 (766)
Index of Class Voting	+41	+38	+33	+50	+33	+37	+39

Per Cent ALP PREFERENCE, SAMPLE NO. 2‡

OCCUPATION TYPE	NEW SOUTH WALES	VICTORIA	QUEENSLAND	SOUTH AUSTRALIA	WESTERN AUSTRALIA	TASMANIA	TOTAL*
1946							
Manual	73 (412)	71 (321)	72 (126)	74 (90)	71 (83)	67 (43)	72 (1065)
Non-Manual	35 (319)	30 (221)	24 (119)	42 (67)	43 (47)	41 (29)	33 (802)
Index of Class Voting	+38	+41	+48	+32	+28	+26	+39

TABLE 7-1 (Continued)

ALP PREFERENCE, SAMPLE NO. 1§

Per Cent

1951

	NEW SOUTH WALES	VICTORIA	QUEENSLAND	SOUTH AUSTRALIA	WESTERN AUSTRALIA	TASMANIA	TOTAL*
Manual	67	69	73	77	73	59	69
	(360)	(264)	(130)	(64)	(59)	(59)	(936)
Non-Manual	29	33	27	30	30	21	30
	(309)	(227)	(110)	(69)	(56)	(34)	(805)
Index of Class Voting	+38	+36	+46	+47	+43	+38	+39

ALP PREFERENCE, SAMPLE NO. 2‡

Per Cent

1951

	NEW SOUTH WALES	VICTORIA	QUEENSLAND	SOUTH AUSTRALIA	WESTERN AUSTRALIA	TASMANIA	TOTAL*
Manual	62	68	65	67	53	66	64
	(378)	(308)	(125)	(89)	(73)	(41)	(1014)
Non-Manual	28	35	34	29	26	29	31
	(299)	(215)	(120)	(62)	(47)	(28)	(771)
Index of Class Voting	+34	+32	+31	+33	+27	+37	+33

1954**

	NEW SOUTH WALES	VICTORIA	QUEENSLAND	SOUTH AUSTRALIA	WESTERN AUSTRALIA	TASMANIA	TOTAL*
Manual	68	69	63	74	68	64	68
	(377)	(307)	(130)	(82)	(66)	(45)	(1007)
Non-Manual	34	40	26	28	27	26	33
	(286)	(208)	(117)	(68)	(45)	(31)	(745)
Index of Class Voting	+34	+29	+37	+46	+41	+38	+35

TABLE 7-1—(Continued)

1955

OCCUPATION TYPE	Per Cent ALP PREFERENCE, SAMPLE NO. 1††							Per Cent ALP PREFERENCE, SAMPLE NO. 2‡‡						
	NEW SOUTH WALES	VICTORIA	QUEENSLAND	SOUTH AUSTRALIA	WESTERN AUSTRALIA	TASMANIA	TOTAL	NEW SOUTH WALES	VICTORIA	QUEENSLAND	SOUTH AUSTRALIA	WESTERN AUSTRALIA	TASMANIA	TOTAL
Manual	65 (371)	65 (306)	68 (130)	80 (87)	...	66 (41)	57 (935)	61 (410)	61 (329)	71 (146)	80 (94)	58 (45)	69 (26)	64 (1050)
Non-Manual	30 (273)	35 (204)	33 (109)	36 (64)	...	32 (28)	24 (678)	29 (309)	27 (292)	29 (149)	37 (81)	23 (29)	31 (32)	29 (892)
Index of Class Voting	+35	+30	+35	+44	...	+34	+33	+32	+34	+42	+43	+35	+38	+35

ALP PREFERENCE, SAMPLE §§ October, 1958

OCCUPATION TYPE	NEW SOUTH WALES	VICTORIA	QUEENSLAND	SOUTH AUSTRALIA	WESTERN AUSTRALIA	TASMANIA	TOTAL
Manual	72 (326)	65 (178)	63 (100)	79 (84)	67 (79)	40 (10)	69 (777)
Non-Manual	37 (316)	38 (196)	28 (98)	23 (83)	44 (50)	22 (27)	35 (770)
Index of Class Voting	+35	+27	+35	+56	+23	+18	+34

TABLE 7-1—(Continued)

Per Cent
ALP PREFERENCE, SAMPLE|||
November, 1958

OCCUPATION TYPE	NEW SOUTH WALES	VICTORIA	QUEENSLAND	SOUTH AUSTRALIA	WESTERN AUSTRALIA	TASMANIA	TOTAL
Manual	70 (334)	73 (225)	70 (90)	74 (81)	63 (59)	73 (30)	71 (819)
Non-Manual	36 (280)	30 (237)	19 (95)	46 (67)	33 (43)	29 (31)	32 (753)
Index of Class Voting	+34	+43	+51	+28	+30	+44	+39

Per Cent
ALP PREFERENCE, SAMPLE##
October, 1960

OCCUPATION TYPE	NEW SOUTH WALES	VICTORIA	QUEENSLAND	SOUTH AUSTRALIA	WESTERN AUSTRALIA	TASMANIA	TOTAL
Manual	68 (321)	65 (208)	64 (90)	84 (92)	55 (38)	85 (26)	68 (775)
Non-Manual	31 (283)	35 (208)	27 (91)	35 (66)	30 (60)	31 (29)	32 (737)
Index of Class Voting	+37	+30	+37	+49	+25	+54	+36

ALP PREFERENCE, SAMPLE***
April, 1961

OCCUPATION TYPE	NEW SOUTH WALES	VICTORIA	QUEENSLAND	SOUTH AUSTRALIA	WESTERN AUSTRALIA	TASMANIA	TOTAL
Manual	65 (320)	64 (238)	61 (113)	72 (107)	64 (67)	70 (33)	65 (878)
Non-Manual	33 (279)	52 (196)	34 (94)	30 (64)	31 (45)	30 (23)	38 (701)
Index of Class Voting	+32	+12	+27	+42	+33	+40	+27

ALP PREFERENCE, SAMPLE†††
December, 1961

OCCUPATION TYPE	NEW SOUTH WALES	VICTORIA	QUEENSLAND	SOUTH AUSTRALIA	WESTERN AUSTRALIA	TASMANIA	TOTAL
Manual	71 (394)	65 (262)	74 (128)	75 (118)	59 (81)	66 (35)	69 (1018)
Non-Manual	35 (321)	36 (233)	41 (117)	37 (65)	38 (63)	17 (24)	36 (822)
Index of Class Voting	+36	+29	+33	+38	+21	+49	+33

* Totals are preferences for the ALP and Liberal Country parties only. Total number of respondents is in parentheses.
† Australian Public Opinion Polls (APOP) Survey No. 45, 1946. Occupational categories are as described in Appendix B.
‡ Recomputed from S. R. Davis, ed., The Government of the Australian States (Melbourne: Longmans, Green, 1960), pp. 621 ff. "Manual" includes skilled, semi-skilled, unskilled, and farm laborers. "Non-manual" includes large and small businessmen, professionals, executives, and white-collar employees.
§ See footnote ‡.
** See footnote ‡.
|| APOP Survey No. 83, 1951.
†† See under ‡. Results are not given for Western Australia because of the high proportion of "Undecideds."
‡‡ APOP Survey No. 140, 1960.
APOP Survey No. 115, 1955.
*** APOP Survey No. 149, 1961.
§§ APOP Survey No. 134, 1958.
††† APOP Survey No. 154, 1961.
||| APOP Survey No. 135, 1958.

TABLE 7–2

Rank Order of Class Voting, Australian States

	NUMBER OF SURVEYS IN WHICH THE STATE RANKED:						RANK-INDEX
	1st	2nd	3rd	4th	5th	6th	SCORE*
South Australia	8	2	1	1	0	1	25
Queensland	2	5	1	2	3	0	38
Tasmania	2	3	2	3	1	2	43
New South Wales	0	3	4	4	1	1	45
Victoria	1	1	2	2	4	3	55
Western Australia	0	1	2	1	4	4	56

* The rank-index score was computed by multiplying each rank number by the number of times a state appeared in that rank and adding. The minimum possible score would have been 13, the maximum, 78, if the states had ranked the same in every survey.

Source: Based on data from Table 7–1. Ties were counted twice in a single rank. Not enough cases were available for Western Australia in one survey.

South Wales in both 1958 and 1961 federal elections. Thus, the religious factor does not counteract class influences. The Right parties are also more unified and better organized in South Australia than elsewhere, having succeeded in merging the social elements supporting the Liberal and Country parties elsewhere into the "Liberal and Country League" in 1933. According to D. W. Rawson, this party is "probably the most impressive political organization in Australia."[23] Thus, the ALP has a united political enemy, and there is little "dilution" of the class bases of politics.

As was noted in Chapter 2 (page 45), the rank order of average level of ALP vote has been: South Australia, New South Wales, Tasmania, Victoria, Western Australia, and Queensland. The only important exception to the rank order of class voting is Queensland, which ranks last in ALP voting, but second in class voting.

Gerrymandering in South Australia and Queensland may help account for both findings. On the state level, South Australia is gerrymandered against Labor, Queensland for Labor, so that the Right has held power in the former state, the Left in the latter, for longer than they should have on the basis of votes. The reaction may have been to turn the voters at the federal level away from the

[23] D. W. Rawson, *Australia Votes: The 1958 Federal Election* (Melbourne: Melbourne University Press, 1961), p. 23.

party holding state power, but also to increase class voting in both states.[24]

In most of the surveys, New South Wales and Victoria—the oldest, most populous, and most industrialized states—have lower levels of class voting than the average in the other states. This is parallel to the finding that in Britain the areas both older and more urbanized have a lower level of class voting. Western Australia, the state with possibly the most regional identity, has the lowest level of class voting, on the average.

New South Wales was the "mother colony" of Australia, and probably special sectional loyalties are most closely associated with national identifications in that state. The clear drop of class voting in Victoria is more difficult to explain, and no attempt will be made here. It might be speculated that the special susceptibility to non-class issues which prompted the emergence of the largely Catholic Democratic Labor party first in Victoria might also have something to do with the decline of class voting, but no evidence to support this is available.

The historic grievances of the smaller "claimant" states against the two central states may reinforce "traditional" class loyalties in somewhat the same way in Australia as they do in Wales and Scotland (as suggested in Chapter 6). But, even if this is true (and Western Australia's level of class voting contradicts this inference), this is not regionalism in the sense of a party loyalty overriding the class bases of politics. Class voting in all of the states remains near or above the 30 per cent level, and in no sense does Australia exhibit political regionalism comparable to that in the American South or in Canadian Quebec.

The pattern of decline of class voting evident for Australia as a whole is not found in all the states, except for Victoria, which contributes disproportionately to the over-all figure of class voting. It cannot be easily concluded that the Victorian path is likely to be followed by the other states, and therefore it is too soon to make any firm predictions about trends in class voting in Australia.

---

[24] One might expect that the class denied victory for "its" party would turn away from the other party, but that the class benefitting from the gerrymander would not be alienated. On the other hand, if a sense of political fair play (part of the political culture) prevailed, both strata might react against the "unfair" party.

WHY A RELIGIOUS PARTY EMERGED IN AUSTRALIA

We may now turn to another problem: The emergence of a political party in 1955 largely based upon Catholics. The reason for focusing upon this party is that it deviates from the secular norm in the Anglo-American political systems. Even in Canada, where religion-based loyalties to political parties are strong, no party openly presents itself as a "religious" party. Neither does the DLP. But the emergence of a factional party based upon Catholics and with the support of part of the Catholic hierarchy and lay organizations such as the Catholic Social Movement suggests the possibility that the traditional class bases of Australian politics may be changing. This is not to say that special religious loyalties to parties have not existed. As will be shown, the Irish Catholics have long shown a special affinity for the ALP, but the development of a special party within the Labor tradition drawing support primarily from Catholics is something new. Is this trend a reversal of traditional patterns? Can we expect other religious parties to emerge? Or is this party a phenomenon peculiar to certain conditions within a class-based political system? The following sections will take up these questions.

In 1955, the Democratic Labor party split off from the Australian Labor party.[25] The nascent DLP had two striking characteristics. First, its constituency was three-quarters Catholic. Second, it arose following a dispute, first between part of the Catholic hierarchy and the ALP and then within the ALP, over anti-communist tactics. Part of the church hierarchy supported a ban on the Communist party, while the ALP leadership had just as vigorously opposed a referendum banning that party in 1951. The split occurred despite the high proportion of Catholics among the ALP leadership. Most Catholics have voted ALP since the split, and the DLP has gotten no more than 10 per cent of the popular vote. Nevertheless, in spite of its relatively small vote and its inability to win united Catholic support (either from the hierarchy or the laity), the DLP succeeded in throwing the 1955, 1958, and 1961 federal elections to the Liberal and Country party coalition which has governed the country since 1949.

The importance of the character of DLP support is indicated by

---

[25] The new party changed its name from the Anti-Communist Labor party in 1958 and will henceforth be referred to consistently as the DLP.

two recent studies of Australian elections. One author of a study of a 1960 by-election asserted that "The DLP's capacity to grow (or even survive) is one of the main factors in the contemporary political situation." And another author says that "the significance of the 1958 election results depends very largely on the sources of support for the DLP."[26]

In view of its largely Catholic support and the issue which sparked its emergence, it seems plausible to portray the Democratic Labor party as essentially a religious movement triggered by a volatile non-economic issue and destined to become as firmly institutionalized as the religious difference between Protestants and Catholics. The Australian political scientist T. C. Truman has interpreted the DLP as part of the world-wide movement of Catholic Action (in Australia the Catholic Social Movement) to "transform secular society into the organic society." According to him, the DLP's policies are "based on Catholic social theory, with great emphasis on 'working proprietorship,' 'decentralisation,' 'rural life,' 'family farms,' 'state aid to denominational schools,' and the like."[27]

But this is not the only perspective on the birth and future of the DLP. It may be suggested that although it is religious in its origins and sponsors, the DLP has significant economic roots in the strains of shifting socio-economic status. Rather than a permanent Australian party, the DLP may be a transitional phenomenon with no guaranteed political future.

CATHOLICS AND AUSTRALIAN POLITICS

Catholic allegiance to the ALP originated out of religious and ethnic identifications which reinforced social class as a source of political loyalties. Most Catholic immigrants to Australia have been Irish, with a historic distrust of England. They have also been predominantly working-class, in a country whose upper classes are English Protestant. Thus, the association of Catholics in Australia with the ALP has both class and ethnic origins.[28]

---

[26] Burns, *op. cit.*, p. 95, and Rawson, *Australia Votes, op. cit.*, 6. 237.

[27] Tom C. Truman, "Catholics and Politics in Australia," *Western Political Quarterly*, XXII (June, 1959), 529.

[28] This section is based upon R. N. Spann, "The Catholic Vote in Australia," in Henry Mayer, ed., *Catholics and the Free Society: An Australian Symposium* (Melbourne: Cheshire, 1961). See also Frank C. Langdon, "The Catholic Anti-Communist Role within Australian Labor," *Western Political Quarterly*, IX (December, 1956), 884–99, and Crisp, *op. cit.*, pp. 84–88.

Until the emergence of the largely-Catholic DLP, three-quarters of the Catholics voted ALP, Catholics comprising almost half of the members of that party. They have held many leading positions in both the party and the trade unions; probably about half of the leaders in the latter also are Catholic. In 1951, 55 per cent of the eighty-two members of the Labor parliamentary group in the House of Representatives were Catholic, more than double the proportion of Catholics in the population. Even after the 1955 Labor split, there were more than thirty Catholics among the seventy-one ALP members elected to the House of Representatives in November, 1958. Among the other parties, there are only an estimated four Catholic members of the federal parliament from the Liberal and Country parties, and only two Catholic Liberals in all of the state parliaments together.[29]

But the most striking feature of this situation of Catholic Labor party leadership is that it is *not* due to any continuing preponderance of Catholics among workers. In 1947 the proportion of Catholics among manual workers was the same as the proportion of Catholics among the employed population (about one-fourth). Church of England members were slightly overrepresented in the manual occupations; Presbyterians were slightly underrepresented.[30] In sum, the Catholics are certainly no longer any lower in objective social status than any other religious group. Clearly, then, in recent years class has not been the primary basis for their disproportionate representation in the ALP. Religion and ethnicity (and traditional party loyalty) have continued to cement these ties.

Traditional loyalties to the ALP may have become strained for those socially mobile Catholics for whom the discrepancy between their bettered economic position and the economic policies of their party has become too great to ignore. Mobility and its consequences have been all the more salient under the impact of the rapid but prosperous industrialization of Australia since World War II.[31]

---

[29] Spann, *op. cit.*, p. 121.

[30] Computed from the *Census of the Commonwealth of Australia* (Canberra: Government Printer, June 30, 1947), I, 770. These census data are also cited in an article by Leicester C. Webb, "Churches and the Australian Community," in E. D. French, ed., *Melbourne Studies in Education, 1958–1959* (Melbourne: Melbourne University Press, 1960), pp. 89–131. Webb suggests that DLP support may reflect the higher social status of Catholics after World War II.

[31] Little evidence is available for these hypotheses, particularly on the precise extent of Catholic social mobility in Australia, but studies of social mobility in

Thus, the postwar ALP can be seen as the focus of considerable dissension, much of it due to economic changes. General prosperity produced a conservative mood, but the ALP's program and organizational support have not changed. Its organizational links to the trade unions and its historic allegiance to socialist objectives have bound the ALP to the still-considerable working classes who have yet to share in the new prosperity. Those Catholics who have indeed moved upward have been placed in a peculiar dilemma. Precisely because their loyalty to Labor is partly religious and ethnic in origin, they are also constrained from shifting to the Right as their purely class interests might dictate.

In addition, however, there is another factor which has inhibited the shift of mobile Catholics to the political Right. The political consequences of mobility are not quite the same for Australians as for Americans. Party and class loyalties have always been more solid in Australia than in the United States (although not more so than in Britain) and have formed more stable and explicit points of anchorage in the social system. This is shown by the openly championed ties of the ALP to the trade unions and the long continuity of party strength in most parliamentary seats in both working-class and middle-class areas.[32] As a consequence, there is a constant emphasis on discipline in the parliamentary fraction which is paralleled by a feeling of guilt among loyal voters who "desert" their party—at least more than is likely in the United States.[33] It seems highly likely, then, that the attitudinal basis for ALP voting—sentiments on labor-supported issues, a sense of class consciousness— has changed among some Australians sooner than their ALP vote.

---

various industrial societies have found that it is everywhere about the same. See S. M. Lipset and R. Bendix, *Social Mobility in Industrial Society* (Berkeley: University of California Press, 1959), pp. 29, 49–56. Particularly in "open societies," of which Australia is certainly one, there seems to be reason to believe that Catholics have moved upward in social status as rapidly as any religious group. On the other hand, as was noted in Chapter 5, there are differences in the mechanisms and types of mobility, which may have affected the Australian Catholics.

[32] See W. K. Rolph, "Federal Party Alignments in Australia" (Unpublished manuscript, Dept. of Political Science, Australian National University, Canberra, 1953) and Overacker, *op. cit.*, pp. 303 ff., for evidence on the solidarity of federal seats in Australia. I am indebted to Henry Mayer for the loan of the Rolph manuscript.

[33] This is the Australian tradition of "mateship." See J. D. B. Miller, "Party Discipline in Australia," *Political Science*, V (March, 1953), 3–15, and V (September, 1953), 21–36.

In a sense, a Labor vote might be the last remaining vestige of a person's identity with the working class, or for that matter with the party itself. In the same way, Democratic identifications may constitute for United States southerners a remaining symbol of regional identity.

It was against this background of historic Catholic allegiances to Labor that the DLP emerged in 1955. Its immediate cause was the dispute over ALP tactics toward Communists which was seized upon by Catholic Action and part of the Catholic hierarchy as justifying the split. Nonetheless, we have seen that many Catholics had probably become reluctant supporters of the ALP, remaining Labor because traditional loyalties opposed their new class interests. It is possible then that the communist issue was only the overt reason why some Catholics switched to the DLP, that the new party provided an opportune facade for the transfer of allegiances to a more economically conservative wing of the political labor movement, namely the Democratic Labor party. The cross-pressures upon upwardly mobile Catholics may have been resolved by a simultaneous vote for a "labor" party and a more Rightist party.

BACKGROUND OF THE 1955 SPLIT IN THE AUSTRALIAN LABOR PARTY

As far back as 1948, the associate editor of the *Catholic Weekly* (a religious organ in the archdiocese of Sydney) warned that a "large-scale clash between Catholic public opinion and the Australian Labour party on socialization and other issues is fast approaching a definite showdown." He raised the prospect of an "independent party based on Christian principles," which would be "the equivalent of the M.R.P. in France, the People's Party in Holland, or the Christian Democratic Party in Italy." He predicted, perhaps prophetically, that such a party would not win seats, but that its effects could be serious enough to "throw the Labour party everywhere into the political wilderness for years to come."[34]

The basic accusation made by part of the Catholic hierarchy against the ALP and which eventually led to the 1955 split was that it was "soft" on communism. The list of charges dates from 1941, when the new Labor government under John Curtin legalized the

---

[34] Quoted in Leicester Webb, *Communism and Democracy in Australia* (New York: Praeger, 1955), pp. 98–99.

Communist party (after it had been outlawed the previous year by the Menzies government). In 1949, during the coal strike precipitated by communist-led unions, the Liberal and Country parties demanded that the party be outlawed. Prime Minister Chifley (the Labor head of the government) opposed it just prior to the federal elections that year. The key issues stressed by Labor's opponents in the 1949 election were the "menace of communism" and the slow action by the Chifley government to end the coal strike, although the Labor government finally did break the strike.

These charges were apparently well received, since the opposition Liberal and Country parties were victors in the 1949 election and promptly passed the Communist Party Dissolution Act of 1950. This was declared invalid by the High Court in March, 1951, by a vote of six to one, and was submitted to the people in a referendum in September of that year. The 1951 referendum on the Communist Dissolution Act, opposed by the ALP, was of deep concern to Catholic leadership. However, the hierarchy's advocacy of outlawing communists did not substantially alter the voting of the average Catholic adherent to Labor. He was apparently more influenced by the official ALP position. Survey data show that, among both manual and non-manual workers, Catholics gave the referendum to outlaw communists the least support of any religious group (Table 7–3). *At this time,* the hierarchy's accusations failed to affect the voting behavior of Catholics. Nevertheless, this was another item on the mounting list of instances in which the ALP was insufficiently willing to favor action against communist organizations and allegedly communist ideas.

TABLE 7–3

Support for Referendum Outlawing the Communist Party, by Occupation Type and Religion, Australia, September, 1951

| OCCUPATION TYPE | PER CENT FOR ANTI-COMMUNIST REFERENDUM | | | |
	Methodist	Catholic	Church of England	Presbyterian
Manual	44 (78)*	32 (141)	37 (251)	47 (79)
Non-Manual	65 (84)	69 (86)	77 (266)	76 (83)

* Total number of respondents is in parentheses.
Source: APOP Survey No. 83.

The situation did not lead to an open break of the Catholic leadership with the ALP until 1954. Until that point, the ALP had continued to cooperate with the Catholics in an attempt to eliminate communist influence from the trade unions. High ALP and union officials had asked the help of the church in defeating the communists during World War II. The Communist party, by controlling most of the important industrial unions in Australia, came close to controlling the Labor party in 1942 and 1943.[35] The Labor party itself, in cooperation with the church, set up "industrial groups" patterned after communist cells which eliminated communist influence in ALP branches in Victoria by 1953. Catholic Action sponsored some of these "groups" within the unions. But the issue of anti-communism united more than just the Catholics.[36]

The ideology of the industrial groups is reflected in the following statement:

> The ideas which the Industrial Groupers have channelled into the Labor movement are the importance of increasing production and the possibility of establishing a productivity index as a measure of wages; the defence of democratic methods in the government of unions, the need for trade unionism to develop methods of joint consultation; decentralisation; the revival and development of Australian agriculture; resistance to Communist expansion, especially in Asia; closer relations and greater dependence on America.[37]

By 1953 these "groups" had almost gained control of the federal ALP, through control of the vital Victorian state executive and strong positions in the state parties of New South Wales and Queensland. According to T. C. Truman, "they would have done this if they had put their motion for making the Industrial Group organization national in scope." Moreover: "Fearing that they could not quite muster a majority of delegates [to the 1954 Federal Conference of the ALP] they deferred the key motion to the 1955 conference."[38]

---

[35] Since the trade unions control the majority of votes in Labor party ruling bodies, control of the trade unions is the key to control of the party.

[36] See also Herbert E. Weiner, "The Reduction of Communist Power in the Australian Trade Unions: A Case Study," *Political Science Quarterly*, LXIX (September, 1954), 390–412.

[37] Quoted from an article by Lloyd Ross in the *Sydney Morning Herald* (January 14, 1955) in an exchange of letters between the Catholic lay leader B. A. Santamaria and a critic of the DLP, Professor H. W. Arndt, in "The Catholic Social Movement," *Australian Journal of Politics and History*, II (May, 1957), 182.

[38] Truman, *op. cit.*, p. 534.

Before the 1955 Conference, however, events rapidly and dramatically changed course. As of 1953, the Catholics, by replacing sufficient communists in the union leadership, had gained considerable leverage themselves. Again, since the unions were the chief bases of power within the ALP, the Catholics threatened to win the war for the party while nearly winning the battle for the unions. Accordingly, ALP federal leader Herbert Evatt removed the Catholic leaders of the Victorian branch of the ALP from office, thereby precipitating the Labor split.

THE FORMATION OF A NEW PARTY

After the largely Catholic leadership of the Victorian Labor party was replaced with "loyalists," the former state executive and members of the "groups" formed the nucleus of the Democratic Labor party. In the December, 1955, federal election, it won over 15 per cent of the popular vote in Victoria (one-third of the Labor vote) and a large proportion of the Catholic vote.[39]

Of the seven ex-Labor members of the federal parliament leading the new party, six were Catholics. The sole Protestant, Mr. Joshua, became the official Leader. Of the seven Victorian Labor representatives who remained in the federal ALP, only two were Catholics. These two loyalists were Mr. Calwell, then Deputy Leader of the federal ALP (Leader, since Mr. Evatt resigned in 1960), who took no part in the purges of the industrial groups, and Mr. Peters, who abandoned the groups at the last minute.

Following its emergence in 1955, the DLP rapidly extended its organization within the Australian electorate. Although it ran candidates only in Victoria in 1955, by 1958 the DLP ran in federal constituencies in all of the six states except South Australia. This extension was aided by the traditional centralization of the Australian parties, by the presence of enough Catholics in almost every state, and by the system of preferential balloting for members of the lower house. This ballot requires electors to indicate ordered

---

[39] The Catholic hierarchy has been seriously split over the new party. One of its leading supporters has been Archbishop Mannix of Melbourne, whose Irish birthplace may account for his greater identification with the Catholics as a militant, politically-involved "out-group." Cardinal Gilroy of New South Wales, a native Australian, opposed the new party, favoring the traditional position of the church that a Catholic may support any party except the Communist, and holding that Catholics should fight within the Labor party. The DLP vote has been lower in New South Wales than in any other state.

preferences for each position in the lower house. If an absolute majority of first preferences is not obtained, second and perhaps third preferences are counted. This encourages minor parties since they can reap protest votes without endangering the major party to which they are closest. In this sense, both the Country party and the DLP may be creatures of the Australian electoral system.

But what have been the political effects of the DLP? Despite the fact that it has in no way threatened to gain dominance in either Labor ranks or the federal government, the DLP has ruined the electoral chances of the ALP. In 1955, the strength of the DLP in the important state of Victoria probably prevented the ALP from winning the 1955 federal election. The *News Weekly,* which often speaks for the Catholic Social Movement, said of the DLP after that election:

> It probably prevented the national disaster of an Evatt Government. The Communist Party will never rule this nation by remote control, pulling the strings of a puppet Labor government.[40]

Also in 1955, the DLP affected the Victorian state elections to the Legislative Assembly. In May, 1955, the second preferences of the DLP (called the Barry Labor party in this instance) led to the downfall of the state Labor government. The Liberal and Country coalition got six seats out of the eighteen which were affected by second preferences. All except one dissident Labor candidate lost— out of forty-four running in sixty-five constituencies.[41]

Again in 1958, the DLP damaged Labor chances at both the federal and state levels. In the federal election, the ALP could have won only if it had gotten every DLP second preference, a "totally unrealistic assumption." Instead, however, most DLP second preferences went to Liberals rather than to the ALP. This was true of 88 per cent of the DLP second preferences in Victoria and 60 per cent in both New South Wales and Tasmania, for example.[42]

Turning to the state level, the Hawke Labor government in Western Australia was ousted in 1959, also because of seats lost on DLP preferences. The DLP contested seventeen state electorates in

[40] Truman, *op. cit.,* p. 528.

[41] See Creighton Burns, "Victoria" from the "Australian Political Chronicle," a regular section of the *Australian Journal of Politics and History,* I (November, 1955), 110–11.

[42] D. W. Rawson, "The Commonwealth," *Australian Journal of Politics and History,* V (May, 1959), 92.

this election, and in four, the second preferences of DLP supporters went to the Liberal-Country coalition. This provided the coalition with its margin of victory over the ALP: twenty-seven seats to twenty-three.[43]

Again in the December 9, 1961 federal election, DLP preferences made some difference in the outcome of the election. Despite a 5 per cent swing to the ALP and its gain of fifteen seats, the Liberal-Country coalition emerged with a majority of two seats, thanks to three won on DLP preferences.[44]

There was no substantial decline in DLP votes in the 1961 election except in Queensland and Western Australia, where its vote dropped over one-third. In Victoria and South Australia its vote rose very slightly, to 15 per cent in the former state.[45]

As these examples attest, the DLP is a movement to be reckoned with even though it is not a real competitor for governmental power in its own right. The DLP has been chiefly an opposition movement hoping to force concessions upon the Labor party, as shown at least by the avowed intentions of the Protestant Federal President, Mr. Joshua. In a speech at the Third Commonwealth Conference of the party in 1959, he said:

> Australia has traditionally been a two-party nation. One of these two parties has always been the Labor Party. Our aim is to unite all whose objectives are fundamentally the same as ours, and to be that Labor party. It has never been our primary purpose to create a permanent third party.[46]

Upon closer examination, this goal of labor unity may be more a reflection of the two-party "norm" than the actual function of the

---

[43] See F. K. Crowley, *State Election* (Perth, published by author, June, 1959), and the same author's notes on the political situation in Western Australia in the *Australian Journal of Politics and History,* V (November, 1959), 243–45.

[44] Joan Rydon, "Some Aspects of Voting in the 1961 Elections," *Australian Journal of Politics and History,* VIII (May, 1962), 98–101. The author cautions that majority voting in place of preferential voting would have changed the pattern of votes, so that it cannot be concluded that the ALP would have won under a different electoral system.

[45] Arguments such as those made in this chapter concerning the character of DLP support need not, of course, apply to all DLP voters. Some of the DLP's support in Victoria may stem from its having been able to convince part of the ALP electorate that it is the legitimate heir of the "Labor party" mantle, since its Victorian leadership came directly from the ALP.

[46] Quoted in Spann, *op. cit.,* p. 141.

DLP. One consequence of the new party's formation may be to alienate ALP supporters who distrust a split, no matter what its origins and ultimate goals. Many working-class people with solid labor loyalties but few ideological concerns feel that there should be a solid labor front. Both Catholics and non-Catholics among this group would rather see a united labor party (regardless of its policies) than the factionalism now evident.

Some evidence of this type of loss of support is apparent from public opinion data. Of the 56 per cent of the electorate not giving their first preferences to the ALP in 1959, 8 per cent would have done so if the party had been united.[47] Presumably a sizable portion of these would have done so regardless of the basis for reunification, whether on Catholic or Evatt terms. This, if true, would demonstrate the dominance of traditional party loyalties over actual issues or the appeal of candidates.

But there is another, more important sense in which the actual function of the DLP may be to reduce the ALP ranks rather than simply to reunite them on more conservative grounds. Unlike the major parties, the DLP was especially concerned with the issues of socialism and communism, on both the federal and state levels. In the federal elections since 1954, these issues were no longer a major point of debate between the major parties. The DLP, however, took steadfast stands against communist influence in the ALP and the trade unions and for the continued non-recognition of Communist China. In the state elections, the DLP raised single-handedly the issue of the ownership of control of new businesses by the state government.[48]

The "Center" character of DLP ideology is indicated by the arguments of its Queensland branch (the Queensland Labor party) in the state campaign of 1960 that Queensland was being squeezed by "monopoly capitalism on the one hand and Marxist inspired socialism on the other."[49]

The ideology of such a Catholic Center party is expressed by a

---

[47] Australian Public Opinion Polls release, February–April, 1959.

[48] This is the view of the 1959 Western Australian state election held by the Australian political scientist D. W. Rawson. See his review of F. K. Crowley, *State Election, op. cit.,* in the *Australian Journal of Politics and History,* V (November, 1959), 263–64.

[49] Charles Grimshaw, "Queensland," in Australian Political Chronicle," *Australian Journal of Politics and History,* VI (November, 1960), 241.

Catholic scholar in a book written soon after World War II. He stressed that the new middle class could be a force superseding class conflicts, and emphasized the concept of "vocational communities" integrated with an organic state in a "natural" hierarchy, resulting in "neither capitalism nor socialism, but something in between."[50] Clearly the leadership and ideology which could give rise to parties like the religious ones of continental Europe exist in Australia; the crucial question is whether the cultural and political conditions which can translate the raw materials into a viable party also exist.

While the issues of communism and socialism have long been the concern of the Catholic church and the demonstrated ideology of DLP spokesmen, it is questionable whether they presage either a shift in ALP policy, or more importantly, a return to the ALP by DLP supporters even in the event of such a shift. As suggested earlier, many Catholic DLP adherents may have been uncomfortable within the ALP because of the social mobility which left no economic basis for their allegiance to the ALP. It may be that the issue of communism was especially significant since it provided an essentially non-economic avenue for withdrawal from the party. This is all the more likely since the DLP was supported by part of the Catholic hierarchy—and Catholicism was one of the original non-economic reasons for allegiance to the DLP.

We are suggesting, then, that the DLP, with its special emphasis on communism and its support from part of the Catholic hierarchy, has had a latent effect. Perhaps in addition to forcing reunification of the ALP on these terms, it has also served as a transition stage for the switching of political allegiances of a sizable number of upwardly mobile and therefore "restive" former members of the ALP. If this is so, the high percentage of DLP second preferences going to the Liberal party may indicate that this group may identify with that party in the future, and not simply that they are presently in strategic opposition to the ALP. The DLP may turn out to be a "temporary" party not because of a future return of its voters to the ALP but because many of its supporters will go on to the Liberal party.

Thus, neither is the DLP a purely religious movement. In fact, it appears to be a mechanism for readjusting the class alignment for

[50] James G. Murtagh, *Australia: The Catholic Chapter* (New York: Sheed & Ward, 1946), pp. 246–49.

Australian politics as a whole by severing the religious and ethnic ties of the mobile Catholics to the ALP.

If these interpretations are correct, they should be supported by data on the socio-economic status of voters from surveys taken during this period. That is, we should find that the DLP did not simply draw support from Catholics in general but rather those particular Catholics who were at odds with typical ALP supporters in their class status. First, however, the general effect of religion upon class voting in Australia will be considered.

RELIGION AND CLASS VOTING

Class voting is higher among Protestants than Catholics in Australia, as it is in the other Anglo-American countries in most surveys. This is shown in Figure 7–3 (based on Table 7–4). In Australia, in contrast to Great Britain, the Catholic deviation is due to a higher Labor vote among both strata, and especially among

TABLE 7–4

Australian Labor Party Preference, by Religion and Occupation Type, Australia, 1951–1961

| OCCUPATION TYPE | PER CENT PREFERRING ALP | | | INDEX OF RELIGIOUS VOTING |
	Catholic	Protestant	Total	
		September, 1951		
Manual	82 (194)*	64 (663)	69 (857)	+18
Non-Manual	48 (126)	25 (600)	29 (726)	+23
TOTAL	69 (320)	46 (1,263)		+23
Index of				
Class Voting	+34	+39	+40	
		December, 1955		
Manual	77 (217)	60 (731)	64 (948)	+17
Non-Manual	42 (160)	25 (656)	28 (816)	+17
TOTAL	52 (377)	44 (1,387)		+8
Index of				
Class Voting	+35	+35	+ 36	

TABLE 7–4—(Continued)

Australian Labor Party Preference, by Religion and Occupation Type, Australia, 1951–1961

OCCUPATION TYPE	PER CENT PREFERRING ALP			INDEX OF RELIGIOUS VOTING
	Catholic	Protestant	Total	
October, 1958				
Manual	67 (207)	61 (569)	63 (776)	+6
Non-Manual	40 (172)	31 (595)	33 (767)	+9
TOTAL	55 (379)	46 (1,164)		+9
Index of				
Class Voting	+27	+30	+30	
November, 1958				
Manual	86 (156)	67 (593)	71 (749)	+19
Non-Manual	48 (114)	28 (573)	31 (687)	+20
TOTAL	70 (270)	59 (1166)		+11
Index of				
Class Voting	+38	+39	+40	
October, 1960				
Manual	77 (155)	65 (550)	68 (705)	+12
Non-Manual	45 (121)	28 (555)	31 (676)	+17
TOTAL	63 (276)	47 (1105)		+16
Index of				
Class Voting	+32	+37	+37	
April, 1961				
Manual	76 (181)	62 (626)	65 (807)	+14
Non-Manual	49 (136)	34 (504)	37 (640)	+15
TOTAL	64 (317)	50 (1130)		+14
Index of				
Class Voting	+27	+28	+28	
December, 1961				
Manual	74 (238)	68 (681)	69 (919)	+6
Non-Manual	55 (135)	31 (598)	35 (733)	+24
TOTAL	67 (373)	50 (1279)		+17
Index of				
Class Voting	+19	+37	+34	

* Total number of respondents is in parentheses.
Source: APOP Surveys Nos. 83, 115, 134, 135, 140, 149, 154.

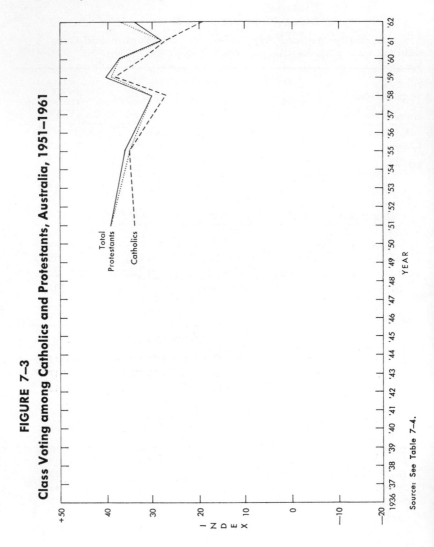

FIGURE 7–3

Class Voting among Catholics and Protestants, Australia, 1951–1961

Source: See Table 7–4.

persons in non-manual occupations. This is a manifestation of religious voting similar to that to be shown in the United States and Canada. Table 7–4 shows that "religious voting" is usually more marked among persons in non-manual occupations than among workers, and that it vacillates considerably. No evidence of either a decline or an increase is indicated.

In order to examine the support for the Democratic Labor party (its vote is omitted from the figures given in Table 7–4), the basic data for Catholics and for the several Protestant denominations will be analyzed in more detail. Table 7–5 shows the support different religious groups gave to "labor" (both ALP and DLP) parties from 1951 to 1961. The support for the DLP is shown separately and then combined with the ALP vote for an over-all "labor" figure.

Clear differences in the patterns of support for the ALP by different religious groups, as well as the changes since 1951, are shown in Table 7–5. The total "labor" vote by the Catholics re-

TABLE 7–5

"Labor" Parties Preference, by Religion, Australia, 1951–1961

	PER CENT PREFERRING "LABOR" PARTIES						
RELIGION	1951	1955			1958		
	ALP	ALP	DLP*	Total Labor†	ALP	DLP	Total Labor
Catholic	69 (320)‡	54	18	72 (454)	52	23	75 (438)
Church of England	49 (749)	43	2	45 (813)	42	4	46 (831)
Presbyterian	40 (229)	38	0	38 (243)	40	4	44 (292)
Methodist	51 (220)	45	3	48 (285)	40	2	42 (451)

	OCTOBER, 1960			APRIL, 1961			DECEMBER, 1961		
RELIGION	ALP	DLP	Total Labor†	ALP	DLP	Total Labor	ALP	DLP	Total Labor
Catholic	53	15	68 (325)	58	10	68 (354)	58	14	72 (434)
Church of England	46	3	49 (678)	51	1	52 (693)	53	2	55 (736)
Presbyterian	42	2	44 (218)	42	2	44 (189)	43	2	45 (274)
Methodist	50	2	52 (209)	48	2	50 (240)	48	3	51 (269)

* The actual DLP vote has consistently been considerably more than that found by APOP surveys of the Australian electorate, and this introduces an unpredictable bias into all of the data here presented. These results are presented in this way with the assumption that those DLP voters who do answer may be typical of those who in this way may be typical of those who do not in their church attendance. See the Melbourne *Herald*, May 3, 1961, for a DLP attack on the Gallup poll for its inaccuracy, and for the Gallup answer, by Mr. Roy Morgan, Director.

† ALP plus DLP equals "Total Labor."

‡ Total number of respondents is in parentheses.

Sources: APOP Surveys Nos. 83, 115, 134, 140, 149, 154.

mained at about two-thirds of all Catholics in this period, and was the highest for any religious group. A big change came with the switch of almost one-fifth of the Catholics to the DLP in 1955. The support of the other religious groups for "labor" parties remained about the same. The new party has not won more than 4 per cent of any non-Catholic group's support in any election from 1955 to 1961. The ALP's support dropped precipitously among the Catholics when the DLP appeared on the political scene, but the ALP in the later surveys still received more support from the Catholics than from any other religious group.

These results are not due to the proportions of manual workers in each religious group. When manual and non-manual workers are examined separately (Table 7–6), Catholics are still far more likely to vote "labor" than any other religious group. As one would expect from the dominance of class politics in Australia, the manual workers in each religious group support the ALP far more than their non-manual brethren, but the Catholics are more heavily "labor" in all strata.

Table 7–6 shows the shifts in the proportions of persons in different religions in manual and non-manual occupations who have preferred one of the "labor" parties. Among manual Catholics, the total "labor" vote (both ALP and DLP) has vacillated but dropped below 80 per cent finally in 1961. Among non-manual Catholics, the total "labor" support has actually increased, although not evenly, from 48 per cent in 1951 to 65 per cent in 1961. Even if the DLP vote is disregarded, however, the ALP vote of Catholics is still higher than that among Protestant denominations (in both strata).

The increase of the over-all "labor" vote among non-manual Catholics implies that some Catholics have moved *back* into "labor" ranks. Given a choice between a Right secular party (the Liberals), a Left secular party (the ALP), and a rightist religious party (the DLP) maintaining the "Labor" name, some non-manual Catholics have chosen the latter. Table 7–6 shows that the proportion of non-manual Catholics voting DLP has ranged from 10 to 26 per cent from 1955 to 1961, while the percentage of manual Catholics voting DLP has actually declined fairly consistently. Many Australian Catholics—both manual and non-manual—seem to be voting according to their religion and according to the political tradition with which that religion has been associated.

Thus, although the DLP represents a move to the Right within

TABLE 7–6

"Labor" Parties Preference, by Occupation Type and Religion, Australia, 1951–1961

OCCUPATION TYPE	PER CENT PREFERRING "LABOR" PARTIES						
	1951	*1955*			*1958*		
	ALP	ALP	DLP	*Total Labor*	ALP	DLP	*Total Labor*
*Manual**							
Catholic	82 (194)†	63	18	81 (265)	67	21	88 (207)
Church of England	69 (401)	59	2	61 (437)	61	5	66 (366)
Presbyterian	59 (112)	53	0	53 (123)	62	5	67 (106)
Methodist	63 (111)	65	3	68 (151)	66	5	71 (106)
Non-Manual‡							
Catholic	48 (126)	35	15	50 (189)	40	26	66 (172)
Church of England	22 (348)	25	2	27 (376)	29	2	31 (348)
Presbyterian	22 (117)	22	0	22 (120)	32	2	34 (120)
Methodist	39 (109)	23	3	26 (134)	31	1	32 (118)

OCCUPATION TYPE	*October, 1960*			*April, 1961*			*December, 1961*		
	ALP	DLP	*Total Labor*	ALP	DLP	*Total Labor*	ALP	DLP	*Total Labor*
Manual									
Catholics	69	11	80 (175)	68	10	78 (202)	67	9	76 (261)
Church of England	67	3	70 (338)	67	1	68 (368)	70	2	72 (402)
Presbyterian	58	3	61 (106)	47	2	49 (97)	60	4	64 (118)
Methodist	58	3	61 (115)	60	1	61 (151)	61	3	64 (161)
Non-Manual									
Catholics	36	19	55 (150)	44	10	54 (152)	43	22	65 (173)
Church of England	26	1	27 (340)	34	2	36 (325)	31	2	33 (334)
Presbyterian	27	2	29 (112)	36	1	37 (92)	29	1	30 (156)
Methodist	39	1	40 (94)	27	2	29 (89)	27	3	30 (108)

* Include skilled, semi-skilled, unskilled, and farm laborers.
† Total number of respondents is in parentheses.
‡ Non-manual workers include professionals, persons in large and small businesses, executives, clerks, and shop assistants. Farm owners are excluded. Totals include "don't knows."
Source: APOP Surveys Nos. 83, 115, 134, 140, 149, 154.

the "labor" tradition, the evidence does not show a decline of the "religious" vote per se. If it can be shown, however, that the Catholic manual workers who deserted the ALP for the DLP are in higher income positions than those who did not leave the ALP, or if DLP voters are more likely to be socially mobile or in non-manual occupations, then there are grounds for regarding the new party as —in function at least—a transition party enabling newly-middle-class Catholics to break their traditional ALP allegiances.

THE SOCIAL BASE OF THE DEMOCRATIC LABOR PARTY

The DLP, as has been shown, drew a large minority of the Catholics from both manual and non-manual strata over to its side in both 1955 and 1958.[51] The occupations of DLP supporters show that the new party draws disproportionately from persons in non-manual occupations, particularly from clerks. The greater appeal of the DLP in 1958 to lower-middle-class persons, especially among Catholics, is shown by Table 7–7, which compares the occupational composition of the DLP and ALP support for both Church of England members and Catholics. Half of the Catholic DLP supporters were in non-manual occupations, and most of these were clerks. By contrast, only about one-third of Catholic and Church of England ALP supporters were in non-manual occupations, and only a quarter of Church of England DLP supporters were non-manual workers.[52] Examining the manual supporters of the parties, it appears that those supporting the DLP are weighted toward the more skilled side. Only 7 per cent of the Catholic DLP supporters were unskilled workers, as compared to between 15 and 26 per cent of the other groups. Thus, the DLP drew disproportionate support from the upper strata of the working class and the lower strata of the middle class in 1958. The lack of similarity of Church of England DLP supporters to Catholic DLP supporters underlines the

---

[51] Party workers, at least in the Brisbane constituency in 1958, were also clearly differentiated by religion. Catholics comprised 8 per cent of the Liberal activitists, 33 per cent of ALP workers, and 82 per cent of QLP workers. (Rawson, *Australia Votes, op. cit.*, p. 211.)

[52] The DLP's few Church of England supporters may have been mainly manual workers voting for it because of some grievance against the ALP and a simultaneous desire to vote for another "labor" party. For these workers, the DLP may serve as an outlet for political grievances in the same way that the Liberal party in England does.

TABLE 7–7

Occupational Composition of ALP and DLP Vote, by Religion, Australia, 1958

	RELIGION			
OCCUPATION	Catholic		Church of England	
	DLP Voters	ALP Voters	DLP Voters	ALP Voters
		(Per Cent)		
Non-Manual				
Professional	.. ⎫	1 ⎫	.. ⎫	1 ⎫
Big Business	5 ⎬ 50	4 ⎬ 34	11 ⎬ 26	6 ⎬ 32
Small Business	1 ⎮	3 ⎮	.. ⎮	4 ⎮
Clerical	44 ⎭	26 ⎭	15 ⎭	21 ⎭
Manual				
Skilled	26 ⎫	26 ⎫	22 ⎫	34 ⎫
Semi-Skilled	16 ⎬ 50	21 ⎬ 66	11 ⎬ 74	16 ⎬ 68
Unskilled	7 ⎮	15 ⎮	26 ⎮	15 ⎮
Farm Labor	1 ⎭	4 ⎭	15 ⎭	3 ⎭
Total Per Cent	100 100	100 100	100 100	100 100
Number	(88)	(207)	(27)	(324)

Of the nine Presbyterians and the six Methodists supporting the DLP in this sample, 67 per cent were manual workers. Farm owners were excluded. This table is presented differently from the preceding ones because only 3 per cent (27 cases) of the Church of England members in the total sample voted DLP.

Source: APOP Survey No. 134.

special appeal of the DLP to particular socio-economic strata among the Catholics.[53]

Up to now only the status characteristics of DLP voters have been examined. It is possible that the finding that DLP voters were largely in lower middle-class and skilled working-class occupations is due to a switch to the DLP of many middle-class persons who voted Liberal in the past. If so, the DLP is not a breakaway from

[53] If former Labor voters in the 1955 survey are examined, the same occupational difference appears. Of Catholic supporters for the DLP in 1955 who had voted in 1954, 66 per cent were in either lower non-manual or skilled occupations, only 20 per cent in semi-skilled and unskilled occupations. Of Protestant ex-Laborites supporting the new party, 35 per cent were in lower non-manual and skilled occupations, 50 per cent in semi-skilled and unskilled occupations. It must be emphasized that we have no evidence that these skilled workers and clerks were socially mobile themselves (or that they were not responding on the basis of their religion).

the ALP (except a breakaway of the leadership), but may represent only the *return* of many Catholics to a labor party which can
also represent their religious and anti-communist sentiments. Table
7–8 provides some evidence that this is not true. Even when we
examine Catholic voters reporting that they switched from the ALP
to the new party, we still find that the new party draws largely
from lower non-manual and skilled working-class occupations.
Among Catholics only, as Table 7–8 shows, switchers from ALP to
the DLP were more likely to be in those occupations than were
solid ALP voters. Of the Catholic 1954 ALP voters who switched
to the DLP in 1955, 66 per cent in 1955 were in either lower non-
manual or skilled occupations, as compared to 56 per cent of the
solid ALP supporters. Thus, even among Catholic former ALP
voters, the DLP voters are in higher status occupations than the
ALP voters. And practically no one switched from Liberal to DLP.

A last check on the validity of the socio-economic differences
between the supporters of the ALP and the DLP is the study of
the relationship between occupation, income level, and switching
from ALP to DLP from 1954 to 1955, among Catholics. Table 7–9
shows that even within selected working-class occupations, Catholic
switchers to the new party were better-off economically than Catholics remaining loyal to the ALP. Among skilled workers, 4 per cent
of Catholic switchers as compared to 12 per cent of Catholic loyalists were in the lowest income category. Among unskilled workers,
13 per cent of Catholic switchers as compared to 29 per cent of
Catholic loyalists were in the lowest income category. Thus, the
DLP seems to have had a special appeal to workers slightly better
off than the average ALP voters, as well as a special appeal to
clerks, as already shown.

Thus, by a variety of measures it has been shown that DLP supporters are in better socio-economic positions than ALP supporters.
It seems justified, therefore, to infer that the party is probably supported by many upwardly mobile Catholics, although little direct
evidence on the mobility of these voters is available. The only available evidence is from a survey of political opinions in a suburban
area of Melbourne, Victoria, the core of support for the DLP. The
results may not be generalizable to Australia as a whole, but the
difference between ALP and DLP voters is striking. Asked how
their "financial position" compared with that of "four or five years
ago," DLP voters were much more inclined than ALP voters to say

TABLE 7–8

Occupational Composition of Solid Voters and Switchers, among Catholics, Australia, 1955*

1954 VOTE	1955 VOTE	OCCUPATION						
		NON-MANUAL		MANUAL		FARM	TOTAL	Number
		Upper	Lower	Skilled	Unskilled *(Per Cent)*			
ALP	ALP	6	22	34	33	6	101	(229)
ALP	Liberal or Country	32	18	14	9	27	100	(22)
ALP	DLP	3	31	35	20	11	100	(74)
Liberal or Country	Liberal or Country	28	31	14	14	14	101	(132)

Source: APOP Survey No. 115, December, 1955.
* Only four persons switched from Liberal or Country to Labor. Retrospective reports are notoriously unreliable, and this evidence must be viewed only as supporting the main argument, not as an independent finding.

TABLE 7–9

Income Level among Catholic Skilled and Unskilled Workers, by 1954 and 1955 Vote, Australia, 1955*

		POOREST INCOME CATEGORY			
1954 VOTE	1955 VOTE	Catholic Skilled Workers		Catholic Unskilled Workers	
		(Per Cent)			
ALP	DLP	4	(26)	13	(15)
ALP	ALP	12	(77)	29	(75)

Source: APOP Survey No. 115, December, 1955.
* Farm and mining areas are excluded. The criteria for income category are those established by Australian Public Opinion Polls. The interviewer determined whether the home has a telephone or a car, and judged the "home, apparent education and demeanor." Since a difference of two cases matters here, the only significance of this table is that it is in accord with pre-existing expectations.

"better," and none said "worse," as Table 7–10 shows. Whether DLP voters were *actually* better off is irrelevant. That they think they are is the crucial fact which may be changing their political loyalties.

In summary, therefore, as D. W. Rawson, the author of a book on the 1958 Australian federal election, puts it, "there seems to be little which is specifically Labour about either DLP membership or the DLP vote . . . its vote comes predominantly and increasingly from

TABLE 7–10

Opinions of Australian Voters on How Their "Financial Position Now Compares with That of Four or Five Years Ago," by Party, West Heidelberg, Victoria, Australia, 1960

OPINION OF FINANCIAL POSITION	LIBERALS	DLP	ALP	ALL VOTERS
		(Per Cent)		
Better Off	61	58	35	46
Same	35	42	38	37
Worse Off	4	. .	27	16
Total Per Cent	100	100	100	99
Total Number	(27)	(12)	(61)	(100)

Source: A survey conducted by members of the West Heidelberg Branch, ALP, in May, 1960. Reported in "Political Opinions: The Darebin Survey," *APSA News*, V (1960), p. 2. DLP voters were also slightly more likely to be in an "above average" income category than ALP voters, although the difference is insignificant, given the small number of cases.

the middle social strata."[54] The leaders as well as the supporters of the DLP are disproportionately of the lower middle class. Most of the few full-time officials are men in their early thirties, who did not experience the depression, and come from lower-middle-class backgrounds. The state presidents are mostly middle-class Catholics. Also, of the six unions affiliated to the DLP, five are lower-middle-class (the Clerks, Teachers, Manufacturing Grocers, Carpenters and Joiners, and Ironworkers).[55]

A 1960 survey in the Victorian constituency of La Trobe (in a by-election) found that the DLP's strongest occupational support came from "the white collar group (39 percent), which, together with the small businessmen (11 percent) and the managers and professionals (10 percent) gave the DLP vote its middle class colour."[56] Two-thirds of the DLP voters were Catholic. Burns summarizes the profile of the characteristic DLP voter as the "skilled or white collar worker, younger and better educated than the average, and most probably a conscientious Roman Catholic."[57] Of special interest in the present connection is Burns's finding that almost none of those intending to vote DLP had voted ALP in 1958. This indicates that there were no further moves away from the ALP since the election—that, therefore, the DLP had its greatest effect upon a specific and susceptible group of middle-class Catholics and was not growing past that point, at least by recruitment from the ALP. Whether the party could sustain itself by recruiting from Liberal Catholics, or by establishing itself as a center-Left or center-Right party without a distinctive religious base is, of course, another question.[58]

RELIGION AND PROSPECTS FOR THE DLP

Showing the socio-economic differences between party supporters does not imply, of course, that there is no religious basis for the

[54] Quoted by Spann, *op. cit.*, p. 134, from D. W. Rawson, "The Elections and How To Go On Losing Them," *Outlook*, III (January, 1959), 2.

[55] Henry Mayer, "The DLP Today: Facts and Hunches," *The Observer* (June 25, 1960), p. 1.

[56] Burns, *op. cit.*, p. 92.

[57] *Ibid.*, p. 93.

[58] For a view of the DLP parallel to that presented here, see Rawson, *Australia Votes, op. cit.*, pp. 6–7, 237–38. Rawson notes that the loyalty of many Catholics to the ALP was "a loyalty which for increasing numbers of them seemed to be in defiance of their class interests" (p. 6).

DLP. As already shown in Table 7–6, the DLP has probably pulled some non-manual Catholics away from a non-Labor vote. DLP supporters are much less secularized in their approach to politics than either the Liberals or the Laborites, according to evidence from another Australian public opinion survey. Of the DLP supporters in a 1960 survey, 62 per cent believed that church leaders did *not* have the right to tell their members they must not vote for certain political parties, as compared to 90 per cent of Liberal and Country party supporters, and 88 per cent of Labor supporters.[59]

The relatively low figure of 62 per cent can also be regarded as evidence of the imperfect isolation of the DLP supporters from the secular norm of the Anglo-American political systems. Fully 62 per cent believed that church leaders did not have the right to instruct their members politically, to turn the implication around. The figure shows therefore not only the difference between DLP supporters and persons supporting the older parties, but also the incomplete identification of the party with the church. According to Henry Mayer, the label "church party" would be fatal for the DLP, and this:

> speaks volumes about the secularization of Australian society and about what people involved in the struggle believe public opinion to be. If there were such a Church party, it would split the Catholics and the Church itself even more than now. We have here a tacit, but I think pretty clear admission that such religious solidarity as does exist among Catholics simply cannot serve as the major basis for political solidarity.[60]

Some recent evidence indicates that religious solidarity is one of the bases for a DLP vote, however.

Catholics, regardless of their party affiliation, are much more likely to be regular church attenders than Protestants, but the DLP voters among the Catholics are far more likely to go to church than their fellow Catholics who support other parties. Table 7–11 shows that 88 per cent of the Catholics indicating that they in-

---

[59] Australian Public Opinion Polls release, August-September, 1960. Catholics were also more likely to assent to the right of church leaders to give political instructions. Of the Catholics, 29 per cent assented to that right; this compared to 9 per cent of Church of England members, 6 per cent of both Presbyterians and Methodists, and none of the Baptists.

[60] Mayer, *op. cit.*, p. 3.

TABLE 7–11

Regular Church-Goers Who Prefer the ALP, DLP, or LCP, by Religion, Australia, 1961

VOTING INTENTION	PER CENT WHO ATTEND CHURCH WEEKLY	
	Catholics	Church of England
ALP	49 (218)*	7 (375)
DLP	88 (40)	11 (9)
Liberal or Country	50 (129)	19 (380)

* Total number of respondents is in parentheses.
Source: APOP Survey No. 149, April, 1961.

tended to vote DLP said that they attended church regularly, as compared to about half of the Liberal and ALP Catholics. By contrast, the few DLP voters belonging to the Church of England were less likely to go to church regularly than Liberals in the same church. These data, taken from a 1961 Gallup poll, show that DLP voters are closely connected to the Catholic church.

Looking at the same data the other way, of Catholics who attend church every week, 11 per cent are DLP voters; whereas Catholics who go to church less regularly or not at all are not much more likely to support the DLP than Protestants of whatever involvement in their church (between 1 and 3 per cent of each group are DLP voters). Clearly, the DLP draws its support from among those Catholics closest to their church. Whether this means that they are more likely to stay with such a party is difficult to tell.

Much of the DLP's support may come from "New Australians"— immigrants from southern and eastern Europe since World War II. If so, then in a sense history may be repeating itself; a low-status minority religious group is taking the path of deviant politics after "old-Australian" Catholics have become politically assimilated. An ecological study of Melbourne electorates found that the DLP vote was highest in the areas with the highest proportion of Catholics *and* the highest proportion of New Australians, particularly those from eastern Europe.[61]

---

[61] James Jupp, "A Note on the Democratic Labor Party Vote in Melbourne," *APSA News,* IV (March, 1959), 10. The author is more confident of the connection between the proportion of Catholics and the DLP vote than between the proportion of immigrants and the DLP vote.

Many of the leaders of one of Canada's third parties—the CCF—were socialist immigrants from Europe. The farm population of Saskatchewan included a high proportion of recent immigrants from European industrial areas, including many trade unionists and Fabian socialists.[62] Their secular tradition partly explains the political direction the CCF took. Possibly the DLP in Australia is similarly supported by Catholic immigrants with strongly anti-communist backgrounds. Unfortunately there is no way of distinguishing these immigrants in the surveys available.

Although much of the support for the DLP can be explained by the special susceptibility of upwardly mobile Catholics to the non-economic issue of communism, the new party cannot be easily dismissed as temporary if a substantial proportion of "New Australians" from eastern European countries have come to support it. These immigrants, from Catholic countries with religious parties, may swerve the party from the goal envisaged by its leaders: pressure upon the ALP to change its leadership and policies. If immigrants are a potential *permanent* social base for a Catholic workers' party (at least until they become assimilated and begin to rise in social status), this constitutes a source of pressure upon the leaders to remain separate. Thus, although the causes of the initial support for the DLP may be due to the strains of the Australian stratification system, support for the DLP coming from a different source which sees the party in different terms may have unanticipated consequences for its stability as a separate party.[63]

Tom C. Truman has argued that "so far from being 'assimilated,' there has arisen in the last twenty years amongst educated Catholics a heightened sense of catholicity and, therefore, of a greater sense of difference from their fellow Australians, which would give stronger (though still not strong enough) support for a specifically

---

[62] S. M. Lipset, *Agrarian Socialism* (Berkeley: University of California Press, 1950), p. 25.

[63] Enough immigrants from largely Catholic countries came to Australia in the postwar years to make this a plausible thesis, although no direct information on where they settled or on their patterns of voting is available. Between 1947 and 1954, there was an increase of 86,000 in the number of persons born in Italy, an increase of 51,000 in the number of persons born in Poland, 50,000 in the number of persons born in Holland. By contrast, there was an increase of 100,000 in the number of "New Australians" born in England and Wales, and 50,000 more born in Germany. See United Nations, *Demographic Yearbook* (New York, 1956), pp. 178–224.

Catholic party than has previously existed."[64] If the Catholics in Australia, by means of their separate educational system, have succeeded in creating a religious subculture, then additional challenges to the secular norm should be observed in other areas. Some indication that this is indeed occurring may be found in the "strike" of Roman Catholic schools in New South Wales in July, 1962, as a protest against the lack of state aid. This was the first direct action taken by Catholics in the drive for aid to their schools.[65]

The persistence of the class factor in Australian politics is shown, however, by the pattern of second preferences exhibited by DLP voters in 1955 (Table 7–12). Higher-status persons were much more likely to give their second preferences to the Liberals than lower-status persons. This is an indication that when and if the new party disappears, many of its supporters will turn to the Liberals and not back to the ALP. (Almost all of these DLP supporters are former ALP voters, even among those in non-manual occupations.)

CONCLUSIONS

In the Australian political system, class cleavages are almost as important for the support for the political parties as they are in

TABLE 7–12

DLP Supporters Who Give Their Second Preferences to the Liberals, by Occupation, Australia, 1955

OCCUPATION	PER CENT LIBERAL SECOND PREFERENCES
Business and Professional	75 (12)*
Clerical	52 (31)
Skilled	61 (39)
Semi-Skilled	43 (21)
Unskilled	33 (12)
TOTAL	54 (115)

* Total number of respondents is in parentheses.
Source: APOP Survey No. 115, December, 1955.

[64] Book Review, in *Australian Journal of Politics and History*, VII (November, 1961), 301.
[65] *New York Times*, July 11, 1962.

Great Britain. Cultural regionalism does not exist, although constitutional and economic regionalism play some role. In view of these similarities to Great Britain and also in view of the pressures bringing minor parties back into the framework of the two-party system and the norm against religious parties, the emergence of a largely-Catholic party in Australia became a problem to explain. It was suggested that the DLP serves one of the several functions possible for a third party in a predominantly class-polarized, two-party system—that of allowing a transition from one class-party to another by maintaining the maximum traditional symbolism while simultaneously breaking the voter from the traditional party and moving him closer to the new party. This function (for upwardly mobile Catholics) contrasts with that of the British Liberal party in Great Britain, discussed in Chapter 6. Whereas the British Liberal party is supported by a constantly changing *composition* but relatively constant *proportion* of the electorate, the DLP is probably supported by a fairly constant constituency. While it exists, it may serve an additional function very similar to that of the British Liberal party. The DLP may be a refuge for voters who are temporarily alienated by the bureaucracy and inertia of the old parties; but this is not its chief function.

It seems plausible to conclude that, in a class-polarized system without substantial ethnic or religious concentration, the Catholics do not form a stable social base for a party, and this is probably true for both Australia and Britain. No religious group in Australia constitutes the kind of distinct social or cultural entity that can form a permanent social base for a political movement. Where a continuing non-economic issue like communism exists, then political lines will not be formed exclusively around "Left-Right" economic lines, but neither will they form along strictly religious lines. The extent to which such parties as the DLP can stabilize themselves around a firm religious base will be an indication of the strength of the secular and two-party pressures in the Anglo-American political systems.

Chapter 8

The United States: The Politics of Diversity

SOCIAL class and political behavior are not as closely associated in the United States as they are in Australia and Great Britain. In several surveys of the national electorate taken from 1952 to 1960, the average level of class voting (the difference in Democratic voting between manual and non-manual occupational strata) was 16 percentage points. This contrasts with average figures of 40 percentage points for Great Britain, 33 for Australia, and 8 for Canada. (See Table 5-2, p. 102.) The national political parties in the United States are not as clearly distinguished by their class support as are the parties in Great Britain and Australia.

DIVERSITY IN THE UNITED STATES

The reasons for the lower level of class voting were discussed in Chapter 5 and will be briefly added to here, although these causes will not be the focus of the chapter. As was suggested earlier, the parties in the United States are not explicitly linked to class organizations and do not appeal for support on the basis of class. However, voters do see the parties as linked to specific class interests, and probably many people vote in accordance with an image of the parties as representing their economic interests. These are perhaps the most important reasons why class voting is relatively low and yet still exists.

A number of characteristics of American society and its political system undoubtedly reduce the level of class voting further. The enormous size of the country, its division into fifty states with real degrees of sovereignty, tremendous ethnic and religious diversity, and a decentralized party structure, all reduce the salience of *national* class divisions as the main bases for party cleavages. The decentralized, undisciplined character of American parties makes them difficult to distinguish from pressure groups or from combinations of interest groups. The party system thus reflects the federal, plural character of both American society and the governmental system. As the author of a recent study of American federalism put it, "a powerful 'pressure group' at the national level may be very closely identified with a State or local party in one or more States, yet prefer to remain aloof from the national party battle in order to maintain freedom to exert pressure upon both parties when tactics require it."[1] That national class divisions exist and divide the parties even as distinctly as they do, is a measure of the degree of economic and political integration the United States has achieved.

The diversity of support for the political parties has been shown by a series of studies of voting—more studies than for any of the other countries considered—and this chapter will not reiterate their findings in detail. The initial study, which set a pattern for subsequent research in both the United States and Great Britain, was *The People's Choice;* this was a survey of voting behavior in Erie County, Ohio, in the 1940 presidential election.[2] Since it embraced only one northern city and its environs, the regional economic and political diversity of the United States presumably did not affect voting behavior. Still, social class, religion, and rural-urban differences were found crucially to affect the political loyalties of voters. Having a low income, being a Catholic, or living in an urban environment, all predisposed voters toward the Democrats; having a high income, being a Protestant, or living in a rural environment predisposed voters toward the Republicans. The study focused on the consequences of "contradictory" social characteristics that presumably pushed people in opposite political directions—the now classic notion of "cross-pressures." A relatively high proportion of persons in Erie County was under cross-pressures, indicating that

---

[1] M. J. C. Vile, *The Structure of American Federalism* (London: Oxford University Press, 1961), p. 92.

[2] P. Lazarsfeld, B. Berelson, and H. Gaudet, *The People's Choice* (New York: Columbia University Press, 1948).

the diversity of sources of political loyalties is great in the United States.[3]

The main problem of this chapter will be not to explain the class or religious or regional bases for party support in the United States but to determine whether class voting has declined since the 1930's, and in which religious or regional groups.

Despite their diversity of support and their ambiguous class base (compared to the British and Australian parties), American political parties are both perceived as supported by, and actually are supported by, persons at different occupational, educational, and income levels, although, as in the other countries, a sizable minority votes for the "other" party. Since voting studies have also made this point clearly, there is no need to go into details. The authors of a study of the 1954 congressional election summarized their results as follows:

> Our data make it evident that a number of the major population categories have a persistent inclination toward one or the other of the two parties. The major theme of this group orientation in voting is social class. The prestige groups—educational, economic— are the most dependable sources of Republican support while the laborers, Negroes, unemployed, and other low-income and low-education groups are the strongest sources of the Democratic vote.[4]

And the parties can be distinguished as representing Left and Right positions. According to Max Beloff:

> If we take the simple view that there is, other things being equal, likely to be one party of the rich and one party of the poor, the Re-

---

[3] Other such voting studies are: B. Berelson, P. Lazarsfeld, and W. McPhee, *Voting* (Chicago: University of Chicago Press, 1954), and a series of studies done by the Survey Research Center at the University of Michigan beginning with the presidential election of 1948. These are reported in A. Campbell, G. Gurin, and W. E. Miller, *The Voter Decides* (Evanston: Row, Peterson, 1954); Angus Campbell and Homer C. Cooper, *Group Differences in Attitudes and Votes* (Ann Arbor: Survey Research Center, The University of Michigan, 1956), and A. Campbell *et al., The American Voter* (New York: Wiley, 1960). For a summary of the findings of many voting studies, see S. M. Lipset, *Political Man* (New York: Doubleday, 1960), chaps. vii, viii, ix.

Systematic comparative study would be necessary to prove that the American electorate is under more cross-pressures than, say, the British electorate, and that this produces more shifting and more apathy. The British voting studies (cited in Chapter 6) show that the effects of cross-pressures are the same in both countries, but their relative magnitude and intensity remain to be analyzed.

[4] Campbell and Cooper, *op. cit.*, p. 35.

publicans fill the bill for the former, and outside the South the Democrats fill it for the latter. The former accept roughly the justice of the present distribution of worldly goods between classes and regions; the latter by and large welcome government intervention to alter it.[5]

The phrases "by and large" and "other things being equal" hide a multitude of contradictions in the policies and voting patterns of Democratic and Republican legislators, but if that statement is accepted as substantially correct, the class bases of the major American parties are understandable. Another compilation of poll data from seven national polls conducted from 1944 to 1952 found that two-and-one-half times as many business and professional people thought the Republicans best served their interests as thought the Democrats did, and that seven times as many unskilled workers and four times as many skilled workers thought the Democrats best served their interests as thought the Republicans did. Whether or not the parties actually served their interests better is, of course, not proved by these images of the parties, but this evidence at least shows that American voting behavior is roughly in line with voters' conceptions of their own interests.[6]

Ideologically, party leaders in the United States are even more divided than voters. A recent study of Democratic and Republican leaders (delegates to national conventions) and followers (a national sample of voters) compared opinions on a number of issues. Republican and Democratic leaders were much farther apart than their followers on issues related to class. The ideology of Republican leaders reflected their managerial, proprietary, and high-status connections; the ideology of Democratic leaders, their labor, minority, low-status, and intellectual connnections.[7]

But, regardless of the current situations, has the association of class and vote declined since the 1930's? It is by now a common-

---

[5] Max Beloff, *The American Federal Government* (New York: Oxford University Press, 1959), pp. 157–58.

[6] Harold Orlans, "Opinion Polls on National Leaders," Series 1953, Report No. 6 (Philadelphia and Washington: Institute for Research in Human Relations), pp. 71–73. The author points out that almost exactly as many white-collar workers pick the Democrats as pick the Republicans, and that this corresponds to their "middle" position.

[7] H. McClosky, P. J. Hoffman, and R. O'Hara, "Issue Conflict and Consensus among Party Leaders and Followers," *American Political Science Review*, LIV (June, 1960), 406–27. The finding holds when various demographic factors are controlled.

place notion that the salience of class for voting was less in the prosperous 1950's than it was in the depressed 1930's.[8] A recent study found a decline of class voting in the period 1948 to 1956, which appears to document the decreasing importance of social class for voting behavior. The authors of *The American Voter* computed an index of "status polarization" which showed that the correlation between the occupational status of respondents and their partisan vote in three separate national surveys in 1948, 1952, and 1956 dropped from 0.44 to 0.26 to 0.12.[9] According to the authors:

> The most striking feature of the polarization trend in the recent past has been the steady and rapid depolarization between 1948 and 1956. This decline occurred in a post-war period when the nation was enjoying a striking ascent to prosperity and a consequent release from the pressing economic concerns that had characterized the Depression.[10]

The way that this decline of "status polarization" is explained is also relevant here, because the authors infer that changes have taken place since the 1930's, although they have no specific evidence of such changes. A substitute for this is evidence on the status polarization (or class voting, the term which will be used henceforth to avoid confusion) among different age-groups. In their 1948 and 1952 surveys, a marked "depression-effect" was found. Persons in their twenties and thirties during the depression of the 1930's (presumably those most affected by it) exhibited the highest level of class voting. In 1956, this was not evident, and the authors conclude that this illustrates the "fading effects of the Depression."[11]

This finding of highest class voting among the depression generation does not contradict the usual inference that persons in such a generation should be more similar in their political attitudes and behavior than persons not sharing this common experience. Another study of American voting behavior which specifically focused upon the problem of generational differences found that the depres-

---

[8] See, for example, V. O. Key, Jr., *Politics, Parties and Pressure Groups* (4th ed.; New York: Crowell, 1958), p. 274.

[9] Campbell *et al., The American Voter, op. cit.,* p. 347. As was discussed in Chapter 4, the method of computing the index of status polarization is identical to that used for my index of class voting.

[10] *Ibid.,* p. 357.

[11] *Ibid.,* p. 359.

sion generation (those who were born in the period 1913–1922) was likely to be more Democratic—regardless of sex, occupation, income, or other social differences.[12] In spite of the Michigan finding that manual and non-manual strata in the depression generation are farther apart in their voting patterns than any other age groups, political consensus is still present. Both strata were affected similarly by the Democratic political currents. These two findings reflect the relative independence of the absolute level of vote for a party from the level of class cleavage.

But the Michigan results may not reflect the actual voting patterns in the 1930's. Their results are for persons interviewed in the 1940's and 1950's, divided by age. That age differences at one point in time truly reflect past behavior and the differential impact of a historical crisis is an inference which may or may not be justified. Data to be presented may clarify the real patterns of class voting and the change in those patterns since the 1930's.

The decline of class voting between 1948 and 1956 is linked by the authors of *The American Voter* to "increasing prosperity and fading memories of the Great Depression of the 1930's." These two factors should imply a continuing decrease of class voting since the 1930's. But the authors must account for another of their own empirical findings—that class-voting was lower in 1944 than in 1948, after which it dropped almost linearly. They suggest that variations in the importance of domestic economic versus foreign policy issues account for this change: When economic issues are important, class voting tends to rise; when non-economic issues, such as foreign policy, are important, class voting tends to drop. ". . . war is a basic public concern that may eclipse those problems of domestic economics leading to cleavage among status interest groups."[13] The authors thus infer what the patterns of class voting *might* have been during the 1930's. Presumably class voting should have been high in the elections of 1932 and 1936, when class issues were dominant. With World War II, "national" issues superseded class ones, and class voting should have been lower in 1940 and 1944. As Campbell *et al.* put it, "Polarization tendencies carrying over from the Great Depression may have been dampened as a result of the national crisis posed by the Second World War, rebounding upward after that conflict was concluded." Domestic economic issues again be-

---

[12] Jane O'Grady, "Political Generations: An Empirical Analysis" (Master's thesis, Department of Sociology, University of California, 1960).

[13] Campbell *et al., The American Voter, op. cit.,* pp. 360–61.

came important, resulting in the rise of class voting in 1948. After this peak, "the renewal of the threat of global war and the outbreak of hostilities in Korea may have acted, in concert with increasing prosperity, to depress the level of status polarization [class voting] once again."[14]

These inferences are logical ones from the standpoint of the data available to the authors of that study and are relevant to the main problem of this chapter: whether class voting has declined since the 1930's. As was mentioned in Chapter 4, this particular problem is not of primary concern to these authors, since they are focusing upon "short-term" fluctuations. These inferences as to declining class voting certainly imply that a long-term decline of the importance of social class in the support of the American parties has taken place. But has it?

TRENDS IN CLASS VOTING SINCE THE 1930'S

Although fluctuations in the level of class voting have occurred in the period 1936 to 1960, there is some evidence that no consistent decline has taken place. Before the evidence for this conclusion is presented, a brief recapitulation of the assumptions upon which the measure of class voting is based is in order.

In estimating the importance of the class bases of politics, shifts to the Right or to the Left should be minimized because they blur the differences between social strata. In such political systems as the Anglo-American ones, shifts usually occur in the same direction in all politically relevant social groups. A shift to the Right such as the Eisenhower victories in 1952 and 1956 could conceivably be regarded as a decline in the importance of social class as a determinant of political behavior. It is probably true that a large vote for Eisenhower among workers meant that class identifications were less important in those elections than in that of 1948, for example. But it is contended here that only if the *gap* between manual and non-manual support of a party has lessened can one speak meaningfully of a decline of class voting. The data presented in *The American Voter* show without question that not only did all social groups vote more Republican in 1952 and 1956 than they did in 1948, but that *in addition* social classes moved closer together. But, was this part of a long-term decline of the importance of the class bases of politics? Or (and this is the thesis of this chapter) was this

[14] *Ibid.*, p. 361.

only a fluctuation within the "normal range" of change of the class bases of American politics, given the social and political structure of American society in this historical period?

Figure 8–1 (based upon data given in Appendix B) shows the level of Democratic voting among manual and non-manual occupational groups from 1936 to 1960. (The gap between the two lines is the level of class voting, portrayed in Figure 5–1, p. 103.) Considerable shifting in the Democratic vote is evident, although class voting was not sharply different in the 1950's from the 1930's. About two-thirds of the manual workers voted Democratic in the three elections between 1936 and 1944; their Democratic vote rose sharply in 1948, dropped just as sharply in 1952 and 1956, then rose back to about 60 per cent in 1960. Among the middle class, the Democratic vote stayed between 40 and 50 per cent between 1936 and 1944, dropped below 40 per cent in the following three elections, and rose again to 46 per cent in 1960. The only election in which both strata moved in sharply opposite directions was 1948, which might be termed a "non-consensual election." If that election had been chosen as the beginning of a time-series, the end of class voting might have been predicted, but data for the longer period indicate that 1948 was exceptional.

No pattern of consistent decline of class voting is thus evident, and its level reached that of Britain and Australia only in the 1948 election. Nor has the level of class voting dropped to the average Canadian level in any election. It may be concluded from the evidence presented in Figure 8–1 that there has been no substantial shift in the class bases of American politics since the 1930's, despite the prosperity since World War II and despite the shifts to the Right in the Eisenhower era.[15]

---

[15] The figures for middle-class and working-class voting patterns given in Heinz Eulau, *Class and Party in the Eisenhower Years* (New York: Free Press of Glencoe, 1962), p. 2, are not comparable to those presented here because Eulau utilized a measure of class based upon a combination of the occupation, income, and education of the respondent. The percentage-point difference in Democratic preferences of the middle class and working class, defined in this way, was 24 in 1952 and only 4 in 1956. Eulau's study was a secondary analysis of the two Michigan election surveys. Actually, for 1956, he dropped income as a component of the class index with the rather curious justification that "it proved so variable as an indicator that it seriously undermined the stability of the index and interfered with the comparability of results" (p. 45). One might ask how results can be comparable if different procedures are used to compute a major index. The variability of the effect of income may reflect the varying effect upon political behavior from election to election of different *components* of stratification.

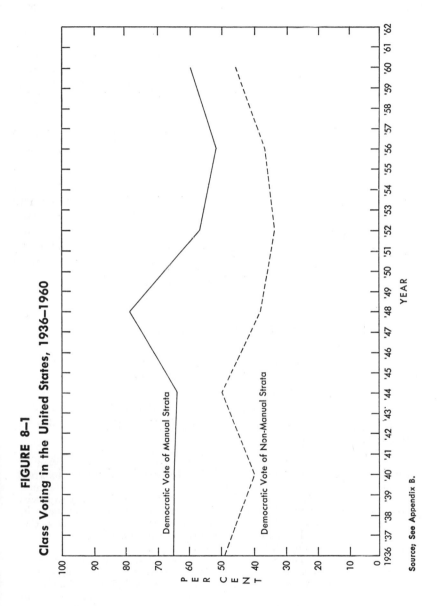

FIGURE 8–1

Class Voting in the United States, 1936–1960

Democratic Vote of Manual Strata

Democratic Vote of Non-Manual Strata

Source; See Appendix B.

The level of class voting found in the various community studies is fairly consistent with the national figures. The 1940 study of Erie County, Ohio, found that class voting was 17. The county at that time had a small and stable population of about 43,000, slightly more than half of which lived in the industrial town of Sandusky. Almost all of the population was native-born white, and the authors described it as largely working-class, with a "cultural and social life . . . perhaps not atypical of the middle western small-town and rural section . . . a 'church town.' "[16]

A later study of the 1948 election in Elmira, New York, found that "the business, professional and white-collar groups supported the Republicans fully 75 per cent; the workers split their vote almost fifty-fifty."[17] Assuming that this description corresponds to a manual-non-manual division, this is a level of class voting of about 24–26, considerably lower than the national level of 41 discovered by a Michigan study. Elmira in 1948 was a Republican community of slightly over 50,000, and class voting might be expected to be lower there than in the larger cities. Detroit in 1957–58 had a level of class voting of 32, much higher than the national level.[18]

The national data also permit some evaluation of the thesis of the authors of *The American Voter* concerning the causes of more short-term fluctuation of class voting. Class voting was not high in 1936, quite the contrary. Two separate national Gallup samples in 1936 show that class voting was as low in that year as in any subsequent year.[19] Figure 8–1 shows that this low level was due to heavy Democratic voting by persons in non-manual occupations. All social strata felt a "need for a change" and voted Democratic accordingly. Social classes were not polarized by the class issues of the 1930's, but were attracted to the party that promised change.

Why the "depression-generation" in the later surveys conducted by the Michigan Survey Research Center exhibited more class vot-

---

[16] Lazarsfeld *et al., The People's Choice, op. cit.,* pp. 10–11. The level of class voting was computed from a table on page 19, which shows that when socio-economic status (as judged by an interviewer) was held constant, occupation made little additional difference in voting patterns.

[17] Berelson *et al., Voting, op. cit.,* p. 57.

[18] Gerhard Lenski, *The Religious Factor* (New York: Doubleday, 1961). The figure was recomputed from a table on page 125. Of course, it is impossible to know whether class voting dropped in either city from 1952 to 1958.

[19] Note that a percentage point difference of at least 8 may be due to errors of calculation, rounding, and other minor errors, so that no stress is laid on individual surveys, elections, or percentages.

ing is an interesting question which cannot be fully explored here. Possibly during such periods of crisis a consensus on the proper political path emerges. But after the crisis is over, the *memory* of the crisis assumes a different meaning for different social strata. In this case, for workers, the memory of the crisis reinforced their Democratic allegiances; for the middle class, it reinforced their Republican attachments, since the actual legislation carried out in the crisis period furthered the centralization of government which many see as furthered by Democratic office-holders.

Thus, the inference by the authors of *The American Voter* that class voting is likely to be higher in elections in which domestic economic issues are salient is weakened by some data from 1936. Their inference is also weakened by the rise of class voting in 1940, an election in which presumably the issues of foreign policy rather than issues of class were dominant. The drop in 1944 is also not consistent, since by that time the issues of national interest were abating, and domestic economic conflicts were again assuming importance. But, the purpose here is not to debate the salience of different issues in different elections. The main point is that no inference that class voting is declining can be made from evidence from great numbers of surveys ranging from 1936 to 1960.

Somewhat unreliable data from 1928 and 1932 reinforce, if anything, the conclusion that class voting has not declined since the 1930's. The League of Women Voters gathered 8,419 interviews in twenty-seven states two weeks prior to the 1932 presidential elections. The difference between the Democratic presidential vote of factory workers, on the one hand, and managers or semi-professionals, on the other, was 10 percentage points in 1928 and 22 points in 1932, as Table 8–1 shows. The Democratic vote went up in all occupational groups from 1928 to 1932 (again showing the consensus that a change was needed), but it increased much more among factory workers, and their greater swing accounts for the increase in class voting.

If any credence at all can be placed in these data, they are further evidence that no decline of class voting has taken place—only a fluctuation around a fairly stable class base for the political parties —since the early 1930's. The League survey is not reported in the United States tables in Appendix B because of the unreliability and lack of comparability of the data. Its sampling accuracy may be judged from its finding that Roosevelt received 30 per cent of the

TABLE 8–1

Democratic Preference, by Occupation, United States, 1928–1932

OCCUPATION	PER CENT VOTING DEMOCRATIC	
	1928	*1932*
Professional	25 (2227)*	30 (2215)
Semi-Professional and Managerial	21 (1701)	28 (1790)
Clerical and Skilled	24 (2130)	35 (2468)
Factory Worker	31 (334)	50 (427)
Difference between Highest and Lowest Percentages	+10	+22

Source: Recomputed from estimates in Samuel P. Hayes, Jr., "The Interrelations of Political Attitudes: IV: Political Attitudes and Party Regularity," *Journal of Social Psychology,* X (1939), 504–5.
Since clerical workers and skilled tradesmen are combined in his tables, it is impossible to compute
a comparable index of class voting. Class voting has been exaggerated, if anything, by using the
manual and non-manual occupational groups which were farthest apart in their Democratic voting.
The respondents were asked how they voted in 1928 and how they intended to vote in 1932. If the
1932 Thomas vote in each occupation is added to the 1932 Roosevelt vote, the parallel percentage-
point difference is +20.
* Total number of respondents in parentheses.

1932 voting preferences in the survey. Nevertheless, differences between occupational groups are, as stated previously, less subject to
sampling error than the actual marginal totals or proportions.

This conclusion holds for congressional as well as presidential elections. Surveys asking about congressional voting in 1946 and 1954,
and party identification (whether a person considers himself a
"Democrat" or a "Republican," regardless of his actual voting intention) in 1954 and 1958 were also available (the data are not
given here in detail), and the index of class voting ranged from 16
to 21. Thus, since several surveys were available for different elections, there can be little doubt that the association of social class
and voting behavior has not permanently changed.

Before we can accept the conclusion that class voting has not declined, it is important to consider where it may have declined or
where it may have actually increased. Trends in various regions of
the United States, as well as among various religious groups, may
offer a clue as to the future role of social class in American politics.
It is not at all clear, for example, that class voting will remain as
low as it is. The disappearance of the loyalties of middle-class
southerners to the Democratic party, when and if it occurs, may
mean a rise of class voting and therefore a realignment of the social

bases of the parties more upon class lines. And the possible dwindling of special religious and ethnic loyalties to the parties may have similar consequences. American political scientist Clinton Rossiter has suggested that in the future:

> the influence of class on political behavior and allegiance may become even more visible than it is today, especially as the influences of ethnology and religion fade ever so slowly but steadily from view. . . . we are still a long way from the class struggle in American politics, but that does not mean that class consciousness is a negligible factor. To the contrary, it must inevitably become a more important factor as Americans become ever more alert to the rewards and symbols of status.[20]

The specific questions which can be answered from the survey data include the following: Has class voting declined or increased in any United States region? and Does this change seem to be related to any pervasive social changes taking place—such as urbanization or industrialization? We might expect that if any trend toward the political re-integration of the South is evident, class voting might have increased in that region since the early 1940's. On the other hand, in the most urbanized and older regions, such as New England or the Middle Atlantic states, class voting might have declined from a formerly high level, somewhat like the pattern in the London metropolitan area of Great Britain. These two trends—in the South and East—might cancel each other out to produce the over-all lack of change of class voting. Or we might find that class voting is higher in the urban South than in the rest of the South and infer that this is a sign of impending change of the social bases of southern politics and an omen of a future national realignment more along class lines.

Similarly, trends in the class voting patterns of Protestants and Catholics may foreshadow the future. It is possible that class voting has dropped among Protestants but increased among Catholics to cancel each other out as far as an over-all index is concerned. The diversity of politics in the United States implies that a single measure of the importance of a single factor for voting behavior is almost meaningless unless the relationship is examined in various other subgroups of the population.

---

[20] Clinton Rossiter, *Parties and Politics in America* (Ithaca: Cornell University Press, 1960), p. 166.

REGIONALISM AND CLASS VOTING

The sectional character of American politics is a commonplace and needs no documentation. Many states, not only in the South, have had a traditional alignment with one of the major parties. This has meant that each of the parties has long cherished a sectional strong-hold within which the other party had little chance of winning legislative representation.

> . . . in 1904 less than one-seventh of the population of the United States lived in states in which the parties contested the election on relatively equal terms, while in 1920 only about 12 million out of 105 million Americans lived in states in which they had a choice between two major parties both of which had some prospect of winning.[21]

And, as V. O. Key puts it:

> Sectionalism . . . contributes to the multiclass composition of each of the major parties, a characteristic bewildering to those who regard only a class politics as "natural." A politics that arrays the people of one section against those of another pulls into one party men of all social strata. A common interest bound the southern banker, merchant, cotton farmer, and wage earner together against the northern combination of finance, manufacturing, and segments of industrial labor.[22]

One major question which can be answered by survey data, but which is not as readily answerable from ecological studies of the voting patterns of social areas, is whether class voting is actually substantially lower in areas such as the South. The second major question of concern here is, of course, whether class voting has declined in any major regions or whether it has increased, particularly in the South. Since the South is the chief example of political regionalism, and since its special role in the Congress has important political consequences for the nation, the voting patterns of the South will be of primary interest in the discussion of regionalism.

Southern politics is a one-party politics dominated by extremely conservative elements which distort the national party pattern by introducing a Right bias within the Democratic party, the major

---

[21] E. E. Schattschneider, "United States: The Functional Approach to Party Government," in Sigmund Neumann, ed., *Modern Political Parties* (Chicago: University of Chicago Press, 1956), pp. 203–4.

[22] Key, *op. cit.*, p. 267.

Left party of the nation. A few examples of the voting patterns of southern Democrats will show this internal contradiction within the Democratic party. On many clearly Left-Right issues in the 1960 Congress, the southern Democrats lined up with the Republicans. In a vote on a housing bill, thirty-five of the forty House Democrats who voted against the bill were southerners. (Only thirteen Republicans voted for the bill.)[23] In a vote on a bill providing relief for areas suffering chronic unemployment, only one of the eleven Democrats voting against it was not a southerner.[24] In the 1962 session, the coalition of southern Democrats and Republicans appeared repeatedly. Typical are examples from House action on two bills on September 20. The House defeated a Republican-led drive to send the foreign aid bill back to committee. Of the sixty-five Democrats who were for referral (against the bill), sixty were southerners.[25] The farm bill, brought up the same day, was passed in spite of twenty-six southerners who were among the thirty-seven Democrats who opposed it.[26] These particular bills indicate again that the southerners are a conservative block on every type of issue, even on those presumably favoring their agricultural constituents.

Add to these voting patterns the dominance of southerners on key committees that determine which legislation shall come before the whole House of Representatives—a dominance due to their long seniority and lack of opposition—and some measure of the strength of the role of the South in American national politics is evident.[27] It is therefore of both practical and theoretical importance if the regional loyalties of southerners are being replaced by political cleavages similar to those exhibited by other regions.

Table 8–2 and Figure 8–2 show the trends and levels of class voting in different United States regions from 1944 to 1960. Table 8–3 summarizes results.

As with previous findings concerning the over-all level of class voting, there is no consistent pattern of change affecting all regions

---

[23] *New York Times*, April 28, 1960, p. 12.

[24] *Ibid.*, May 7, 1960, p. 8.

[25] *Ibid.*, September 21, 1962, p. 5. Of the thirty-four Republicans against referral, nineteen were from heavily urbanized states.

[26] *Ibid.*, September 21, 1962, p. 4. Only two Republicans favored the farm bill.

[27] See V. O. Key, Jr., *Southern Politics in State and Nation* (New York: Knopf, 1949), Part 2.

TABLE 8–2

Democratic Preference, by Occupation Type and Region, United States, 1944–1960

OCCUPATION TYPE	NEW ENGLAND	MIDDLE ATLANTIC	EAST CENTRAL	WEST CENTRAL	SOUTH	MOUNTAIN	PACIFIC	TOTAL
1944								
Manual	77 (109)*	62 (330)	62 (257)	68 (139)	75 (103)	62 (71)	71 (110)	66 (1,119)
Non-Manual	48 (93)	50 (268)	38 (231)	38 (118)	64 (108)	33 (57)	45 (85)	46 (960)
Index of Class Voting	+29	+12	+24	+30	+11	+29	+26	+20
1948								
Manual	54 (94)	47 (319)	51 (243)	55 (117)	69 (81)	54 (69)	50 (114)	52 (1,037)
Non-Manual	29 (88)	31 (249)	27 (255)	30 (113)	53 (86)	47 (38)	32 (112)	32 (941)
Index of Class Voting	+25	+16	+24	+25	+16	+7	+18	+20
1952 (Sample No. 1)								
Manual	55 (56)	53 (137)	55 (156)	59 (73)	57 (189)	62 (21)	60 (65)	56 (697)
Non-Manual	29 (34)	30 (97)	30 (128)	33 (54)	47 (122)	27 (11)	27 (56)	34 (502)
Index of Class Voting	+26	+23	+25	+26	+10	+35	+33	+22
1952 (Sample No. 2)								
Manual	46 (140)	43 (488)	44 (460)	51 (178)	47 (665)	45 (69)	54 (224)	47 (2,224)
Non-Manual	23 (110)	31 (386)	28 (336)	20 (136)	36 (429)	20 (75)	36 (208)	30 (1,681)
Index of Class Voting	+23	+12	+16	+31	+11	+25	+18	+17

TABLE 8-2—(Continued)

OCCUPATION TYPE	NEW ENGLAND	MIDDLE ATLANTIC	EAST CENTRAL	WEST CENTRAL	SOUTH	MOUNTAIN	PACIFIC	TOTAL
1956								
Manual	38 (42)	47 (104)	46 (65)	61 (46)	53 (105)	62 (16)	65 (49)	52 (427)
Non-Manual	14 (22)	30 (70)	39 (46)	30 (33)	50 (44)	37 (8)	46 (39)	36 (262)
Index of Class Voting	+24	+17	+ 7	+31	+ 3	+25	+19	+16
1960 (Sample No. 1)								
Manual	67 (67)	64 (370)	57 (302)	54 (120)	60 (317)	62 (37)	53 (137)	60 (1,350)
Non-Manual	68 (97)	57 (295)	30 (228)	36 (121)	42 (173)	48 (60)	42 (154)	45 (1,128)
Index of Class Voting	− 1	+ 7	+27	+18	+18	+14	+11	+15
1960 (Sample No. 2)								
Manual	60 (43)	61 (147)	64 (179)	60 (53)	56 (190)	72 (29)	57 (70)	60 (711)
Non-Manual	50 (52)	52 (198)	43 (167)	34 (76)	47 (258)	52 (44)	44 (141)	46 (936)
Index of Class Voting	+10	+ 9	+21	+26	+ 9	+20	+13	+14

Sources: 1944: AIPO Survey No. 323. 1948: AIPO Survey No. 423; 1952: Sample No. 1—Michigan 1952 Survey, otherwise reported in A. Campbell, G. Gurin, and W. Miller, The Voter Decides (Evanston: Row, Peterson, 1954), Sample No. 2—tabulated from the IBM cards available for the survey reported in Samuel Stouffer, Communism, Conformity and Civil Liberties (New York: Doubleday, 1955); 1956: AIPO Survey No. 573; 1960: AIPO Survey No. 636K and Roper Survey No. 75. With one exception, the regions correspond to the census classification.

* Total number of respondents is in parentheses.

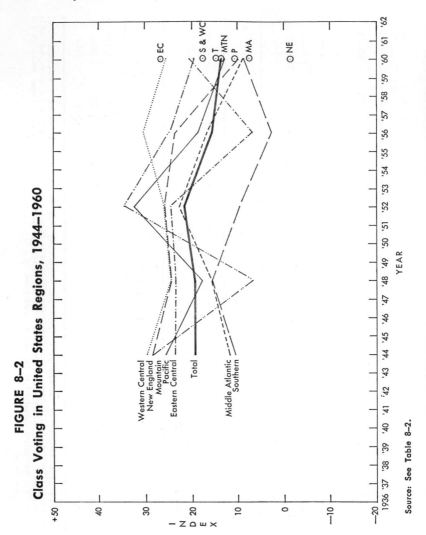

FIGURE 8–2

Class Voting in United States Regions, 1944–1960

Source: See Table 8–2.

similarly. The political diversity of America remains great in this respect—that the degree of variation of class voting over time within and between the major regions of the country is considerable. The Eisenhower elections marked not a dwindling of this difference, but an intensification of it. If the single survey available for 1948 is representative of the electoral shifts in that year, the major regions —save for the "Mountain" region—drew closer together in that year—a "class" election—than in any other between 1944 and 1960.[28]

In these surveys, the over-all level of class voting varied between 14 and 22, while the highest level reached achieved in any region was 35, and the lowest was —1. Unfortunately, sampling error is so great for particular regional figures that trends within regions cannot be regarded as reliable, and the few generalizations to be offered must be regarded as speculative. An attempt to discern some regular difference between regions in the average level of class voting is presented in Table 8–3.

Table 8–3 lists the number of times each region was found in a certain rank when the level of class voting was computed for each region. It is noteworthy that most of the sharpest deviations from the usual pattern were found in 1960 surveys, particularly in regions where a pro-Catholic or anti-Catholic effect might have been expected: New England and the South. Class voting in New England was actually —1 in one survey. Further analysis by religion

TABLE 8–3

Rank Order of Class Voting in United States Regions

REGION*	FREQUENCY OF RANK							RANK-INDEX SCORE†
	1st	2nd	3rd	4th	5th	6th	7th	
West Central	5	1	1					10
Mountain	1	3	1	1			1	14
New England	1	1	3		1‡		1‡	24
East Central	1‡	1‡	1	1	2	1		26
Pacific		1		4	2			28
Mid-Atlantic					2	5		40
South		1‡			1	2	3	40

* See Appendix D for the composition of the regions based on the various definitions.
† Ties were counted twice; then the next rank was skipped. The maximum possible index score is +49; the minimum, +7.
‡ The deviations from the usual rank order found in two 1960 surveys.
Source: Derived from Table 8–2.

---

[28] These inferences are advanced with caution. The definitions of regions are not consistent for every survey, and in the single 1948 survey available, the rise of the over-all level of class voting found in the Michigan survey does not appear. Even so, the regional pattern which it portrays may be found in other 1948 surveys.

showed that this effect was indeed due to the Catholic vote, since class voting among Protestants was +22. Class voting in the South was higher in this election than in any since 1948, and the South ranked second in level of 1960 class voting in at least one survey.

No dwindling of the political diversity of America's regions appears from these data, therefore, and no apparent trend toward the reintegration of the South is found. There is also little evidence that the more urbanized regions such as New England or the Middle Atlantic states have high levels of class voting. As suggested in Chapter 5, it seemed plausible to predict that class voting would be higher rather than lower in the regions both older and more urbanized in the United States, unlike Great Britain, because of the disappearance in urban and long-settled areas of various parochial political loyalties interfering with the emergence of class-based politics. No pattern of that kind seems to exist in the United States as yet.[29]

No detailed exploration of the regional regularities can be undertaken. It seems probably, however, that they are not accidental, and that certain historical and structural features of these regions could be found to account for the differences. The consistently low level of class voting in the South is no surprise and easily explained. But why does the West North Central region exhibit almost the highest consistent pattern of class voting? These are the midwest agrarian states, which are largely Republican: Minnesota, Iowa, Missouri, North and South Dakota, Nebraska, and Kansas. Clearly

---

[29] New England and the Middle Atlantic states have denser populations, a greater proportion of their populations employed in manufacturing, and more manufacturing establishments per 1,000 population than other regions, but not any higher proportion of "urban" population. (See *The World Almanac and Book of Facts* [New York, 1962], pp. 255, 280–96, 693. The original data are from the Census.) The East North Central states did not differ much from New England on any measure. Urbanization may be an excessively crude measure for our purposes, and there are too few regions to be able to determine a meaningful rank order.

An ecological study of a smaller unit—congressional districts—in four election years (1944 to 1950) found that the correlation between the percentage of laborers in a district and the percentage of the Democratic vote was greater in urban than in rural areas. (Duncan Macrae, Jr., "Occupations and the Congressional Vote, 1940–1950," *American Sociological Review*, XX [June, 1955], 333.) The author suggests that there is a stronger spirit of community and of cohesion that cuts across class lines in rural areas and small towns. The regional data available to the present author are apparently too "coarse" to exhibit the same result.

this is not a "regionalism" like that of the South, because both strata are not pulled over to a single party. On the contrary, as Table 8–2 indicates, the Democratic vote of manual workers is usually above the average; that of non-manuals, usually below. For some of these states, the high level of class voting may reflect the historical patterns of agrarian revolts, expressed through the Nonpartisan League in North Dakota and the socialist traditions of Minnesota.[30] But, whatever the cause, class voting in this midwest region is usually as high as in the London metropolitan area of Great Britain or in urban Australia.

The vacillations of the mountain region (the strip along the Rocky Mountains from Montana to New Mexico) are not so easily laid to a particular historical tradition and may merely reflect the small numbers of cases (the fewest in any region) or the heterogeneity of the region. But, as will be noted in the case of the Prairie provinces in Canada, part of this vacillation may be due to the frontier character of the region. Further research might be able to pin down some of the reasons for this and other regional regularities of political behavior.[31]

Although national surveys offer no evidence that the South, at least, is becoming more like other regions in its level of class voting —and is therefore losing its special regional allegiance to the Democratic party—other studies indicate that such a change may be imminent. The Republican vote has steadily climbed in the South and may be derived from middle-class more than from working-class persons.[32]

Also, to some extent southern political distinctiveness may be due to its character as a "backward" area and not to true differences in the allegiances of similar kinds of voters. Evidence to this effect is that urban Republicanism in the South has become quite similar to

---

[30] It must be noted that these data do not include farmers, but only manual and non-manual occupations. As will be seen in the next chapter, the agrarian movements of Canada's prairie provinces, next door to North Dakota, have *not* resulted in consistently high levels of class voting as measured by the index.

[31] The Mountain and West Central or North Central states not only have either high or vacillating levels of class voting, but also have had greater swings back and forth between the major parties than the other regions. See Harold F. Gosnell, *Grass Roots Politics* (Washington, D. C.: American Council on Public Affairs, 1942), pp. 13–17.

[32] A gradual equalization of the contribution of different regions to the vote of the major parties from 1896 to 1952 is shown in Paul T. David, "The Changing Party Pattern," *Antioch Review*, XVI (Fall, 1956), 338–41.

urban Republicanism elsewhere.[33] The higher Democratic percentages in the South may increasingly come from rural Democratic loyalties (which are Republican elsewhere) and which will be as hard to change as any rural traditionalisms.

The authors of *The American Voter* note that "generally speaking, [status] polarization is lower in the South than in other regions of the nation," but their data show that "Between 1952 and 1956 . . . when levels [of status polarization] were declining elsewhere, there was an actual increase of polarization in the South, from a coefficient not much above zero to a point of clear significance in 1956."[34] In a footnote, they suggest that "this trend may reflect growing industrialization and urbanization in the South, processes that are likely in the long run to blur traditional differences in political behavior generally." This suggestion reflects a hypothesis which the present author shares: Class voting should increase if and when the influence of the traditional regional, ethnic, and religious loyalties to party dwindles.

Also, "status voting [was] more prevalent among *weak* party identifiers than among strong in the South in 1952," with a smaller but consistent such relationship in 1956.[35] This might indicate that persons who are breaking away from their Democratic identifications are predominantly middle-class and are the voters who are both least strongly identified with the Democrats and those whose shift to the Republicans accounts for the increasing class voting (or status polarization) in the South in 1952 and 1956 shown by *The American Voter* data.

Some evidence that the South may yet split along national lines when two parties develop there is given in recent unpublished studies by Herbert McClosky. He found that the Republicans in the South were even more conservative on a number of issues (and even more authoritarian) than the southern Democrats. The southern Republicans have therefore not been the natural home of lib-

---

[33] See Donald S. Strong, *Urban Republicanism in the South* (Birmingham: University of Alabama, Bureau of Public Administration, 1960), for an ecological study of several southern cities. The author concluded that "Prosperous southerners are now showing the same political preferences as their economic counterparts outside the South. Here one may see the abandonment of ancient loyalties forged a century ago and their replacement by voting based on calculations of class advantage" (p. 57).

[34] Campbell *et al.*, *The American Voter, op. cit.*, pp. 367–68.

[35] *Ibid.*, p. 368. Italics in original.

erals hoping to express their disagreement with the control of the Democratic party in the South by conservatives. The national two-party split between Left and Right is repeated in the South, the main difference being that *both* party elites are further to the Right than their northern counterparts. This indicates that changes tending to bring the South into two-party competition will not result in a liberal Republican party and a conservative Democratic party, but rather the same alignment as the rest of the nation.

In 1962, the congressional elections afforded further evidence of the dwindling importance of the traditional regional strongholds of both parties. The Republicans gained four more House seats in the South, won the governorship in Oklahoma for the first time in history, and nearly won a number of formerly safe Democratic seats. The Democrats in turn penetrated into hitherto safe Republican strongholds in New England, and Wisconsin possessed two Democratic senators for the first time.[36]

RELIGION AND CLASS VOTING

The continuing diversity of American politics is also shown by religious differences in class voting. As before, the main questions here are: Has class voting dropped among either Protestants or Catholics, and what possible significance do shifts by either grouping have for a future trend in class voting?

Evidence from six surveys in five different presidential elections indicates that class voting may be declining slightly among Protestants, but that non-class factors affect the voting behavior of Catholics so much that no clear trend exists. Table 8–4 and Figure 8–3 show the vacillations of class voting among Catholics and an apparent slight decline among Protestants.[37]

The decline found among Protestants is not sharp, and the margin for error is such that we must conclude that for Protestants as

---

[36] See the *New York Times,* November 8, 1962, for a summary of the election results.

[37] Here, as with the data on regionalism, the lack of more than one survey for each election makes the evidence on trends rather speculative. Since the more complete evidence from fifteen surveys shows no consistent decline of class-voting over-all, and the Protestant trend parallels the slight decline over-all found in these selected surveys—except for the 1960 estimate—it is possible that the Protestant decline of class voting is merely a function of the slight over-all decline found in these particular surveys.

TABLE 8–4

Democratic Preference, by Religion and Occupation Type, United States, 1944–1960

OCCUPATION TYPE	PER CENT PREFERRING DEMOCRATS			RELIGIOUS VOTING INDEX OF
	Catholic	Protestant	Total	
		1944		
Manual	78 (245)*	60 (530)	66 (1104)	+18
Non-Manual	59 (165)	37 (537)	46 (949)	+22
TOTAL	70 (410)	48 (1067)		+22
Index of Class Voting	+19	+23	+20	
		1948		
Manual	58 (316)	49 (674)	52 (1032)	+9
Non-Manual	50 (215)	24 (643)	32 (936)	+26
TOTAL	54 (531)	37 (1317)		+17
Index of Class Voting	+8	+25	+20	
		1952, Sample No. 1		
Manual	52 (540)	44 (1598)	47 (2224)	+8
Non-Manual	34 (347)	25 (1168)	30 (1681)	+9
TOTAL	45 (887)	36 (2766)		+9
Index of Class Voting	+18	+19	+17	
		1952, Sample No. 2		
Manual	64 (196)	52 (461)	56 (697)	+12
Non-Manual	38 (101)	28 (344)	34 (502)	+10
TOTAL	55 (297)	42 (805)		+13
Index of Class Voting	+26	+24	+22	
		1956		
Manual	59 (118)	49 (300)	52 (422)	+10
Non-Manual	48 (67)	29 (170)	36 (256)	+19
TOTAL	55 (185)	41 (470)		+14
Index of Class Voting	+11	+20	+16	

TABLE 8–4—(Continued)
Democratic Preference, by Religion and Occupation Type, United States, 1944–1960

OCCUPATION TYPE	PER CENT PREFERRING DEMOCRATS			INDEX OF RELIGIOUS VOTING
	Catholic	Protestant	Total	
		1960, Sample No. 1		
Manual	79 (214)	51 (444)	60 (711)	+28
Non-Manual	73 (233)	32 (600)	46 (936)	+41
TOTAL	76 (447)	40 (1044)		+36
Index of Class Voting	+6	+19	+14	
		1960, Sample No. 2		
Manual	85 (385)	47 (869)	60 (1356)	+38
Non-Manual	75 (282)	29 (741)	45 (1128)	+46
TOTAL	81 (667)	38 (1610)		+43
Index of Class Voting	+10	+18	+15	

Sources: 1944: AIPO Survey Nos. 323, 423; 1952: Sample No. 1, Past vote, asked in the "Stouffer Study" in 1954, Sample No. 2, recomputed from the Michigan study of the 1952 election, reported in A. Campbell, G. Gurin, and W. Miller, The Voter Decides (Evanston: Row, Peterson, 1954); 1956: AIPO Survey No. 573; 1960: AIPO Survey No. 636K and Roper Survey No. 7S (Sample Nos. 1 and 2). Discrepancies of totals are due to inclusion of Jews and persons in other religions or with no religion in the totals. The designation "index of religious voting" assumes that the percentage-point difference between the voting preferences of Protestants and Catholics, holding social class constant, reflects the degree to which religious affiliation affects political behavior. The Michigan voting studies found a level of religious voting (as measured by this indicator) of 14 in 1956 and 44 in 1960, identical or very close to the Gallup figures. See Philip E. Converse, "Religion and Politics: The 1960 Elections" (Ann Arbor: Survey Research Center, University of Michigan, dittoed, August, 1961).

* Total number of respondents is in parentheses.

well as for the total electorate in the United States, there is no evidence of any change in class voting. As a matter of fact, the level of Protestant class voting is more consistent than the Catholic and implies that much of the vacillation of class voting, possibly even in earlier years, has been due to the greater shifting of Catholics than Protestants.

Protestants have exhibited a higher level of class voting than Catholics in each election except in 1952. The general pattern is consistent with the presumed ethnic and minority sentiments among Catholics which override class sentiments as bases for political

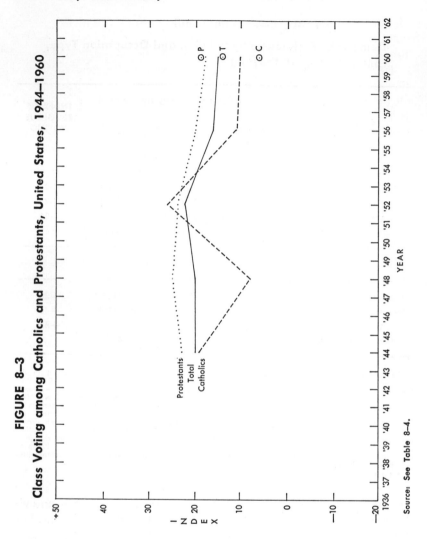

FIGURE 8–3

Class Voting among Catholics and Protestants, United States, 1944–1960

Source: See Table 8–4.

loyalties. If only the 1944, 1948, and 1952 data were available, it would appear that Protestants and Catholics were becoming just alike in their levels of class voting, since a pattern of convergence culminated in actually higher class voting among Catholics than among Protestants in 1952.[38] This change was due to a rise of Cath-

---

[38] This is shown by both of the two surveys available which asked about the 1952 vote of respondents.

olic class voting—not to a drop of Protestant class voting. More specifically, it was due to a pull of the Catholic middle class to the Republican nominee.

The 1952 election was the only one in which the religious deviation of both manual and non-manual Catholics was about equal. In all of the other surveys, Catholic non-manuals were much farther from Protestant non-manuals than Catholic manuals were from Protestant manuals. Catholicism seems in the United States to have more political consequences for persons in non-manual occupations than for manual workers. Because non-manual occupations are less identified as a particular social class (they are less homogeneous than working-class occupations), non-class loyalties and identifications affect the political behavior of persons in non-manual occupations more easily. But in 1952, this possible process affecting religious voting failed to operate. Non-manual persons in different religions were, for the only time, more alike than manual persons in different religions. In 1956 and 1960, they returned to the usual pattern. This 1952 deviation may have been due to the "strong foreign policy appeal to the ethnic groups, especially the Catholics and Germans."[39] The 1952 data indicate that such an appeal, if it was the cause of this Republican shift among the middle-class Catholics, did not affect Catholic workers, who were tied to the Democrats by both class and religious loyalties; thus class voting among Catholics increased to a point above that of the Protestants for the only time in sixteen years.

Whether class is defined objectively or subjectively, class voting was higher in 1952 among Catholics than among Protestants, as Table 8–5 shows. Although the Democratic vote within similar strata, defined *both* by subjective and objective class, was higher for Catholics than for Protestants (except among non-manual middle-class identifiers, among whom the Democratic vote was uniformly low), both objective or subjective class made more difference for the politics of the Catholics than of the Protestants. Holding occupation constant, the association of subjective class identification with voting was higher among Catholics than among Protestants. Holding subjective class identification constant, the association of occupation and voting was higher among Catholics than among Protestants. This is additional evidence that the lack of difference

---

[39] Lipset, *op. cit.*, p. 297.

TABLE 8–5

Democratic Preference, by Religion, Occupation Type, and Subjective Class Identification, United States, 1952

| OCCUPATION TYPE | SUBJECTIVE CLASS IDENTIFICATION | | | INDEX OF SUBJECTIVE CLASS VOTING |
	Working	Middle	Total	
		Protestants		
Manual	54 (314)*	39 (88)	52 (422)	+15
Non-Manual	45 (126)	23 (185)	29 (330)	+22
TOTAL	52 (440)	25 (273)		+27
Index of Objective Class Voting	+9	+16	+23	
		Catholics		
Manual	68 (144)	47 (34)	65 (184)	+21
Non-Manual	52 (46)	22 (50)	38 (98)	+30
TOTAL	64 (190)	32 (84)		+32
Index of Objective Class Voting	+16	+25	+27	

Source: Michigan 1952 Survey. Persons declaring that there were no classes in the United States are not included in the totals. Further analysis of the same survey which considers the effect of class identification upon political behavior appears in Heinz Eulau, *Class and Party in the Eisenhower Years* (New York: The Free Press of Glencoe, 1962). Eulau uses a different index of class, so that his results are not precisely comparable.
* Total number of respondents is in parentheses.

between Catholics and Protestants in 1952 was not spurious, and that class overrode the religious factor more in that year than in others before or since.[40]

In 1960, class voting among Catholics did not change appreciably

[40] However, Oscar Glantz found sharp differences between Protestants and Catholics in a Philadelphia study shortly after the 1952 election, even when subjective social class and social status were controlled. Differences in political preferences were considerably less among persons in the two religions sharing a pro-business or pro-labor ideology, and, among persons with both high-status and a pro-business orientation, the religious difference in political preferences disappeared. This finding parallels that in Table 8–5, showing that middle-class Catholics (both objectively and subjectively) were no more Democratic than middle-class Protestants. These data were recomputed from Oscar Glantz, "Protestant and Catholic Voting Behavior in a Metropolitan Area," *Public Opinion Quarterly*, XXIII (Spring, 1959), 73–82.

from the 1956 level, but the association of religion and voting went up sharply, undoubtedly because of the candidacy of a Catholic for President. Whether this swing was enough to offset anti-Catholic shifts is a moot point.[41] Even manual Protestants did not give the Democratic candidate a majority. Whether the victory of a Catholic candidate will finally end Catholic minority consciousness is an open question. American political scientist Peter H. Odegard suggests that "minority" consciousness may be the chief cause of the Catholic deviation:

> As consciousness of "minority" status declines for any religious group, one may assume that other factors than religion will play a larger and larger role in determining voting behavior. That is to say, as intensity of religious identity or distinction declines, economic and social status may be expected to increase in importance in explaining voting behavior. As this occurs among American Catholics and Jews, their party preferences will be less and less influenced by religion and more by other factors. They should then become indistinguishable from the preferences of others of the same or similar economic and social status, regardless of religious affiliation.[42]

Although certainly this argument is plausible and should hold for the regional as well as the religious deviations from class voting in the United States, no evidence of a consistent increase of class voting or a decline of the religious deviation is as yet manifest. It might be noted that only among non-manual persons identifying themselves as middle-class did the religious difference in voting behavior disappear, as is indicated by Table 8–5. Not only objectively higher status but a subjective sense of being part of the "great middle class" is required to rid Catholics of their sense of minority consciousness and, as a consequence, of their Democratic loyalties.

---

[41] See Philip E. Converse, "Religion and Politics: The 1960 Elections" (Survey Research Center, University of Michigan, August, 1961), and P. E. Converse, A. Campbell, W. E. Miller, and D. E. Stokes, "Stability and Change in 1960: A Reinstating Election," *American Political Science Review*, LV (June, 1961), 269–80. These authors conclude from their careful analysis of a 1960 national survey that Kennedy suffered a net loss of slightly more than 2 per cent of the national vote, with a 4 per cent gain from Catholics and a 6 per cent loss from Protestants (p. 278).

[42] Peter H. Odegard, "Catholicism and Elections in the United States," in P. H. Odegard, ed., *Religion and Politics* (Published for the Eagleton Institute of Politics at Rutgers, the State University, by Oceana Publications, Inc., 1960), pp. 120–21.

Obviously much more could be said about various political cleavages in the American electorate, but this chapter has focused on whether any consistent pattern of decline or increase of class voting was evident in general, within various regions, or within the two major religious divisions.[43]

CONCLUSION

No evidence of either a decline of class voting or any substantial change in the pattern of class voting among major United States regions or religious groups has been found. The diversity of American politics, remarked on by most political observers, remains as great as ever. Some signs of regional economic and political integration have been cited which may mean the pulling of the South into line with other parts of the country, but the outcome is not yet visible in any increase of class voting in that region. The 1960 election marked the greatest difference of Protestant and Catholic voting behavior since 1944, even when similar occupational groups were compared; therefore there is no sign yet of any decline of this source of non-class voting.

But despite this continuing diversity, data from a number of surveys from 1936 to 1960 have shown no unmistakable decline of class voting in the United States since 1936, despite the move to the Right in the Eisenhower period. As S. M. Lipset has said, "such factors as occupational status, income and the class character of the district in which people live probably distinguish the support of the two major parties more clearly now than at any other period in American history since the Civil War."[44] The data in this chapter reinforce the conclusion that there has not yet been, in V. O. Key's phrase, a "secular realignment" of the class bases of the political parties in the United States.[45]

Another incidental conclusion of the attempt to investigate changes of patterns of voting over time is that as wide a time-span

---

[43] It should be emphasized, however, that there is more variation politically within Protestantism than between Protestants in general and Catholics. See Wesley and Beverly Allinsmith, "Religious Affiliation and Politico-Economic Attitude: A Study of Eight Major U. S. Religious Groups," *Public Opinion Quarterly*, XII (Fall, 1948), 377–89.

[44] Lipset, *op. cit.*, p. 304.

[45] Key, "Secular Realignment and the Party System," *Journal of Politics*, XXI (May, 1959), 198–210.

as possible must be taken into account when attempting to assess not only political change but also the particular political behavior of a social group. The exceptional behavior of middle-class Catholics in 1952 is a case in point. If the only evidence for their political behavior were taken from that election, many false generalizations concerning the decline of religious deviations could be erected. Especially when the political realignment of entire social groups (rather than of individuals) is the research focus, as many surveys as possible over a broad range of time are necessary.

The lack of any consistent decline of class voting since 1936 does not necessarily mean that class loyalties and consciousness have remained strong. Workers might continue to vote Democratic and businessmen, Republican, but the sense of identification of this behavior with class interests might be becoming obscure and weak. Such a change could occur within both parties and social classes: the parties themselves could be moving ever closer together in their platforms and appeals, and/or occupational groups could be moving closer together in their values, styles of life, and political perspectives. An important line of research is implied by these possible changes: to determine what changes of political values and attitudes can take place *without* any substantial shift in the actual political alignment of a social group. The data on class voting give no direct clue to these changes, but they do give pause to the easy conclusion that the Eisenhower swing and postwar prosperity of the United States greatly modified the class differential in voting behavior.

Chapter 9

Canada: Pure Non-Class Politics?

THE association of social class and voting behavior, as measured by the index of class voting, is lower in Canada than in any of the other Anglo-American countries. Preliminary evidence for this assertion was presented in Chapter 5, where it was shown that in ten separate surveys of the Canadian electorate taken between 1952 and 1961 the percentage point difference between the non-manual and manual vote for either of the two major Canadian Left parties —the Liberal or New Democratic (formerly the Cooperative Commonwealth Federation, or CCF) parties—was lower than was an analogous index computed for the other countries. Class voting is low in Canada whether education, income, or occupation are used, singly or in combination, as the measure of social class position. Class voting is also lower in all regions and in either major religious grouping than it is in Britain or Australia.[1]

The discovery that class voting is relatively low does not imply that class interests do not exist in Canadian society. Class cleavages

[1] Few class differences were found in a recent analysis of social characteristics of three of the Canadian parties (all except Social Credit) in 1960. See S. Peter Regenstreif, "Some Aspects of National Party Support in Canada," *Canadian Journal of Economics and Political Science*, XXIX (February, 1963), 59–75. His results were based upon a sample of 1,000 party supporters derived from mailing lists compiled by the parties themselves. Since only 18 per cent of the sample returned the questionnaires, he does not claim to have a representative sample of all Canadian voters. CCF supporters were slightly more likely to be skilled workers, and Progressive-Conservative voters were slightly more likely to be in high income brackets than were supporters of the other parties. Clear evidence of religious voting was found.

do exist in Canada and are expressed in political demands and through political parties, but they do not result in sharply divergent support by social classes for the major national parties. Presentation of the data supporting this conclusion, discussions of why this is so in Canada, and predictions of changes are the subjects of this chapter.

It might be argued that the low level of class voting in Canada implies that it is in the forefront of a trend in all of the Anglo-American countries away from class politics. If these societies are wealthy and possess expanding middle classes with no solid class identifications, then surely a country which has a low level of class voting will stay that way. I suggest, on the contrary (and this point will be developed in Chapter 11), that class voting in Canada is less than should be expected in a country with its type of stratification, and that therefore class voting may be expected to increase if social changes follow certain paths.

The reasons for this prediction depend upon the causes for the low level of class voting. Class voting is low in Canada because the political parties are identified as representatives of regional, religious, and ethnic groupings rather than as representatives of national class interests, and this, in turn, is due to a relative lack of national integration. If, however, the conditions sustaining non-class solidarities are disappearing and a national identity is emerging, tendencies toward an increase in the level of class voting should be evident, and this chapter will consider some of the evidence available for such changes in the period 1940 to 1961.

THE ASSOCIATION OF CLASS AND PARTY IN CANADA

Regardless of whether the bases of support for the Liberal or the New Democratic party are examined separately or together, little distinctive connection of social class with party loyalties appears. The New Democratic party has more of a distinctive class basis than the Liberal party. Figure 9–1 (in which the figures are given for the voting of both occupational strata for each party in fifteen surveys from 1940 to 1961) shows that no matter what the level of New Democratic party voting has been, it has always gained more support from manual than from non-manual workers. New Democratic support among non-manuals has ranged from 4 to 15 per cent from 1940 to 1961, but among manual workers it has ranged from 9

FIGURE 9–1
Class Voting in Canada, 1940–1961

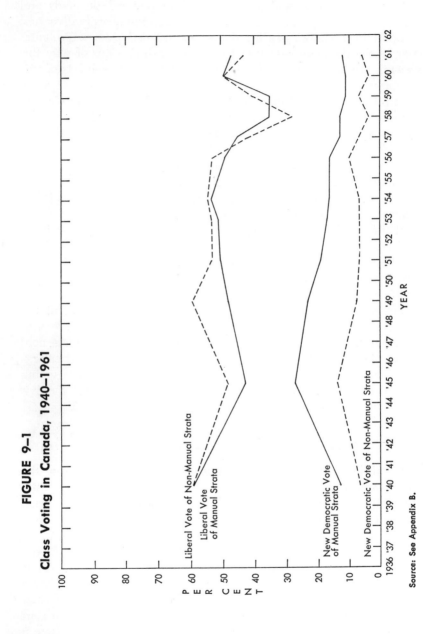

Liberal Vote of Non-Manual Strata

Liberal Vote of Manual Strata

New Democratic Vote of Manual Strata

New Democratic Vote of Non-Manual Strata

PERCENT

YEAR

Source: See Appendix B.

to 28 per cent—higher than the non-manual percentage in every survey.[2]

This is not true for the Liberal party. In eight of the fifteen surveys, non-manual persons gave the Liberal party more support than manual workers did; in one-third of the surveys the percentages were identical or nearly so. The point is that the way the support for the two "Left" parties—the Liberal and the New Democratic parties—has been combined in most of the tables which follow does not account for the lack of class voting which exists in Canada.

The New Democratic party draws its support primarily from skilled workers and union members but receives little support from better-educated and better-off persons in non-manual occupations. It might be expected that if the New Democratic party manages to become the major Left party in Canada, class politics would be sharply accentuated. The Liberal party—a "center-Left" party like the Democratic party in the United States—does not draw any kind of distinctive class support. Therefore, including the New Democratic party with the Liberal party in computing measures of class voting actually increases the statistic of class voting. If only the Liberal party is considered—on the grounds that it is the major "Left" party in Canada and the only one capable of forming a government—the class bases of the Canadian party system are even more indistinct. In the data presented in subsequent tables, the Liberal and New Democratic parties are classed together as Left parties, but their historical distinctiveness and separate roles must of course be taken into account in more detailed analyses of Canadian political behavior.[3]

---

[2] See Leo Zakuta, "The Radical Political Movement in Canada," in S. D. Clark, ed., *Urbanism and the Changing Canadian Society* (Toronto: University of Toronto Press, 1961), pp. 135–50, for an assessment of the past and the future of the CCF (New Democratic) party. Zakuta attempts to explain why the CCF became more "worldly" (had less involvement by amateurs and was less ideological) even though it failed to become a major party—a phenomenon found in this party alone among Western social-democratic parties. The NDP was formed in 1961 in an explicit attempt to create a national Left party which could replace the Liberals.

[3] It must be kept in mind that the data on class voting do not refer to voting based on subjective class identifications. It is entirely possible (although no evidence is available to test it) that the high level of Liberal voting by manual workers prior to 1957 was due to an identification of their class interests with the Liberal party and that the high level of Liberal voting by non-manual workers was due to a great diversity of non-class motives, or even some class motives, in cases where the Liberal party served some business interests.

Figure 5–1 (p. 103) gives the trends in class voting in Canada from 1940 (as ascertained from a question on past vote asked in 1945) to 1961 from fifteen separate surveys and compares them with the three other Anglo-American countries. (See Appendix B for the data upon which both Figures 5–1 and 9–1 are based.)

The general pattern visible in Figure 5–1 up to 1956 is one of stable and low class voting; but from 1957 to 1961, considerable vacillation appears, even when surveys are taken only three months apart (January and March, 1961). There is therefore no stable trend of change in the period, either upward or downward, although the average level in the 1957–61 period would seem to be higher. The high probability of sampling error for any or all of the surveys precludes any inferences from any of the particular swings, however.[4]

The reasons for Canada's low level of class voting depend partly upon its lack of legitimacy as a nation, and this historical background will be discussed briefly before the character of the parties is analyzed.

THE PROBLEM OF CANADIAN NATIONAL INTEGRATION

Canada is not a nation in the full sense of a socially unified people possessing a consciousness of nationality and a sense of patriotism. Although the Canadian state has the instruments of national sovereignty, it has neither the embedded symbols of legitimacy nor the deep loyalties to the political community which Americans and Britishers take for granted. As Alexander Brady has put it, Canada is an "aggregation of sectional communities."[5]

Settled from England and France, Canada came together into a federal nation not out of a revolutionary situation which molded a national mentality and solidarity, but out of more mundane eco-

---

[4] It may be noted, however, that these data do not support Jewett's assertion that "a Conservative landslide, as in 1958, can almost obliterate age, sex, and class lines," at least insofar as class is concerned. See Pauline Jewett, "Voting in the 1960 Federal By-Elections at Peterborough and Niagara Falls: Who Voted New Party and Why?" *Canadian Journal of Economics and Political Science,* XXVIII (February, 1962), 47. Instead, persons in manual and nonmanual occupations were farther apart in their voting patterns than ever before in this period (at least as measured by the index of class voting).

[5] Alexander Brady, *Democracy in the Dominions* (Toronto: University of Toronto Press, 1947), p. 83.

nomic interests. According to Brady, the 1867 federal union of the four provinces of Ontario, Quebec, New Brunswick, and Nova Scotia was "not the child of an aggressive democratic impulse or a powerful mass pressure," but was the result of a desire to provide a large area for free trade and to render extensive railway construction possible.[6] Thus, no great pressure was present for integration of the Canadian people into a single national political culture which could have welded the French into a strong "Canadian" nation encompassing both descendants of English and French cultural heritage. The federal union therefore gave maximum guarantees to French desire for political and cultural autonomy.

That Canada had no revolution for independence has made the nation susceptible to many influences further hindering the development of national legitimacy. Canada has remained in the British Commonwealth, and, while this national pseudo-legitimacy has reinforced a sense of national unity, it has also prevented the development of truly national solidarity. Many British immigrants still consider themselves British citizens, not Canadians. Much of Canada's population has come from the United States, but these immigrants have not been forced to become integrated into a national culture in the same way that immigrants to the United States have been, and therefore they have retained their national loyalties to the United States. The dual national identity of much of the population, with many having primary political identification with either the United States, Britain, or Quebec, has weakened the chances for the development of a sense of *national* Canadianism. (Quebecers consider themselves the truly *Canadian* Canadians, but this is defined not as national integration but as the preservation of provincial autonomy.)

The failure of the bourgeois revolution to carry through completely in Canada meant that quite different political cultures have dominated the various regions. "Central and eastern, in contrast with western, Canada have had essentially counter-revolutionary traditions, represented by the United Empire loyalists and by the church in French Canada, which escaped the influences of the French revolution."[7]

Paradoxically, as Canada has become more independent of the

---

[6] *Ibid.*, pp. 41–42.

[7] Harold A. Innis, *Essays in Canadian Economic History* (Toronto: University of Toronto Press, 1956), p. 406.

Commonwealth (both because of the strengthening of nationalist forces and because of the weakening of the Commonwealth itself), autonomist and regional political forces have been strengthened. As long as Canada was securely linked to Britain, the lack of national legitimacy was not a severe problem. In a sense, Canada "borrowed" legitimacy from the Crown and those British institutions which it adopted, and the *modus vivendi* which allowed Quebec autonomy within the framework of essentially English institutions was effective. But, as Canada broke some of its links with the Empire, by gaining the power to amend its own "constitution" (the British North America Act) for example, the influence of the United States has replaced that of Britain, and this influence has no historic legitimacy at all. As a result, centrifugal tendencies have developed which have not been restrained by a parallel development of nationalism. The United States, with even more internal diversities than Canada—even more local autonomy, many more political units smaller than the nation, greater size, a similar "dissident" region in the South—can maintain unity because of its national identity, well defined by its Revolution and firmly established by its Civil War.

Under these conditions, parliamentary government and a monarchy may have been essential for a necessary minimum of national unity in Canada. Lacking the homogeneous political culture or the legitimacy of either the United States or England, "only the objective reality of a monarchy and the permanent force of monarchical institutions could form the centre and pivot of unity" in Canada, a country of "economic hazard, external dependence, and plural culture."[8]

Canada, thus, is a sovereign state possessing consensus, but there is no sense of legitimacy for a single nation (see p. 3). Formed because political unification was needed to allow economic exploitation of her western regions, Canada has never possessed either the symbols of national legitimacy or the strong sentiments which reinforce it. Canada has no generally accepted national anthem and no flag; and, until recently, the Privy Council of England held ultimate jurisdiction over its laws. These items are merely symptoms of the lack of acceptance of the Canadian nation as the proper and right political jurisdiction over its citizens. Canada's dual ties with the Commonwealth and with the United States, combined with the circumstances of its formation and the existence of Quebec, have

---

[8] W. L. Morton, *The Canadian Identity* (Madison: University of Wisconsin Press, 1961), p. 111.

prevented the reinforcement of state sovereignty by national integration.[9]

WHY CLASS VOTING IS LOW IN CANADA

Class voting is low in Canada because the political parties are identified with regional and religious rather than class groupings. Neither class nor national identities are well developed, and the major diffuse solidarities or attachments of people are to regional and religious identities. As will be shown later, religious voting is considerably higher than class voting. Evidence from surveys will show that the voting differences between Protestants and Catholics within similar occupations are considerably greater than voting differences between different occupational strata within the same religion.

This evidence of the non-class-linked bases of party support underlines the fundamental cause of low class voting in Canada. Embedded within a nation where the majority is Protestant and British-linked is the enclave of traditionalist, French-speaking, Catholic Quebec. Unlike the social cleavages in the other Anglo-American countries, which crosscut each other, Quebec unifies several crucial cleavages—ethnic, language, cultural, religious, and even (to some extent) class—and these are bulwarked by a semi-autonomous political unit coexistent with the boundaries of the separate culture.[10] This situation, which emerged for historical rea-

---

[9] Opposition, developing in recent years, to the United States' ownership of Canadian industry and to the United States' political influence which this makes possible, may be a sign of increasing national legitimacy, albeit in a negative way. And, in English Canada at least, textbooks have been recently criticized as too "American"; a Royal Commission investigated the situation in British Columbia, and Ontario moved to rid itself of all United States-produced textbooks. *New York Times,* December 10, 1961.

[10] The political fact of federalism is probably more important than the social facts of religious and ethnic differences in accounting for Quebec separatism. The gradual assimilation of French-Canadian immigrants into New England shows that the unique "values" of the French-Canadians do not prevent the disintegration of ethnic solidarity. Probably the early autonomy of the French Catholic community in Canada within the barriers of political boundaries allowed the development of a community so large as to prevent cultural absorption. See George F. Theriault, "The Franco-Americans of New England," in Mason Wade, ed., *Canadian Dualism* (Toronto: Toronto University Press, 1960), pp. 392–411. Some of the conditions favoring or preventing ethnic assimilation are discussed (with special reference to Canada) by Stanley Lieberson, "A Societal Theory of Race and Ethnic Relations," *American Sociological Review,* XXVI (December, 1961), 902–10.

sons beyond the range of this chapter, has fundamentally shaped the Canadian political system. The necessities of maintaining minimum political consensus have given Quebec a veto-power over the expansion of national government. As a consequence, the provinces have retained a high degree of political autonomy, and regional loyalties have been easier to maintain.[11] It must be noted that the political and cultural barriers dividing Ontario and Quebec are not reinforced by geographic barriers. ". . . the industrial and economic heart of Canada . . . is geographically and economically united by its common system of waterways."[12]

The political parties in Canada have been identified with opposite sides of these primary social cleavages. The Progressive-Conservative party has been identified as the party of English or Irish Protestants and as the party of government centralization in Ottawa. The Liberal party has been identified as the party of French-speaking Catholics and as the party of provincial autonomy. (These images do not correspond to their behavior when in office, and the tensions of practice and popular image produce recurrent difficulties.) *Les deux races* of Canada have shaped the identities of the political parties.[13]

Class issues have been important in Canadian politics, but not in a way which has produced a national cleavage along class lines. Canada's "empire"—the Prairie provinces—has been the source of a struggle between the frontier farmer and eastern finance, which is the second major historical factor shaping the pattern of political cleavages in Canada. Many of the policies of the Canadian government have been designed to aid the economic development of the western provinces. The Canadian Pacific Railway, financially supported by the government and pressed for by the Conservative party under John A. Macdonald, and even confederation itself have been explained as devices to further the economic expansion

---

[11] See Dennis H. Wrong, "Parties and Voting in Canada," *Political Science Quarterly*, LXXIII (September, 1958), 397–412, and "The Pattern of Party Voting in Canada," *Public Opinion Quarterly*, XXI (Summer, 1957), 252–64, for parallel interpretations of Canadian parties and voting patterns.

[12] K. A. MacKirdy, "Geography and Federalism in Australia and Canada," *The Australian Geographer*, VI (March, 1953), 44.

[13] See, for treatments of Canadian political institutions which emphasize the consequences of regional and religious diversity, Alexander Brady, *op. cit.*, R. MacGregor Dawson, *The Government of Canada* (2nd ed.; Toronto: The University of Toronto Press, 1954), and H. McD. Clokie, *Canadian Government and Politics* (Toronto: Longmans, Green, 1944).

and exploitation of the West. Because of the interregional character of this conflict, the political consequences have been the formation of various agrarian protest parties, among them the Progressive party, the Social Credit party and the Cooperative Commonwealth Federation, all centered in the western provinces.[14] (The United States has had similar agrarian protest parties, centered in the Middle West.)

These regional class movements have not had the broad political impact on the United States that they have had on Canada, however. The regional parties in Canada have persisted more strongly, have been more numerous, and have managed to become national parties, even if weak. This is probably due to two major factors: the primary importance of the Quebec French–Ontario English split in the Canadian political system and Canada's system of parliamentary government. The fundamental conflict of *les deux races* in Canada has shaped political institutions, as already suggested, along lines favoring autonomist movements. This autonomist tendency, originally due to the need to compromise the demand for Quebec autonomy, has been built into Canadian institutions since the 1867 Confederation. This tendency has made it easier for other kinds of regional movements to fragment the political system further; it has made it more difficult for Ottawa to act as a unifying force.

The system of parliamentary government in Canada has also favored regional parties. Parliamentary government was transferred bodily from Great Britain, where it was appropriated for a homogeneous society. In Canada the discipline which it enforced upon the parties was not appropriate for the dual society, and the outcome—again because reaching some minimum agreement remained more important than splitting up the nation—was a series of provincial parties, not able to satisfy their demands because flexible national parties of the American type did not exist.[15]

---

[14] Western Canada's secession movement in the 1930's was based, not upon a drive for regional autonomy, but upon economic grievances, like Western Australia's similar secession attempt in the same period. See S. M. Lipset, *Agrarian Socialism* (Berkeley: University of California Press, 1950), pp. 81–82. William L. Morton asserts that the Social Credit and the Cooperative Commonwealth movements were class- and not sectionally-oriented. *The Progressive Party in Canada* (Toronto: Toronto University Press, 1950), p. 287.

[15] See Seymour M. Lipset, "Party Systems and the Representation of Social Groups," *European Journal of Sociology*, I (1960), 50–85.

Thus, both the autonomist pressure of Quebec and parliamentary government favored the emergence of a series of "third" parties in the western provinces. As suggested, probably the regional class conflict would not have had the impact it had if it had not been for the pre-existing bias of Canadian political institutions toward, paradoxically, *both* autonomy and centralization. The existence of centralized parties and government in the midst of a strongly federalized nation created tensions which are still unresolved. The existence of the Canadian political state probably required, in its formative period, a centralized government. The provincial parties, in turn, allow the release of strains between the centralized parliamentary system and the dominance of religious, ethnic, and regional cleavages.

The major parties have not been as sharply differentiated into Left and Right as have the major parties in Australia and Great Britain. Some historical bases for a class division do exist, but they are muffled by the stronger tendencies toward regional and religious bases of politics. Having a region (Quebec) which supports the major Left party but which represents conservative forces has consequences for Canada that are different from those produced by the South in the United States. Quebec probably exerts far more pull to the Right upon the Liberal party than the South does upon the Democratic party because Quebec is so much larger than the South relative to the rest of the nation. The Liberals may therefore be more inhibited from taking Left positions than are the Democrats, on the national level, although both are considerably influenced by the presence of such large conservative blocs.

Although the major parties are not distinctly Left and Right in their policies and appeals, they have, by that very token, been an integrating force in Canadian society, since they emphasize regional, religious, and ethnic representation and compromises rather than either universalistic or class representation. This indicates that the parties in Canada have not merely been the instruments of diverse social groups, but that party membership and identification may have served as an independent basis for whatever integration the nation has achieved.

Another reason for the absence of national class politics may be that a national class structure is probably not as visible in Canada as it is in the more homogeneous countries. In Great Britain, for example, status distinctions align with class distinctions rather than cut across them. In Canada sometimes the English-French status distinction cuts across the working-class–middle-class distinction, but sometimes they reinforce each other. An important class basis for an ethnic vote thus may exist in Quebec. A study of inter-generational mobility in urban Quebec found that mobility was considerably higher among English-Canadians than among French-Canadians. This is one of those cases where the two factors cannot be easily separated.[16]

Thus, a number of factors have prevented the emergence of national parties based predominantly upon social classes in Canada. Underlying every other factor is the existence of Quebec, with its cultural separatism, which reinforces provincial autonomy and sets up an ethnic and religious cleavage cutting across class lines. The lack of legitimacy of the nation, the lack of differentiation of the parties into clearly Left and Right polarities, and the lack of visibility of a national class structure, are secondary factors. Whatever class politics Canada possesses is largely channeled through the regional parties.[17]

Once established, the legitimacy of ethnic pluralism may long sustain voting patterns based upon ethnic membership, although some authors suggest that national region-wide ethnic solidarity in voting is unlikely: "it is possible that ethnic political assimilation can occur at the national level while ethnic differentiation becomes a feature of political *behavior* at provincial and municipal levels."[18]

If the conditions restraining the emergence of class voting are changing, then it may increase. If the social changes connected with industrialization and urbanization are having the same ho-

---

[16] See Yves de Jocas and Guy Rocher, "Inter-Generation Occupational Mobility in the Province of Quebec," *Canadian Journal of Economics and Political Science*, XXIII (February, 1957), 66.

[17] Not all Canadian political scientists and historians accept the view that Canada is so split by regional and ethnic cleavages and that class interests do not penetrate to the national political parties. In the view of such men as H. A. Innis, S. D. Clark, A. R. M. Lower, and F. H. Underhill, a part of French-Canadian regional politics is due to the regions' economic subordination to the Anglo-Saxon business group, not merely to their concern for cultural autonomy. They emphasize also that prairie politics is a response to the economic exploitation of the West by eastern business and financial interests. See especially, Innis, *op. cit.*, Frank H. Underhill, *In Search of Canadian Liberalism* (Toronto: Macmillan, 1960).

[18] Frank G. Vallee, Mildred Schwartz, and Frank Darknell, "Ethnic Assimilation and Differentiation in Canada," *Canadian Journal of Economics and Political Science*, XXIII (November, 1957), 548. Italics in original.

mogenizing and secularizing effects upon Canada as they have had upon other countries, then the bases for religious and regional voting may be disappearing.

The cleavages still dividing Canadian political life were discussed by André Siegfried, the great French political scientist, in his book *The Race Question in Canada*, published in 1907.[19] Siegfried asserted that the "purity" of political life in Canada suffers from the necessity to "prevent the formation of homogeneous parties, divided according to creed or race or class." The result has been the formation of "entirely harmless parties" made up of "heterogeneous elements: employers and labourers, townsmen and peasants . . ."[20] Canadian parties have thus been characterized for at least sixty years by a lack of both doctrine and a stable class base. Only lack of understanding of the historical roots and functions of the Canadian party system could lead a political journalist in 1962 to describe the election as a "referendum on everything and on nothing, for the great issues of national policy have been obscured by a smoke screen of petty quarrels and accusations."[21] Such a statement assumes a degree of national integration not yet achieved in Canada.

REGIONALISM AND CHANGES IN CLASS VOTING

If class voting has increased in some or all regions of Canada, this might be evidence that a rise is a national trend and not one confined to particular areas where class grievances might be particularly relevant in this period. Evidence for a nationwide increase of class voting might indicate that the structural bases of politics are changing, not merely the temporary relevance of class issues. However, Table 9–1 and Figure 9–2 show no consistent increase of class voting in any major region of Canada in this period.

As in the case of the national figures, only the over-all relationships have much meaning, not the specific figures. The numbers of cases, particularly in the smaller provinces or regions, are too small to allow any inferences about changes in class voting in, say, British

---

[19] London: Eveleigh Nash.

[20] *Ibid.*, p. 143. Siegfried discusses the reasons for lack of class consciousness on p. 224 ff.

[21] William H. Hessler, "The Canadians Go to the Polls," *The Reporter*, June 7, 1962, pp. 30–32.

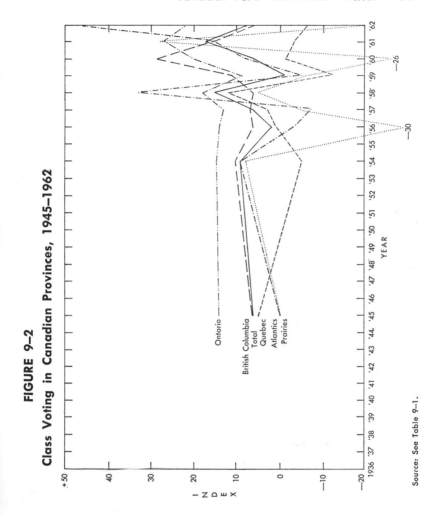

FIGURE 9-2

Class Voting in Canadian Provinces, 1945-1962

Source: See Table 9-1.

Columbia versus the Atlantic provinces. The more or less consistent rank order of the provinces and the consistently higher level of class voting in Ontario are the two main findings worth discussing. (See Table 9-2 for a summary of the crude rank order visible from the data of Table 9-1.)

In general, the results are what might be expected from knowledge of the political history of the provinces. Ontario has the highest level of class voting in six of the ten surveys here reported;

TABLE 9–1

Liberal or New Democratic Preference, by Region and Occupation Type, Canada, 1945–1961

OCCUPATION TYPE	PER CENT OF LIBERAL OR NDP VOTERS					
	Atlantics	Quebec	Ontario	Prairies	British Columbia	Total
May, 1945						
Manual	62 (55)*	82 (103)	68 (203)	68 (97)	75 (49)	71 (505)
Non-Manual	62 (37)	77 (129)	54 (226)	68 (122)	69 (59)	65 (573)
Index of Class Voting	0	+5	+14	0	+6	+6
September, 1954						
Manual	75 (69)	64 (129)	68 (199)	68 (81)	69 (84)	69 (562)
Non-Manual	66 (82)	69 (186)	53 (240)	60 (107)	56 (69)	60 (684)
Index of Class Voting	+9	−5	+15	+8	+13	+9
July, 1956						
Manual	61 (41)	70 (120)	65 (162)	44 (36)	70 (27)	65 (385)
Non-Manual	64 (45)	69 (180)	51 (187)	74 (92)	64 (31)	63 (534)
Index of Class Voting	−3	+1	+14	−30	+6	+2
May, 1957						
Manual	56 (88)	79 (200)	60 (283)	52 (83)	37 (60)	62 (714)
Non-Manual	63 (76)	76 (160)	47 (239)	57 (91)	30 (73)	56 (639)
Index of Class Voting	−7	+3	+13	−5	+7	+6
March, 1958						
Manual	63 (43)	51 (109)	48 (169)	30 (53)	48 (48)	48 (422)
Non-Manual	30 (33)	39 (111)	30 (119)	25 (55)	42 (26)	33 (344)
Index of Class Voting	+33	+12	+18	+5	+6	+15

TABLE 9–1—(Continued)

OCCUPATION TYPE	PER CENT OF LIBERAL OR NDP VOTERS					
	Atlantics	Quebec	Ontario	Prairies	British Columbia	Total
	November, 1959					
Manual	56 (27)	44 (66)	52 (89)	35 (54)	47 (17)	46 (253)
Non-Manual	61 (18)	56 (48)	43 (95)	41 (34)	36 (14)	47 (209)
Index of Class Voting	—5	—12	+9	—6	+11	—1
	November, 1960					
Manual	48 (21)	68 (53)	66 (50)	41 (29)	69 (16)	60 (169)
Non-Manual	40 (20)	69 (36)	46 (63)	67 (30)	40 (15)	54 (164)
Index of Class Voting	+8	—1	+20	—26	+29	+6
	January, 1961					
Manual	67 (12)	50 (50)	73 (66)	61 (33)	69 (26)	64 (187)
Non-Manual	52 (25)	53 (55)	46 (82)	33 (33)	54 (13)	47 (208)
Index of Class Voting	+15	—3	+27	+28	+15	+17
	March, 1961					
Manual	55 (29)	48 (42)	67 (49)	37 (35)	85 (13)	55 (168)
Non-Manual	64 (11)	56 (34)	45 (75)	45 (22)	64 (14)	51 (156)
Index of Class Voting	—9	—8	+22	—8	+21	+4
	November, 1961					
Manual	69 (13)	57 (51)	69 (59)	26 (23)	56 (16)	58 (162)
Non-Manual	23 (13)	63 (49)	47 (55)	46 (26)	50 (12)	50 (155)
Index of Class Voting	+46	—6	+22	—20	+6	+8

Source: CIPO Surveys Nos. 142, 238, 250, 258, 266, 279, 285, 286, 287, and 292. The Prairies include Saskatchewan, Alberta, and Manitoba. The Atlantics include New Brunswick, Nova Scotia, Newfoundland, and Prince Edward Island.
* Total number of respondents is in parentheses.

TABLE 9–2

Rank Order of Class Voting in Canadian Regions

REGIONS IN TENTATIVE RANK ORDER	NUMBER OF SURVEYS IN WHICH THE REGION RANKED:					
	1st	2nd	3rd	4th	5th	RANK-INDEX SCORE*
Ontario	6	4	0	0	0	14
British Columbia	2	5	2	1	0	22
Atlantics	2	1	3	2	2	31
Quebec	0	1	4	2	3	37
Prairies	1	0	1	3	5	41

Source: A summary of the data given in Table 9–1. Since the samples in the provinces are so small and so subject to sampling error, no statistical measure of the rank order is appropriate. The consistency of the results from survey to survey indicates that these data may correspond to the actual level of class voting in the provinces, however—although the high level of inconsistency found in the Atlantics, for example, may indicate either variations from sample to sample or real vacillations of political support.

* The ranks were summed to obtain the rank-index score.

British Columbia is second-highest in five of the ten. The Atlantic provinces vacillate considerably, being highest in two and lowest in three. Quebec is almost consistently low, as are the Prairie provinces.

Class voting is particularly low in the Prairies, despite their history of rural class struggles, probably partly because the non-manual strata which normally vote Conservative in Ontario have swung over to the Liberal party as the chief protection against the socialist CCF. The Liberal party may have benefitted from its "center" position by appealing to the lower strata where the Conservatives are strong and to the higher strata where the CCF and now the NDP have been strong.[22]

Ontario's relatively high level (close to the United States level of class voting or higher, in some surveys) indicates that Canada is not immune from such bases for political cleavages. The consistently higher level of class voting in Ontario is not surprising. Ontario is the most urbanized and industrialized region of

---

[22] Whether the erratic pattern exhibited by the Prairies is due to the peculiarities of the sample or some "real" factor is unknown. Probably the political behavior of manual and non-manual workers is erratic in areas where politics is oriented toward farming issues and most of the population is in agricultural occupations. Even as farmers constitute a marginal and volatile economic group within the national political system, so other strata constitute marginal and volatile economic groups within areas dominated by farming interests.

the country.[23] The very political fragmentation of Canada means that a province like Ontario approaches closely a "nation" in its own right. Ottawa, the capital of Canada, is located in Ontario, and this undoubtedly reinforces the sense of identity with the nation as a political *unity* (not simply a congeries of autonomous provinces) which reduces the importance of "local" identities, such as those important in Quebec. Also, Ontario has a long heritage of association with Great Britain, and much of its population comes from the United Kingdom. (More of the population of the Atlantic provinces comes from England, but those small provinces have a history of opposition to the "domination" of Ontario and therefore reveal "regional" patterns of voting.) In other words, the "regional" identity of Ontario is almost identical with a "national" identity and does not interfere with the development of the patterns of class voting.

The differential patterns of provincial versus Dominion class voting would provide an additional clue to changes in class voting in Canada, although data are not available to the author. If the focus of class cleavages has been at the provincial level, then class voting should have been higher at the provincial level than at the Dominion level in the 1930's and 1940's. But if regional and parochial loyalties are being replaced by class loyalties at the national level, then class voting should not be higher at the Dominion level. If this is true, this would be further evidence that a realignment of the class bases of Canadian politics is indeed taking place. A survey of Quebec voting in the 1960 provincial elections found no class voting, however, contradicting this suggestion that the focus of class politics in Quebec, at least, may be at the provincial, rather than the national, level.[24]

Some evidence is available showing that consistent voting for the same party at Dominion and provincial levels is increasing. This may indicate that the opposition of provincial and national interests is no longer as important as it has been in the past, at least in producing such "contradictory" patterns of political behavior. Table 9–3 shows that the proportion of persons supporting a Dominion

[23] Data on the degree of urbanization of the provinces will be presented later. Ontario has the most telephones per 1,000 population and the most surfaced roads for its land areas as well. See the *Canada Yearbook, 1957–1958* (Ottawa: Dominion Bureau of Statistics), pp. 834, 889. These indicate that its population is the least "isolated."

[24] See Groupe de Recherches Sociales, *Les Électeurs Québécois* (Montreal, 1960), esp. pp. 50–62.

TABLE 9–3

Dominion Party Supporters Who Backed the Same Party
at the Provincial Level, Canada, 1945–1958

| | PER CENT BACKING SAME PROVINCIAL PARTY | | | | | |
| DOMINION | Canada | | Quebec | | Ontario | |
PARTY	1945	1958	1945	1958	1945	1958
Conservative	68 (361)*	80 (394)	47 (38)	48 (132)	79 (175)	95 (185)
Liberal	72 (537)	83 (186)	75 (159)	79 (67)	67 (176)	85 (76)
CCF	70 (239)	94 (16)	56 (16)	.. (1)	75 (85)	100 (12)
Social Credit	74 (47)	.. (5)	50 (10)	.. (3)	.. (1)	.. (1)

Sources: CIPO Surveys Nos. 142 and 270. For 1945, federal voting intention and past vote in a provincial election are the basis for these data. For 1958, voting intention was used in both. Many persons supporting a party on one level were undecided on the other level. Non-voters are excluded. Of the *Bloc Populaire* supporters in Quebec in 1945, 91 per cent supported the provincial *Union Nationale*.
* Total number of respondents backing a given Dominion party is in parentheses.

party who also supported the same party at the provincial level increased from 1945 to 1958 and that this was true nationally and in Ontario, but not in Quebec. Again, we may infer that the impulse toward regionalism is weakest in Ontario. (The exact proportions of voters cannot be inferred from this table, only the relative proportions in the two different surveys.)

As already suggested in other chapters, the social changes connected with urbanization—industrialization, the disappearance of the special economic character of a province, the erosion of parochial and local loyalties—may well be connected with an increase of class voting. If the provinces with special reasons for regional politics are becoming urbanized, then a number of causes of regionalism may be dwindling in importance. Table 9–4 shows that the greatest urbanization has taken place in two of the Prairie provinces, those most subject to regional, class-based political movements. In this period, Quebec has become one of the most urbanized provinces, indicating that over-all urbanization as such does not immediately break down cultural regionalism. The greatest urbanization took place in Alberta, the original home of Social Credit, which was 33 per cent urban in 1941 but 57 per cent urban in 1956. Manitoba in 1956 was close to the level of urbanism that Ontario had reached in 1941. In 1956, Ontario, British Columbia, and Quebec were the most urbanized provinces.

Also, if class voting is higher in more urban areas, we have more

TABLE 9–4

Urban Population in the Canadian Provinces, 1941–1956

PROVINCE	URBAN PER CENT OF POPULATION			PER CENT CHANGE	RATIO
	1941	*1951*	*1956*	*1941–1956*	*1956–1941*
Atlantics					
Newfoundland	37	43	45	+ 8	1.22
Prince Edward I.	22	25	30	+ 8	1.36
Nova Scotia	50	54	57	+ 7	1.14
New Brunswick	38	42	46	+ 8	1.21
Quebec	62	66	70	+ 8	1.13
Ontario	68	71	76	+ 8	1.12
Prairies					
Manitoba	49	57	60	+11	1.22
Saskatchewan	21	30	36	+15	1.71
Alberta	33	50	57	+24	1.73
British Columbia	67	68	73	+ 6	1.09
CANADA	56	62	67	+11	1.20

Source: *Canada Yearbook* (Ottawa: Dominion Bureau of Statistics). The 1956 figures are taken from the 1957–58 volume, p. 122. The 1941 and 1951 figures are computed from the 1952–53 volume, p. 144. All definitions of the urban population refer to the 1951 definition.

reason to believe that urbanization will indeed result in a decrease of the parochial bases of politics dominant in Canada at the present time. Several surveys show that class voting is indeed higher in cities over 30,000 than in towns under that size, but no consistent increase according to city size occurs. Actually, the Left vote of manual workers (particularly the CCF vote) is much higher in cities of 30,000 to 100,000 population than in cities over 100,000. Reasons for this cannot be explored here, since the only relevant point is that class voting does seem to be higher in urban areas.[25]

There is some evidence that political regionalism in Canada is dwindling. The shifts of voting for or against the government party have become more similar in the major regions of Canada in the period 1921–1958. The standard deviation from the average swing was smaller at each election except the one in 1958, which was

[25] The data will not be given here in detail, but 1954, 1957, and 1958 surveys show that class voting is higher in all city-size categories of over 30,000 than in those under 30,000 with one exception (in the 1958 survey, class voting was second-highest in the 2,000 to 10,000 category). In a 1945 survey, no such consistency appears, so a change in the effect of urbanism may have occurred.

marked, however, by a remarkably uniform swing of all regions to the Conservative party. The Conservative vote in 1958 varied only from 49 to 56 per cent in the five regions. Scarrow suggests that Canada is becoming more "politically homogeneous" and concludes that by-elections may come more to reflect national trends than heretofore.[26]

REGIONALISM IN QUEBEC

Thus, the basis for a national class politics is laid by a number of important social changes taking place in Canada. But the changes mentioned are only relevant to the economic character of the provinces—therefore mainly to the Prairies-Eastern cleavage. Perhaps more important is the question of the cultural bases of regionalism in Quebec. Are there any social changes which may create the bases for a class politics on national lines?

Quebec social structure has in fact been changing faster than its political structure. Its rate of economic growth since World War II has been faster than any province except Ontario. And, as already seen, it is now highly urbanized. "While the number of individuals employed in agriculture remained almost stationary between 1890 and 1950, the urban population rose by 500 percent, reversing the former 2:1 rural-urban ratio."[27] This means, as it means wherever urbanization takes place, that the objective conditions reinforcing the isolation of Quebec are disappearing. Quebecers are becoming more geographically mobile, and the increasing contact with Anglo-Saxons has produced greater acceptance of them in predominantly English cities. According to F. Alexander:

> . . . French-Canadian visitors now command respect where once they provoked rude or hostile comment as foreigners. Of this change I was assured by older French-Canadian residents of Montreal and Quebec who nowadays travel westward as part of the increasing vacational and business mobility of the contemporary Canadian. The improved facilities for this interprovincial travel are themselves only another manifestation of the impact of the industrial revolution on the once self-contained and isolated French-Canadian province.[28]

[26] Howard A. Scarrow, "By-Elections and Public Opinion in Canada," *Public Opinion Quarterly*, XXV (Spring, 1961), 89–91.

[27] Walter O. Filley, "Social Structure and Canadian Political Parties: The Quebec Case," *Western Political Quarterly*, IX (December, 1956), 909.

[28] Fred Alexander, "André Siegfried: A 20th Century de Tocqueville," *Australian Journal of Politics and History*, VI (May, 1960), 25.

The class divisions within Quebec are also assuming more and more "national" patterns. As Filley puts it, there is an "increasing awareness of class differentiation." The formerly "self-sufficient *habitant* more and more approximates the North-American farmer-entrepreneur." The middle class has expanded, and the clerical-professional elite no longer holds its position unchallenged.[29]

The industrial working class has grown and also changed its character, becoming less aware of itself as "French" and "Catholic" and more conscious of its common interests with other Canadian workers. Evidence for this may be seen in both the growth of trade-union organization and the political changes taking place in recent years. Quebec workers, because of their acceptance of Catholic economic and political ideology, for a long time accepted a passive role. The early trade unions were rejected because of their English and American taint, and the first Catholic unions were little more than company unions until World War II.[30] The French-Catholic labor federation (the CTCC—*Confederation de Travail Canadien et Catholique*) organized the largest bloc of French-speaking workers and began to work with the Canadian Labor Congress after the latter was formed in 1956 at the same time as the AFL and the CIO merged in the United States. The 1958 Annual Congress of the CTCC authorized negotiations for affiliation with the CLC.[31] The changing psychology of French industrial workers is illustrated by a statement by the secretary-general of the CTCC, M. Jean Marchand: "Twenty years ago we French-Canadian workers bitterly hated our English employers. Now we merely hate our employers."[32]

A consequence of these changes has been the dwindling appeal of nationalism. The anti-labor policies of the *Union Nationale*, especially the crushing of an asbestos strike in 1949, finally resulted in political action on the part of the CTCC, previously politically inactive. In the next provincial elections, one-half of the Liberals winning may have owed their victories to the backing of the Catholic labor organization.[33]

Changes in Quebec policies vis-à-vis the Dominion government following the death of the *Union Nationale* leader, Maurice

[29] Filley, *loc. cit.*
[30] *Ibid.*, p. 910.
[31] Alexander, *op. cit.*, p. 21.
[32] *Ibid.* Professor Alexander interviewed M. Marchand.
[33] Filley, *op. cit.*, p. 910. See also H. F. Quinn, "The Changing Pattern of Quebec Politics," *Canadian Forum*, XXXII (September, 1952), 129–30.

Duplessis, also possibly indicate a new political integration of Quebec with the rest of Canada. (These changes also demonstrate the way in which one man possessing the aura of nationalist legitimacy can delay political changes beyond the time when social changes have produced a population ready to accept the new forms of politics.) Although the new premier, Paul Sauvé, and his successor, Antonio Barrette (who took office in January, 1960), were nominally also *Union Nationale,* their policies broke with some of the keystones established by M. Duplessis as barriers to federal "penetration." Sauvé immediately began negotiating with the Dominion government for the release of funds held for Quebec universities. The funds had been refused by Duplessis for fear of increasing Dominion influence over the Catholic-dominated Quebec educational system. Participation in the federal hospital insurance plan and liberalization of the labor relations laws were also considered by the new regime.[34]

Obviously, these few social and political changes are not enough to assure social and political integration of Quebec into Canada, and this study cannot go more deeply into the problem. But the signs are that the isolation of Quebec is breaking down, and ethnic and religious solidarities interfering with class voting may be weakening.

RELIGION AND CLASS VOTING

Table 9–5 and Figure 9–3 present the data on class voting among Protestants and Catholics in nine surveys. In eight of the nine, class voting was higher among Protestants than among Catholics. The "religious effect" is also evident in this table, since the voting for the Liberal and New Democratic parties (mainly the Liberals) is consistently considerably higher among both manual and non-manual Catholics than among Protestants in the same social class position.

Within both Quebec and Ontario, however, Protestants are more likely to vote according to their class than Catholics; this is shown in at least one 1957 survey, data from which appear in Table 9–6. But as might be expected, Catholics were slightly more likely to vote according to their class in Ontario than in Quebec. Differences between the two religions were strong in both provinces, however,

---

[34] See the *New York Times,* November 19 and 22, 1959 and January 6 and 7, 1960. The *Union Nationale* finally lost provincial power to the Liberals in 1960.

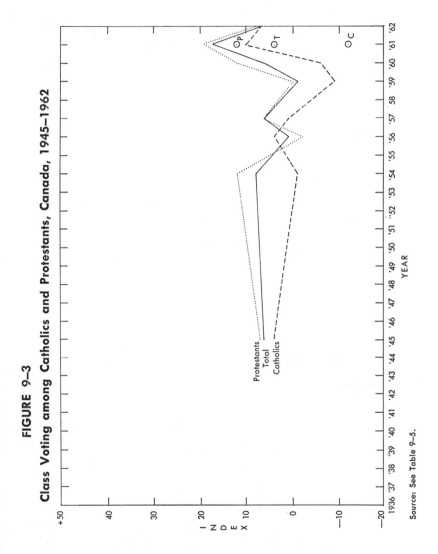

FIGURE 9–3

Class Voting among Catholics and Protestants, Canada, 1945–1962

Source: See Table 9–5.

TABLE 9–5

Liberal and New Democratic Preference, by Religion and Occupation Type, Canada, 1945–1961

OCCUPATION TYPE	PER CENT PREFERRING LIBERAL OR NEW DEMOCRATIC PARTIES			RELIGIOUS VOTING INDEX
	Catholics	*Protestants*	*Total*	
		May, 1945		
Manual	85 (164)*	63 (297)	71 (503)	+22
Non-Manual	81 (161)	56 (348)	65 (565)	+25
TOTAL	83 (325)	59 (645)	67 (1068)	+24
Index of Class Voting	+4	+7	+6	
		September, 1954		
Manual	71 (223)	64 (311)	68 (551)	+7
Non-Manual	72 (255)	52 (396)	60 (677)	+20
TOTAL	72 (478)	57 (707)	64 (1228)	+15
Index of Class Voting	—1	+12	+8	
		July, 1956		
Manual	74 (176)	55 (198)	64 (380)	+19
Non-Manual	70 (208)	57 (310)	63 (534)	+13
TOTAL	72 (384)	56 (508)	63 (914)	+16
Index of Class Voting	+4	—2	+1	
		May, 1957		
Manual	76 (321)	50 (392)	62 (713)	+26
Non-Manual	75 (232)	44 (388)	56 (637)	+31
TOTAL	76 (553)	47 (780)	59 (1350)	+29
Index of Class Voting	+1	+6	+6	
		November, 1959		
Manual	56 (108)	37 (141)	46 (253)	+19
Non-Manual	65 (60)	37 (142)	47 (209)	+28
TOTAL	59 (168)	37 (283)	46 (462)	+22
Index of Class Voting	—9	0	—1	

TABLE 9–5—(Continued)

Liberal and New Democratic Preference, by Religion and Occupation Type, Canada, 1945–1961—(Continued)

OCCUPATION TYPE	PER CENT PREFERRING LIBERAL OR NEW DEMOCRATIC PARTIES			
	Catholics	Protestants	Total	RELIGIOUS VOTING INDEX
		November, 1960		
Manual	69 (75)	53 (87)	60 (169)	+16
Non-Manual	75 (52)	41 (106)	54 (164)	+34
TOTAL	72 (127)	47 (193)	57 (337)	+25
Index of Class Voting	—6	+12	+6	
		January, 1961		
Manual	70 (92)	54 (88)	64 (187)	+16
Non-Manual	60 (86)	35 (109)	47 (208)	+25
TOTAL	65 (178)	44 (197)	55 (395)	+21
Index of Class Voting	+10	+19	+17	
		March, 1961		
Manual	58 (65)	53 (102)	55 (168)	+5
Non-Manual	70 (40)	41 (109)	51 (156)	+29
TOTAL	63 (105)	47 (211)	53 (324)	+16
Index of Class Voting	—12	+12	+4	
		November, 1961		
Manual	67 (72)	51 (84)	59 (162)	+16
Non-Manual	60 (45)	43 (100)	52 (155)	+17
TOTAL	64 (117)	47 (184)	55 (317)	+17
Index of Class Voting	+7	+8	+7	

Source: CIPO Surveys Nos. 142, 238, 250, 258, 279, 285, 286, 287, 292. Discrepancies in the totals are due to omission of persons belonging to other religions or not answering.

* Total number of respondents in parentheses.

TABLE 9–6

Liberal or CCF Preference, by Religion and Occupation Type, Quebec and Ontario, Canada, 1957

OCCUPATION TYPE	PER CENT PREFERRING LIBERAL OR CCF PARTIES			RELIGIOUS VOTING INDEX
	Catholic	Protestant	Total	
			Quebec	
Manual	82 (180)*	61 (13)	81 (193)	+21
Non-Manual	80 (117)	44 (18)	76 (137)	+36
TOTAL	81 (297)	52 (31)		+29
Index of Class Voting	+2	+17	+5	
			Ontario	
Manual	89 (62)	53 (212)	61 (274)	+36
Non-Manual	82 (33)	38 (160)	47 (203)	+44
TOTAL	86 (95)	47 (372)		+39
Index of Class Voting	+7	+15	+14	

Source: CIPO Survey No. 258 (May, 1957).
* Total number of respondents in parentheses.

since the differences between the religions within similar strata were consistently larger than the differences between classes within the same religion.[35]

[35] A survey of the federal constituency of Kingston, Ontario, in 1953 and 1955 found sharp differences between the political preferences of Catholics and Protestants (particularly United Church members). The author did not report a control for social class. See John Meisel, "Religious Affiliation and Electoral Behaviour: A Case Study," *Canadian Journal of Economics and Political Science*, XXII (November, 1956), 481–96.

Meisel, contrary to the predictions of the "cross-pressures" hypothesis, did not find that the Catholics had a lower turnout rate than the Protestants, although the constituency is strongly Conservative, and the Catholics were heavily Liberal. This is probably because there was no "breakage effect," the term used by the authors of the 1948 (Elmira, New York) voting study for the consequences of lack of political homogeneity within the "primary" (family and friends) political environment of voters. Only if friends and family disagreed did the political climate of the New York community affect the turnout rate and the direction of voting. It is likely that few Kingston Catholics were exposed to Conservative friends and relatives; therefore they were not really exposed to cross-pressure from the dominant Conservative climate. If this solidary political environment is breaking up, we would expect not only a drop in the Liberal vote of Catholics, but also a drop in their turnout rate as they become subjected to contradictory political influences. See Bernard Berelson *et al.*, *Voting* (Chicago: University of Chicago Press, 1954), pp. 98–101, for a discussion of the "breakage effect."

Although the French in Canada are overrepresented in the lower occupational groups,[36] this cannot account for the lower level of class voting in Quebec or among Catholics because the index of class voting is designed to compensate for the relative proportions of persons in different occupational strata. In other words, even though there may be an association of social class with religion in Canada, this cannot be considered to be a "class" basis for Quebec's adherence to the Liberal party because among Catholics within Quebec, there is still little political cleavage along occupational lines. That Quebec regionalism may not have an entirely religious basis is implied by the higher level of Liberal vote in Quebec than in Ontario among Protestants in both social strata.

Although there is no evidence of an increase in class voting among either Protestants and Catholics, the secularization of Canadian society might increase class voting by reducing the importance of religious influences upon behavior generally and upon political behavior specifically. A possible indication of the consequences of secularization is available from a 1957 Canadian survey which asked whether respondents listened to religious services on radio or television. If it can be inferred that persons who never or rarely listened were more secular in their general orientation than persons who regularly listened, and if it can be predicted that Canada, and specifically Quebec, will become more secularized, then this is some evidence that class voting may increase in Canada. In this survey (CIPO No. 258, May, 1957), the over-all level of class voting among Catholics was +1; among Protestants, +6. Among persons who never listened to such religious services, however, class voting among Catholics was +10; among Protestants, +13. The religious effect was still present, however, since within manual occupations, voting for the Liberal and CCF parties was 30 per cent higher among Catholics than among Protestants; within non-manual occupations, it was 33 per cent higher. (These data are not presented in any table.)

Indirect evidence of secularization in Canada is afforded by an increase in the proportion of interfaith marriages occurring in every

---

[36] Bernard Blishen, "The Construction and Use of an Occupational Class Scale," *Canadian Journal of Economics and Political Science,* XXIV (November, 1958), 530–31. Blishen reported that 34 per cent of persons of British origin are found in the two lowest occupational categories of seven, but that almost 50 per cent of the persons of French origin were in the two lowest categories.

province including Quebec from 1922 to 1957.[37] Even when the amount and changes of the distribution of religious groups within the provinces were allowed for, it was found that the proportions of marriages of persons of different faiths increased fairly steadily over the thirty-year period. This finding held true for both Protestant and Catholic brides and grooms. The author suggests that this change may reflect "diminutions of ingroup solidarity among the predominantly Catholic group of French origin and the predominantly Protestant group of British origin as well as a lessening of association between religious and social-class differences."[38]

Changes in Quebec are by no means all in the direction of increasing cultural assimilation and secularization, however. On the one hand, in addition to the changes already mentioned, Quebec is feeling the impact of the demand for more educational opportunities (in itself an indication of modernization), and part of those in the movement desire secularized education. On the other hand, a new secessionist group has arisen, demanding various nationalist actions.[39]

THE 1957–1962 CANADIAN ELECTIONS AND CLASS VOTING

The possible significance of the social changes taking place in Canada for a fundamental realignment of Canadian politics must not be overstated. The three Canadian elections in 1957, 1958, and 1962 showed that the bases of politics remain primarily regional. It continued to be true that "a party, to be successful, must draw its support from two or more regions" of Canada.[40]

Of the 1957 election, a study concluded that the voting results showed the continuing importance of regional and religious factors in Canadian politics:

> the Liberals' areas of special strength were French Canada, "frontier" constituencies, and those in which the population was not predominantly of British origin. The Conservatives consolidated their traditional strongholds, particularly in Ontario, and scored impressive gains in almost all other sections of the country. The in-

---

[37] David M. Heer, "The Trend of Interfaith Marriages in Canada: 1922–1957," *American Sociological Review*, XXVII (April, 1962), 245–50.
[38] *Ibid.*, p. 250.
[39] *New York Times*, November 14 and 20, 1961.
[40] Clokie, *op. cit.*, p. 80.

crease in their strength was greatest in the metropolitan areas (except in Quebec), in Nova Scotia, British Columbia and the Prairies, although in this region the third parties remained in a strong position. On the whole, the appeal of the Conservative party was greatest in non-French, Protestant and British constituencies, although many areas containing non-Anglo-Saxon and non-French majorities gave Mr. Diefenbaker strong support.[41]

The continuing dual loyalty of French-Canadians is well illustrated by a phrase in a speech by the Liberal Prime Minister M. St. Laurent during the campaign. Speaking in Roberval, Quebec, concerning a railway line extension, he said:

It grated me to see that all this railway expansion would direct business to Toronto or Montreal. Of course we are all part of one and the same country, but we all have our own little homeland. Frankly, it is more as a Quebecer than as Prime Minister of Canada that I put my weight behind the demands of your citizens here.[42]

Appealing for votes on the basis of "our little homeland" is clearly only possible where local loyalties are still much stronger than national ones, and is probably inconceivable in Australia or Great Britain, although less so in the United States.

The conflict between national development under the initiative of the Dominion government and provincial autonomy was continually present during the election campaign, and the fact that *both* major parties felt it necessary to present themselves as representing *both* the best interests of the nation and those of the provinces shows not only the still-fundamental ambiguity of political jurisdictions in Canada, but also the political necessities of remaining "on the fence."

The Conservative party played both tunes—national development and provincial rights—against the Liberals. They asserted that the government had become excessively centralist. According to one of their leaflets, this led to a "deliberate policy of invasion of the major taxation fields in order to shut out the provinces and municipalities from their main source of income and to force them to beg for handouts from Ottawa." According to Meisel, "in the province of Quebec the same argument took the form of attacks on

---

[41] John Meisel, *The Canadian General Election of 1957* (Toronto: University of Toronto Press, 1962), p. 266.

[42] From a speech on May 29, 1957, just before the Dominion election in June. Quoted in *ibid.*, p. 115.

the government for allegedly having violated provincial rights."
Although no precise proposals for changing Dominion-provincial
relations were announced, Mr. Diefenbaker in a speech promised to
call a Dominion-provincial conference "to bring about a settlement
[of Dominon-provincial differences] not in the spirit of arrogant
domination, as displayed by the present government, but in the
spirit of unity and amity, with mutual tolerance and respect."[43]

The Liberals tried to play both tunes also. They tried to show
that the "Conservative party was still very much an Ontario party,
pressing the interests of the central provinces at the expense of the
peripheral ones. In contrast, the Liberal party was frequently referred to as a truly national party—one which had always taken a
national viewpoint and could be counted upon to continue doing so
in the future."[44]

The Conservative leaders used Left-Right issues in an attempt to
break their identification as the party of privilege, according to
Meisel. The Liberals' were attacked as raising old-age pensions
"insufficiently" (from forty to forty-six dollars in 1956). Diefenbaker
attacked this as "insufficient, inequitable, niggardly." This kind of
campaign rhetoric achieved a:

> two-fold purpose; it branded the Liberals as a party no longer
> sympathetic to the underdog, to the group Mr. Diefenbaker once
> characterized as the "humble men and women across this country
> who desire some one to speak for them in Parliament." Secondly, it
> enabled the Conservatives to divest themselves of the lingering
> stigma of being a party of privilege. Mr. Diefenbaker was prob-
> ably the first Conservative leader in this century to succeed in mak-
> ing creditable Conservative promises of social reform.[45]

If this Conservative appeal was successful, it should have had
the result of reducing class voting by reducing the distinction—
already blurred—between the parties along Left-Right lines. If
class voting went up in 1958, when the Conservatives won by a
considerably larger margin than they had in 1957, possibly a structural realignment is actually taking place. Manual workers switched
over less to the Conservatives than non-manual workers did, in spite
of the Conservative appeal on Left issues such as the old-age
pensions.

---

[43] Quoted in *ibid.*, p. 55.
[44] Quoted in *ibid.*, p. 56.
[45] *Ibid.*, p. 54.

But after all, it could be said that the Conservatives did win and that this move to the Right in and of itself means a reduction of the class bases of Canadian politics, regardless of the relative degree of change in different occupational strata. This general argument was dealt with in Chapter 4, but it is still relevant. It can be refuted only through evidence from the next several elections in Canada. If class voting remains high or goes higher despite over-all moves either to the Right or to the Left, and if the patterns of voting in Quebec become like those in the rest of the nation, and if Protestants and Catholics move closer together, then it can be more confidently asserted that a structural realignment of Canadian politics has taken place.

Another argument which sees the Conservative, and particularly Diefenbaker's, victories as negating rather than furthering the increase of class voting in Canada may be briefly considered. Mr. Diefenbaker campaigned in the style of a charismatic leader, and it could be argued that this created a "mass" rather than a "class" appeal. Diefenbaker spoke like a revivalist preacher, according to Meisel, with a "stream of consciousness" speaking style incorporating much Christian imagery and rather incoherent sentences ("sacred trust, unrepentant taskmasters, brotherhood, destiny, vision, faith," etc.). Much had an "apocalyptic aura about it."[46]

In contrast, M. St. Laurent was staid and bureaucratic, merely citing figures of Liberal accomplishments. St. Laurent constantly used the analogy of the family, seeing the problems of the state as "essentially those of a family man coping with the decisions confronting any normal family."[47]

But the question is: Does the "mass" appeal which Diefenbaker made contradict the prediction made here that the class bases of the Canadian parties are likely to become more clear—not more ambiguous? In the first place, the role of the party leader is more important in a non-class system like Canada's than in a class-based political system like Australia's or Great Britain's. Particularly when a new leader, like Mr. Diefenbaker, is assuming party leadership, he needs to establish himself as a personality, not merely as the

---

[46] *Ibid.*, p. 156.

[47] The analogy to a family is probably a good one. The provinces are seen as members of a family in a non-class system. In a family, differences are not those of basic interests, which must be compromised, but those of giving representation to different members, respecting individual differences, and so on. See *ibid.*, p. 353.

head of a bureaucratized alternative government. If this is so, then Mr. Diefenbaker's campaign oratory is part of a historical pattern of Canadian politics and does not necessarily imply a swing further away from a class-based politics toward a kind of personal demagoguery supposedly appealing to uprooted suburbanites; it is merely a continuation of historical patterns.

The succession crisis is perennial in Canadian politics, partly because party loyalties are not mediated by identification of the parties with stable economic interests and by class-organizations which support a party and are identified with it. Instead, the parties are bound together by a leader. As Clokie says, "In the nature of the system, therefore, the transition from the dominance of one leader to a new one presents the chief threat to party unity." After Macdonald's death in 1891 and after the retirement of Mr. Bennett in 1938, the Conservative party suffered severe succession crises.[48]

The role of the party leader is more important in Canada than in even the United States, where the President is the focus of national loyalties. Where class is absent as a disciplining, unifying force behind the parties (even where parliamentary discipline and cabinet government exist), charisma unites the various regions behind a leader. As Clokie puts it:

> The dominant position of the party leader in Canadian politics has often been commented on by foreign observers. It is far greater than in Britain where the adherence to party principles or programme competes with loyalty to the leader as a bond of partisanship. It is also greater than in the United States where party candidates are nominated locally without any obligation to support the national leader of the party. In Canada more than anywhere else it is possible to define a party as being a body of supporters following a given leader. Parliamentary elections are primarily occasions on which the electors choose between party leaders and prospective prime ministers.[49]

Whether this is still the case in Canada is an important question. Mr. Diefenbaker's campaign tactics may be evidence that the establishment of personal leadership is still vital for a Canadian politician. On the other hand, possibly Mr. Diefenbaker's "mass" appeal has a different significance. If Canada is on the verge of achieving national integration and if the parochial loyalties of Quebec are

---

[48] Clokie, *op. cit.*, p. 92.
[49] *Ibid.*, p. 91.

dwindling, possibly the charismatic appeal of Diefenbaker or other leaders may be serving the same function for Canada that the charismatic leadership of men such as Nkrumah of Ghana, Mboya of Kenya, and Sukarno of Indonesia serve for their countries. Charismatic leadership may overcome "tribal" loyalties (whether those of the Ashanti or of Quebecers) in the interests of national legitimacy. If this is so, the Diefenbaker charisma (or that of Réal Caouette, the newly emergent Social Credit leader in Quebec) may be a transition phenomenon—from local, parochial loyalties to those based more upon social class and centered on the nation rather than the provinces.[50]

The June, 1962, election did not indicate any drastic alteration of the traditional bases of Canadian politics. The Progressive-Conservative vote dropped from 53 to 37 per cent, but its seats dropped from 208 to 116, leaving the Canadian Parliament deadlocked. In the 1962 Parliament, the Liberals had 99 seats; Social Credit, 30 (26 in Quebec); and the New Democratic party, 19. Class voting, according to a pre-election Canadian Institute of Public Opinion survey, was only +7 over-all (−10 in Quebec and +17 in Ontario, +1 among Catholics, and +11 among Protestants).[51] No change in the general character of party support was evident in this election.

The volatility of Quebec voting was again dramatically evident in the 1962 election. After having been a Liberal stronghold for many years, Quebec went heavily Progressive-Conservative in 1958; and in 1962, twenty-six of the fifty-four Quebec seats outside of Montreal went to the Social Credit party, led by Réal Caouette, who was apparently another charismatic figure such as Diefenbaker

---

[50] Another analysis of the 1958 Conservative victory, although not stressing a change toward a class alignment, suggests a reason for the defection of Liberals to the Conservatives which is consistent with the hypothesis that class voting actually increased. Middle-class people saw that another "respectable" party besides the Liberals had a chance to win. "These Liberals intensely disliked the radical theories of the Socreds [the author's term for the Social Credit party] and similarly feared the socialism and inevitable high taxes that accompanied the doctrines of the C.C.F. . . ." See P. Regenstreif, "The Canadian General Election of 1958," *Western Political Quarterly*, XIII (June, 1960), 367.

[51] See R. Alford, "Political Cleavages in the 1962 Canadian Election," in John Meisel, ed., *Papers on the 1962 Canadian General Election* (forthcoming), for a detailed analysis of the voting patterns in this election from the perspective of this chapter. The April, 1963 election left Parliament still deadlocked, although the Liberals were able to form a government.

was in 1957.[52] Again, this lack of solid party support may reflect a transition state in which traditional allegiances to church and region have been weakened but no new and stable bases for party loyalty have yet emerged. It may be noted that twenty of the twenty-one Montreal seats went to the "traditional" Quebec party, the Liberals. It is possible that these urban Liberal loyalties are not traditionalist at all, but reflect class cleavages.

CONCLUSIONS

Although the evidence which has been presented here is not conclusive, it is rather consistent. Class voting has not consistently increased in Canada from its low level as contrasted with the other Anglo-American countries; this is true despite a number of social changes in Canadian life which seem to imply a decline of regional loyalties. The decreasing isolation of Quebec and the increasing economic integration of the nation may indicate that a national pattern of higher levels of class voting may yet come to exist. A contrary indication is that religious voting was actually higher in Ontario than in Quebec—at least in one 1957 survey—implying that the Catholics outside of the province of Quebec are still as much or more likely to vote according to their religion than those within the "Catholic" province.

Whether only temporary shifts of the class bases of Canadian politics have occurred in the 1958 to 1961 period or whether a more or less permanent realignment is occurring, depends on other evidence that regional and religiously based political identities are weakening and class and national identities strengthening.

The example of Canada shows clearly the connection between a national identity and the emergence of national political parties polarized around distinctive class bases. The lower level of class voting for the national parties in Canada than in any of the other Anglo-American countries can probably be explained as mainly due to the lack of legitimacy of the Canadian nation and the lack of differentiation of the major parties along Left-Right lines.

Although class voting has not increased in the 1945–1961 period, the social foundations which imply an increase of class politics are

---

[52] See the *New York Times,* June 20, 1962, p. 8, and the *Toronto Globe and Mail,* June 20, 1962, p. 7, for descriptions of Mr. Caouette's oratory and sloganeering. His hometown nickname is "Tonnerre"—the thunder.

being laid. Canada is becoming more urbanized and industrialized particularly in some of the provinces which have had deviant politics. Although few data were available on the changing class bases, certain inferential evidence was given. More "secularized" persons exhibit more class voting, and class voting is higher in urban areas. If further changes toward urbanization and secularization can be predicted as Quebec and the Prairies continue to industrialize, then possibly class voting in Canada will rise.[53] The breakdown of the isolation of Quebec is also apparently occurring, and if Quebec becomes more politically integrated with the rest of the nation, this additional factor pulling Canadian politics away from class lines may become less important. It is difficult to show close connections between cause and effect in a single case because so many forces are operating in different directions. Even in the area of trade union organization, it cannot be assumed that the overwhelming trend is toward secularization. The Protestant trade unions in Holland sent an organizer to Canada after World War II, and "as a result of his work a small but increasing number of Protestant locals has been founded."[54]

The tendency toward regionalism in Canada cannot be attributed either to the recent origin of the nation (its "immaturity"), the distance of the western populations from the major political centers in the East, or to the existence of a federal nation. All of these also exist in Australia, but without the consequences of an exaggerated regionalism such as Canada's. Australia became a nation in 1901, some thirty years after Canada. Its states and the clusters of populations within them are equally separated by great distances. Australia is also a federal nation. Therefore, the main factors sustaining

---

[53] But see Norman W. Taylor, "The Effects of Industrialization—Its Opportunities and Consequences—Upon French-Canadian Society," *The Journal of Economic History*, XX (December, 1960), 638–47, for a discussion of the way in which French-Canadian ascriptive and particularistic values have affected the speed and manner in which Quebec has industrialized. At certain stages of industrial and urban development, regional and cultural antagonisms may actually be accentuated. Before 1914, for example, the surplus labor force of rural Quebec moved to industrial centers in the United States. When this labor force began to be absorbed by the new industrial centers in the province, the problems of French-English economic and political relationships were raised anew since the "safety-valve" of migration was gone. See S. D. Clark, *The Social Development of Canada* (Toronto: University of Toronto Press, 1942), pp. 389–91.

[54] Michael P. Fogarty, *Christian Democracy in Western Europe, 1820–1953* (London: Routledge & Kegan Paul, 1957), p. 214.

Canadian political regionalism—and (in turn) its lack of class voting—are its economic and social heterogeneity—unless Canada's
"frontier," something Australia never had, is of crucial importance.
If these are losing importance as factors affecting party loyalties
with the rise of national and class identities, then class voting will
probably increase.[55]

---

[55] A number of the topics of concern here are discussed, briefly and provoca-
tively, by Professor Fred Alexander in *Canadians and Foreign Policy* (Toronto: University of Toronto Press, 1960). In spite of its title, the book discusses the future of the New Democratic party and the social forces unifying
Canada. He asserts that the high cost of coast-to-coast Canadian Broadcasting
Corporation programs is consciously paid as the price of creating a Canadian
national identity. As will be noted in Chapter 11, the consequence may actually
be the opposite.

Chapter 10

The Consequences of Class Polarization

THE association of social class with voting behavior and the effect of regionalism and religious membership upon class voting have been examined in Great Britain, Australia, the United States, and Canada. This chapter will summarize the assumptions and the main empirical findings of the preceding chapters and suggest some possible political and social consequences and correlates of varying levels and kinds of political cleavages in these countries. Singled out for special consideration will be the role of the "third party" in these "two-party" systems.

THE ASSUMPTIONS OF THIS STUDY

The main questions guiding the study were: How much do levels of class voting diverge in four Anglo-American countries—all of which are economically developed with high levels of consensus upon the form of government? And: To what extent do religious and regional loyalties to party affect class voting? The empirical approach to answers to these questions involved certain assumptions which will be reviewed here before the findings are summarized.

The four Anglo-American countries have a common political culture and a limited range of political cleavages. In none of the countries is there an important threat to the basic constitutional and parliamentary framework. Political conflict therefore focuses on the political parties and upon alternative policies to be pursued by the government dominated by one of the major parties. Contrasting these four societies, which are remarkably alike in many respects when compared to preindustrial or totalitarian societies but remarkably different in their political histories, may clarify the problems of political stability and change in stable two-party systems and also contribute to a more general theory of cleavage and change in democratic political systems.

A certain level of class voting is to be expected because of the nature of both the stratification and political orders. Deprived groups seek redress through political action. In a democratic system, political parties provide representation for many different groups. Such representation would not be necessary, however, if the ruling order were not challenged in some respects. Party *systems* (as distinct from *parties*) arose and continue partly in order to provide access by less privileged groups to decisions made by authoritative agencies—mainly government. Before the rise of mass parties of the Left in the nineteenth century, there were "parties" of the Right—rival coalitions of ruling groups—but no party systems as such institutionalizing competition for majority support.

An important point of view in modern political thought holds that parties need not be representatives of social classes. Parties, in this view, can constitute competing bodies of men seeking political power but need not represent any given set of interests or coalition of such interests. This is the economist Joseph Schumpeter's view of the essence of democracy. Democracy is a political form which need not have any class content.[1] The competing political factions need not represent *any* set of interests consistently but need only be alternative sets of leaders for the given political unit—be it organization, party, or nation.

If social classes in the Western democracies become so shifting and blurred that no social interests with a degree of stability can be distinguished, then we might expect that democracy in these countries will come to resemble Schumpeter's model. Support for a party would not be predictable from either an assessment of the legislative behavior of its representatives or an analysis of stratification among the electorate. The United States and Canada, among these four countries, are closest to the state of affairs where neither parties nor electorate can be divided sharply into Left and Right, have nots and haves.

But an objective basis for class voting does still exist in the character of the stratification order. The similarities of these four coun-

---

[1] See Joseph Schumpeter, *Capitalism, Socialism and Democracy* (New York: Harper, 1947), p. 269.

tries described in Chapter 1 suggest that if rational and structural factors were the only variables affecting voting behavior, the social bases of politics in these countries should be coming to be more *similar*. Class voting may decline ultimately, but there seems to be little reason to suppose that it will disappear as long as these societies remain stratified.

A number of methodological assumptions concerning ways of measuring class position, voting behavior, and the extent of religious and regional political loyalties have been made. Since public opinion surveys were the main source of data for the study, occupational status, divided into manual and non-manual occupations, was used as the measure of class divisions. Voting intention in a national election as indicated in answers to interviewer's questions was the measure of actual voting behavior.

Whether religious allegiances and identifications are the real basis for the differences discovered in the political behavior of Protestants and Catholics is difficult to know with certainty. Examination of religious differences within various age-groups, regions, and so forth, has shown that differences in political behavior between religious groups exist, but this is still a major assumption. Wherever religious differences were found in *both* manual and non-manual occupations, it has been assumed that this was actually a religious difference and not one which could be accounted for by other non-religious factors.

Similarly, it is difficult to know whether the apparent regional differences in political behavior are actually due to specifically regional identifications and loyalties. As with the case of religious differences, it has been assumed that if a regional difference was found within both manual and non-manual occupations (as evidenced by extremely high or low levels of class voting), this was due to some special character of the region as a cultural or social entity.

Given these assumptions, which may seriously qualify the generality of the conclusions which can be drawn from the data, the findings of the study may now be briefly summarized.

REGIONALISM, RELIGION, AND CLASS VOTING

Great Britain not only has the highest level of class voting of any of the four Anglo-American countries, but class factors appear to be the only significant ones—at least in comparison to factors relevant in the other countries. Voting is highly correlated with occupation, education, income, and subjective class identification, whether considered separately or together. The greatest regional variations in class voting occur in Wales and Scotland, the areas with the greatest sectional identification and cultural identity. Unlike the regions with similar kinds of identities in the United States and Canada—the South and Quebec—class voting is generally higher in those regions, indicating that whatever effect the regional loyalties have, they do not produce alignments of both strata behind one party. Similarly, class voting was not uniformly lower among the Catholics in England than among Protestants, in contrast to the other countries. The pattern of religious deviation from class voting is different in Great Britain from that in any of the other countries, where the Left party received disproportionate support from both manual and non-manual Catholics. Catholic identifications in England do not express themselves in allegiances to one party.

Great Britain, therefore, has a relatively "pure" class politics. Regional and religious loyalties tend not to be expressed through political parties, but, in a sense, may become demands upon the whole political system. If the Scots want more representation in parliament, they will demand it of the government, not of any party. The political parties are no longer mediators of any parochial or sectional interests except class interests (which can also be parochial and sectional, but in a different sense).

Perhaps the most surprising empirical finding was that class voting has not declined in Great Britain in the period 1943 to 1959, but, if anything, has actually increased. Manual workers were no less likely to vote Labour in 1959 than they were in 1943, and a decline in Labour votes occurred among persons in non-manual occupations. If blurring of social class lines has taken place in Great Britain, it has not yet reduced class voting. One single piece of evidence that a decline of class voting may occur was found: Class voting was lowest in the London and Southern region, including the London metropolitan area, where educational opportunities have been more equalized for the classes and which probably is better-off economically than other areas. If such social changes continue, the lower level of class voting around London may presage the future decline of class voting in Britain. (The low level of class voting in the London area is due to a low Labour vote among manual workers. See Table 6–5, Chapter 6.)

The level of class voting in Australia is somewhat lower than in Great Britain, but the Catholics, regardless of their occupation, are far more likely than Protestants to be Labor supporters. Regional loyalties are not important in Australian politics, but the older and more urbanized states—New South Wales and Victoria—exhibit lower levels of class voting. A special study of the largely Catholic Democratic Labor party which emerged in 1955 found that the DLP served as a vehicle for the transition of upwardly mobile Catholics away from the old Labor party in an era in which their ethnic and religious loyalties had become politically less relevant. Although a slight decline of class voting occurred in Australia between 1943 and 1961, it was due largely to a drop in Victoria. Overall trends in Australia do not, therefore, support the hypothesis of a decline of the importance of the class bases of politics.

In the United States, the level of class voting has vacillated considerably between 1936 and 1960. It rose to high points in 1940 and 1948 but remained higher in the 1956 and 1960 elections than it was in 1936, when both manual and non-manual strata were attracted to Roosevelt. Class voting is lowest in the South, where sectional loyalty overrides social class as a basis for political cleavage. No decline of the southern deviation was evident from these data.

The importance of religious voting has also vacillated considerably, though the Catholics are usually pulled over to the Democratic party. This was not true in 1952, however, when non-manual Catholics voted Republican to almost the same extent as non-manual Protestants. Any decline of the "Catholic vote" through secular assimilation was obscured by the 1960 election, which marked the greatest difference between Protestant and Catholic voting (in both strata) of any election since 1944. As was suggested in Chapter 8, whether the achievement of the Presidency by a Catholic will mark the end of Catholic minority consciousness, and therefore the end of their distinctive political behavior, is an open question.

In Canada, non-class factors assume a paramount role. Class voting in Canada has, since 1943, been consistently lower than in any of the other three countries. Economic and cultural heterogeneity, and the political veto-power exercised by the French-Catholic cultural "island" of Quebec—signs of a weakly integrated nation—are probably the major factors reducing class alignments around the parties, although class interests and struggles are by no means absent from Canadian political history.

A little evidence of an increase of class voting in Canada was found in the 1957–1961 period, despite the swing of all social groups toward the Progressive-Conservative party and its leader, John Diefenbaker. Signs of a breakdown of the extreme regionalism characteristic of Canadian politics may indicate, however, that the absence of class voting in Canada is not a sign of its having reached political and social maturity, but rather a sign that it may yet come to exhibit the forms of political cleavage characteristic of more homogeneous nations.

In sum, where class factors are paramount in determining national political cleavages, religious and regional loyalties do not significantly affect political behavior. Where social classes do not support the national parties in sharply different degrees, regional and religious loyalties are strong. In addition, there is no evidence that class voting is decreasing substantially in any of the four countries.

SOME CONSEQUENCES AND CORRELATES OF CLASS POLARIZATION

Australia and Great Britain—with fairly high levels of class voting and low regional or religious voting— may be called the more "class-polarized" political systems, while the United States and Canada may be called the less class-polarized systems. As might be expected, labor union membership is greater in the more class-polarized countries, although Australia and Britain are not differentiated in this respect, nor are Canada and the United States.[2] It seems probable that the relative strength of labor unionism is both a cause and a consequence of class politics. The level of self-identification of manual workers as "working class" is also in the same order as the level of class voting according to one study of

---

[2] The percentage of labor union membership in Great Britain, Australia, the United States, and Canada, respectively, listed in their order of class voting, was in 1957 approximately: 42, 45, 26, and 23 (using the total labor force as a base), and 19, 18, 10, and 9 (using the total population as a base). Figures were compiled from the *Worldmark Encyclopedia of the Nations* (New York: Worldmark, 1960).

three of these countries.[3] Undoubtedly the integration of class and party serves to clarify the character of the stratification system, for workers at least.

A number of political and social processes seem to differ in a way logically related to these various measures of the extent to which these political systems are polarized around class bases. Localism, particularism, and informal bases for political action seem to be more prevalent in the less class-polarized systems, as will be described. No systematic evidence exists for these generalizations, but some suggestive regularities appear.

In the more class-polarized systems, Great Britain and Australia, politics has become bureaucratized, and "mass parties"—parties organized around branches, with individual membership, and a centralized, tightly organized form—have emerged. Australia and Great Britain have party systems organized around "mass" parties; the United States and Canada have party systems organized on a "cadre" or "honoratioren" basis.[4] The parties in the latter two nations are led by "notables" and lack the strength and solidarity of party organization characteristic of mass parties. Instead, party organization practically disappears between elections. Both of the major parties in Canada and the United States are more like "honoratioren" parties than either of the major parties in Australia and Great Britain, and it may be suggested that the rise of a working-class party organized along disciplined lines forces the more conservative party in each country to organize likewise in self-defense.

The effect of parties strongly organized on a class basis is to spread party organization to every political level. The parties in both Australia and Great Britain are far more likely to operate on

---

[3] See page 30 for the method of computing this measure, reported in William Buchanan and Hadley Cantril, *How Nations See Each Other* (Urbana: University of Illinois Press, 1953), p. 14. The index figures for those in manual occupations were: Britain, —76; Australia, —61; United States, —57.

[4] The terms are those of Maurice Duverger and Sigmund Neumann. Duverger asserts that the distinction between cadre and mass parties "corresponds approximately with the distinction between Right and Left, Middle-class and Workers' Parties," and suggests that the rise of mass parties coincided with the rise of working-class movements seeking to gain political representation outside of the existing ruling elites. See Maurice Duverger, *Political Parties* (London: Methuen, 1954), pp. 63–71, and Sigmund Neumann, "Toward a Comparative Study of Political Parties," in S. Neumann, ed. *Modern Political Parties* (Chicago: University of Chicago Press, 1956), p. 401.

local and city levels than are the parties in the United States and Canada.[5] The dominance of party and class also reduces the importance of informal pressure groups because political influence and decisions are more likely to be expressed through formal party and governmental organizations.

The contrast between the "hometown boy" politics of Canada and the United States, found in exaggerated form in the South, and rural politics in Australia is evident from a study of an Australian country constituency, Eden-Monaro, in the election of 1955. Few of the candidates benefited from their hometown votes, and the authors concluded that "there is no automatic process which gives a candidate an advantage in the district around his home, except perhaps over a very limited area indeed."[6] On the other hand, in spite of national centralization of the Canadian parties, "they have not always fought their engagements on purely national issues, and it has been by no means uncommon to have the fates of Dominion Governments decided by a series of local skirmishes which have borne little real relationship to each other."[7] Thus, localized issues and personalities in the United States and Canada probably have nationally decisive consequences far more than they do in Britain and Australia.[8]

---

[5] See Delbert C. Miller, "Decision-Making Cliques in Community Power Structures: A Comparative Study of an American and an English City," *American Journal of Sociology*, LXIV (November, 1958), 299–310. In "English City," representatives of different institutions (party, economic, and others) function "in relatively independent roles," as contrasted with the American city, which has a highly stratified single elite (p. 310). I suggest that a part of these differences is due to the dominance of class in British politics. Many American cities undoubtedly exhibit the "British" pattern, although no such comparative studies have been published.

[6] Donald W. Rawson and Susan M. Holtzinger, *Politics in Eden-Monaro* (Melbourne: Heinemann, 1958), p. 147. While local influences are important in Great Britain—especially in rather traditional Conservative-dominated towns such as Glossop—the parties are organized both for national and local elections. See A. H. Birch, *Small-town Politics* (London: Oxford University Press, 1959), pp. 98–100.

[7] Robert MacGregor Dawson, *The Government of Canada* (2nd ed.; Toronto: University of Toronto Press, 1954), p. 497.

[8] There may also be differential consequences for the attitudes of voters. W. E. Miller found that, in the United States, political motivations and attitudes of Democrats were quite different in strongly Republican counties than in Democratic counties, and vice versa. I would expect such "local" effects to be much less in Australia and Britain, but no studies have been done on this problem. See W. E. Miller, "One-Party Politics and the Voter," *American Political Science Review*, L (September, 1956), 707–25.

It may be possible to ascribe differences in the operations of government bureaucracies and even the legal systems in these countries to differential pressure toward regionalism and decentralization (and therefore away from effective bureaucratization at the national level). A comparative analysis of parliamentary supervision of delegated legislation (rules enacted by government departments within a general framework of parliamentary legislation) in Britain, New Zealand, Australia, and Canada found that the efficacy of such supervision was greatest in Britain and least in Canada, the same order as that of class polarization.[9] Where regionalism is less evident, effective control of bureaucracies may be easier to establish. "Federalization" of bureaucracies undoubtedly increases what seem from an administrative point of view to be "inconsistencies" and "arbitrary decisions." It may be significant that Australia's system of supervision was judged to be more effective than Canada's. Federalism in and of itself apparently does not interfere with effective control of bureaucratic decision-making.

Particularism also penetrates the judicial systems of less class-polarized countries in various ways. To take only one example, choice of which United States Supreme Court justice is to write an opinion may sometimes be determined by his sectional, religious, or party identification. In one classic case, Justice Frankfurter was first assigned the writing of the opinion in a case overturning Texas' "white primary." The assignment was later given to Justice Reed, after Justice Jackson wrote a revealing letter to the Chief Justice which asserted that the combination of Frankfurter's being a Jew, from New England (the home of abolitionism) and not a strong Democrat might "grate on Southern sensibilities." Reed, in contrast, was a Kentuckian, a Protestant, and an old-time Democrat.[10] Such explicit revelations of the particularistic bases of judicial actions are infrequent, but they reveal something of the character of the legal and political system when they appear. The British courts, by contrast, undoubtedly consider the consequences of judicial actions for

---

[9] See John E. Kersell, *Parliamentary Supervision of Delegated Legislation* (London: Stevens & Sons, 1960). Kersell does not make an explicit general comparison, but his judgments concerning the relative immunity of political heads of departments from criticism (p. 4), and the elaborateness of the supervisory machinery and the date of its development (chap. vii) are consistent with the ordering above.

[10] Quoted in Henry J. Abraham, *The Judicial Process* (New York: Oxford University Press, 1962), p. 187.

various regional and religious groupings, but probably do not take into account the personal characteristics of judges in such a manner.

Even such a purely legal process as judicial review, supposedly based on precedent and justice, may come to be influenced by considerations of "expediency" (which group a decision will affect and what its political consequences will be) rather than "principle" (which underlying values or precedents, applied to this case, will be accepted by most politically-relevant groups) where regional and religious factors are more important than class. The courts in a consensual system cannot act as if laws have universal application or derivation when in fact they are not accepted by certain segments of the society. Class probably does not have the same effect because class interests can be more readily split, compromised, and handled than can regional and religious values.

The localism and particularism of the less class-polarized systems probably increases the proportion of the electorate likely to see informal pressure as effectively able to influence local politics. Persons in the United States are more likely than persons in Great Britain at every level of education to indicate that they would undertake political action through informal channels (Table 10–1). Where class is the dominant basis of political cleavage, parties and government tend to be less influenced by informal and particularistic loyalties. Decisions are taken as compromises between more or less "rational" interest considerations and reflect the pressures of formally organized groups, rather than informal ones.

Note also from Table 10–1 that in the United States, higher education increases the proportion willing to enlist informal support, while in Great Britain, education has no such effect. Despite the lower proportion of British citizens who view informal action as appropriate, better-educated Britishers are no more likely than poorly-educated ones to use informal political channels. The difference between the United States and Britain is not, therefore, due to differences between low and high status persons; it is probably a true difference between the two political systems.

Differences between low and high status groups in political participation and in what might be called a sense of "political efficacy" are also smaller in the more class-polarized systems. A comparative study of Norway and the United States found no status differences in the proportion of politically active persons in the former country, but substantial differences in the latter. The authors interpreted this

TABLE 10–1

"Local Competents" Who Would Enlist the Support of An Informal Group to Influence a Local Regulation They Thought Was Unjust, by Education, United States and Great Britain

COUNTRY	PER CENT WHO WOULD ENLIST SUPPORT, BY EDUCATION				
	Primary or less	Some Secondary	Some College or More	Total	PERCENTAGE-POINT RANGE
United States	63	75	81	73 (747)*	+18
Great Britain	41	46	45	43 (727)	+ 5
Percentage-Point Difference	+22	+29	+36	+30	

Source: Sidney Verba, "Political Participation and Strategies of Influence: A Comparative Study," *Acta Sociologica*, VI (1962), 31, 39. Other countries included in the study were Germany, Italy, and Mexico. The year the surveys were conducted was not given.
* To make the samples more comparable, the figures are only for persons considered politically "competent" from answers to questions concerning their political information.
* Total number of respondents is in parentheses.

in terms of a difference of the institutional setting of participation in the two countries, particularly the difference in "status polarization" (or class voting, as I have termed it). They suggest that in more class-polarized countries, "citizens of little formal education and in lower-status occupations would be under a minimum of cross-pressures and would feel much less discouraged from taking on active roles in the political organizations they would give their vote."[11]

Further evidence that the usual differences in political participation between status-groups dwindle in more class-polarized systems is that lower-status persons in Great Britain are more convinced of the efficacy of political action than similarly placed persons in the United States. Persons with low education in Great Britain are considerably more likely to feel that they can "do something" about an unjust local law than persons with similar education in the United States, while persons with more education do not

[11] Stein Rokkan and Angus Campbell, "Norway and the United States of America," *International Social Science Journal*, XII (1960), 69–99. I have computed an index of class voting from their data, given in Table 9; the figure for the United States is +14; for Norway, +47 (combining the Socialist and Communist parties) (p. 88). Norway's class voting level is thus close to Britain's. The political distinctiveness of the working class in Norway is much greater than that of the British working class, however. See page 84 above.

differ in the two countries (Table 10–2). Middle-class persons have a higher sense of political efficacy than lower-class persons do in both countries, and the difference between the countries appears only in the less-educated stratum.

Another consequence of the existence of mass parties based upon social classes seems to be an increase of universalism as a basic political principle. The non-rational and particularistic aspects of politics are probably less evident in the more class-polarized systems. One illustration of this may be differences in the degree of political corruption—nepotism and graft—between the Anglo-American countries. One analysis of Australian society suggests, "Although the extent of political corruption is difficult to estimate, the Australian record would appear to be reasonably good compared with that of the United States and the Latin American republics, but considerably poorer than that of Britain."[12] Since political corruption is particularly widespread in Canadian Quebec, the more class-polarized countries also seem to have less political corruption.[13] Universalism in political procedures may be associated with the bureaucratization and interest-cleavages more characteristic of class politics than of regional and religious politics.

Another aspect of universalism in politics is the way voters judge candidates. In the more class-polarized system of Great Britain, voters are much less likely to let particularistic factors influence their voting decision than are voters in the less class-polarized system of the United States. Some evidence for this is afforded by a 1958 Gallup survey in both countries which asked whether certain personal characteristics of political candidates (being a Catholic, a

---

[12] R. Taft and K. Walker, "Australia," in Arnold M. Rose, ed., *The Institutions of Advanced Societies* (Minneapolis: University of Minnesota Press, 1958), p. 159.

[13] Since Quebec comprises one-third of Canada, its high level of political corruption may be considered evidence of the differential between Canada and the other English-speaking countries (if we may consider Canada as a nation—and therefore the attributes of its component parts as in some degree reflections of the whole). Trudeau considers Quebec corruption to reflect the lack of commitment by Quebecers to the institutions and morality of democracy. The manipulation of those institutions by the English in the early years of Canada produced such a reaction. See Pierre E. Trudeau, "Some Obstacles to Democracy in Quebec," in Mason Wade, ed., *Canadian Dualism* (Toronto: University of Toronto Press, 1960), pp. 244–47. Articles in the *New York Times,* November 19 and 22, 1959, following the death of Quebec Premier Maurice Duplessis, noted that observers did not expect a change in the spoils system characteristic of Quebec politics.

TABLE 10–2

Respondents Who Say That They Can Remedy a Local Regulation They Consider Unjust, by Education, United States and Great Britain

COUNTRY	PER CENT WHO BELIEVE THEY CAN REMEDY A LOCAL REGULATION, BY EDUCATION			
	Primary or Less	Some Secondary	Some College or More	Total
		(Per Cent)		
United States	58	82	94	77 (970)*
Great Britain	73	84	92	77 (963)

Source: Sidney Verba, "Political Participation and Strategies of Influence: A Comparative Study," *Acta Sociologica*, VI (1962), 26, 38.
* Total number of respondents in parentheses.

Jew, a "colored" person, a woman, or an atheist) would interfere with their voting for that candidate. On each score, voters in the United States were less likely to say that they would vote for such a candidate (Table 10–3). Whether a voter was Catholic or Jewish made the least difference to the voters of both countries, and this factor showed the least difference between the countries. The difference between the countries was sharpest on the matter of atheism. Less than one-fifth of United States voters would vote for an atheist, while almost one-half of British voters would not care. Despite the differences between the countries, the rank order of importance

TABLE 10–3

People Willing to Vote for a Qualified Candidate Who Happens to Have Certain Social Characteristics, United States and Great Britain, 1958

CHARACTERISTIC OF THE CANDIDATE	PER CENT OF RESPONDENTS		
	Britain	United States	Percentage-Point Difference
Catholic	82	68	+14
Jewish	71	62	+ 9
Woman	76	52	+24
Colored	61	38	+23
Atheist	45	18	+27

Source: BIPO release, November, 1958.

of these personal characteristics of candidates was nearly the same in both countries, showing the similarity of social values in the two countries, despite the higher level of universalism in Great Britain.

The domination of class politics in countries such as Australia and Great Britain, which possess high degrees of effectiveness and legitimacy, has meant that both the major parties are pulled far to the Left.[14] On domestic economic and welfare issues, at least, the Right parties of Australia and Great Britain (the Liberal and Conservative parties, respectively) have accepted legislation which would be regarded as almost outright communism by many American voters.

Where the relative power of Left forces is greater, another consequence may be that lower-income groups are able to secure more of the national product than where the Left has less power. A preliminary study indicates that although Britain has a lower level of economic growth and development than the United States, the proportion of British national income going to workers is slightly higher. Political power may compensate somewhat for the relatively poorer economic situation of Britain.[15]

Another consequence of different levels of class polarization may have been a quicker shift to the Right in the more class-polarized systems. The conservative shift after World War II took place sooner in the countries with higher levels of class voting. In Australia, the Liberal party took power in 1949, and in Great Britain the Conservative party won in 1950, while the Republicans won in the United States in 1952, and the Progressive-Conservatives in Canada, in 1957. Assuming that the switch to a more conservative party reflects social trends in each country in the prosperous era after World War II, several characteristics of the social and political systems of these countries may account for this pattern.[16]

First, it may be suggested that a switch of a class-based system in a conservative direction because of prosperity occurs more rap-

---

[14] See S. M. Lipset, *Political Man* (New York: Doubleday, 1960), pp. 77–83.

[15] See S. M. Miller and Herrington Bryce, "Social Mobility and Economic Growth and Structure," *Kölner Zeitschrift fur Soziologie* (forthcoming). Britain was lower than the United States in percentage increase in national product (1900–1950), percentage increase in national product per capita (same years), and current product per man-hour (United States dollars); however, it was higher in percentage of national income paid to "employees."

[16] Particular historical and political features of elections in each country obviously may have speeded up or slowed down conservative drifts. If Eisenhower had won on the Democratic ticket in 1952, clearly the Republican trend would have been invisible.

idly than a switch of a political system based upon regional, religious, and ethnic solidarities. Class-based political allegiances may actually change more readily than others once the demands of working-class groups (trade unions and parties) for legitimacy and bargaining rights are won.

Second, in societies which are more homogeneous, such as Australia and Great Britain, there are fewer "solid seats," and fewer regional strongholds; therefore, a relatively smaller switch of group allegiances to a party produces quicker and more massive political consequences.

Another consequence of a high level of class polarization may be the reduction of either the number or the intensity of strikes, which may seem paradoxical. But, given the similar class structures and political cultures of these countries, we might expect to find that where class interests are not expressed explicitly through political parties, they are more likely to be demonstrated elsewhere—as in strikes. Where, on the contrary, a labor party exists and there is a relatively sharp political division of social classes, class issues will tend to be moved from the bargaining arena to the political arena.

Among these four countries, there should thus be a greater incidence or intensity of strikes in Canada and the United States than in Australia and Britain. On the other hand, the original factors producing class voting (in Chapter 5 class voting was found to be higher in relatively poorer countries with fewer educational opportunities and lower growth rates) would seem also to produce high strike rates. However, a study of strikes in fifteen countries found that in the United States and Canada there is a "moderately high propensity to strike as well as a relatively long duration" for those strikes that occur. In contrast, in the United Kingdom there is a "nominal propensity to strike and a low or moderate duration of strikes."[17] Australia has a unique pattern of numerous but short strikes. The authors attribute this to the lack of constitutional powers available to the Commonwealth government to carry out labor's objectives through political action. Therefore, Australian labor, unlike British labor, was unable to translate its potential power into effective intervention in the collective bargaining process.[18]

---

[17] Arthur M. Ross and Paul T. Hartman, *Changing Patterns of Industrial Conflict* (New York: Wiley, 1960), pp. 72, 77.

[18] Ross and Hartman agree that more and longer strikes should be associated with the absence of a labor party. Where no such party exists, collective bargaining is normally settled by a trial of economic strength. *Ibid.*, p. 163.

Both Britain and Australia have relatively short strikes; both Canada and the United States have relatively long ones.[19] In the latter two countries, a grievance which reaches the point of a strike may tend to last longer in part because workers are under less political control than they are in the other countries. Not only does a labor party encourage compulsory collective bargaining, but it must restrain strikes as the price of respectability in a consensual system. Potential governmental power in such a system carries with it responsibilities not only to serve the workers but to discipline them.

To summarize, clear differences in the consequences and correlates of class polarization have been shown. The more class-polarized systems are more likely to have strongly organized and disciplined parties extending their influence even to the city level. Where workers have a party clearly appealing to their interests, their participation and sense of political efficacy is as great as middle-class persons. Where class polarization is greater, politics tends to be more universalistic, in the sense that political corruption is less evident and candidates are not as likely to be rejected on the grounds of personal characteristics. Political shifts may take place more readily in the more class-polarized systems, which are also more homogeneous and have fewer regional one-party bastions. Overt class conflict in the form of strikes is less evident in the class-polarized systems—which possess labor parties with greater control over collective bargaining, and have a higher level of trade union organization.

THE FUNCTIONS OF THIRD PARTIES

The role of the third parties in systems which differ in the relative importance of various political cleavages requires some mention. "Third" parties—any small party besides the two major parties —serve a number of functions in the Anglo-American countries, as long as they remain third parties. The following discussion does not attempt to deal with the conditions under which a party rises to majority status, an eventuality difficult in two-party systems, but only with its role as a "third" party. If it should attain majority sta-

---

[19] The average number of working days lost annually per striker between 1948 and 1956 was four in Britain, three in Australia, fifteen in the United States, and nineteen in Canada. *Ibid.*, p. 27.

tus, there may be pressures within the system which produce a new "third" party.

The functions of third parties may conveniently be considered under three headings: those performed for social groups, those for other parties, and those for the total political system. For social groups, third parties may serve as a "half-way house" during a process of change of loyalties from one of the major parties to the other; they may also function as a political outlet for "marginal" groups of one kind or another or as a temporary channel for the expression of grievances arising from the attempt to coalesce diverse interests within two parties.

For the other political parties, third parties sometimes serve as an instrument for invidious comparison ("If you don't vote for us, see what you will get") and sometimes as a testing ground for potential vote-getting issues. The major party can then move in and take over the issue.

For the total political system, third parties, especially where the two parties are fairly rigidly organized, can add an element of flexibility by preventing the majority party from an assured victory, or by exerting pressure from the "outside" upon the two alternative potential governments. At this point, only the possible bases of appeal to social groups will be considered.

In the case of the Anglo-American countries, third parties in the more class-polarized systems—Britain and Australia—seem to serve social groups primarily as transition parties or as outlets for the strains of highly stratified societies. In both cases, the third parties seem to have more of an "ideological" than a "representative" character, the latter being more typical of the United States and Canada. Following are some examples in each country.

Where major pressures exist for a new alignment of voters and where the main parties seem incapable of providing representation because of historic ties with "enemy" groups, a third party may emerge which functions as a transition party, even though the issues and appeals upon which it is based do not explicitly indicate this. (Other conditions will determine whether this transition party is able to stabilize itself as a permanent addition to the party system.)

This function for a minor party implies that political parties to some extent become historically associated with different subcultures. Loyalty to a party may become associated with loyalty to a social group and subculture, not with a distinctive political ideology. Where social changes alter the position of a group, whether by changing either its socio-economic position or its sense of minority consciousness, identification with the traditional party may contradict the actual economic interests of many members of the group. But breaking with the party represents a break with traditional cultural loyalties. It is this strain which may be reflected in the emergence of third parties under a number of circumstances.

The principal example of this type of third party examined here has been the Democratic Labor party in Australia, which represents no stable economic interest (as does the Country party). Although this party may have an ideological base in anti-communism and an organizational base in the Catholic Social Movement, it was suggested in Chapter 7 that much of the support for the DLP is due to its function as a transition party for upwardly mobile Catholics.

Especially where the parties are closely identified with social classes, it is difficult for upwardly mobile persons to change to the "enemy" party. Loyalties shared with friends and family and long-held ideas about the "proper" political party to support interfere with a switch to a more conservative party. And yet, precisely because class interests are so closely identified with parties in such a system, it becomes imperative to break the loyalty to the old party. In such a situation, the political tensions induced by social mobility find a natural outlet in the third party.

In Australia, therefore, it was possible for middle-class or upper-income Catholics to switch from the Australian Labor party to the Democratic Labor party. By this move, the cross-pressures were eased; they voted both "Labor" and for a more rightist party at the same time.

Analogous pressures may account for part of the support for third parties in the United States and Canada. In North Dakota, voters for the Non-Partisan League went to the LaFollette Progressives before finally changing to the Republicans.[20] The southern Dixiecrats (or future similar movements) may serve a similar function. It is not possible for southern conservatives to switch directly to the Republicans, long considered an enemy, and a Dixiecrat vote

---

[20] See Edward N. Doan, *The LaFollettes and the Wisconsin Idea* (New York: Rinehart, 1947), p. 6, and Herbert E. Gaston, *The Nonpartisan League* (New York: Harcourt, 1920).

may allow Democratic loyalties to weaken and prepare the way for Republican inroads into the South.

In the federal systems, vote-splitting may serve the same transitional function as the third party in more centralized systems. Probably the Catholics in the United States do not form the kind of solid voting bloc which makes necessary the transitional device of the third party. Catholics may move away from their traditional Democratic voting patterns earlier on the presidential level than on the local and state levels. The Presidency may be in one sense "above" partisanship, or at least farther removed from party in symbol and aura than local and state offices. The same may be true for the southern Democrats who deserted their party in 1952 and 1956 to vote for Eisenhower but remained true on the state level.

In Canada, Protestant Conservatives in Saskatchewan may have switched over to the CCF because they could not bring themselves to vote for the Liberals, long identified with the French-Catholics.[21]

The second function, that of serving as an outlet for the tensions of a rigidly stratified society, is best seen in the British Liberal party, discussed in Chapter 6. The Liberal party may be a "safety valve" for disgruntled Labourites and Conservatives who feel that their party no longer serves them or is encrusted with bureaucracy. A protest vote in by-elections may not only serve as a warning to the major parties that they cannot count on solid support, it may also encourage the third party sufficiently to keep it alive.

The tensions between class position and political allegiance seem likely to be considerably greater in the countries with high levels of class voting. Conversely, cross-pressures based upon regional and religious conflicts with political allegiances are undoubtedly greater in Canada and the United States. One would expect, therefore, that the consequences of cross-pressures—withdrawal from the political system, apathy, non-voting, delayed decisions—would have different bases in the two types of systems.

As already suggested, third parties in more class-polarized two-party systems may tend to be *ideological* in character, instead of being tied to a specific interest group. In some cases this ideological tendency may be permanent, as may be the case with the British Liberal party. It represents certain elements of the middle class and working class that may always object to the centralized bu-

---

[21] See S. M. Lipset, *Agrarian Socialism* (Berkeley and Los Angeles: University of California Press, 1950), pp. 163–65.

reaucracies of the major parties and would look for a new political home if the Liberal party as it exists were absorbed or changed. This streak of individualism may be a persistent tendency not to be erased by any easy concession, particular legislation, or overture. In other cases (and the Australian Democratic Labor party may also exhibit this in part) the ideological tendency may be temporary, stemming from the status or other social position of one or another group, and finding political expression in party form for various historical reasons. In Australia, the Catholics—particularly New Australian immigrants from eastern Europe—may hold an extremely anti-communist ideology which does not easily accept the compromises usual within the Australian party system. This ideology is not, however, a permanent feature of the stratification system, as the other can be considered, but is a temporary by-product of social changes such as immigration or historically specific social mobility.

In less class-polarized systems primarily based upon regional support, third parties may tend to play a *representative* role. The geographical bases of the parties concentrate support from ethnic, religious, or economic groups in one area and cause political support to be seen not as a matter of ideology, more or less divorced from specific groups, but as a matter of pleasing the special interests or values of a group. (See Chapter 11 for a discussion of the various bases of regionalism.)

Third parties with a representative role need not be transitional parties in the above sense, but may represent a stable regional economic interest where that interest has access to a political party or a unit of government. This is the case in Canada, where perennial Dominion-provincial conflicts, combined with the dominance of wheat farming in the Prairie provinces, have produced a series of third parties, recent ones being Social Credit (in Alberta and British Columbia, and in 1962, in Quebec) and the CCF in Saskatchewan.[22] This type of regionalism has a parallel in Australia in the Country party, which is stably supported by well-to-do farmers in rural constituencies. The United States has had its regional third parties also, mainly agrarian, which have served to gain representation and concessions from the major parties.

The third main function of third parties in such systems may be

---

[22] See especially James R. Mallory, *Social Credit and the Federal Power in Canada* (Toronto: University of Toronto Press, 1954), and S. M. Lipset, *Agrarian Socialism, op. cit.*

to provide a *political outlet* for social groups which are "marginal" in some way to the main strata of the society. Among specific occupations, clerks and small shopkeepers are marginal to the solid middle-class occupations, and skilled workers and foremen are marginal to the solid working-class occupations. Among religions, the Catholics and the Jews are marginal to the dominant Protestant denominations. Depending on the relevance of one or another basis of political cleavage, we would expect to find that such marginal groups are more likely than others to support whatever third parties come to exist for other reasons. (The same prediction would hold for regions within the nations—especially where, as in Quebec, Catholics are the dominant group. There, Protestants should disproportionately support third parties.) Again, the Australian Democratic Labor party provides evidence for this, since the clerks and skilled workers gave greater support to the party than other strata. This party is an example of the reinforcement of the three separate bases for third party support, since it plays a transitional, an ideological, and a marginal role. These functions are independent, however, since marginal groups may remain marginal and need not be either in transition or possess a distinctive ideology. Marginality may reflect a more or less permanent condition in relation to the main social institutions of a modern society. In a country such as Canada, in which more important forces are stabilizing the minor parties, such a function as this may remain relatively hidden.

The difference in the electoral system of Australia and the other countries raises the possibility that a third party in one system may be functionally comparable to a pressure group in another. As was noted in Chapter 7, the "third" parties in Australia—both the Democratic Labor party and the Country party—may be creatures of the preferential ballot. If this is so, possibly a third party in Australia may not really be more significant than a pressure group of Catholics or farmers in the United States. The disciplined major parties coupled with the preferential ballot in Australia force the particular pressure to take the form of a new party. Because the interest group is organized into a visible "party," it seems more consequential than if its activities had remained less public. Because a party seems more impressive than a pressure group—it runs candidates and engages in campaign rhetoric—it is easy to assume that the social or political base which underlies it is more substantial and the consequences for the political system more fundamental than those of the pressure group. Yet they may not actually differ greatly. The political instruments available to groups to accomplish the same purposes may differ in a fairly rigid system from those in a system with flexible, coalition politics like the United States. This is part of the problem of comparative analysis—to assess the actual comparability of function and consequences of quite different institutions.

Chapter 11

Modernization and Class Polarization

IT WAS shown in Chapter 5 that a number of differences between these countries in the level of "modernization" were related to the level of class voting. These were the character and mechanisms of mobility, the degree of traditionalism, the level of income, the degree of urbanization, and the level of transformation of the labor force into an industrial one. It was suggested that contradictions between elements of modernization in a given society might account for different levels of class voting—the less wealthy but more urbanized and industrialized societies exhibiting higher class voting, for example. Although "modernization" is certainly not a simple unilinear process of change, it may be useful to explore some of the intervening changes which may connect industrialization and urbanization with the kinds of political cleavages characteristic of these societies.

These intervening changes are probably consequences of industrialization and urbanization which produce pervasive pressures upon the societies to change in certain ways. Stated most generally and baldly, industrialization and urbanization may encourage national economic integration, cultural assimilation, national political integration, and secularization. The first three are aspects of the balance between regionalism and national unification; the last has a different character. This chapter will first show that the level of class polarization is indeed related to differences in the degree to which these countries exhibit various forms of regionalism and degrees of secularization. Some of the evidence of changes and the consequences which these changes may have for the forms of political cleavage likely to exist in the near future will then be considered.[1]

Class polarization of the support for national parties seems to be most evident in the countries where a national political identity has replaced political identities centered on regional or religious loyalties. The aspects of modernization mentioned above favor the emergence of national political identities and thus favor class polarization of the parties—up to a certain point. These societies, as this chapter will suggest, may all be moving toward a common level of structurally based class cleavages—cleavages which remain while traditional political identities dwindle in importance.

A national communications system may be a necessary instrument of national integration, given a minimum level of industrialization and urbanization. Unless some means of communications exists between regions, no common political action can develop, regardless of common interests or values. Likewise, no true sense of national identity can exist unless there can be regular interchanges of ideas, people, and goods between the various regions of a nation. The expansion of national organizations of all kinds, whether business, recreational, trade union, or otherwise, contributes to the communication of ideas and grievances; it creates the possibility of the formation of a national public opinion.[2] No extensive comparative evidence bearing on this point will be given, but it may be noted that the countries with lower levels of regionalism are also those with higher circulations of newspapers per capita.[3]

---

[1] For a parallel mode of analysis, see Leslie Lipson, "Party Systems in the United Kingdom and the Older Commonwealth: Causes, Resemblances, and Variations," *Political Studies* (Oxford), VII (1959), 12–31. His concern is with the connection of the degree of homogeneity of the social structure with the cohesiveness of the political system. As he puts it, "a party system is certain to be influenced by the groupings in society, and is likely to reproduce either their complexity or their simplicity" (p. 23).

[2] Karl Deutsch develops this idea in *Nationalism and Social Communication.* (New York: Wiley, 1953).

[3] Newspaper copies distributed per 1,000 population in 1957 were: Great Britain, 573; Australia, 381; United States, 337; and Canada, 244. United Nations *Statistical Yearbook* (New York, 1958), pp. 545–60. For Weber's discussion of the prerequisites of nationhood, including communications of common sentiments, see Hans H. Gerth and C. Wright Mills, eds., *From Max Weber: Essays in Sociology* (New York: Oxford University Press, 1946), p. 178.

POLITICAL AND SOCIAL CHARACTERISTICS OF THE ANGLO-AMERICAN COUNTRIES

Economic regionalism, cultural regionalism, federalism, and secularism are four social and political characteristics associated with different levels of class polarization in the Anglo-American countries. As was discussed in Chapter 2, in a country with *economic regionalism*, one or more regions is dominated by agriculture, and the others are heavily industrialized and urbanized (i.e., regions are *internally* homogeneous). In a country with *cultural regionalism*, a majority of the population in one or more regions differs in religion, language, and/or ethnic background from the majority of the population in other regions. In a federal country (one with what might be called *constitutional regionalism*), units of government "lower" than the nation have a certain degree of autonomy which is constitutionally or traditionally guaranteed. Finally, in a *secularized* country, a sizable proportion of the population is not bound into a religious community or does not accept a set of religious beliefs as a guiding philosophy.

The generalizations to follow apply specifically only to the four Anglo-American countries. Whether they would hold for other countries with different political cultures and levels of social and economic development must remain problematic. The degree of regionalism or secularism is meaningful only in a comparative context, it must again be emphasized. All of these countries possess regions with special economic and cultural characteristics which are not likely to disappear. Ecological and geographical factors insure that mining, agricultural, and industrial concentrations stamp the populations of certain areas with a certain social character, as do the historical concentrations of certain ethnic and religious groupings. These regional elements exist in every country; thus only crude comparisons of "more or less" can be made.

Similarly, all political units above a certain size are comprised of different levels of political jurisdiction and authority, whether or not they are organized into a formal federal system. The lower levels of power possess certain specific jurisdictions of their own which cannot easily be challenged. Even the British unitary state has its county and borough governments which strive to maintain their jurisdictions vis-à-vis the national government. Thus, the distinction between federal and unitary states is a matter of degree. Secularism is also a matter of degree. Clearly no absolute determination of how "secular" a society is can be made.

Economic Regionalism

Economic regionalism is more characteristic of the less class-polarized political systems. Canada, with its wheat-growing Prairie provinces and heretofore agricultural Quebec, and the United States, with its underdeveloped South and areas of various agricultural and industrial concentration, are far more diverse economically than either Australia or Great Britain. Each state in Australia has its share of primary industry, but no state is dominated by either agriculture or any industry to the point where a sectional interest as great as those in the United States or Canada has developed.[4] The extremely small percentage of persons dependent upon agriculture in Great Britain—less than 6 per cent—means, almost in itself, that no area could be dominated by an agricultural interest. The mining economy of Wales approaches an economically homogeneous character more closely than any other British region.

Economic regionalism can lead to a "disguised" class politics if one social class is dominant in a particular region and supports one political party because of its economic interests. Agricultural areas, particularly agricultural areas dominated by small farmers, are probably not as likely to be sharply stratified as are industrial areas. Industrialized agriculture probably tends to resemble areas of heavy industry more closely and to have similar patterns of class conflict.

Cultural Regionalism

Cultural regionalism is more characteristic of the less class-polarized political systems. Canada, with its concentration of French-Catholics in Quebec and multitudes of immigrants, and the United States, with its ethnic groups, are far more diverse culturally than either Australia or Great Britain. Until World War II, Australia was composed primarily of persons of northern European descent. Since its Catholics are distributed fairly evenly throughout the six states, they do not form a distinct cultural community in the way that Canadian Catholics do. Britain has more cultural regionalism than Australia, but probably less than the United States and Canada.

---

[4] According to Kenneth MacKirdy, "the distribution of economic activities bears less relation to the boundaries of Australian states than it does to those of Canadian provinces." See MacKirdy, "The Federalization of the Australian Cabinet, 1901–1939," *Canadian Journal of Economics and Political Science,* XXIII (May, 1957), 223.

Unlike the Australian states, regions in Great Britain—Northern Ireland, Scotland, and Wales—have majorities with distinctive cultural and ethnic heritages. In Northern Ireland, the counterreaction to the pull toward the Irish Free State has produced political regionalism—overwhelming support for the Ulster Unionists. But the distinctive cultures of Wales and Scotland are not associated with political regionalism like that of the United States and Canada.

Possibly a more realistic way of evaluating British cultural regionalism is to point out that the sharp status differentiation of British society may override any sense of specific cultural identity. As was noted in Chapter 6, a worker in Britain probably feels himself to be a worker before he feels himself to be a Welshman or a Scotsman. Class- and status-identities override cultural boundaries.

Federalism

Federalism is, again, more characteristic of the less class-polarized political systems. As we have seen, the Canadian provinces possess possibly even greater legitimacy than that of the federal Dominion. In addition, Canadian provincial jurisdictions have been reinforced by judicial decisions. In the United States, "states' rights" are deeply embedded in the political system, not only by constitutional requirement but through acceptance by the electorate of existing distributions of jurisdiction and power between state and federal levels. By contrast, the Australian federal system is much weaker, being neither as powerful nor held to be as legitimate vis-à-vis the Commonwealth government as either the American states or the Canadian provinces. And, of course, Britain is not a federal state at all. Its local governments exist as agencies of the national government, and although such governments tend to build up jurisdictions which are not easily challenged, such "federal" tendencies do not have either the great legitimacy or the constitutional and legal bulwarks of the truly federal systems.

Some evidence that the states in Australia are far weaker vis-à-vis the national government than the states (or provinces) in the United States and Canada is afforded by the relative proportion of state revenues coming from federal grants. The financial dependence of federal units upon the national government is a fairly direct index of the relative power of the two political levels. As Table 11–1 shows, far less revenue in the states of the United States and Canada comes from federal grants than is the case with the revenues of the states in Australia.

TABLE 11–1

State Revenues Coming from Federal Grants, Australia, United States, Canada, 1950–1951

COUNTRY	STATE REVENUES FROM FEDERAL GRANTS (Per Cent)	TOTAL STATE REVENUES (Millions)
Australia	61	$181.2
United States	20	$11,264
Canada	14	$1,048

Source: A. H. Birch, *Federalism, Finance and Social Legislation* (London: Clarendon, 1955), pp. 262, 263, 269. The Canadian provinces are considered "states" in the above table. It may be noted that the federal contribution in the United States jumped from 13 per cent in 1942 and 10 per cent in 1945 to 20 per cent in 1950 and 19 per cent in 1951.

The strength of federalism is linked to the degree of economic and cultural regionalism, but these are factors which must be kept distinct because they need not coexist. Federalism in Australia is undoubtedly weakened by the absence of any social group seeking to defend its autonomy and integrity by using the federal machinery, but federalism is nevertheless likely to remain a structural characteristic of the Australian political system.

The cultural and social differences between Canada and Australia produce a different *kind* of federal state. A statement by the British Columbian premier shows the contrast in the degree of "social unity" in Canada and Australia. Asserting the need for provincial sovereignty at a Dominion-provincial conference called to iron out jurisdictional problems, the premier said:

> It may be accepted as axiomatic . . . that there are five economic and social units comprising the confederation of the Dominion of Canada. . . . Each of these units is distinctive, and there is nothing to be gained and much to be lost in attempting to bring them to a common level.

According to the British sociologist A. H. Birch, such a speech "could not conceivably have been made by the premier of an Australian state."[5]

The extent to which the legitimacy of regionalism goes in Canada

---

[5] A. H. Birch, *Federalism, Finance and Social Legislation in Canada, Australia and the United States* (Oxford: Clarendon, 1955), p. 146 (the above quotation from the premier appears on the same page). Birch also notes that "the feeling of community among Australians demands a much greater degree of equality as in the services provided for citizens, wherever they happen to live, than does the feeling of community among Canadians."

is indicated by an apparently serious move by a British Columbia newspaper to campaign for the secession of Vancouver Island, including the capital city, from British Columbia.[6]

Both Canadian and Australian political scientists are concerned with the problem of federalism, but their concern is significantly different. In Australia, the issue is whether the states should be abolished, or, if not, then what their particular subsidiary role should be. The states are not seen as valued political entities (at least in contrast with Canada's), but only as administrative units to be retained if they serve certain economic or political purposes, and whether they serve such purposes is usually seriously questioned. In line with the socialist–anti-socialist cleavage in Australia and the corresponding use of the states as a barrier to socialist action on the federal level, the states are seen as serving specific economic interests, not as bastions of cultural values or as homelands of specific peoples.[7]

In Canada, by contrast, the problem historically has been almost the opposite: How can a national government be sustained in the face of seemingly immovable provincial sovereignty? The position of Quebec that the national government was merely a "treaty" between separate sovereign powers joining together for certain limited purposes has meant, as was discussed in Chapter 9, that the Canadian national government has not yet attained real legitimacy.[8]

Such differences affect the functioning of many national institutions. The varying images of how the public broadcasting systems, for example, should serve the function of binding together the nation are illustrated by differences between the functions held up as important for the systems in Canada and Australia. "In Canada . . . the public and private sectors have historically been called upon to form one vast national broadcasting system in order to bind together the people through the wave-lengths . . . the need for this

---

[6] Kenneth A. MacKirdy, "Geography and Federalism in Australia and Canada," *The Australian Geographer*, VI (March, 1953), 42. The author comments that such a campaign "could have no counterpart in Australia."

[7] Most Australian political scientists would agree that "the States are no longer vital political entities in any basic sense." S. J. Butlin, "The Problem of Federal Finance," *Economic Record*, XXX (May, 1954), 11. See also P. H. Partridge, "The Politics of Federalism," in G. Sawer, ed., *Federalism: An Australian Jubilee Study* (Melbourne: F. W. Cheshire, 1952), p. 195.

[8] See F. R. Scott, "French-Canada and Canadian Federalism," in A. R. M. Lower *et al.*, *Evolving Canadian Federalism* (Durham: Duke University Press, 1958), pp. 80–81. Changes are occurring, but the point here is simply the contrast with Australia.

concept of a unified national system has not been as pressing 'down under.' "[9] It is suggested here that it is because of the greater *need* to have symbols of national unity in Canada as against Australia that such an image of a unifying function arises.

Paradoxically, although up to a certain point a national communications system may further national integration, such a system may also be turned to the service of regional separatism. Although conceived of as an instrument for unifying Canada, the Canadian Broadcasting System may now actually solidify French and English cultural separatism, since "the services of the national system are now so comprehensive that the great bulk of Canadians, whether English- or French-speaking, need never listen to broadcasts or telecasts in a language other than their own."[10] Clearly, such a situation can only occur where the cultural bases for the political deviation of a group—a separate language and culture—are reinforced by the holding of a regional stronghold by that group.

In the United States, the existing division of powers between the federal government and the states is accepted, by and large, and the *existence* of neither the federal government nor the states is in question. To be sure, the relative jurisdiction of the states and the federal government over many questions is in constant dispute, with continuing legal battles between interest groups differently advantaged by the division of powers, but the legitimacy of neither states nor nation is in doubt.

Thus, the more class-polarized political systems—Great Britain and Australia—either are unitary nations or have weak federal units which are financially subordinate to the national government and are not really legitimate political entities. The less class-polarized political systems—the United States and Canada—have strongly established federal units, and in Canada there is even more emphasis on the national government as the creature of the provincial will.[11]

---

[9] W. H. N. Hull, "The Public Control of Broadcasting: The Canadian and Australian Experiences," *Canadian Journal of Economics and Political Science,* XXVIII (February, 1962), 118.

[10] Norman Ward, "The National Political Scene," in Mason Wade, ed., *Canadian Dualism* (Toronto: University of Toronto Press, 1960), p. 274.

[11] It might be speculated that it was the American Civil War which finally established the legitimacy of the American national government without question. In Canada, a civil war was avoided, with the result that the possibility of secession has never finally been resolved. The maintenance of consensus may have actually prevented the achievement of national legitimacy.

Secularism

The less class-polarized political systems are less secularized than the more class-polarized systems. A high level of religiosity in a country may reduce the tendency for politics to be polarized around interest or class lines, although the evidence is of the grossest kind.

An International Gallup poll in 1948 asked persons in these four countries (and others) whether they believed in God, went to church, and believed in life after death. As Table 11–2 shows, the

TABLE 11–2

Religiosity of Persons in the Four Anglo-American Countries, 1948

COUNTRY	PER CENT WHO BELIEVE IN LIFE AFTER DEATH	PER CENT WHO GO TO CHURCH
United Kingdom	49	30
Australia	63	35
United States	68	..
Canada	78	69

Source: Australian Public Opinion Polls release, February–March, 1948. Whether the person went to church was not asked in the United States. There was no difference between Australia, Canada, and the United States in the percentage of respondents who indicated that they believed in God—about 95 per cent answered yes; of Britishers, 84 per cent answered yes. Parallel findings for the United States and Great Britain are given in Michael Argyle, *Religious Behaviour* (London: Routledge & Kegan Paul, 1958), pp. 35–38.

countries in which fewest people went to church or believed in life after death are also the countries with more class-polarized political systems. The rank order of religiosity is the same as the rank order of class voting.[12]

Part of these differences may be due to the greater proportion of Catholics in the less secular countries, since Catholics in modernizing societies are usually more likely to maintain religious beliefs and practices than Protestants. And, as we have seen, the Catholics pro-

---

[12] S. D. Clark has noted that "in few countries in the Western world has religion exerted as great an influence upon the development of the community as it has in Canada," and concludes that the burden of maintaining religious establishments has actually retarded economic development in Canada. See S. D. Clark, "The Religious Factor in Canadian Economic Development," in *Economic Growth: A Symposium* (Supplement VII, *The Journal of Economic History*, 1947), pp. 90–94.

vide a major religious deviation from patterns of class voting. The supremacy of national jurisdictions over religious ones in the Anglo-American countries as contrasted with continental European areas may be due to the Protestant character of the majority in the former countries. Protestantism may produce a pressure for national identities overriding religious and regional identities, and class politics may emerge more readily where this has taken place. As Max Weber asserted, in a different context, "normally, Protestantism . . . absolutely legitimated the state as a divine institution and hence violence as a means. Protestantism, especially, legitimated the authoritarian state."[13]

In sum, nations with high levels of cultural and economic regionalism, strongly embedded federal units, and a low level of secularization, tend to have low levels of class voting and high levels of regional and religious voting, and vice versa.

That class and national identities tend to be associated is not accidental. Where regions within a nation are economically homogeneous—relatively unstratified or with a dominant economic stratum—an ideology of homogeneous interests will arise together with a tradition of one-party voting which may override actual class stratification as a basis for political orientations. If economic regionalism is reinforced by cultural barriers—language, religion, etc. —it will be more difficult for national and class identities to develop. If economic and cultural bases for regionalism are further reinforced by the protection of a coexisting political unit (as in the federal nations), it will be even more difficult for national and class identities to penetrate sectional loyalties.

POSSIBLE CHANGES IN THE POLITICAL AND SOCIAL FACTORS AFFECTING ANGLO-AMERICAN POLITICS

If class, national, and secular identities are closely related, then we may inquire further about possible changes in some of the factors affecting the emergence of such identities. Specifically, are there trends away from economic and cultural regionalism or federalism and toward secularism? Are such changes likely to produce actually *higher* levels of class voting, not lower levels? Some suggestions have been given in the chapters on each country as to the path of possible change, and they will be summarized here.

---

[13] Gerth and Mills, eds., *op. cit.*, p. 124.

Decline of Economic Regionalism

Probably the most important economic changes reducing this type of regionalism are the industrialization of formerly agricultural regions and the economic integration of the nation—the development of national ownership of industries and a national marketing system. Such moves away from economic regionalism tend to produce economic cleavages and conflicts on the national rather than local or state (provincial) level and may tend therefore to focus political issues at the national level. In the absence of sharp cultural conflicts, such an economic system may produce parties polarized around Left-Right economic issues and around social classes. Such changes are clearly long-range, and no easy correlation of cause and effect can be found.

An aspect of the general decline of economic regionalism is the narrowing of the differences in the wages paid for the same kind of work from region to region. Such a narrowing, found in the United States and Australia and probably also in Great Britain and Canada, has been attributed to the "increased dispersion of manufacturing industry around the nation and the reduced importance in some areas of a large localized supply of agricultural workers" and possibly also to trade union policy favoring the reduction of regional wage differentials.[14]

As already noted, both Great Britain and Australia have less economic regionalism than the United States and Canada, but changes are taking place in the latter countries in a similar direction. The examples of the industrialization of Quebec and the South are probably the most outstanding, but even the Prairie provinces, as shown in Chapter 9, are becoming more urbanized and therefore presumably more industrialized. Some research has shown that the United States and Canada are becoming economically more homogeneous, that the major regions are deviating less and less from the national average on a number of indexes of economic development.[15]

A study of changes in the location of manufacturing activity in

---

[14] See Clark Kerr, "Wage Relationships—The Comparative Impact of Market and Power Forces," in John T. Dunlop, ed., *The Theory of Wage Determination* (New York: St. Martin's Press, 1957), p. 177, for a summary of sources on interarea wage differentials.

[15] See Roderick D. McKenzie, *The Metropolitan Community* (New York: McGraw-Hill, 1933), pp. 118–20. Robert Wenkert, Department of Sociology, University of California at Berkeley, has shown in an unpublished paper that the trends computed by McKenzie up to 1930 have continued to 1950.

the United States from 1929 to 1954 found that the more industrialized areas (the northeastern states) lost ground relatively while
the less industrialized areas (the South and West) gained, thus indicating a trend toward national economic homogeneity.[16] Another
detailed study concluded, from analysis of population and economic
indicators for United States regions, that "the economic growth of
the nation has reduced disparities in levels of living among the regions."[17] Although provincial comparisons were not made, one study
of the spread of industry to previously non-industrialized areas in
Canada found substantial shifts.[18]

As noted in Chapter 6, to some extent variations in class voting
in the British regions can be accounted for by the concentration of
industries in certain regions, notably Wales. Since 1939 industrial
diversification of British regions, most notably Wales, has increased.[19]. It seems probable that as these changes occur, the degree of regional variation in British class voting will drop even
lower than it is.

The hypothesis that economic regionalism is decreasing because
of the tendency for the level of urbanization and industrialization
to become equalized is contradicted by the suggestion of some econ-
omists and geographers that the urban-industrial areas of a nation
tend to attract further economic growth, and that a country does
not in fact move in the direction of regional equalization of industrial or urban development. According to Ullman, "initial location
advantages at a critical stage of change become magnified in the
course of development."[20] Ullman shows that the "core area" of the
United States remains the northeastern bloc of states, with 7 per

---

[16] See Victor R. Fuchs, "Changes in the Location of United States Manufacturing since 1929," *Journal of Regional Sciences,* I (Spring, 1959), 1–17.

[17] Harvey S. Perloff *et al., Regions, Resources and Economic Growth* (Baltimore: Johns Hopkins University Press, 1960), p. 285.

[18] The author analyzed both "diffusion" (the growth of manufacturing in
secondary industrial areas and non-industrial areas) and "dispersion" (shifts of
industry from large cities to smaller ones, or from both to non-urban areas).
See David W. Slater, "Decentralization of Urban Peoples and Manufacturing
Activity in Canada," *Canadian Journal of Economics and Political Science,*
XXVII (February, 1961), 72–85.

[19] C. E. V. Leser, "Changes in Level and Diversity of Employment in Regions of Great Britain 1939–1947," *Economic Journal,* LIX (September, 1949),
326–42.

[20] Edward L. Ullman, "Regional Development and the Geography of Concentration," *Papers and Proceedings of the Regional Science Association,* IV
(1958), 196.

cent of the population, but 70 per cent of the industry in 1950. What this point may mean, however, is not that there is no continuing concentration of industry in one area, but that *all* areas become transformed into urban areas, with either industry or industrialized agriculture as an economic base. After a certain "threshold" of urban-industrial development is passed, it may not make sense to speak of concentration of industry because the consequences for social and political organization may be substantially the same for all areas past the threshold level.[21]

Decline of Cultural Regionalism

Urbanized and industrialized societies, particularly those which are fairly "evenly" developed, tend to have uniform and high rates of geographical mobility and tend to develop networks of mass communications which contribute to the breakdown of parochial communities integrated around special subcultures. As already shown, Great Britain and Australia are already more culturally homogeneous than the United States and Canada, but trends toward homogeneity are evident in the latter countries and may remove this particular barrier to class and national identities. As was suggested in Chapter 9, Quebec is no longer the isolated province that it was fifty years ago, and rapid transportation, social mobility, and mass communications are breaking down the isolation of ethnic and religious subcultures in the United States.

A detailed study of patterns of segregation of ethnic groups in urban areas of the United States concluded that "the general trend has been towards declining residential segregation of ethnic groups from the native white population. . . ."[22]

---

[21] Ullman (*ibid.,* p. 189) suggests that if several individual countries were created out of the present United States, "development might *increase* in the smaller units, but *decrease* in the present core area." Conversely, if Canada were part of the United States, probably "urban development, metropolitan services and some transport . . . would be lower" (p. 188). (Italics in original.) If such is the case (clearly, evidence would be difficult to obtain), then national integration might encourage the economic development of regions less than the disintegration of existing boundaries would. There is some evidence that balanced industrial development in Australia was hindered by its ties to the Commonwealth.

[22] Stanley Lieberson, *Ethnic Patterns in American Cities* (New York: Free Press of Glencoe, 1963), p. 45. The study was based primarily on data concerning immigration; it utilized ward data for 1910 and 1920 and census tract data for 1930 and 1950 from ten United States cities. The author also found that second-generation immigrants were less segregated than were the first generation—in 1930, at least.

There is some evidence, on the other hand, that ethnic pluralism has increased in Australia and Canada, because of the influx of many nationalities since World War II. The lack of pressure toward ethnic assimilation has allowed them to maintain a separate existence. The number of newspapers, for example, in languages other than English or French has tripled in Canada since the 1930's, while the opposite is probably true in the United States.[23] Whether these new groups are concentrated in such a way as to accentuate political regionalism in either Australia or Canada is as yet unknown.

In Britain, the national press, movies, and geographic mobility are leading to cultural assimilation of all of the minority peoples. ". . . in Scotland as in Wales the silent process of assimilation has steadily continued. It has become harder every year for an Englishman on his way to Scotland to be aware that he has crossed the border."[24]

Decline of Federalism

Under the impact of war, depressions, and the demand for more social legislation, the national governments of all of these four countries have become more centralized, taking over more and more functions from lower levels of government. In the process, the states and provinces of the federal systems have lost much of their actual power. The contradiction between actual centralizing tendencies and the lagging legitimacy of national jurisdictions, particularly in Canada, has produced inevitable tensions and political conflicts.

Such centralizing tendencies are not only evident in the more federalized systems—the United States and Canada—but also in the already more centralized nations.

In Great Britain, local government has been steadily losing functions to the central government. "Under post-war legislation, the minor authorities have lost all their previous direct powers in the important fields of education . . . of the police and fire services, of

---

[23] See Frank G. Vallee, Mildred Schwartz, and Frank Darknell, "Ethnic Assimilation and Differentiation in Canada," *Canadian Journal of Economics and Political Science,* XXIII (November, 1957), 540–49. In the United States, there were 1,092 newspapers in foreign languages in 1940 and only 695 in 1949. See Joseph Roucek, "The Foreign-Language Press and Radio," in Francis J. Brown and Joseph Roucek, eds., *One America* (New York: Prentice-Hall, 1952), p. 391.

[24] Sir Reginald Coupland, *Welsh and Scottish Nationalism: A Study* (London: Collins, 1954), p. 383.

gas and electricity, of the health services, and of town and country planning."[25] This change has been taking place despite the fact that the local governments have long been merely agencies of the central government and not autonomous units.[26]

In Australia, the centralization of effective power in the hands of the Commonwealth government has also been taking place, despite the lack of willingness of the electorate to vote for amendment of the Constitution to allow actual legislative dominance by the national government.[27]

Since the main concern here is whether centralizing processes have taken place in the non-class-polarized political systems, it is more relevant, however, to see whether similar processes are occurring in the United States and Canada. There seems to be little doubt that they have, although no systematic evidence can be presented here. Even in Canada, "new ideas of state control . . . have tended to reverse the developments of three-quarters of a century and place increasing powers in the hands of the Dominion."[28] The centralizing tendencies in the United States political system, whether occurring under Democratic or Republican auspices, have been noted by many observers and need not be further documented here. A general survey of changes of political jurisdictions in federal nations concludes that there is a near-universal tendency for power in federal nations to move to the federal level at the expense of state or provincial governments.[29] And a survey of a number of federal nations concludes that:

> In Australia, Canada, and the United States, then, there has clearly appeared a tendency to seek increasing power in the community [national] legislature over the production of goods, and especially over the labor relations involved in their production. The efforts, at first unsuccessful and then successful, to persuade the United States Supreme Court to give a construction of the commerce power which reaches that objective; the unsuccessful attempts in

---

[25] Peter Self, "New Prospects for Local Government," *Political Quarterly,* XXVIII (1957), 27.

[26] See W. O. Hart, "The White Paper on Local Government," *Public Law* (London), I (1956), 336–49.

[27] See L. F. Crisp, "Centenaries of the Australian States," *Parliamentary Affairs,* X (1957), 180–94.

[28] Robert MacGregor Dawson, *The Government of Canada* (2nd ed.; Toronto: University of Toronto Press, 1954), p. 96.

[29] Arthur E. Sutherland, "Attrition of State Powers in Federal Nations," *Juridical Review* (Edinburgh), III, New Series (1958), 111–33.

Canada to attain that end through the use of the treaty-making power; and the efforts of the Australian Parliament to extend its powers over production and labor relations by passing proposals for constitutional alteration, which were rejected by the electors— these may be taken to indicate a substantial opinion that the increasingly close integration of the economic activities of a modern federal nation makes necessary a considerable measure of community [national] control over production and labor relations.[30]

Such a statement, although applying specifically to production and labor relations, indicates the close connection of the growing economic homogeneity of these countries with the growing importance of the national government and the dwindling importance of the federalized units.[31] And, as the actual focus of political issues moves to the national level, the lines of political cleavage around the political parties seem likely to become increasingly drawn on a class basis.

It is difficult to know whether the actual balance of power between the Canadian federal government and the provinces has shifted toward the national level. Probably there are contradictory trends. An analysis of trends from the publication in 1945 of the Rowell-Sirois Commission report to 1961 reveals no clear-cut direction of change, although change has taken place. Without making any overt statement of principle contradicting the Rowell-Sirois recommendations that certain measures be taken to guarantee provincial autonomy, the federal government has informally assumed more power, largely through the mechanism of grants to the provinces to which specific conditions are attached. Another postwar development, the expansion of *ad hoc* committees linking federal and provincial executives and bureaucracies, may or may not indicate increased federal influence.[32]

---

[30] Arthur E. Sutherland, "Commerce, Transportation, and Customs," in Robert R. Bowie and Carl J. Friedrich, eds., *Studies in Federalism* (Boston: Little, Brown, 1954), p. 328. See also, A. H. Birch, *op. cit.*, pp. 288–89.

[31] For a similar position, see Kenneth C. Wheare, *Federal Government* (2nd ed.; London: Oxford University Press, 1951), pp. 255–58, and Arthur W. Macmahon, ed., *Federalism: Mature and Emergent* (New York: Doubleday, 1955), especially the chapter by David Truman.

[32] D. V. Smiley, "The Rowell-Sirois Report, Provincial Autonomy, and Postwar Canadian Federalism," *Canadian Journal of Economics and Political Science*, XXVIII (February, 1962), 54–69. Smiley emphasizes that some legislation enacted by the Canadian Parliament in 1949 and 1954 delegated federal authority to executive agencies under provincial jurisdiction—a move away from federal control.

It should be noted that the shift of government expenditures from state to federal levels measures only certain aspects of government centralization, particularly those relating to economic and social welfare legislation. In the United States, at least, "the provisions of those bodies of law which regulate the relationship between the individual and the state and the relationships between individuals—the general body of criminal and civil law—these remain overwhelmingly a matter of State law."[33]

Secularization

Whether there is any tendency for these societies to become more secularized and whether such secularization helps to create a different kind of political orientation, specifically a greater tendency to vote according to class rather than region or religion, are really open questions. That urbanization and industrialization tend to break down "traditional" loyalties of all kinds, specifically religious ones, has long been a cliché of sociological theorizing about broad trends of social change since the Industrial Revolution. As with all clichés, this may have a germ of basic truth, but it is vastly oversimplified. Statistics showing increasing church attendance in the United States and showing the increase of the size of the Catholic communities in all of these countries could probably be given as indexes of an opposite trend. Probably a number of indexes showing *either* secularization or increasing religiosity could be constructed. In any case, it cannot be assumed that inevitable processes of social change will push the United States and Canada in the Australian and British direction (assuming that the latter two are actually more secularized).

But even if an increase in the degree of secularization could be established, it would still be difficult to show the connection of this with the changing bases of political orientations. It is certainly plausible that if religious communities lose their solidarity, political loyalties will increasingly become unrelated to religious loyalties. In such a case, the religious community might remain intact, but politics and religion would be severed.

---

[33] See M. J. C. Vile, *The Structure of American Federalism* (London: Oxford University Press, 1961), p. 6. Vile correctly emphasizes that the United States remains a "federal country in spirit, in its way of life, and in its Constitution," despite centralizing tendencies in certain types of governmental activity (p. 1).

It could plausibly be argued that the level of secularism is about as high as it will get. Secularization may be associated with processes of modernization at earlier stages of development—when the religious basis of community organization was disappearing. The tremendous geographic mobility in the early stages of industrialization necessarily broke the solidary ties to traditional religious and ethnic communities, especially since transportation and communication were not well developed. Such a connection between mobility and the breakdown of ethnic and religious solidarities may not exist in the most "modernized" societies.

Apart from the question of secularization, religion would seem to be a far more permanent potential basis of political cleavage than regionalism, and a basis of cleavage much less affected by the social and political changes being discussed. Religious loyalties are not based upon a territorial identification, but are ideological and value-laden. For this reason, the process of secularization must be seen as quite different from the breakdown of other "traditional" identifications such as those with a regional subculture.[34]

I have suggested that a number of changes are taking place in the very factors which are apparently associated with levels of class, religious, and regional voting. All of the Anglo-American countries are becoming more culturally and economically homogeneous and more centralized politically, although not necessarily more secular. Since these factors were originally associated with the more class-polarized systems, does this mean that class voting will rise in the countries where it has historically been low—the United States and Canada—and remain high in Australia and Great Britain? The next section is devoted to a discussion of the changes to be expected in class voting and the possibilities of convergence of the social bases of Anglo-American politics.

POSSIBLE CHANGES IN THE LEVEL OF CLASS VOTING

The analysis thus far does not imply that a disappearance of class voting in the Anglo-American countries is likely, but rather that a *convergence* of the social bases of political support may take place —a decline of religious and regional voting in those countries where

---

[34] Such is actually the case in a number of continental European countries where the religious–non-religious cleavage cuts across the Left-Right cleavage. The Christian ecumenical movements and the Christian Democratic parties of Europe are movements with a broad religious base.

it is high and a move toward similar levels of class voting reflecting both the structured cleavages of economic interests and pressures upon parties to respond to the cleavages dominant at any given time.

The hypothesis of convergence is not securely buttressed by the empirical data which have been given, but it is supported by an interconnected set of propositions and some evidence. No evidence of decline of religious and regional voting has been found in the United States, and little evidence has been presented to indicate a decline of religious voting in Canada. Yet social changes which seem to be connected with such a decline are occurring and may reduce deviations from "interest" politics. If these societies are likely to become more economically and culturally homogeneous, if the national governments are likely to become more and more the central focus of political cleavages, if a pervasive process of secularization is taking place, we may expect a decline of religious and regional voting. A lower level of religious and regional voting has been shown to be associated with higher levels of class voting, and therefore we may expect a further rise of class voting in Canada, for example, as the nation becomes more economically and culturally homogeneous.

Some indirect evidence bearing on these hypotheses can be given. In the chapters on Australia and Great Britain, it was suggested that the regions both older and more urbanized exhibited the *lowest* levels of class voting, while in Canada similar regions exhibited the *highest* levels of class voting. The implications of this finding may indicate the likelihood of a convergence of the social bases of Anglo-American politics. The characteristics that really account for the empirical pattern are difficult to determine. It is possible both that the oldest and most "British" regions are likely to be similar in their patterns of political cleavage and that the more urbanized, more wealthy, more "modern" regions are likely to be similar. Whether structural cleavages dominate in such regions in the absence of traditionalism or whether these regions are historically similar in their social and ethnic composition and therefore merely exhibit another version of traditional political allegiances, is a moot question.

Figure 11–1, drawn from data presented in the chapters on the several countries, summarizes the trends in class voting in the regions that are both older and more urbanized. A pattern of con-

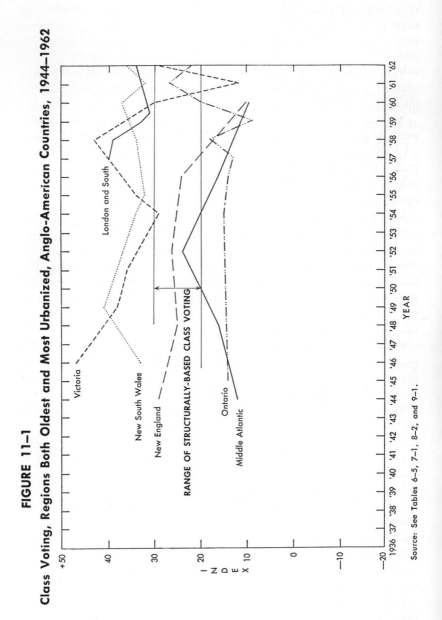

FIGURE 11–1

Class Voting, Regions Both Oldest and Most Urbanized, Anglo-American Countries, 1944–1962

Source: See Tables 6–5, 7–1, 8–2, and 9–1.

vergence appears, despite the maintenance of approximately the same rank order of class voting. Australia and Great Britain still have higher levels of class voting than the United States and Canada, showing that pressures of the total system still probably override the tendency for regional convergence. (Since the number of surveys was limited and, particularly for Britain, cover only a brief time-span, these generalizations can only be speculative.)

Victoria and New South Wales are the oldest, most urbanized, and most industrialized states of Australia; yet they have had the lowest levels of class voting of any of the states except Western Australia. The London and Southern region of Great Britain is the most urbanized area of the nation, and yet in 1958–59, it had the lowest level of class voting of any region. The New England and Middle Atlantic regions are the oldest and most industrialized areas of the United States. (As noted in Chapter 8, the evidence on regionalism in the United States is inconclusive.) Ontario in Canada contains the capital of the nation. All of these regions are in some sense identified as "central" regions of the nation and are closely associated with the national identity—or better, they lack any sectional identity. New South Wales and Victoria are the "eastern" states which financially and politically dominate Australia. New South Wales contains the national capital, Canberra, as does the London region of Great Britain. The New England and Middle Atlantic regions in the United States were the first settled and still may be the areas which lack distinct sectional identities. Ontario, as noted, contains Ottawa, the capital of Canada, and is also probably the province most closely linked with Canada's incipient national identity.

Class voting may not be extremely high where there is the least sectional identity. Rather, voting may be based upon structured interest cleavages where a national identity has replaced various local and parochial political loyalties. In such regions, the structural similarities of the stratification and political systems in these four countries produce similar patterns of political cleavage. To put it another way, class voting may be approaching the same level in the oldest and most urbanized regions in each country. This may show that historic differences in party organization, appeals, and loyalties are becoming less important than the nature of interest-cleavages in determining political support. The structural bases for political cleavage may override traditional loyalties and even vast differences in the history and organization of the parties.

The dotted lines in Figure 11–1 represent extensions of the most recent trends in the level of class voting exhibited on the available survey data, and, as the graph shows, they roughly converge. What may be called the range of structurally-based class voting is shown crudely by two lines drawn between the 20- and 30-percentage-point difference in the support of manual and non-manual strata for 'a major political party. This range represents a theoretical prediction of what the divergence of the class bases of support for the parties is likely to be in these countries, given the existing economic and political framework, the lack of any extreme conditions such as a war or a depression which would alter all of the conditions upon which the generalizations of this study are premised, and the assumption that all of these countries are becoming more economically and culturally homogeneous.

The Middle Atlantic region of the United States is the one region both old and highly urbanized which does not fit the pattern predicted. This region, containing New York, Pennsylvania, and New Jersey, is as old as New England, early a center of political power, and, in fact, it contained early capital cities (New York and Philadelphia). The region is both more urbanized and industrialized than the general British level. However, the patterns of class voting revealed by the data available are not consistent with the prediction that they should fall within the range of structurally-based class voting, since the Middle Atlantic region fell well below the lower level in 1944, 1948, and 1960. The data do not allow further exploration of this deviation—except that the 1960 drop is not due in this case, unlike that of New England, to the Catholic vote. Both Protestants and Catholics had low levels of class voting in the Middle Atlantic region in 1960. (It is possible, however, that Gallup inclusion of states bordering on the south in this region accounts for this particular finding.)

It may be noted that the sharp decline of New England in the 1960 election is due entirely to the Catholic vote across class lines for Kennedy (according to Gallup No. 636K). In the one survey in which barely enough cases were available to allow an examination of the effect of religion upon class voting within regions, class voting in 1960 among Catholics in New England was +6, among Protestants, +22. If the prediction made in Chapter 8 that Catholic "citizenship" has at last been validated by the achievement of the Presidency and therefore that religious voting may be expected to decline, voting patterns in New England may yet converge in the same manner as similar regions in the other countries.

But, is there not a contradiction between these findings and the correlations of gross social characteristics of these countries and their levels of class voting, discussed briefly at the end of Chapter 5? If urbanization and a lack of traditional sectional loyalties produce higher levels of class voting in Australia and Great Britain than in the United States and Canada, then why should the older and more urbanized regions not have the highest levels of class voting? This holds only for the United States and Canada, not for Great Britain and Australia, where the more urbanized regions show less class voting.

One problem in reconciling the apparently different consequences of these sets of factors is a methodological one. It is difficult to know whether the same factors which make for a difference between these political systems considered as wholes should have similar consequences for subsystems within the whole. It is entirely possible that for very good reasons, the "more urbanized" societies should have higher levels of class voting than "less urbanized" societies, but that "more urbanized" regions (within "more urbanized" societies) should have lower levels of class voting than "less urbanized" regions, and vice versa, for regions within "less urbanized" societies. Part of the difficulty may be a semantic one, that urbanism is much too diffuse and inclusive a "factor," and that actually different elements of urbanization, not necessarily always consistent elements, may have different consequences, depending upon the character or level of the system.

High levels of class voting in Australia and England may not reflect the actual economic interests involved in political struggles, but rather a form of traditionalism. The traditional loyalties characteristic of the nations with high levels of class voting may be peculiar to countries with long histories of labor parties, and a deep association of upper-status groups with the Right parties. If these traditionalized class loyalties dwindle under the impact of the same rationalizing forces of urbanism and industrialism that may yet reduce religious and regional loyalties in the United States and Canada, the structural similarities of interest cleavages may come to be the decisive ones. Thus, the early urbanism and dominance of class issues in Australia and Great Britain may have produced higher levels of traditionalized class voting. But further stages of political change are also most evident in the more urbanized areas of these countries. Urban areas are centers of innovation, and the ideologies which spawn there spread to the rest of the country and become traditionalized. But change does not cease, and certain urban areas are continually innovating.

The breakdown of traditional loyalties of all kinds, both those based upon solid class identifications and those based on solid regional or religious identification, suggests another kind of evidence for the possible convergence of the social bases of Anglo-American politics. If structural cleavages are likely to become the main bases for political loyalties, and if *subjective* class identifications are likely to become similar in these countries (specifically the blurring of the solid class loyalties of Britishers), we may expect that class voting among persons with similar class identifications is becoming similar and, in fact, should be within the suggested range of structurally-induced class voting.

Table 11–3 shows that class voting in Britain and the United States is much more similar among persons identifying themselves as "middle-class" than among the total electorate (30 and 21 respectively). If we assume that patterns of both structural cleavages and of subjective class identifications are moving toward similarity in the two countries, then these figures show a convergence. Note that the levels of class voting are at the extreme ends of the range of structurally based class voting, with Britain still remaining higher. And, although the Left vote in the United States is lower among middle-class identifiers, the level of class voting is *not* reduced sharply by considering only persons identifying themselves as middle-class (from 23 over-all to 21). This lack of a drop indicates that an increased blurring of class lines in the United States would not further reduce class voting. Class voting in the United States is probably as low as it is likely to get, even given the existing stratification order and political system, and will probably increase if religious and regional deviations disappear or diminish. On the other hand, the high level of class voting in Great Britain is partly due to the solid class identifications of manual workers. If the image of the Labour party as a class party becomes less sharp, or if the working class absorbs middle-class identifications, class voting may be expected to decline in Britain. (The data on working-class identifications are included in Table 11–3 for the sake of completeness but are not relevant here.)

TABLE 11–3

Labour or Democratic Preference, by Occupation Type
and Subjective Class Identification, Great Britain (1957),
United States (1952)

	PER CENT PREFERRING LABOUR OR DEMOCRATIC PARTIES SUBJECTIVE CLASS IDENTIFICATION*					
OCCUPATION TYPE	WORKING-CLASS		MIDDLE-CLASS		TOTAL	
	United States	*Great Britain*	*United States*	*Great Britain*	*United States*	*Great Britain*
Manual	59 (482)	78 (454)	45 (143)	50 (269)	57 (642)	67 (737)
Non-Manual	49 (191)	52 (457)	24 (267)	20 (85)	34 (480)	24 (551)
Index of *Class Voting*	+10	+26	+21	+30	+23	+43

Sources: BIPO Survey No. 1717, February, 1957, and the Michigan Survey Research Center Survey of the 1952 United States presidential election.
* The table includes all those as "middle-class" who identified themselves as lower middle-class, middle-class, or upper middle-class. Only those specifically calling themselves "working-class" are included as such. Discrepancies in the totals are due to omission of persons rejecting the whole idea of social classes or not answering. The total proportion preferring Labour in the British survey was 48 per cent; the total proportion preferring the Democratic party in the United States survey was 47 per cent.

Sketchy evidence has been presented which indicates that a "normal" level of class voting may come to exist in countries with moderate political cultures and relatively open class systems. Figure 11–2 summarizes the major substantive findings of this study. The four countries are positioned according to the empirical data on their levels of class, regional, and religious voting. The arrows indicate the possible path of political change, converging on a theoretical position representing the common structural bases of cleavage. Religious and regional voting will probably not increase, but will vary around a low level. The social and economic variances among regions are also not likely to increase.[35]

The empirical findings summarized in Figure 11–2 indicate the possibilities of a process of political realignment in these four countries which may have important common aspects. In Great Britain, class voting may decline as the society becomes even more eco-

---

[35] If regions develop into special economic areas because of their special resources, even when highly urbanized and industrialized, we may expect differential patterns of voting. But, this would not be "regionalism" in the sense meant here, but a special form of class- or interest-cleavage such as is found in the Prairie provinces in Canada, where there is no special non-class loyalty producing the regional deviation.

nomically and culturally homogeneous and traditional class loyalties wither. In Australia, the Catholic deviation will probably dwindle, and class voting is likely to drop slightly. (The level of class voting in Australia is already not much higher than the predicted high-point of the range of structured class voting, which may indicate that traditional status distinctions reinforcing class identifications in Great Britain are less operative in Australia.) In the United States and Canada, the average level of class voting will probably increase as regional and religious deviations decrease.

Two extreme possibilities are also visible on Figure 11–2. Where religious and regional voting *and* class voting are high, the conditions for a breakdown of political consensus—and therefore a fragmentation of the boundaries of the existing political community— exist.[36] At the other extreme, where none of these cleavages exists, a "mass society" is approximated. Here, the political parties are mere bureaucratic entities competing for power. They have no solid base in allegiances to groups intervening between individual and nation, whether these groups are based upon regional, religious, or class loyalties. It is an open question whether such a situation is potentially dangerous for the continuation of a given political structure. In any case, it seems an unlikely possibility for these four countries.[37]

Where transitional processes are occurring, as possibly in Canada, there may be a breakdown of ethnic and religious political loyalties without any immediate replacement by class-based ones, and we may expect considerable instability—a lack of "rhyme or reason"— in electoral behavior. Party in the English-speaking countries is not securely linked to ideology, so that group affiliation is the main basis for the stability of party loyalties. If the main group affilia-

---

[36] Obviously Quebec came very close to this at several historical points, and the factors which have affected the relations between Quebec and the Canadian Dominion have important implications for the understanding of the integration of political systems. Wherever such an extreme conflict exists between national and regional loyalties and jurisdictions, the conditions maintaining or undermining a given political system can be discovered more readily than where little conflict exists.

[37] See William Kornhauser, *The Politics of Mass Society* (Glencoe: Free Press, 1959) for the view, ultimately deriving from Alexis de Tocqueville, that the masses in such a political system are easily manipulated by political elites and that the political elites in turn cannot easily isolate themselves from irresponsible influence from the masses.

FIGURE 11–2
The Future Social Bases of Anglo-American Politics

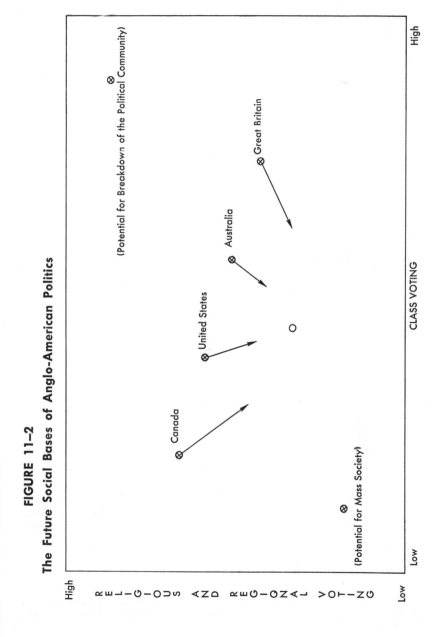

tions providing the historic ground for the strength of a party in an area are weakening, there may literally be no conditions stabilizing party allegiances. This may be particularly true if geographic mobility is high, because a person may move into an area where few of the traditional party symbols have meaning for him. A Britisher moving from north to south England is moored to his traditional party by the anchor of the national similarity of political symbols. An Ontarian moving to Manitoba or British Columbia, or a Quebecer moving to Alberta has no ready-made links reinforcing his tie to traditional party loyalties.

To the extent that large-scale social changes are taking place, the structure of government seems to be becoming more centralized to deal with problems increasingly defined as national in scope, and the structure of society seems to be becoming more homogeneous, less parochial, less traditionalistic. We may expect that parties will change in a similar direction. They will become more dominated by a nationally-organized central committee and local branches will become less autonomous. Parties will pursue the electorate brandishing national issues, similarly defined, in every region, and they will receive the support of similar kinds of people in every region.

One final note on the gap between the available survey data and the kinds of generalizations attempted in this study: Survey data, by imposing separate treatment of "factors" and "variables," cannot portray adequately the actual interplay of class, regional, and religious aspects of political cleavages, particularly where only four cases exist for analysis. To take a remote example of the actual interconnections of these factors, the chairman of the Irish Home Rule Parliamentary party in 1874, Isaac Butt, was a Conservative Protestant who tried to convince Irish Protestants of the gentry that regional separatism would mean neither Catholic domination nor "class" domination by agrarian radicals.[38] Here is a merger of the three aspects of political cleavage in a way which is neither profitable nor possible to separate—in a single case—by devising separate measures of "class" or "religious" bases of political action. The intention in this study has not been to isolate a given factor except insofar as its role can therefore be more clearly seen in a comparative framework.

---

[38] See Lawrence J. McCaffrey, "Isaac Butt and the Home Rule Movement: A Study in Conservative Nationalism," *Review of Politics*, XXII (January, 1960), 72–95.

CONCLUSION

Social classes in the sense of great diffuse blocs of people in generalized conflict may no longer exist in these societies. But social classes in the sense of groups in similar objective situations organizing to pursue collective interests remain powerful political forces. Such a shift in the reality delineated by the term "social class" is of vital importance in understanding the nature of political cleavages in these societies, although the data on class voting may not directly reveal a shift from solidarities based upon deep identification with a class over generations to solidarities based upon rather transitory interests of individuals. The member of the United Auto Workers Union or the National Association of Manufacturers or the Farmers' Union is now less a member of a solidary "class" and more a member of an "interest" or "status" group. The view that the achievement of industrial and political "citizenship" by workers was an important de-revolutionizing force is essentially the view that workers are now a "status group" and not a "class." But to view them this way is not to imply that deep conflicts of interest have been eliminated; it is merely to evaluate the role of such conflicts differently.[39]

"Class" conflicts of the old variety may actually sustain regional, ethnic, and religious political loyalties, contrary to what Marx believed about the secularizing and generalizing power of class interests. Because social classes developed in particularistic association with certain cultural traits, the religious, ethnic, and regional identities associated with traditional class identities remain alive as long as the class identifications do. Thus, the dwindling of particularistic and parochial loyalties to political parties may occur only as social classes change their character.

The intellectual perspective of the present study is close to that stated by Reinhard Bendix, who suggests that when the struggle over the distribution of national sovereignty is settled, politics becomes a struggle over the distribution of the national product. In the terms I have been using, the disappearance of regional and parochial political loyalties allows class identities to develop. Bendix postulates a centralized national government as a feature of the type

---

[39] See Ralf Dahrendorf, *Class and Class Conflict in Industrial Society* (Stanford: Stanford University Press, 1959) for a similar point of view.

of political system characteristic of modern Western societies. As he puts it:

> Centralization means that such major functions as the adjudication of legal disputes, the collection of revenue, the control of currency, military recruitment, the organization of the postal system and others have been removed from the political struggle in the sense that they cannot be parcelled out among competing jurisdictions or appropriated on a hereditary basis by privileged status-groups. Under these circumstances politics are no longer a struggle over the distribution of the national sovereignty; instead they have tended to become a struggle over the distribution of the national product and hence over the policies guiding the administration of centralized government functions.[40]

Here Bendix is distinguishing the stable Western democracies from other less legitimate and stable nations. Certainly in his comparative context this statement adequately describes all four of the Anglo-American countries. Yet, as this study has shown, legitimacy and centralization are still problematic in these countries. The relations of political units to each other and the importance of various group-formations in politics are changing and unresolved. National parties struggling over the distribution of the national product cannot really emerge in Canada, for example, until the relative jurisdictions of the provinces and their subordination to the Dominion government has become settled. Clearly these processes are interrelated: those factors which further national legitimacy also break down regional and religious ties to political parties, so these are not causal sequences in a strict sense. The process of balancing between the various group interests in a society, their demands for representation, and the maintenance of the legitimacy of the national government is a complicated and uneven one.

Basic to the views expressed here has been the assumption, already mentioned in Chapter 1, of a number of competing social interests and social values, each borne by a sizable section of the population and each seeking legitimacy for its goals. Nothing is gained by viewing these struggles of social groups for cultural autonomy, or political groups for jurisdiction, as deriving their legitimacy from a single set of values. This assumption merely clouds analysis of the actual conflicts of values and interests. Such a set of

---

[40] Reinhard Bendix, "Social Stratification and the Political Community," *European Journal of Sociology,* I (1960), 181–213.

general values may exist but must not be assumed to exist merely because a given social and political system continues to operate and to hang together.

The evidence that the political parties in these systems may come to be more clearly based upon class cleavages is not prima facie evidence of imminent danger to the existing political institutions. Under conditions of highly developed industrialism, class cleavages may actually be the cleavages which are most easily compromised and the ones most likely to retain national unity and political consensus (regardless of the level of class voting). Regional and religious loyalties are not easily compromised because they rest on differences of "values," not "interests." Such cleavages may be inherently more disintegrative and less flexible than class ones. Regions within which sectional, religious, or ethnic sentiments override the class bases of politics are usually backward economically, less equalitarian, and rejecting of civil liberties and urban ways of life. Although these four nations are higher on the scales of legitimacy and economic development than most other nations, even they have their "backward areas" and groups.

Some traditional political theorists have emphasized the need to *restrict* the power of the national state, afraid that increasing power would become irresponsible. They have neglected the need for mechanisms to *generate* national power. This has been due to the fear that class allegiances would be far more rigid than any other cleavage between social groups and that a pure class politics (supposedly implicit in universal suffrage together with working-class political organization) would endanger the stability of democratic polities. This is the source of the idea that the more cross-cutting cleavages the better: ethnic, religious, regional, federal, etc., so that the supposedly most uncompromising cleavage—class—would lose its political effectiveness.

However, class allegiances may actually be more flexible than non-class loyalties. A consensual system divided along non-class lines may have a politics of *stalemate* as well as a politics of moderation. (Canada in 1962 and 1963 may well have exhibited such a stalemate.) New mechanisms of consensus can come into existence when class politics is dominant, obviating many of the needs for cross-cutting allegiances. But the continuation in the less class-polarized systems of institutional devices for limiting the concentration of power has meant that a solid majority for a party representing a consistent set of national policies cannot be gained. Power is fragmented rather than generated and is not easily applied to social goals. Such fragmentation of power is probably evidence of the dominance of Right political forces in this historical period. It need not be assumed that the return of Left forces to power and a resulting emphasis upon generating rather than restricting national power will renew old forms of class conflict and endanger the stability of the political system.

One requirement of a general theory of political systems would be an empirical demonstration that the same processes of change are evident under similar conditions in all political systems. Part of this study may be considered an effort to show that the contrast between the most developed and the underdeveloped areas is not absolute, but that the same kinds of processes of political change are going on. As has been shown," premodern" structures (parochial and local loyalties) persist even within modern political systems, although the former ("primary" and "informal" in character) may tend to be affected and "modernized" by the "secondary" and "formal" patterns of the latter. The political scientist Gabriel Almond correctly emphasizes that "all political systems—the developed Western ones as well as the less-developed nonWestern ones—are transitional systems, or systems in which cultural change is taking place."[41] This transition is away from domination of the political system by "non-rational" alliances and coalitions—whether religious, ethnic, or regional (or even class, under certain conditions), but always parochial and narrow in outlook and demands.

Since government, party, and society are partially autonomous institutional and cultural areas, changes in them may to some extent occur independently. Centralization of government may occur without a corresponding decrease of economic or cultural regionalism; a sense of national identity may increase without a corresponding establishment of a political boundary encompassing the new "community." Since social change seldom proceeds with a smooth correspondence of all the "parts" of society, we may expect that there will be continual tensions between processes taking place at dif-

---

[41] Gabriel Almond and James S. Coleman, eds., *The Politics of the Developing Areas* (Princeton: Princeton University Press, 1960), p. 24. Almond suggests that there has been an "unfortunate theoretical polarization" of industrial and agrarian types of societies and of the types of action, values, and orientations characteristic of each (p. 23).

ferent levels in several of these areas. It is the *discrepancies* between these processes which form the concrete historical facts of social life and which may be the source of changes in the political loyalties of different social groups of concern here. Quebec, for example, is now highly industrialized and urbanized; yet it maintains its urge for cultural integrity and, therefore, for political autonomy. But its industrial character means also that demands are made upon the government to intervene in industrial disputes and to assume the function of regulating the economy. A series of changes in the relations of the province to the Canadian Dominion and of local industry to national industry is set in motion which may alter in subtle ways the character of social life and culture.

Saying this does not imply that there is one form of social and political life which is best fitted to the character of a modernized society. The range of variation of social and political organization which an industrial, urbanized society can "tolerate" is undoubtedly immensely wider than any of these societies exhibit. Nevertheless, the view that there are pressures for cultural assimilation, for a decline of various forms of regionalism, and toward a politics of interest-conflict affords insight into social and political changes. It is not necessary to assume that this process will reach a final and uniform conclusion—complete social and cultural homogeneity with a unitary and centralized nation-state—in order to see that there may be fairly uniform pressures and tensions in such societies, pressures and tensions which need not have the same outcomes but which groups seeking political power must take into account in their actions.

APPENDIXES

Appendix A

Surveys Tabulated Especially for this Study

TABLE A–1 List of Surveys Tabulated[a]

ORGANIZATION OR STUDY	IDENTIFYING SYMBOL	DATE OF SURVEY	APPROXIMATE SAMPLE SIZE	SOURCE FOR THE DATA[b]
		Great Britain		
Social Surveys, Ltd. (SS)	104	December, 1943	1,800	Roper
SS	CS 1717	February, 1957	1,900	SRC
SS	CQ 36	August, 1957	1,000	SRC
SS	CQ 58	January, 1958	1,000	SRC
SS	CQ 82	August, 1958	2,000	SRC
SS	CQ 103	February, 1959	1,000	SRC
SS	CQ 116	May, 1959	1,000	SRC
SS	CQ 118	June, 1959	1,000	SRC
SS	CQ 275	June, 1962	1,000	Social Surveys, Ltd.
		Australia		
Australian Public Opinion Polls (APOP)	45	September, 1946	2,000	SRC
APOP	83	September, 1951	2,000	SRC
APOP	115	December, 1955	2,000	SRC
APOP	134	October, 1958	2,200	Roper
APOP	135	November, 1958	2,200	Roper
APOP	140	October, 1960	2,100	APOP
APOP	149	April, 1961	2,000	APOP
APOP	154	December, 1961	2,000	APOP

TABLE A–1—*(Continued)*

ORGANIZATION OR STUDY	IDENTIFYING SYMBOL	DATE OF SURVEY	APPROXIMATE SAMPLE SIZE	SOURCE FOR THE DATA[b]
United States				
American Institute of Public Opinion (AIPO)	53	September, 1936	5,600	SRC
AIPO	56	November, 1936	2,700	SRC
AIPO	323	July, 1944	2,500	Roper
AIPO	423	August, 1948	2,000	Roper
Fortune (Elmo Roper)	70	September, 1948		Roper
Survey Research Center, Univ. of Michigan	Michigan 1952 study[c]	1952	1,600	SRC
Fund for the Republic	"Stouffer study"[d]	1954	5,000	SRC
Roper Commercial	65	October, 1956	3,000	Roper
AIPO	573	October, 1956	1,000	Roper
AIPO	636K	September, 1960	3,600	Roper
Roper	75	October, 1960	3,000	Roper
Canada				
Canadian Institute of Public Opinion (CIPO)	142	May, 1945	1,500	Roper
CIPO	212	August, 1951	1,500	Roper
CIPO	238	September, 1954	1,500	SRC
CIPO	250	July, 1956	1,100	SRC
CIPO	258	May, 1957	1,500	Roper
CIPO	266	May, 1958	900	Roper
CIPO	270	August, 1958	1,000	Roper
CIPO	278	September, 1959	690	Roper
CIPO	279	November, 1959	680	Roper
CIPO	285	November, 1960	680	Roper
CIPO	286	January, 1961	680	Roper
CIPO	287	March, 1961	670	Roper
CIPO	292	November, 1961	680	CIPO

[a] Sources for data appearing in published reports and cited in the body of the study are not given here. Only surveys from which data were especially tabulated for this study are listed in this Appendix.

[b] The source for the data refers to the location of the IBM decks and code books from which the tabulations were made. "Roper" refers to the Roper Public Opinion Research Center, Williams College, Williamstown, Massachusetts. "SRC" refers to the Survey Research Center, University of California, Berkeley. Some surveys were obtained from the organizations originally conducting them.

[c] Results from the Michigan 1952 study are published in A. Campbell, G. Gurin, and W. E. Miller, *The Voter Decides* (Evanston: Row, Peterson, 1954).

[d] Results from the "Stouffer study," sponsored by the Fund for the Republic, are reported in Samuel Stouffer, *Communism, Conformity and Civil Liberties* (New York: Doubleday, 1955).

Appendix B

Preference for Each Party, by Occupation Type,
Great Britain, Australia, United States, Canada,
Various Surveys, 1936–1962
Indexes of Class Voting*

---

* See Chapter 4, pp. 79–86, for a discussion of the index of class voting.

TABLE B–1

Labour, Liberal, and Conservative Party Preferences, by Occupation Type, Great Britain, 1943–1962[a]

OCCUPATION AND VOTE	PER CENT PREFERRING												
	1943[b]	1945[c]	1950[d]	1951[e]	1955[f] Sample No. 1	1955 No. 2	1957 Sample No. 1[g]	1957 No. 2[h]	1958 Sample No. 1[i]	1958 No. 2[j]	1959 Sample No. 1[k]	1959 No. 2[l]	1962[m]
Manual													
Labour	60	68	65	65	62	65	67	67	67	64	63	57	57
Liberal	12				6	3	9	7	8	11	10	13	19
Conservative	28	32	35	35	32	32	24	26	25	24	27	30	24
TOTAL NUMBER	(1064)				(847)	(383)	(398)	(737)	(415)	(892)	(398)	(871)	(537)
Non-Manual													
Labour	37	31	25	23	23	23	24	24	26	22	19	21	22
Liberal	10				6	4	13	12	7	21	9	12	29
Conservative	53	69	75	77	70	73	63	64	67	57	72	67	49
TOTAL NUMBER	(378)				(650)	(289)	(282)	(551)	(344)	(703)	(309)	(606)	(434)
Total													
Labour	54	55	52	51	45	47	49	42	48	45	44	42	41
Liberal	12				6	3	10	9	8	16	9	13	24
Conservative	34	45	48	49	48	50	40	49	44	39	47	45	35
TOTAL NUMBER	(1442)				(1497)	(672)	(680)	(1288)	(759)	(1594)	(706)	(1477)	(971)
Index of Class Voting	+23	+37	+40	+42	+39	+42	+43	+43	+41	+42	+44	+36	+35

ᵃ The figures taken from 1957 to 1962 polls of the British Institute of Public Opinion (BIPO) are based on answers to the question: "If there were a General Election tomorrow, how would you vote?" Questions for earlier polls are indicated in the following footnotes. For the 1957–62 polls, the occupational categories were as follows (the standard Gallup split in this period): "Manual" (factory, transport, building, farm, and other), "Non-Manual" (professional, director, proprietor, manager, shop, personal service, office and others, student). Housewives are included under their husbands' occupation.

For all of the figures, undecided persons and persons voting for other parties were excluded. This has the effect of assuming that they split in the same way as the persons who had made up their minds.

The index of class voting is computed by subtracting the Labour vote of persons in non-manual occupations from the Labour vote of those in manual occupations. For a discussion of the index, see Chapter 4.

ᵇ British Institute of Public Opinion (BIPO) Survey No. 104, December, 1943. "Labour" includes the following categories of responses to the question: "If there were a General Election tomorrow, how would you vote?": Left, Labour, National Labour, and Against the Government. "Conservative" includes Conservative, National, Churchill, and For the Government. Only the answer "Liberal" was classified as "Liberal." "Non-Manual" occupations include professionals, salaried persons and executives, and proprietors (shop or business). "Manual" includes all those working for weekly wages in factories, heavy industry, transport, mining, and agriculture. Housewives were allocated to "manual" or "non-manual" categories according to their socio-economic level in order to achieve maximum comparability with other surveys in which housewives were included under their husbands' occupations. Class voting among men in this survey was +30; among women, +16, which may indicate errors of classification of women according to socio-economic level, since none of the 1957 –62 surveys shows any sharp sex differences in voting.

ᶜ The figures for 1945, 1950, and 1951 are recomputed from estimates presented in John Bonham, *The Middle-Class Vote* (London: Faber & Faber, 1954), p. 168. They are not exactly comparable to the other figures, since Bonham included the Liberal voters, non-voters, and voters for other minor parties in a category "neither Conservative nor Labour." Therefore, the figures in this table are based on a two-party, not a three-party, total. Also, Bonham excluded voters not in clearly "non-manual" and "wage-earning" occupations, comprising an "intermediate" class of mixed or doubtful status. Both of these differences in computation probably tend to exaggerate the extent of class voting discovered from Bonham's data as compared to the method used elsewhere. Since the Liberals draw almost equally from both strata and since the persons in status positions marginal to both major strata tend to split their votes fairly evenly, Bonham's data include mainly those persons likely to vote in accordance with a class predisposition. Also, from the statistical point of view, the percentage differences are likely to be greater when the base is composed of only two rather than three or four categories. Thus, strictly comparable data would probably show greater differences in class voting from the 1950–51 period to the 1957–62 period than are indicated here. Bonham's data are also derived from BIPO surveys.

ᵈ See footnote c.

ᵉ See footnote c.

ᶠ These figures are derived from two BIPO polls which asked: "How did you vote in the last General Election in 1959?" Sample No. 1 is taken from CQ 82, August, 1958; Sample No. 2 is from CQ 103, February, 1959. Note that no percentage differs by more than 3 points in the two polls. The most consistent drop-off is in the Liberal vote, since only two-thirds or one-half as many reported having voted Liberal in the previous election in the later poll as compared to the earlier one.

ᵍ BIPO No. CQ 36, August, 1957.

ʰ BIPO No. 1717, February, 1957.

ⁱ BIPO No. CQ 58, January, 1958.

ʲ BIPO No. CQ 82, August, 1958.

ᵏ BIPO No. CQ 103, February, 1959.

ˡ BIPO Nos. 116 and 118, May–June, 1959 (combined). If the vote for only the two major parties is considered, class voting rises to +41. Differences between the other countries are therefore minimized by computing the index for the total three-party vote.

ᵐ BIPO No. CQ 275, June, 1962.

TABLE B-2

Labor, Democratic Labor, Liberal, and Country Party Preferences, by Occupation Type, Australia, 1943–1961[a]

PER CENT PREFERRING

OCCUPATION AND VOTE	1943[b]	1946		1949[e]	1951		1954		1955				1958		1960[p]	1961	
		No.1[c]	No.2[d]		No.1[f]	No.2[g]	No.1[h]	No.2[i]	No.1[j]	No.2[k]	No.3[l]	No.4[m]	No.1[n]	No.2[o]		No.1[q]	No.2[r]
Manual																	
Labor	83	72	72	68	69	64	68	69	60	67	70	70	63	66	65	63	66
DLP	..	..	..	..	..	..	..	..	7	..	4	4	9	8	5	3	5
Liberal	17	28	28	32	31	36	32	31	29	33	26	26	28	26	30	34	29
Country									4								
TOTAL NUMBER	(1131)	(1225)	(1065)	(1032)	(936)	(1014)	(1007)	(1156)	(1124)	(934)	(838)	(829)	(854)	(886)	(815)	(905)	(1068)
Non-Manual																	
Labor	41	35	33	29	30	31	33	34	28	33	35	33	32	30	30	36	34
DLP	..	..	..	..	..	..	..	..	5	..	4	5	7	7	5	4	6
Liberal	59	65	67	71	70	69	67	66	62	67	61	62	61	63	65	60	60
Country									5								
TOTAL NUMBER	(673)	(734)	(802)	(766)	(805)	(771)	(745)	(1033)	(934)	(678)	(806)	(744)	(828)	(807)	(775)	(731)	(874)
Total																	
Labor	68	58	55	51	51	50	53	52	45	53	53	53	48	49	48	51	52
DLP	..	..	..	..	..	..	..	..	6	..	4	4	8	7	5	4	5
Liberal	32	42	45	49	49	50	47	48	45	47	43	43	44	44	47	45	43
Country									4								
TOTAL NUMBER	(1804)	(1959)	(1867)	(1798)	(1741)	(1785)	(1752)	(2189)	(2058)	(1613)	(1644)	(1573)	(1682)	(1693)	(1590)	(1636)	(1942)
Index of Class Voting	+42	+37	+39	+39	+39	+33	+35	+35	+32	+34	+35	+37	+31	+36	+35	+27	+32

Note: For each occupation group the Liberal and Country figures are bracketed together (reported as a combined percentage) except in Sample No. 1 of 1955, where they are shown separately.

a Totals exclude voters for minor parties other than those mentioned, and exclude those who did not indicate a party preference. "Manual" occupations include skilled, semi-skilled, and unskilled workers, and farm laborers. "Non-manual" occupations include professionals, owners and executives of large businesses, small businessmen, clerks, and shop assistants. Farm owners, pensioners, and servicemen are excluded. In some surveys, persons selecting the Country party were not distinguished from those selecting the Liberal party. The index of class voting is the percentage point difference between the vote of manual and non-manual occupational groups for the major Labor party.

b Australian Public Opinion Polls (APOP), Survey No. 45, September 21, 1946. The question was: "Would you mind telling me which party or candidate you voted for at the last Federal election?" in 1943. The United Australia party was succeeded by the Liberal party in 1944, but is referred to as the "Liberal" party in this table.

c APOP No. 45. The question was: "The next question is an experiment to see if we can forecast the Federal election. Judging by how you feel now, which party and candidate are you likely to vote for?" The interview was terminated if, in response to an additional question, "How do you think you are likely to vote?" there was still no answer.

d From S. R. Davis, *The Government of the Australian States* (Melbourne: Longmans, Green, 1960), pp. 621 ff. The figures are approximate since the percentages are computed from an average sample size for each of the five surveys ranging from 1946 to 1955. Occupational categories are the same as in other surveys. In the 1955 figures, DLP voters are not distinguished from ALP. Only votes for the major parties are included, which accounts for variations in the number of cases.

e See footnote d.

f APOP Survey No. 83, September 13, 1951. The question was: "Would you mind telling me which party or candidate you voted for at the last Federal election?" The last election was held on April 28, 1951, six months previously.

g See footnote d.

h See footnote d.

i APOP Survey No. 115, December 3, 1955. The question was: "Would you mind telling me which party or candidate you voted for at the last Federal election?" which took place on May 29, 1954.

j APOP No. 115. The question was: "The next question is to see how accurately we can forecast the coming Federal election for the House of Representatives. Judging by how you feel now, which party are you likely to vote for: the ALP, or Anti-Communist Labor, or Liberal, Country, Communist or somebody else?" The interviewers were to ask, if the respondent was evasive: "Well, which side are you leaning toward at present?" The election was one week later, December 10, 1955.

k See footnote c.

l APOP Survey No. 134, October 28, 1958 (the election was November 22, 1958). The question dealt with the past vote of the respondent, and was in the same form as in previous surveys.

m APOP Survey No. 135, November 12, 1958 (past vote).

n APOP No. 134 (voting intention).

o APOP No. 135 (voting intention).

p APOP No. 140, October 9, 1960 (voting intention).

q APOP No. 149, April 7, 1961 (voting intention).

r APOP No. 154, December 1, 1961 (voting intention).

TABLE B-3

Democratic and Republican Party Preferences, by Occupation Type, United States, 1936–1960[a]

OCCUPATION AND VOTE	1936 Sample No. 1[b]	No. 2[c]	1940[d]	1944 Sample No. 1[e]	No. 2[f]	No. 3[g]	1948 No. 1[h]	Sample No. 2[i]	No. 3[j]	1952 Sample No. 1[k]	No. 2[l]	1956 Sample No. 1[m]	No. 2[n]	1960 Sample No. 1[o]	No. 2[p]
Manual															
Democratic	63	67	65	59	64	67	52	56	79	57	47	52	52	60	60
Republican	37	33	35	41	36	33	48	44	21	43	53	48	48	40	40
TOTAL NUMBER	(3318)	(1279)	..	..	(502)	(1105)	(1036)	(766)	(224)	(642)	(2118)	(537)	(427)	(1356)	(711)
Non-Manual															
Democratic	47	52	40	41	50	46	32	27	38	34	30	39	36	45	46
Republican	53	48	60	59	50	54	68	73	62	66	70	61	64	55	54
TOTAL NUMBER	(700)	(391)	..	..	(824)	(945)	(939)	(773)	(180)	(480)	(1676)	(667)	(262)	(1128)	(936)
Total															
Democratic	60	64	53	51	53	57	43	42	56	47	39	55	54	53	52
Republican	40	36	47	49	47	43	57	58	44	53	61	45	46	47	48
TOTAL NUMBER	(4018)	(1670)	..	..	(1576)	(2050)	(1975)	(1539)	(404)	(1122)	(3794)	(1204)	(689)	(2484)	(1647)
Index of Class Voting	+16	+15	+25	+18	+14	+21	+20	+29	+41	+23	+17	+13	+16	+15	+14

[a] Farmers are excluded from both manual and non-manual occupational groups in all of the following figures. Farmers do appear in certain of the percentages pertaining to the total samples, where the data were not available in a form allowing their elimination. The totals of manual and non-manual workers are always those of persons choosing a presidential nominee of one of the major parties, the Democratic and Republican parties. Undecided persons, or those choosing a minor party, do not appear in the totals. The index of class voting is the percentage point difference between the vote of manual and non-manual occupation types for the Democratic party.

[b] American Institute of Public Opinion (AIPO) Survey No. 53, September 26, 1936. Professionals and businessmen comprise the "non-manuals," skilled and unskilled workers, the "manuals." Unemployed workers are excluded, but if they are included as manuals, the index of class voting would be +20.

[c] AIPO Survey No. 56, November 4, 1936. Occupations are the same as in footnote b. If unemployed workers were included as manuals, the index of class voting would be +17.

[d] Estimated from a table in Hadley Cantril and Mildred Strunk, *Public Opinion: 1935–1946* (Princeton: Princeton University Press, 1949), p. 602. For the purpose of the estimate, the numbers of cases in each occupation within the non-manual or manual categories were assumed to be equal. Professionals, proprietors, and white-collar workers were included as non-manual, and skilled, semi-skilled and unskilled workers as manual. The question, asked October 22, 1940, by the Gallup organization, was, "If the presidential election were held today, would you vote for Willkie or Roosevelt?" The total is of the two major parties.

[e] *Ibid.*, p. 627. Identical results were obtained from two nationwide samples, in July and August of 1944. The question was similar to the above. Since the number of cases was not given, the same procedure for estimating the proportion of manual and non-manual workers used above was repeated.

[f] From Sheldon H. Korchin, *Psychological Variables in the Behavior of Voters* (Ph.D. dissertation, Harvard University, 1946). I am indebted to Dr. Philip Converse of the Survey Research Center, University of Michigan, for these data. Non-manual includes white-collar and service workers. The survey was done by the National Opinion Research Center, University of Chicago.

[g] American Institute of Public Opinion Survey No. 323, July 18, 1944. The question was: "If the presidential election were being held today how would you vote—for Dewey or for Roosevelt?" Manual occupations include skilled, semi-skilled, and unskilled workers; domestic servants; and protective service workers. Non-manual occupations include executive, white-collar, small business, semi-professional, and professional positions.

[h] AIPO Survey No. 423, August 11, 1948, IBM cards for this survey were made available to the writer by the Roper Public Opinion Research Center, Williamstown, Massachusetts. The question was: "If the presidential election were being held today, how would you vote—for Dewey, for Truman, or for Wallace?" (As noted above, Wallace and Thurmond voters and undecided persons are excluded.) In addition, persons who indicated that they were "leaning" toward Dewey or Truman were included. Occupational categories are the same as those reported in footnote d.

[i] Fortune poll No. 70 (Elmo Roper organization), September, 1948. The question was: "If the election were being held today, which candidate for President do you think you'd vote for: Harry S. Truman, Thomas E. Dewey, Henry Wallace, Norman Thomas, Strom Thurmond, or who?" Non-manual occupations include professional, proprietary (other than farm), salaried (minor and executive). Manual occupations included all those working for wages. Retired and unemployed persons, students, and housewives were excluded.

[j] Recomputed from A. Campbell, G. Gurin, and W. E. Miller, *The Voter Decides* (Evanston: Row, Peterson, 1954), pp. 72–73. The total refers to all persons expressing a party choice, not just voters. Class voting for voters only was +44. Non-manual occupations include professionals, managers, and other white-collar persons. Manual occupations include skilled, semi-skilled, and unskilled. Farm operators are excluded. The data from the 1948 and 1952 Michigan studies are the only ones based upon true probability samples of the American electorate.

[k] Computed from the IBM cards available from the 1952 Michigan survey reported in *ibid.*

[l] Computed from the IBM cards available from the study otherwise reported in Samuel Stouffer, *Communism, Conformity and Civil Liberties* (New York: Doubleday, 1955). The question was: "Whom did you favor for President in 1952: Eisenhower or Stevenson?" asked in May and June of 1954. Persons who did not remember or who voted for someone else are excluded. Non-manual occupations include professionals, proprietors, managers and officials, and clerical and sales workers. Manual occupations include craftsmen, foremen, operatives, service workers, and farm laborers. Farm owners and managers are excluded.

[m] Roper Commercial poll No. 65, October, 1956. The tabulations were performed by the Roper Public Opinion Research Center, Williamstown, Massachusetts. Farm proprietors and "homemakers" are excluded. Non-manual occupations included professionals, executives, store proprietors, and white-collar workers. Manual occupations included factory, non-factory, and farm laborers. The question was: "If the election were being held today, who do you think you would vote for: Eisenhower and Nixon on the Republican ticket, or Stevenson and Kefauver on the Democratic ticket?"

[n] AIPO Survey No. 573, October, 1956, made available to the writer by the Roper Public Opinion Research Center. The question was: "If the presidential election were being held today, which candidates would you vote for—Eisenhower and Nixon, Stevenson and Kefauver, or Byrd and Jenner?" (The last were excluded, as well as undecideds, as already noted.) Manual occupations included skilled, unskilled, and service workers, and other laborers. Non-manual included executives, clerical and sales people, and professionals. Housewives were included under their husbands' occupation.

[o] AIPO No. 636K, September, 1960.

[p] Roper No. 75, October, 1960.

TABLE B-4

Liberal, Conservative, New Democratic, and Social Credit Party Preferences, By Occupation Type, Canada, 1940–1961

PER CENT PREFERRING

OCCUPATION AND VOTE	1940[a]	1945 Sample No. 1[b]	1945 Sample No. 2[c]	1949[d]	1951[e]	1953[f]	1954[g]	1956[h]	1957 Sample No. 1[i]	1957 Sample No. 2[j]	1958[k]	1959[l]	1960[m]	1961 No. 1[n]	1961 Sample No. 2[o]	1961 No. 3[p]
Manual																
Liberal	59	43	42	48	50	51	53	49	51	39	35	35	49	52	39	49
Conservative	28	24	28	25	26	26	22	30	31	43	50	45	32	26	35	35
New Democratic	13	28	26	23	19	17	16	16	11	15	13	11	11	12	16	9
Social Credit	..	5	4	4	5	6	9	5	7	3	2	9	8	10	10	7
TOTAL NUMBER	(478)	(505)	(1097)	(1050)	(478)	(1206)	(562)	(383)	(713)	(358)	(375)	(253)	(169)	(187)	(168)	(162)
Non-Manual																
Liberal	59	50	47	59	53	53	54	53	46	38	28	40	49	43	41	46
Conservative	34	33	35	31	38	34	33	34	41	52	66	48	40	47	45	43
New Democratic	7	15	13	8	7	7	7	10	7	6	4	7	4	4	10	4
Social Credit	..	2	5	2	2	6	6	3	5	4	2	5	7	6	4	7
TOTAL NUMBER	(548)	(567)	(1230)	(1307)	(593)	(1231)	(684)	(527)	(542)	(312)	(308)	(209)	(164)	(208)	(156)	(155)
Total																
Liberal	59	47	45	54	51	52	53	51	49	38	32	37	49	47	40	47
Conservative	31	29	32	28	33	30	29	32	35	47	57	46	36	37	40	39
New Democratic	10	21	19	15	13	12	11	12	10	11	9	10	8	8	13	7
Social Credit	..	2	4	3	3	6	7	5	6	4	2	7	7	8	7	7
TOTAL NUMBER	(1026)	(1072)	(2357)	(2327)	(1071)	(2437)	(1248)	(910)	(1255)	(670)	(683)	(462)	(333)	(395)	(324)	(317)
Index of Class Voting[q]	+6	+6	+8	+4	+9	+8	+8	+2	+9	+10	+16	−1	+7	+17	+4	+8

a Past vote (in the 1940 Dominion election) asked on **Canadian Institute of P**ublic Opinion (CIPO) Survey No. 142, May, 1945. The question was: "**Do you** remember for certain whether you voted in the 1940 Dominion election? (If yes.) Did you vote for the Conservative, Liberal, CCF, or other candidate?" Non-manual occupations included professional, executive, small business, and white-collar. Manual occupations included skilled, unskilled, domestic service, and "other", manual (such as waitress, janitor, etc.). The total is of the three parties.

b Voting intention, asked on CIPO Survey No. 142, May, 1945. The question was: "If a Dominion election were held today, would you vote for the candidate of the Progressive-Conservative, Liberal, CCF, Social Credit, Labor-Progressive, Bloc Populaire, or other party?" The occupation categories are the same as above. If the Bloc Populaire is included as a "Left" party (albeit a nationalist one), the level of class voting is +9. Ten per cent of the manual workers and 7 per cent of the non-manuals, all in Quebec, supported it.

c I am indebted to Seymour Martin Lipset for the data from this 1945 poll and the following data for 1949 and 1953. The exact question is not known. The occupations are the same as given above.

d See footnote c.

e CIPO Survey No. 212, August, 1951. The question was the voting intention of the respondent, and the occupational categories are as given above.

f See footnote c.

g CIPO Survey No. 238, September 8, 1954. The election was the previous August 10, 1954. The question was: "If a Dominion election were held today, which party's candidate do you think you would favor?" A question was also asked about their vote the month before, and the distribution of the answers shows that the index of class voting does not depend upon the particular form of the question asked and that it is a relatively stable measure. While the total number of manual and non-manual persons included in the figures given in Table IV was 1,246, for the "past vote" question it would have been only 1,095. Nevertheless the index of class voting for the "past vote" question was +8, only one point different from the results for the "voting intention" question. The total manual vote for the Liberal and CCF parties was 70 and 69 per cent for the two questions respectively, and the non-manual vote was 62 and 60 per cent. This also shows that the 20 per cent of undecideds on the "voting intention" question does not noticeably affect the index.

h CIPO Survey No. 250, July, 1956. The question was: "If a Dominion election were held today, which party's candidate do you think you would favor?" Manual occupations included skilled, semi-skilled and unskilled labor. Non-manual occupations included professionals, executives, small businessmen, clerical and sales workers, teachers and government employees.

i Voting intention, CIPO Survey No. 258, May, 1957. The question was: "If a Federal election were being held today, which party's candidate do you think you would favor?" Non-manual occupations were major and junior executives, owners of large and small businesses, professionals and semi-professionals, clerical workers, service and inside salesmen, and outside salesmen. Manual occupations included skilled labor or tradesmen, and unskilled laborers. The election was June 10, 1957.

j Past vote, CIPO Survey No. 266-X, March 15, 1958. Of persons who said they had voted in the 1957 election, the question asked was: "Which party did the candidate for whom you voted represent?" The occupational categories are the same in this as in the previous survey cited.

k Voting intention, CIPO Survey No. 266-X, March 15, 1958. The election was March 31, 1958.

l Voting intention in CIPO No. 279, November, 1959. The CIPO occupational code from No. 275 to at least No. 292 is: professional, business executive (owners and managers), salespeople, clerical and white-collar (all of these are here classified as non-manual), skilled labor, unskilled labor (these are classified as manual), farmer, widow and spinster, pensioned and retired, unemployed, armed forces, and student (the last six categories are excluded from the tables).

m CIPO No. 285, November, 1960, (voting intention).

n CIPO No. 286, January, 1961, (voting intention).

o CIPO No. 287, March, 1961, (voting intention).

p CIPO No. 292, November, 1961, (voting intention).

q The index of class voting was computed by subtracting the percentage of persons in non-manual occupations preferring the New Democratic (CCF in surveys prior to 1961) party or the Liberal party from the percentage of manual workers preferring the same parties. Farmers are included in neither stratum. The occupations comprising the manual and non-manual strata are given in footnotes above.

Undecided persons and voters for minor parties are excluded from all totals, but their inclusion would not affect the relationships reported, despite the high proportion of "undecideds," sometimes as much as 30 per cent of the sample. The reason for (and the effects of) this phenomenon in the Canadian political system will be the subject of a future article.

Appendix C

The Definition of Religion

SINCE the data for this study are interviews of representative samples of respondents in each country, religious affiliation is determined from answers to a direct question. Typical questions are: "What religion do you belong to?" (United States: Roper No. 65), "What is your religious preference: Protestant, Roman Catholic, or Jewish?" (United States: Gallup and the Stouffer study), "Would you mind telling me if you are Roman Catholic, Protestant or Jewish?" (Canadian Institute of Public Opinion), "Would you mind telling me your religion?" (Australian Public Opinion Polls), and "What religious denomination do you belong to?" (British Institute of Public Opinion).

Such questions may evoke diverse and not necessarily equivalent answers. The reply "Catholic" or "Protestant" does not inform us of the person's intensity of religious commitment or involvement, but is only a crude reflection of self-identified membership in a religious community, broadly defined. It is assumed that a group of persons answering that they are "Catholic" in response to any of the questions above possess experiences and backgrounds different from those of a group answering "Protestant" and that such differences will appear in different kinds of political behavior—if religious affiliation is politically relevant.

For the purposes of this study, respondents were divided into "Protestant" and "Catholic." In some surveys, no other denominations or religions were coded (except Jewish, for which too few cases were available for analysis); but in some surveys, Lutherans,

Methodists, Presbyterians, and other Protestant denominations were distinguished. These were all lumped into a single "Protestant" category, despite the finding from some research that the political differences within Protestantism are as great as those between Protestants and Catholics. Nevertheless, in view of the scope of the cross-national comparisons being made over time, no finer differentiation than this could be attempted.

Appendix D

The Definition of Regions

EACH respondent in each of these national samples was interviewed in an area of the country which is called here a "region." Only presence, and not actual residence, in a region determined the classification of respondents, but probably relatively few persons were interviewed in regions in which they do not live.

Regions cannot be identified in a precisely similar way for all of the Anglo-American countries because of lack of data and because of their differing political structures. The theoretically relevant criterion which comes closest to being empirically possible with the survey data is that of "potential nation," but not a potential nation in the sense that there is any great likelihood of secession. Certain regions within each country are potential nations, because they have special cultural identities (Wales and Scotland), because they actually have some degree of sovereignty (Ontario and New South Wales), or because they have both (Quebec and the South). This definition is the kind most relevant to the concerns of the present study because political loyalties which stem from strong regional identifications may cross-cut class loyalties. Therefore, the boundaries of regions have been defined to approximate either political or cultural unities smaller than the present national boundaries.

The problem of definition is least difficult in Canada and Australia, since they are both federal nations with few enough political units that the survey data can be tabulated separately by province or state.

AUSTRALIA: REGIONS ARE STATES

In the case of Australia, each of the six states was considered separately with respect to the level of class voting.
New South Wales
Victoria
Queensland
Western Australia
South Australia
Tasmania

CANADA: REGIONAL CLASSIFICATION OF PROVINCES

In the case of Canada, a lack of sufficient cases in certain provinces forced a combination for purposes of analysis of the data. Three western provinces with a common wheat economy and history of opposition to the larger eastern provinces are called the "Prairie Provinces." Four of the small eastern provinces are considered together as the "Atlantic Provinces."
Prairie Provinces: Alberta, Saskatchewan, Manitoba
Atlantic Provinces: Prince Edward Island, Nova Scotia, New Brunswick, Newfoundland
Ontario
Quebec
British Columbia

UNITED STATES: REGIONAL CLASSIFICATION OF STATES

Although the United States is also a federal nation, groups of states are classified as regions, partly because of the lack of enough data to analyze fifty units separately, but also because of the appropriateness of defining an entire bloc of states—the "South" or "New England"—as a region from the point of view of their cultural or economic identity and potential political unity. Unfortunately, the various surveys do not use exactly the same states for their definition of regions, so that the region called "West North Central," may include Kansas in some surveys but not in others. The Middle Atlantic region in the Gallup surveys includes Maryland, Delaware, and West Virginia, in addition to the three states called "Middle Atlantic" in the "Stouffer study" (see Appendix A): New York, New

Jersey, and Pennsylvania. Including the border states of Maryland, Delaware, and West Virginia in the Middle Atlantic region tends to increase the Democratic percentage as shown by the Gallup survey as contrasted to the Stouffer survey, which classifies them into the South Atlantic region. This example is given to underline the caution with which particular regional differences in class voting should be regarded.

Following are the regional classifications used by the Stouffer study and by the Gallup surveys.

Gallup Classification

New England: Maine, New Hampshire, Vermont, Massachusetts, Rhode Island, Connecticut

Middle Atlantic: New York, New Jersey, Pennsylvania, Maryland, Delaware, West Virginia, District of Columbia

East Central: Ohio, Michigan, Indiana, Illinois

West Central: Wisconsin, Minnesota, Iowa, Missouri, North Dakota, South Dakota, Nebraska, Kansas

Southern: Virginia, North Carolina, South Carolina, Georgia, Florida, Kentucky, Tennessee, Alabama, Mississippi, Arkansas, Louisiana, Oklahoma, Texas

Rocky Mountain: Montana, Arizona, Colorado, Idaho, Wyoming, Utah, Nevada, New Mexico

Pacific: California, Washington, Oregon

The Gallup classification differs slightly, as has been noted, from that used in the Stouffer study. The latter is exactly the same as that used by the United States Census, as follows:

Stouffer and Census Classification

New England: Maine, New Hampshire, Vermont, Massachusetts, Rhode Island, Connecticut

Middle Atlantic: New York, New Jersey, Pennsylvania

East North Central: Ohio, Indiana, Illinois, Michigan, Wisconsin

West North Central: Minnesota, Iowa, Missouri, North Dakota, South Dakota, Nebraska, Kansas

South Atlantic: Delaware, Maryland, District of Columbia, Virginia, West Virginia, North Carolina, South Carolina, Georgia, Florida

East South Central: Kentucky, Tennessee, Alabama, Mississippi

West South Central: Arkansas, Louisiana, Oklahoma, Texas

Mountain: Montana, Idaho, Wyoming, Colorado, New Mexico, Arizona, Utah, Nevada

Pacific: Washington, Oregon, California

For purposes of analyzing the survey data, the South Atlantic, East South Central, and West South Central regions were combined into one "Southern" region from the Stouffer study. No finer breakdown was possible from the data for this study, but for further research the Gallup coding procedures permit analyzing the data by separate states, given enough cases.

GREAT BRITAIN: REGIONAL CLASSIFICATION OF COUNTIES

In Great Britain, since it is not a federal nation, census regions must be used as the closest possible approximation of political units. In the case of Wales and Scotland, the census unit coincides with the cultural boundaries with the greatest political relevance. Following are the counties comprising the British regions, as used by the British Institute of Public Opinion (Social Surveys, Ltd.) after 1959. Only two surveys (CQ 116 and CQ 118) used in this study were made after that date, but this classification of counties is not substantially different than the previous one. No respondents were interviewed in Northern Ireland.

Northern: Cumberland, Durham, Northumberland, Westmorland, Yorkshire (North Riding)

East and West Ridings: Yorkshire (East Riding), Yorkshire (West Riding)

North-Western: Cheshire, Derbyshire (part of), Lancashire

North Midland: Derbyshire (part of), Leicestershire, Lincolnshire, Northamptonshire, Nottinghamshire, Soke of Peterborough, Rutland

Midland: Herefordshire, Shropshire, Staffordshire, Warwickshire, Worcestershire

Eastern: Bedfordshire, Cambridgeshire, Isle of Ely, Essex (part of), Hertfordshire (part of), Huntingdonshire, Norfolk, East Suffolk, West Suffolk

London and South Eastern: Essex (part of), Hertfordshire (part of), Kent, London (administrative county), Middlesex, Surrey, East Sussex, West Sussex

Southern: Berkshire, Buckinghamshire, Dorsetshire (part of), Hampshire, Oxfordshire, Isle of Wight

Southwestern: Cornwall, Devonshire, Dorsetshire (part of), Gloucestershire, Somersetshire, Wiltshire

Scotland

Wales

In the tables based upon the survey data, the above regions are combined into "Northern" (the first three above), "Midlands" (the next three), "London and Southern" (the next three). Wales and Scotland are tabulated separately.

Appendix E

Alternative Methods of Percentaging the Index of Class Voting

THE three possible ways of percentaging the index of class voting involve separate assumptions as to the nature of change in a consensual political system.[1]

A simple percentage difference between two groups (the method used for the index of class voting) assumes that it is easy to shift from one group to another no matter what the absolute level of support at any given time. To take an example, if 80 per cent of manual workers vote Democratic and 40 per cent of the non-manual workers vote Democratic in a given election, and then 90 and 50 per cent vote Democratic respectively in the next election, measuring the change as "10 percentage points difference" assumes that *both* groups can easily swing back the other way. Such a computation assumes that there is no point within the range of possibilities at which some qualitative change takes place which makes it more difficult to swing back. If, however, the 90 per cent Democratic vote by manual workers means a sharp increase of class consciousness and the 90 per cent figure level becomes stable, then the percentage difference would not reveal the qualitative shift in the nature of party loyalties. Thus an assumption of political consensus and the ever-present possibility of large-scale shifts in *either* di-

---

[1] These assumptions and computations are discussed in Hans Zeisel, *Say It with Figures* (4th ed.; New York: Harper, 1957), chap. i. See also P. F. Lazarsfeld and A. H. Barton, "Qualitative Measurement in the Social Sciences: Classification, Typologies, and Indices," in D. Lerner and H. Lasswell, eds., *The Policy Sciences* (Stanford: Stanford University Press, 1951), pp. 155–92.

rection by either stratum underlies this particular computation of an index of class voting.

The second way of computing a percentage change starts with the base figure at "Time$_1$" and measures change from that point. Thus if the first method were symbolized by "Time$_2$ — Time$_1$" (i.e., 90 per cent minus 80 per cent equals 10 percentage points), the second method would be: $\dfrac{\text{Time}_2 - \text{Time}_1}{\text{Time}_1}$. This method embodies the assumption that once a certain point of unanimity is reached, it is more difficult for further change to take place. If only a few people vote a certain way, then it is easier for more people to vote that way. Taking the same figures as before, this method of computation would show that there was a one-eighth increase in the Democratic vote among manual workers (from 80 to 90 per cent) but one-fourth among non-manual workers (from 40 to 50 per cent). The greater index figure for the non-manuals reflects the assumption that adding 10 per cent to the original 40 per cent of non-manuals voting Democratic was more significant than adding 10 per cent to the original 80 per cent of the manuals voting Democratic. There is no reason to assume for the Anglo-American countries that this difference in the significance of shifts exists.

The third way of computing a percentage change assumes that once a certain point of unanimity is reached, it is easy to go the rest of the way. If we assume that social pressure might increase the uniformity of political behavior, then once 90 per cent of the manual workers vote Democratic, reaching 100 per cent might be easy. (The second method assumes a saturation point, that most of the people "available" for convincing have been reached, and that any increase is more difficult.) The computation for the third method is as follows: $\dfrac{\text{Time}_2 - \text{Time}_1}{100 - \text{Time}_1}$. Here, using the same figures as before, it develops that one-half (10 per cent) of the 20 per cent of the manual workers not yet voting Democratic in the first election have changed over, but that only one-sixth of the non-manuals not yet voting Democratic have been won over. The greater index figure for the manual workers reflects the assumption that votes are easier to win where there are more potential voters. This assumption does not seem valid for the Anglo-American countries either for the excellent empirical reason that rarely does any stratum give more than 70 per cent of its votes to any given party.

BIBLIOGRAPHY

1. COMPARATIVE STUDIES

Aitken, Hugh G. J., and others. *The American Economic Impact on Canada*. Durham, N.C.: Duke University Press, 1959.

―――, ed. *The State and Economic Growth*. New York: Social Science Research Council, 1959.

Alexander, Fred. *Moving Frontiers, An American Theme and Its Application to Australian History*. Melbourne: Melbourne University Press, 1947.

―――. *Canadians and Foreign Policy*. Toronto: University of Toronto Press, 1960.

―――. "André Siegfried: A 20th Century de Tocqueville," *Australian Journal of Politics and History*, VI (May, 1960), 14–27.

Almond, Gabriel. "Comparative Political Systems," in Heinz Eulau and others, eds. *Political Behavior: A Reader in Theory and Research*. Glencoe: Free Press, 1956, pp. 34–42.

―――, and Coleman, James S., eds. *The Politics of the Developing Areas*. Princeton: Princeton University Press, 1960.

Argyle, Michael. *Religious Behavior*. Glencoe: Free Press, 1959.

Ashworth, William. *A Short History of the International Economy, 1850–1950*. London: Longmans, Green, 1952.

Birch, Anthony H. *Federalism, Finance and Social Legislation in Canada, Australia and the United States*. Oxford: Clarendon Press, 1955.

Bowie, Robert R., and Friedrich, Carl J., eds. *Studies in Federalism.* Boston: Little, Brown, 1954.

Brady, Alexander. *Democracy in the Dominions.* 2nd ed.; Toronto: University of Toronto Press, 1952 (1st ed., 1947).

Bryce, James. *Modern Democracies.* New York: Macmillan, 1929.

Buchanan, W., and Cantril, H. *How Nations See Each Other: A Study in Public Opinion.* Urbana: University of Illinois Press, 1953.

Burks, R. V. "Catholic Parties in Latin Europe," *Journal of Modern History,* XXIV (September, 1952), 269–86.

Clark, Colin. *The Conditions of Economic Progress.* 3rd ed.; London: Macmillan, 1957 (1st ed., 1940).

Converse, Philip E., and Dupeux, Georges. "Politicization of the Electorate in France and the United States," *Public Opinion Quarterly,* XXVI (Spring, 1962), 1–24.

Cutright, Phillips. "National Political Development: Measurement and Analysis," *American Sociological Review,* XXVIII (April, 1963), 253–65.

Daudt, H. *Floating Voters and the Floating Vote: A Critical Analysis of American and English Election Studies.* Leiden, Netherlands: H. E. Stenfert Kroese N. V., 1961.

Davis, Morris, and Verba, S. "Party Affiliation and International Opinions in Britain and France, 1947–1956," *Public Opinion Quarterly,* XXIV (Winter, 1960), 590–605.

Duverger, Maurice. *Political Parties.* London: Methuen, 1954.

Fogarty, Michael P. *Christian Democracy in Western Europe, 1820–1953.* London: Routledge & Kegan Paul, 1957.

Galenson, Walter, and Zellner, Arnold. "International Comparison of Unemployment Rates," in National Bureau of Economic Research. *The Measurement and Behavior of Unemployment.* Princeton: Princeton University Press, 1957, pp. 439–583.

Goodrich, Carter. "The Australian and American Labour Movements," *Economic Record,* IV (November, 1928), 193–208.

Heaton, Herbert. "Other Wests than Ours," *The Tasks of Economic History,* Supplement VI of *The Journal of Economic History* (1946), pp. 50–62.

Hull, W. H. N. "The Public Control of Broadcasting: The Canadian and Australian Experiences," *Canadian Journal of Economics and Political Science,* XXVIII (February, 1962), 114–26.

Inkeles, A., and Rossi, Peter. "National Comparisons of Occupational Prestige," *American Journal of Sociology*, LXI (January, 1956), 329–39.

International Urban Research. *The World's Metropolitan Areas*. Berkeley and Los Angeles: University of California Press, 1959.

Kerr, Clark. "Wage Relationships—The Comparative Impact of Market and Power Forces," in John T. Dunlop, ed. *The Theory of Wage Determination*. New York: St. Martin's Press, 1957, pp. 173–93.

Kersell, John E. *Parliamentary Supervision of Delegated Legislation*. London: Stevens, 1960.

Kuznets, Simon. "Quantitative Aspects of the Economic Growth of Nations, V: Capital Formation Proportions: International Comparisons for Recent Years," *Economic Development and Cultural Change*, VIII, Part II (July, 1960), 1–96.

———. "Quantitative Aspects of the Economic Growth of Nations, VI: Long-Term Trends in Capital Formation Proportions," *Economic Development and Cultural Change*, IX, Part II (July, 1961), 1–124.

Lipset, Seymour M. *Political Man*. New York: Doubleday, 1960.

———, and Bendix, Reinhard. *Social Mobility in Industrial Society*. Berkeley: University of California Press, 1959.

———, and Linz, Juan. *The Social Bases of Political Diversity in the Western Democracies*. Unpublished manuscript, Center for Advanced Study in the Behavioral Sciences, Palo Alto, Calif., 1956.

Lipson, Leslie. "Party Systems in the United Kingdom and the Older Commonwealth: Causes, Resemblances and Variations," *Political Studies* (Oxford), VII (1959), 12–31.

MacKirdy, Kenneth A. "Geography and Federalism in Australia and Canada," *The Australian Geographer*, VI (March, 1953), 38–47.

———. *Regionalism: Canada and Australia*. Unpublished Ph.D. dissertation, University of Toronto, 1959.

Matthews, Donald R. *The Social Background of Political Decision-Makers*. New York: Random House, 1954.

Miller, Delbert C. "Decision-making Cliques in Community Power Structures: A Comparative Study of an American and an English

City," *American Journal of Sociology,* LXIV (November, 1958), 299–310.

Miller, S. M. "Comparative Social Mobility: A Trend Report and Bibliography," *Current Sociology,* IX (1960), 1–89.

————, and Bryce, Herrington. "Social Mobility and Economic Growth and Structure," *Kölner Zeitschrift für Soziologie,* forthcoming.

Neumann, Sigmund. "Toward a Comparative Study of Political Parties," in S. Neumann, ed. *Modern Political Parties.* Chicago: University of Chicago Press, 1956.

Overacker, Louise. "The British and New Zealand Labour Parties: A Comparison," *Political Science* (New Zealand), I (March, 1957), 23–36; II (September, 1957), 15–33.

Rokkan, Stein, and Campbell, Angus. "Norway and the United States of America," *International Social Science Journal,* XII (1960), 69–99.

Rose, Arnold M., ed. *The Institutions of Advanced Societies.* Minneapolis: University of Minnesota Press, 1958.

Ross, Arthur M., and Hartman, Paul T. *Changing Patterns of Industrial Conflict.* New York: Wiley, 1960.

Sharp, Paul F. "Three Frontiers: Some Comparative Studies of Canadian, American, and Australian Settlement," *Pacific Historical Review,* XXIV (November, 1955), 369–77.

Stone, Richard. "A Comparison of the Economic Structure of Regions Based on the Concept of Distance," *Journal of Regional Science,* II (Fall, 1960), 1–20.

Sutherland, Arthur E. "Attrition of State Powers in Federal Nations," *Juridical Review* (Edinburgh), III (1958), 111–13.

Turner, Ralph H. "Sponsored and Contest Mobility and the School System," *American Sociological Review,* XXV (December, 1960), 855–68.

Ullman, Edward L. "Regional Development and the Geography of Concentration," *Papers and Proceedings of the Regional Science Association,* XIV (1958), 179–99.

Verba, Sidney. "Political Participation and Strategies of Influence: A Comparative Study," in Stein Rokkan, ed. *Approaches to the Study of Political Participation.* Bergen: The Christian Michelsen Institute, 1962, pp. 22–42. Also published in *Acta Sociologica,* Vol. VI, fasc. 1–2 (1962).

Weber, Adna F. *The Growth of Cities in the 19th Century.* Columbia University Studies in History, Economics and Public Law, Vol. XI. New York: Macmillan, 1899.

Wheare, Kenneth C. *Federal Government*. 2nd ed.; London: Oxford University Press, 1951.

Wilkinson, Thomas O. "Urban Structure and Industrialization," *American Sociological Review*, XXV (June, 1960), 356–63.

Wyman, Walker D., and Kroeber, Clifton B., eds. *The Frontier in Perspective*. Madison: University of Wisconsin Press, 1957.

2. GENERAL AND THEORETICAL WORKS

Abraham, Henry J. *The Judicial Process*. New York: Oxford University Press, 1962.

Bendix, Reinhard. *Max Weber: An Intellectual Portrait*. New York: Doubleday, 1960.

———. "Social Stratification and the Political Community," *European Journal of Sociology*, I (1960), 183–213.

Blumer, Herbert. "Public Opinion and Public Opinion Polling," *American Sociological Review*, XIII (October, 1948), 542–54.

Bock, Kenneth E. *The Acceptance of Histories*. University of California Publications in Sociology and Social Institutions, Vol. 3, No. 1. Berkeley and Los Angeles: University of California Press, 1956.

Dahrendorf, Ralf. *Class and Class Conflict in Industrial Society*. Stanford: Stanford University Press, 1959.

Deutsch, Karl W. *Nationalism and Social Communication: An Inquiry into the Foundations of Nationality*. New York: Wiley, 1953.

Easterbrook, W. T. "Long-Period Comparative Study: Some Historical Cases," *Journal of Economic History*, XVII (December, 1957), 571–95.

Eckstein, Harry. *A Theory of Stable Democracy*. Research Monograph No. 10. Princeton: Center of International Studies, 1961.

Eysenck, Hans J. *The Psychology of Politics*. London: Routledge & Kegan Paul, 1954.

Feldman, A. H. "Economic Development and Social Mobility," *Economic Development and Cultural Change*, VIII (April, 1960), 311–21.

Gerth, Hans, and Mills, C. Wright, eds. *From Max Weber, Essays in Sociology*. New York: Oxford University Press, 1946.

Key, V. O., Jr. *Politics, Parties and Pressure Groups.* 4th ed.; New York: Thomas Y. Crowell, 1958.

Kornhauser, William. *The Politics of Mass Society.* Glencoe: Free Press, 1959.

Leiserson, Avery. "The Place of Parties in the Study of Politics," *American Political Science Review,* LI (December, 1957), 943–54.

Lieberson, Stanley. "A Societal Theory of Race and Ethnic Relations," *American Sociological Review,* XXVI (December, 1961), 902–10.

Lipset, S. M. "Democracy and Social Structure," Unpublished manuscript, University of California, Berkeley, 1962.

———. "Party Systems and the Representation of Social Groups," *European Journal of Sociology,* I (1960), 50–85.

MacIver, R. M. *The Web of Government.* New York: Macmillan, 1947.

Macmahon, Arthur W., ed. *Federalism: Mature and Emergent.* New York: Doubleday, 1955.

Marshall, Thomas H. *Citizenship and Social Class.* London: Cambridge University Press, 1950.

Merton, Robert K. *Social Theory and Social Structure.* Glencoe: Free Press, 1957.

Moore, Barrington, Jr. *Political Power and Social Theory.* Cambridge: Harvard University Press, 1958.

Padover, Saul K., ed. *The Complete Madison.* New York: Harper, 1953.

Schumpeter, Joseph. *Capitalism, Socialism and Democracy.* New York: Harper, 1947.

Stockwell, Edward G. "The Measurement of Economic Development," *Economic Development and Cultural Change,* VIII (July, 1960, Part I), 419–32.

Tocqueville, Alexis de. *Democracy in America.* New York: Vintage Books, 1954.

Weber, Max. *The Theory of Social and Economic Organization.* Glencoe: Free Press, 1947.

3. METHODOLOGY AND STRATIFICATION

Davies, A. F. "Concepts of Social Class," *Australian Journal of Politics and History,* II (November, 1956), 84–93.

Duncan, O. D., and Duncan, Beverly. "Residential Distribution and

Occupational Stratification," *American Journal of Sociology,* LX (March, 1955), 493–503.

Gibbs, Jack P., and Davis, Kingsley. "Conventional versus Metropolitan Data in the International Study of Urbanization," *American Sociological Review,* XXIII (October, 1958), 504–14.

Goffman, Irwin W. "Status Consistency and Preference for Change in Power Distribution," *American Sociological Review,* XXII (June, 1957), 275–81.

Hartshorne, Richard. "The Functional Approach in Political Geography," *Annals of Association of American Geographers,* XL (June, 1950), 95–130.

Hochbaum, G., and others. "Socioeconomic Variables in a Large City," *American Journal of Sociology,* LXI (July, 1955), 31–38.

Hyman, Herbert H. "Toward a Theory of Public Opinion," *Public Opinion Quarterly,* XXI (Spring, 1957), 54–60.

Kahl, Joseph A., and Davis, James A. "A Comparison of Indices of Socioeconomic Status," *American Sociological Review,* XX (June, 1955), 317–25.

Key, V. O., Jr. "The Politically Relevant in Surveys," *Public Opinion Quarterly,* XXIV (Spring, 1960), 54–62.

Kornhauser, Arthur. "Public Opinion and Social Class," *American Journal of Sociology,* LV (January, 1950), 333–46.

Landecker, Werner. "Class Boundaries," *American Sociological Review,* XXV (December, 1960), 868–77.

———. "Class Crystallization and Class Consciousness," *American Sociological Review,* XXVIII (April, 1963), 219–29.

Lazarsfeld, Paul F., and Barton, Allen H. "Qualitative Measurement in the Social Sciences: Classification, Typologies and Indices," in Daniel Lerner and Harold Lasswell, eds. *The Policy Sciences.* Stanford University Press, 1951, pp. 155–92.

Lenski, Gerhard E. "Status Crystallization: A Non-Vertical Dimension of Social Status," *American Sociological Review,* XIX (August, 1954), 405–13.

Lewis, Oscar. "Comparisons in Cultural Anthropology," *The Yearbook of Anthropology.* New York: Wenner-Gren Foundation for Anthropological Research, 1955, 259–92.

Park, George K., and Soltow, Lee. "Politics and Social Structure in a Norwegian Village," *American Journal of Sociology,* LXVII (September, 1961), 152–64.

Reiss, Albert J., Jr., and others. *Occupations and Social Status.* New York: Free Press of Glencoe, 1961.

Reissman, Leonard. *Class in American Society.* Glencoe: Free Press, 1959.

Sjoberg, Gideon. "The Comparative Method in the Social Sciences," *Philosophy of Science,* XXII (April, 1955), 106–17.

Williams, Thomas Rhys. "A Critique of Some Assumptions of Social Survey Research," *Public Opinion Quarterly,* XXIII (Spring, 1959), 55–63.

Zeisel, Hans. *Say It with Figures.* New York: Harper, 1957.

4. AUSTRALIA

Arndt, H. W., and Santamaria, B. A. "Letters on 'The Catholic Social Movement,'" *Australian Journal of Politics and History,* II (May, 1957), 181–95.

Australia. *Census of the Commonwealth of Australia.* Canberra: Government Printer, June 30, 1947.

Australian Public Opinion Polls. Melbourne releases, 1946–1961.

Blackton, Charles S. "The Dawn of Australian National Feeling, 1850–1856," *Pacific Historical Review,* XXIV (May, 1955), 121–39.

Burns, Creighton. *Parties and People.* Melbourne: Melbourne University Press, 1961.

Butlin, S. J. "The Problem of Federal Finance," *Economic Record,* XXX (May, 1954), 7–18.

Crisp, Leslie F. *The Parliamentary Government of the Commonwealth of Australia.* London: Longmans, Green, 1949.

———. *The Australian Federal Labour Party, 1901–1951.* London: Longmans, Green, 1955.

———. "Centenaries of the Australian States," *Parliamentary Affairs,* X (1957), 180–94.

Crowley, F. K. *State Election.* Perth: published by author, June, 1959.

Davis, Solomon R., ed. *The Government of the Australian States.* London: Longmans, Green, 1960.

Duncan, Walter G. K., ed. *Trends in Australian Politics.* Sydney: Angus & Robertson, 1935.

Fitzpatrick, Brian. *The British Empire in Australia: An Economic History.* Melbourne: Melbourne University Press, 1941.

Garnett, A. Campbell. *Freedom and Planning in Australia.* Madison: University of Wisconsin Press, 1949.

Grimshaw, Charles. "Queensland," in the "Australian Political Chronicle," *Australian Journal of Politics and History,* VI (November, 1960), 241–45.

Hetherington, R., and Reid, R. L. *The South Australian Elections 1959.* Adelaide: Rigby, 1962.

Jupp, James. "A Note on the Democratic Labour Party Vote in Melbourne," *Australian Political Science Association News,* IV (March, 1959), 6–10.

Langdon, Frank C. "The Catholic Anti-Communist Role within Australian Labor," *Western Political Quarterly,* IX (December, 1956), 884–99.

MacKirdy, Kenneth A. "The Federalization of the Australian Cabinet, 1901–1939," *Canadian Journal of Economics and Political Science,* XXIII (May, 1957), 216–26.

Mayer, Henry. "The D.L.P. Today: Facts and Hunches," *The Observer* (Australia) (June 25, 1960), pp. 1–4.

Miller, John D. B. "Party Discipline in Australia," *Political Science,* V (March, 1953), 3–15; and V (September, 1953), 21–36.

———. *Australian Government and Politics.* London: Duckworth, 1954; 2nd ed., 1959.

Murtagh, James G. *Australia: The Catholic Chapter.* New York: Sheed & Ward, 1946.

Oeser, O. A., and Hammond, S. B. *Social Structure and Personality in a City.* London: Routledge & Kegan Paul, 1954.

Overacker, Louise. *The Australian Party System.* New Haven: Yale University Press, 1952.

Rawson, Donald W., and Holtzinger, Susan M. *Politics in Eden-Monaro.* Australian National University, Social Science Monographs, 11. Melbourne: Heinemann, 1958.

Rawson, Donald W. *Australia Votes: The 1958 Federal Election.* Melbourne: Melbourne University Press, 1961.

———. "Labour, Socialism and the Working Class," *Australian Journal of Politics and History,* VII (May, 1961), 75–94.

Robinson, K. W. "Sixty Years of Federation in Australia," *The Geographical Review,* LI (January, 1961), 1–20.

Rolph, W. K. "Federal Party Alignments in Australia." Unpublished manuscript, Department of Political Science, Australian National University, Canberra, 1953.

Rosecrance, R. N. "The Radical Tradition in Australia: An Interpretation," *The Review of Politics,* XXII (January, 1960), 115–32.

Sawer, Geoffrey, ed. *Federalism: An Australian Jubilee Study.* Melbourne: F. W. Cheshire, 1961.

———. *Australian Government Today.* Melbourne: Melbourne University Press, 1961.

———, and others. *Federalism in Australia.* Melbourne and London: F. W. Cheshire, 1949.

Sayle, Murray. "As Far as You Can Go," *Encounter,* XIV (May, 1960), 19–34.

Spann, R. N. "The Catholic Vote in Australia," in Henry Mayer, ed. *Catholics and the Free Society: An Australian Symposium.* Melbourne: F. W. Cheshire, 1961, pp. 115–41.

Taft, Ronald. "The Social Grading of Occupations in Australia," *British Journal of Sociology,* IV (June, 1953), 181–88.

Truman, Tom C. "Catholics and Politics in Australia," *Western Political Quarterly,* XII (June, 1959), 527–34.

Ward, Russel. "Social Roots of Australian Nationalism," *Australian Journal of Politics and History,* I (May, 1956), 179–95.

———. *The Australian Legend.* Melbourne: Oxford University Press, 1958.

Webb, Leicester C. "Churches and the Australian Community," in E. D. French, ed. *Melbourne Studies in Education, 1958–1959.* Melbourne: Melbourne University Press, 1960, pp. 89–131.

———. *Communism and Democracy in Australia.* New York: Praeger, 1955.

———. "Politics and Polity." Inaugural lecture at Australian National University, Canberra, 1960.

Weiner, Herbert E. "The Reduction of Communist Power in the Australian Trade Unions: A Case Study," *Political Science Quarterly,* LXIX (September, 1954), 390–412.

5. CANADA

Beck, J. M., and Dooley, D. J. "Party Images in Canada," *Queen's Quarterly,* LXXVII (August, 1960), 431–88.

Blishen, Bernard R. "The Construction and Use of an Occupational Class Scale," *Canadian Journal of Economics and Political Science,* XXIV (November, 1958), 521–31.

Brunet, Michel. "The British Conquest: Canadian Social Scientists and the Fate of the Canadians," *Canadian Historical Review*, XL (June, 1959), 93–107.

Clark, Samuel D. *Movements of Political Protest in Canada, 1640–1840*. Toronto: University of Toronto Press, 1959.

――――. "The Religious Factor in Canadian Economic Development," *Economic Growth: A Symposium*. Supplement VII of *The Journal of Economic History* (1947), 89–103.

――――. *The Social Development of Canada*. Toronto: University of Toronto Press, 1942.

――――., ed. *Urbanism and the Changing Canadian Society*. Toronto: University of Toronto Press, 1961.

Clokie, H. McD. *Canadian Government and Politics*. Toronto: Longmans, Green, 1944.

Dawson, Robert McGregor. *The Government of Canada*. 2nd ed.; Toronto: University of Toronto Press, 1954 (1st ed., 1947).

Eayrs, James. *The Art of the Possible: Government and Foreign Policy in Canada*. Toronto: University of Toronto Press, 1961.

Filley, Walter O. "Social Structure and Canadian Political Parties: The Quebec Case," *Western Political Quarterly*, IX (December, 1956), 900–14.

Grant, Douglas, ed. *Quebec Today*. Toronto: University of Toronto Press, 1960.

Groupe de Recherches Sociales. *Les Électeurs Québécois*. Montreal, 1960.

Guindon, Hubert. "The Social Evolution of Quebec Reconsidered," *Canadian Journal of Economics and Political Science*, XXVI (November, 1960), 533–52.

Heer, David M. "The Trend of Interfaith Marriages in Canada: 1922–1957," *American Sociological Review*, XXVII (April, 1962), 245–50.

Hessler, William H. "The Canadians Go to the Polls," *The Reporter*, June 7, 1962, pp. 30–32.

Hughes, Everett C. *French Canada in Transition*. Chicago: University of Chicago Press, 1943.

Innis, Harold A. *Essays in Canadian Economic History*. Toronto: University of Toronto Press, 1956.

Jewett, Pauline. "Voting in the 1960 Federal By-Elections at Peterborough and Niagara Falls: Who Voted New Party and Why?" *Canadian Journal of Economics and Political Science*, XXVIII (February, 1962), 35–53.

Jocas, Yves de, and Rocher, Guy. "Inter-Generation Occupational Mobility in the Province of Quebec," *Canadian Journal of Economics and Political Science*, XXIII (February, 1957), 57–68.

Lipset, Seymour M. *Agrarian Socialism*. Berkeley: University of California Press, 1950.

Lower, Arthur R. M., and Scott, F. R., and others. *Evolving Canadian Federalism*. Durham, N.C.: Duke University Press, 1958.

Mallory, James R. *Social Credit and the Federal Power in Canada*. Toronto: University of Toronto Press, 1954.

McHenry, Dean E. *The Third Force in Canada*. Berkeley and Los Angeles: University of California Press, 1950.

Meisel, John. "Religious Affiliation and Electoral Behavior: A Case Study," *Canadian Journal of Economics and Political Science*, XXII (November, 1956), 481–96.

———. *The Canadian General Election of 1957*. Toronto: University of Toronto Press, 1962.

Morton, William L. *The Canadian Identity*. Madison: University of Wisconsin Press, 1961.

———. *The Progressive Party in Canada*. Toronto: University of Toronto Press, 1950.

Quinn, Herbert F. "The Changing Pattern of Quebec Politics," *Canadian Forum*, XXXII (September, 1952), 129–30.

Regenstreif, S. Peter. "The Canadian General Election of 1958," *Western Political Quarterly*, XIII (June, 1960), 349–74.

———. "Some Aspects of National Party Support in Canada," *Canadian Journal of Economics and Political Science*, XXIX (February, 1963), 59–75.

Scarrow, Howard A. "By-Elections and Public Opinion in Canada," *Public Opinion Quarterly*, XXV (Spring, 1961), 79–91.

———. *Canada Votes: A Handbook of Federal and Provincial Election Data*. New Orleans: Hauser Press, 1962.

Sharp, Paul F. *The Agrarian Revolt in Western Canada*. Minneapolis: University of Minnesota Press, 1948.

Siegfried, André. *The Race Question in Canada*. London: Eveleigh Nash, 1907.

Slater, David W. "Decentralization of Urban Peoples and Manufacturing Activity in Canada," *Canadian Journal of Economics and Political Science*, XXVII (February, 1961), 72–85.

Smiley, Donald V. "The Rowell-Sirois Report, Provincial Autonomy and Postwar Canadian Federalism," *Canadian Journal of Economics and Political Science,* XXVIII (February, 1962), 54–69.

Taylor, Norman W. "The Effects of Industrialization—Its Opportunities and Consequences—Upon French-Canadian Society," *Journal of Economic History,* XX (December, 1960), 638–47.

Underhill, Frank H. *In Search of Canadian Liberalism.* Toronto: Macmillan, 1960.

Vallee, Frank G., and others. "Ethnic Assimilation and Differentiation in Canada," *Canadian Journal of Economics and Political Science,* XXIII (November, 1957), 540–49.

Wade, Mason. *The French Canadians, 1760–1945.* London: Macmillan, 1955.

——, ed. *Canadian Dualism.* Toronto: University of Toronto Press, 1960.

Ward, Norman. *The Canadian House of Commons: Representation.* Toronto: University of Toronto Press, 1950.

Wrong, Dennis H. "The Pattern of Party Voting in Canada," *Public Opinion Quarterly,* XXI (Summer, 1957), 252–64.

——. "Ontario Provincial Elections: 1934–55: A Preliminary Survey of Voting," *Canadian Journal of Economics and Political Science,* XXIII (August, 1957), 395–403.

——. "Parties and Voting in Canada," *Political Science Quarterly,* LXXIII (September, 1958), 397–412.

6. GREAT BRITAIN

Abrams, Mark. "Social Class in British Politics," *Public Opinion Quarterly,* XXV (Fall, 1961), 342–50.

——, and others. *Must Labour Lose?* London: Penguin Books, 1960.

Beer, Samuel H. "Pressure Groups and Parties in Britain," *American Political Science Review,* L (March, 1956), 1–23.

Benney, Mark, and others. *How People Vote.* London: Routledge & Kegan Paul, 1956.

Birch, Anthony H. *Small Town Politics.* London: Oxford University Press, 1959.

Bonham, John. *The Middle-Class Vote.* London: Faber & Faber, 1954.

Brady, Alexander. "The British Governing Class and Democracy," *Canadian Journal of Economics and Political Science,* XX (November, 1954), 405–20.

Brennan, Tom, and others. *Social Change in Southwest Wales.* London: Watts, 1954.

Burns, J. H. "The Scottish Committees of the House of Commons, 1948–1959," *Political Studies* (Oxford), VIII (1960), 272–96.

Burrell, Sidney A. "The Scottish Separatist Movements: A Present Assessment," *Political Science Quarterly,* LXX (September, 1955), 358–67.

Butler, David E. *The British General Election of 1951.* London: Macmillan, 1952.

————, and Rose, Richard. *The British General Election of 1959.* London: Macmillan, 1960.

Cairncross, Alexander K. *The Scottish Economy.* London: Cambridge University Press, 1954.

Campbell, P., and others. "Voting Behavior in Droylsden in October, 1951," *The Manchester School of Economics and Social Studies,* XX (January, 1952), 57–65.

Campion, Lord, and others. *Parliament: A Survey.* London: George Allen & Unwin, 1952.

Cleary, E. J., and Pollins, H. "Liberal Voting at the General Election of 1951," *Sociological Review,* I (December, 1953), 27–41.

Cole, G. D. H. "The Conception of the Middle Classes," *British Journal of Sociology,* I (December, 1950), 275–90.

Coupland, Sir Reginald. *Welsh and Scottish Nationalism: A Study.* London: Collins, 1954.

Crosland, C. A. R. *The Future of Socialism.* New York: Macmillan, 1957.

————. "New Moods, Old Problems," *Encounter,* XVI (February, 1961), 2–10.

Dickinson, Robert E. *City, Region and Regionalism.* London: Kegan Paul, Trench, Trubner, 1947.

Finer, Samuel C., and others. *Backbench Opinion in the House of Commons, 1955–1959.* London: Pergamon, 1961.

Fogarty, Michael P. *Prospects of the Industrial Areas of Great Britain.* London: Methuen, 1945.

Fothersgill, P. "The Liberal Predicament," *Political Quarterly,* XXIV (1953), 243–49.

Glass, David V., ed. *Social Mobility in Britain.* London: Routledge & Kegan Paul, 1954.

Hart, W. O. "The White Paper on Local Government," *Public Law* (London), I (1956), 336–49.

Highet, John. "Scottish Religious Adherence," *British Journal of Sociology,* IV (June, 1953), 142–59.

Holt, A. "The Liberal Attitude to Contemporary Problems," *Political Quarterly,* XXIV (1953), 249–58.

Holt, Edgar. *Protest in Arms.* New York: Coward-McCann, 1961.

Jennings, Sir Ivor. *Party Politics, I: Appeal to the People.* Cambridge: Cambridge University Press, 1960.

———. *Party Politics, II: The Growth of Parties.* Cambridge: Cambridge University Press, 1961.

Krebhiel, Edward. "Geographic Influences in British Elections," *The Geographical Review,* II (December, 1916), 419–32.

Leser, C. E. V. "Changes in Level and Diversity of Employment in Regions of Great Britain, 1939–1947," *Economic Journal,* LIX (September, 1949), 326–42.

Lipson, Leslie, "The Two Party System in British Politics," *American Political Science Review,* XLVII (June, 1953), 337–58.

———. "Common Ground and Emerging Conflict between the British Parties," *Political Quarterly,* XXVII (1956), 182–94.

Lloyd George, M. "Regional Parliaments," *Parliamentary Affairs,* VIII (1955), 430–35.

Lockwood, David. " 'The 'New Working Class,' " *European Journal of Sociology,* I (1960), 248–59.

McCaffrey, Lawrence J. "Isaac Butt and the Home Rule Movement: A Study in Conservative Nationalism," *Review of Politics,* XXII (January, 1960), 72–95.

McCallum, R. B. "The Liberal Outlook," in Morris Ginsberg, ed. *Law and Opinion in England in the 20th Century.* Berkeley: University of California Press, 1959, pp. 63–78.

McKenzie, Robert T. *British Political Parties.* London: Heinemann, 1955.

———, and Silver, Allan. "Conservatism, Industrialism and the Working Class Tory in England." Paper prepared for the Fifth World Congress of Sociology, Washington, D.C., September, 1962.

Miliband, Ralph. *Parliamentary Socialism: A Study in the Politics of Labour.* London: George Allen & Unwin, 1961.

Milne, Robert S., and Mackenzie, H. C. *Straight Fight.* London: Chiswick Press, 1954.

————. *Marginal Seat: 1955.* London: Hansard Society for Parliamentary Government, 1958.

Nicholas, Herbert G. *The British General Election of 1950.* London: Macmillan, 1951.

Orwell, George. *The Road to Wigan Pier.* London: Victor Gollancz, 1937.

Pollock, James K., and others. *British Election Studies, 1950.* Ann Arbor: George Wahr, 1951.

Prescott, J. R. V. "The Function and Methods of Electoral Geography," *Annals of the Association of American Geographers,* XLIX (September, 1959), 296–304.

Schnore, Leo F. "Metropolitan Development in the United Kingdom," *Economic Geography,* XXXVIII (July, 1962), 215–33.

Self, Peter. "New Prospects for Local Government," *Political Quarterly,* XXVIII (1957), 20–31.

Smellie, Kingsley B. *The British Way of Life.* New York: Praeger, 1955.

Stacey, Margaret. *Tradition and Change: A Study of Banbury.* London: Oxford University Press, 1960.

Steiner, George. "The Decline of the Labour Party," *The Reporter,* September 29, 1960, pp. 33–40.

7. UNITED STATES

Allinsmith, Wesley, and Allinsmith, Beverly. "Religious Affiliation and Politico-Economic Attitude: A Study of Eight Major U. S. Religious Groups," *Public Opinion Quarterly,* XII (Fall, 1948), 377–89.

Anderson, H. D., and Davidson, P. E. *Ballots and the Democratic Class Struggle.* Stanford: Stanford University Press, 1943.

Bailey, Stephen K. *The Condition of Our National Political Parties.* An Occasional Paper of the Center for the Study of Democratic Institutions, 1959.

Beloff, Max. *The American Federal Government.* New York: Oxford University Press, 1959.

Benson, Edward G., and Perry, Paul. "Analysis of Democratic-Republican Strength by Population Groups," *Public Opinion Quarterly,* IV (September, 1940), 464–73.

Berelson, Bernard, and others. *Voting.* Chicago: University of Chicago Press, 1954.

Bogue, Donald J. *The Structure of the Metropolitan Community.* Ann Arbor: Horace H. Rackham School of Graduate Studies, University of Michigan, 1950.

Brogan, D. W. *Politics in America.* New York: Doubleday Anchor, 1960 (first published, 1954).

Campbell, Angus, and others. *The American Voter.* New York: Wiley, 1960.

Campbell, Angus, and Cooper, H. C. *Group Differences in Attitudes and Votes.* Ann Arbor: Survey Research Center, 1956.

Campbell, Angus, and others. *The Voter Decides.* Evanston: Row, Peterson, 1954.

Chinoy, Ely. "Social Mobility Trends in the United States," *American Sociological Review,* XX (April, 1955), 180–86.

Converse, Philip. "Religion and Politics: The 1960 Election." Unpublished manuscript, Survey Research Center, University of Michigan, 1961.

———. "The Shifting Role of Class in Political Attitudes and Behavior," in E. Maccoby and others, eds. *Readings in Social Psychology.* 3rd ed.; New York: Holt, 1958, pp. 388–99.

———, and others. "Stability and Change in 1960: A Reinstating Election," *American Political Science Review,* LV (June, 1961), 269–80.

David, Paul T. "The Changing Party Pattern," *Antioch Review,* XVI (Fall, 1956), 333–50.

Doan, Edward N. *The La Follettes and the Wisconsin Idea.* New York: Rinehart, 1947.

Eulau, Heinz. *Class and Party in the Eisenhower Years.* New York: Free Press of Glencoe, 1962.

———. "Identification with Class and Political Perspectives," *Journal of Politics,* XVIII (May, 1956), 232–53.

Fuchs, Victor R. "Changes in the Location of United States Manufacturing since 1929," *Journal of Regional Science,* I (Spring, 1959), 1–17.

Gaston, Herbert E. *The Nonpartisan League.* New York: Harcourt, 1920.

Glantz, Oscar. "Unitary Political Behavior and Differential Motivation," *Western Political Quarterly,* X (1957), 833–47.

————. "Protestant and Catholic Voting Behavior in a Metropolitan Area," *Public Opinion Quarterly*, XXIII (Spring, 1959), 73–82.

Gosnell, Harold F. *Grass Roots Politics*. Washington, D. C.: American Council on Public Affairs, 1942.

Harrington, Michael. *The Other America*. New York: Macmillan, 1962.

Hayes, Samuel P., Jr. "The Interrelations of Political Attitudes, IV: Political Attitudes and Party Regularity," *Journal of Social Psychology*, X (1939), 503–52.

Holcombe, A. N. *The Middle Class in American Politics*. Cambridge: Harvard University Press, 1940.

————. *The New Party Politics*. New York: Norton, 1933.

Key, V. O., Jr. "Secular Realignment and the Party System," *Journal of Politics*, XXI (May, 1959), 198–210.

————. *Southern Politics in State and Nation*. New York: Knopf, 1949.

————, and Munger, Frank. "Social Determinism and Electoral Decision: The Case of Indiana," in Eugene Burdick and Arthur J. Brodbeck. *American Voting Behavior*. Glencoe: Free Press, 1959, pp. 281–300.

Korchin, S. J. "Psychological Variables in the Behavior of Voters." Unpublished Ph.D. dissertation, Department of Social Relations, Harvard University, 1946.

Lazarsfeld, Paul, and others. *The People's Choice*. New York: Columbia University Press, 1948.

Lenski, Gerhard. *The Religious Factor*. New York: Doubleday, 1961.

Lerner, Max. *America as a Civilization*. New York: Simon & Schuster, 1957.

Lieberson, Stanley. *Ethnic Patterns in American Cities*. New York: Free Press of Glencoe, 1963.

McClosky, Herbert, and others. "Issue Conflict and Consensus among Party Leaders and Followers," *American Political Science Review*, LIV (June, 1960), 406–27.

MacRae, Duncan, Jr. "Occupations and the Congressional Vote, 1940–1950," *American Sociological Review*, XX (June, 1955), 332–40.

McKenzie, Roderick D. *The Metropolitan Community.* New York: McGraw-Hill, 1933.

Mayer, Kurt. "Recent Changes in the Class Structure of the United States," *Transactions of the Third World Congress of Sociology,* 1956, pp. 66–80.

Miller, Warren E. "One-Party Politics and the Voter," *American Political Science Review,* L (September, 1956), 707–25.

Morgan, James N., and others. *Income and Welfare in the United States.* New York: McGraw-Hill, 1962.

Odegard, Peter H., ed. *Religion and Politics.* Published for the Eagleton Institute of Politics at Rutgers, The State University, by Oceana Publications, Inc., 1960.

O'Grady, Jane. "Political Generations: An Empirical Analysis." Unpublished Master's thesis, Department of Sociology, University of California, Berkeley, 1960.

Orlans, Harold. "Opinion Polls on National Leaders." Institute Report No. 6. Philadelphia and Washington: Institute for Research in Human Relations, Series 1953.

Perloff, Harvey S., and others. *Regions, Resources and Economic Growth.* Baltimore: The Johns Hopkins Press, 1960. Published for Resources for the Future, Inc.

Rossiter, Clinton. *Parties and Politics in America.* Ithaca: Cornell University Press, 1960.

Schattschneider, E. E. "United States: The Functional Approach to Party Government," in Sigmund Neumann, ed. *Modern Political Parties.* Chicago: University of Chicago Press, 1956, pp. 194–215.

———. *Party Government.* New York: Farrar & Rinehart, 1942.

Smith, Henry Nash. *Virgin Land: The American West as Symbol and Myth.* New York: Vintage Books, 1957.

Stouffer, Samuel. *Communism, Conformity and Civil Liberties.* New York: Doubleday, 1955.

Strong, Donald S. *Urban Republicanism in the South.* Birmingham: University of Alabama, Bureau of Public Administration, 1960.

Vile, M. J. C. *The Structure of American Federalism.* London: Oxford University Press, 1961.

Wright, John K. "Voting Habits in the United States: A Note on Two Maps," *The Geographical Review,* XXII (October, 1932), 666–72.

8. MISCELLANEOUS

Canada. *Yearbook*. Ottawa: Dominion Bureau of Statistics, 1953, 1957, 1958.

Cantril, Hadley, and Strunk, Mildred, eds. *Public Opinion, 1935–1946*. Princeton: Princeton University Press, 1951.

Great Britain. "Occupation Tables," *Census 1951*. London: H. M. Stationery Office, 1956.

———. "General Report," *Census 1951*. London: H. M. Stationery Office, 1958.

Milne, Robert S. "Voting in Wellington Central, 1957," *Political Science* (New Zealand), X (September, 1958), 31–64.

Mitchell, Austin. "Dunedin Central," *Political Science* (New Zealand), XIV (March, 1962), 27–80.

New York Times, various issues.

Schoeffler, Herbert. *Wirkungen der Reformation*. Frankfurt am Main: Vittorio Klostermann, 1960.

Siegfried, André. *Tableau Politique de la France de l'ouest sous la Troisième République*. Paris: Librairie Armand Colin, 1913.

Times, The, of London. *Guide to the House of Commons*. London, 1945, 1950, 1951, 1955, 1959.

United Nations. *A Preliminary Report on the World Social Situation*. New York, 1952.

———. *Demographic Yearbook*. New York, 1956.

———. *Statistical Yearbook*. New York, 1958.

———. *National and Per Capita Income in Seventy Countries, 1949*. Statistical Papers, Series E, No. 1. New York, 1950.

UNESCO. *World Survey of Education*. Paris, 1955.

United States. *Historical Statistics of the United States, Colonial Times to 1957*. Washington, D. C.: United States Bureau of the Census, 1960.

World Almanac and Book of Facts, The. New York, 1962.

Worldmark Encyclopedia of the Nations. New York: Worldmark Press, 1960.

Index

SUBJECT INDEX